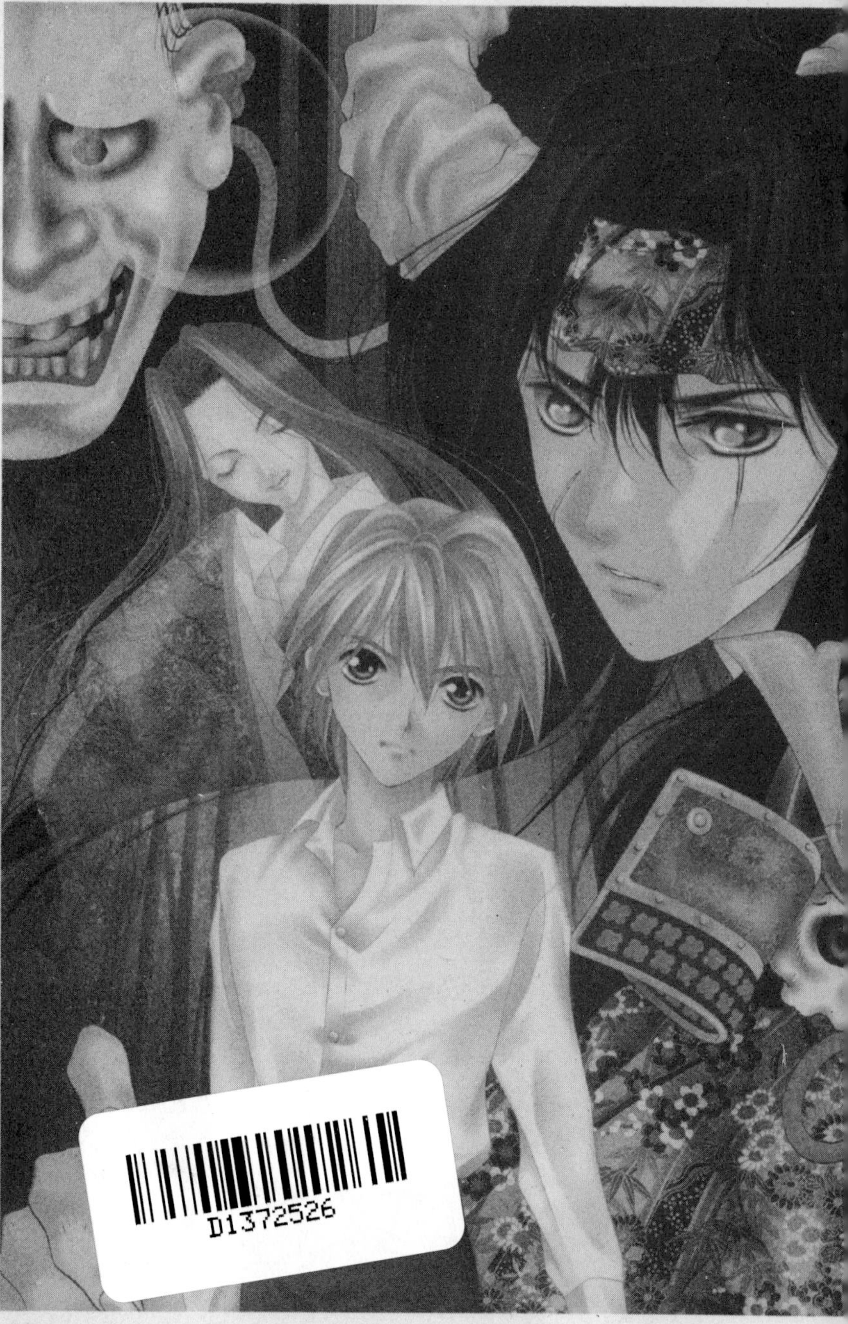

Sengoku Nights Vol. 2
Created by Kei Kusonoki & Kaoru Ohashi

Translation - Althea Nibley
English Adaptation - Aaron Sparrow
Copy Editor - Peter Ahlstrom
Retouch and Lettering - Peter Sattler
Production Artist - Mike Estacio
Cover Design - Kyle Plummer

Editor - Aaron Suhr
Digital Imaging Manager - Chris Buford
Production Managers - Jennifer Miller
Managing Editor - Lindsey Johnston
VP of Production - Ron Klamert
Publisher and E.I.C. - Mike Kiley
President and C.O.O. - John Parker
C.E.O. and Chief Creative Officer - Stuart Levy

A  Manga

TOKYOPOP Inc.
5900 Wilshire Blvd. Suite 2000
Los Angeles, CA 90036

E-mail: info@TOKYOPOP.com
Come visit us online at www.TOKYOPOP.com

ISBN: 1-59532-946-3

First TOKYOPOP printing: April 2006
10 9 8 7 6 5 4 3 2 1
Printed in the USA

Created By:
Kei Kusunoki & Kaoru Ohashi

Sengoku Nights

Vol. 2

Volume 2

Created by
Kei Kusunoki & Kaoru Ohashi

HAMBURG // LONDON // LOS ANGELES // TOKYO

Created By:
Kei Kusunoki & Kaoru Ohashi

Sengoku Nights Vol. 2

Table of Contents

This work is fiction. It has no relation to any real persons, groups, or events.

Summary of Volume 1

Kowai Mountain: Birthplace of the legend of the witch Oni-hime. It is said that after making a pact with a demon and killing many people, she sealed all the curses placed upon her in the mountain and died, only to be reincarnated as high school student Masayoshi Kurozuka. Masayoshi is attacked by the vengeful ghosts of the past as Oni-hime's reincarnation. Unfortunately for Masayoshi, the seal on the mountain is broken by land developers, and he finds himself the target of the demon hordes' vengeance. As Oni-hime, Masayoshi is protected by the god of the land, Nozuchi no Mikoto, and the spiritual medium Mizuki, who is able to drive away the evil spirits. Now, deluged with the memories of a past life not his own, he has learned that the one who made a pact with the demons was not Oni-Hime, but the princess' father...

MASAYOSHI
KUROZUKA

NOZUCHI NO
MIKOTO

MIZUKI THE
EXORCIST

GRANDMA

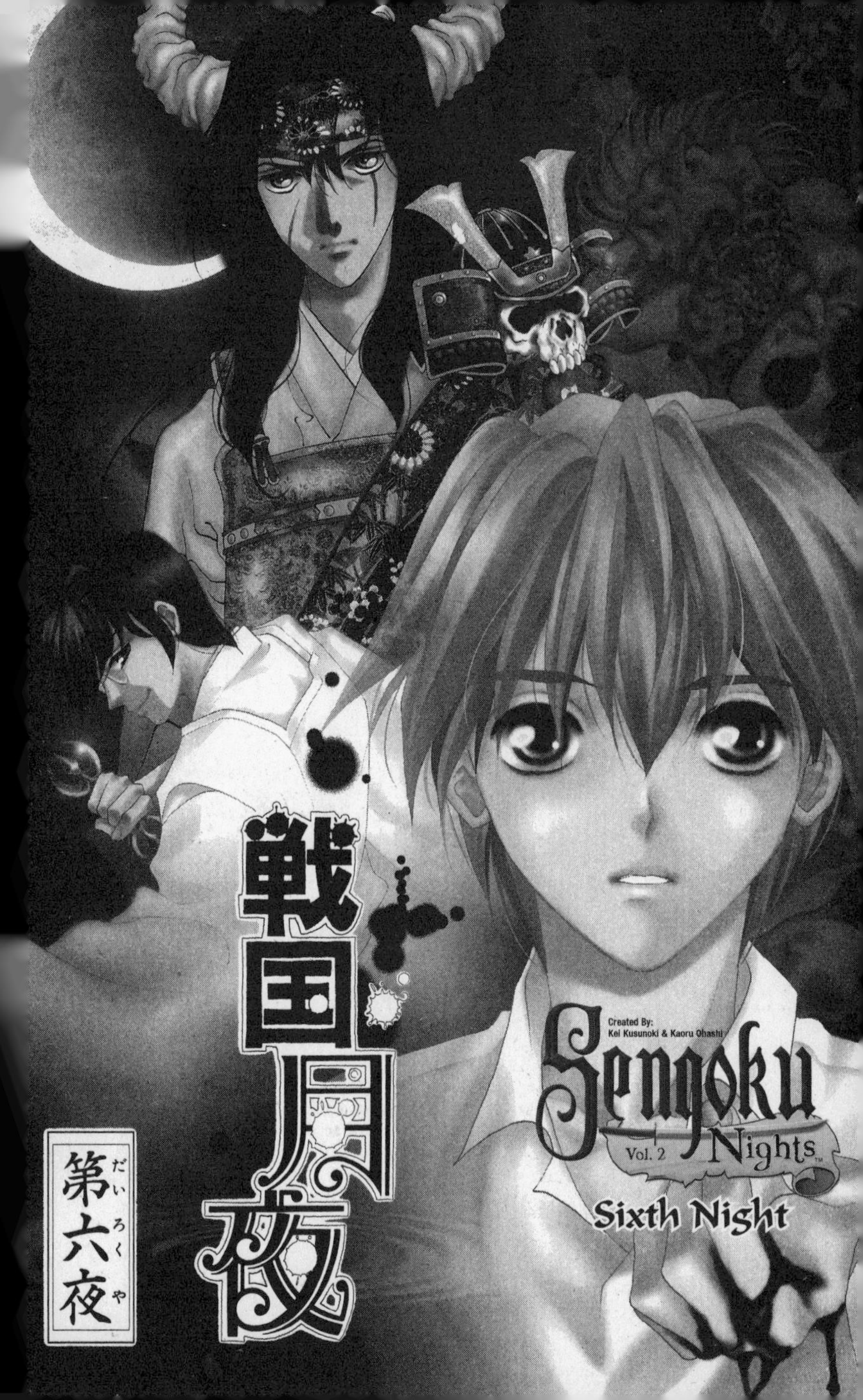

第六夜（だいろくや）
戦国闇夜
Created By:
Kei Kusunoki & Kaoru Ohashi
Sengoku Nights
Vol. 2
Sixth Night

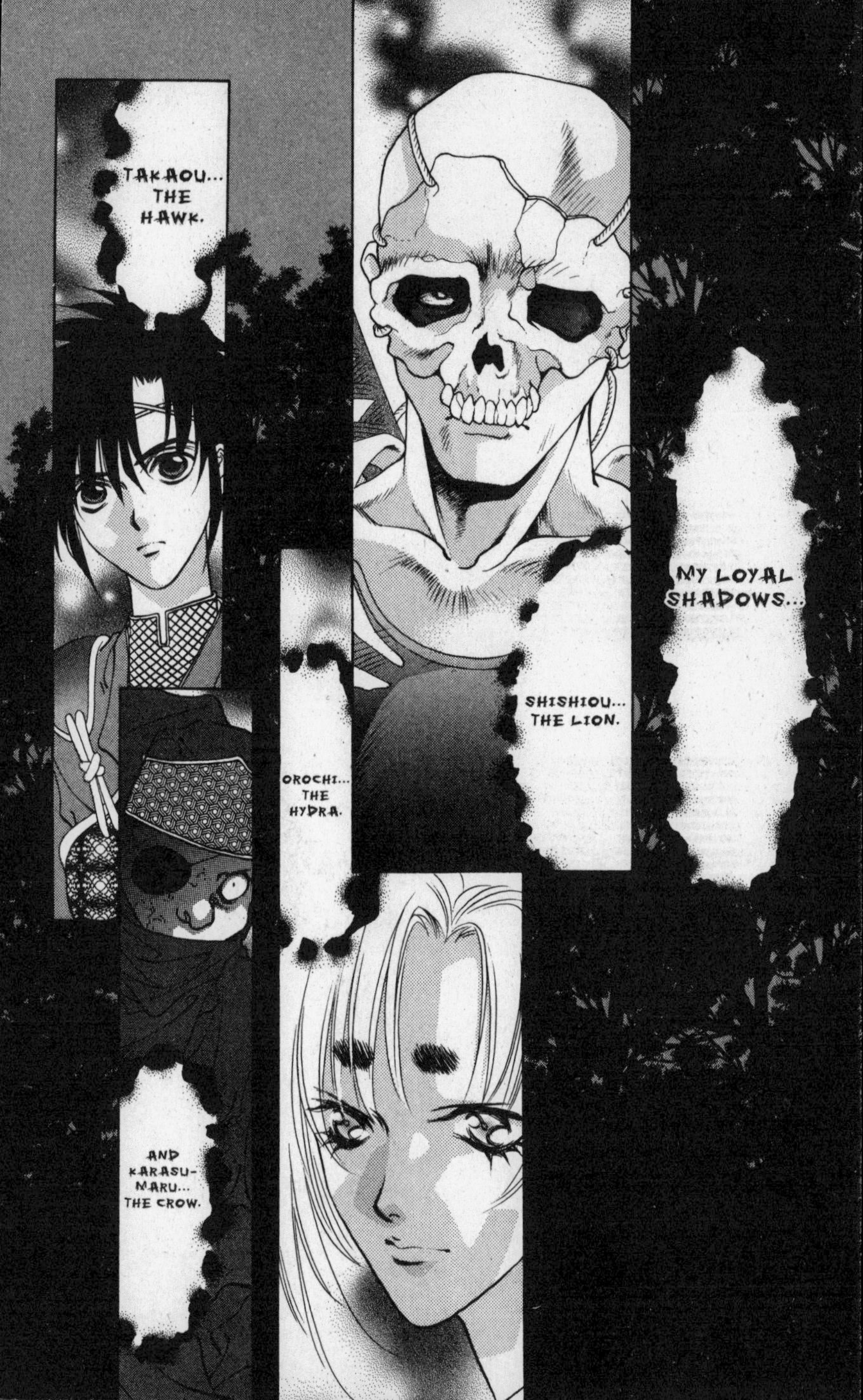
MY LOYAL SHADOWS...
SHISHIOU... THE LION.
TAKAOU... THE HAWK.
OROCHI... THE HYDRA.
AND KARASU-MARU... THE CROW.

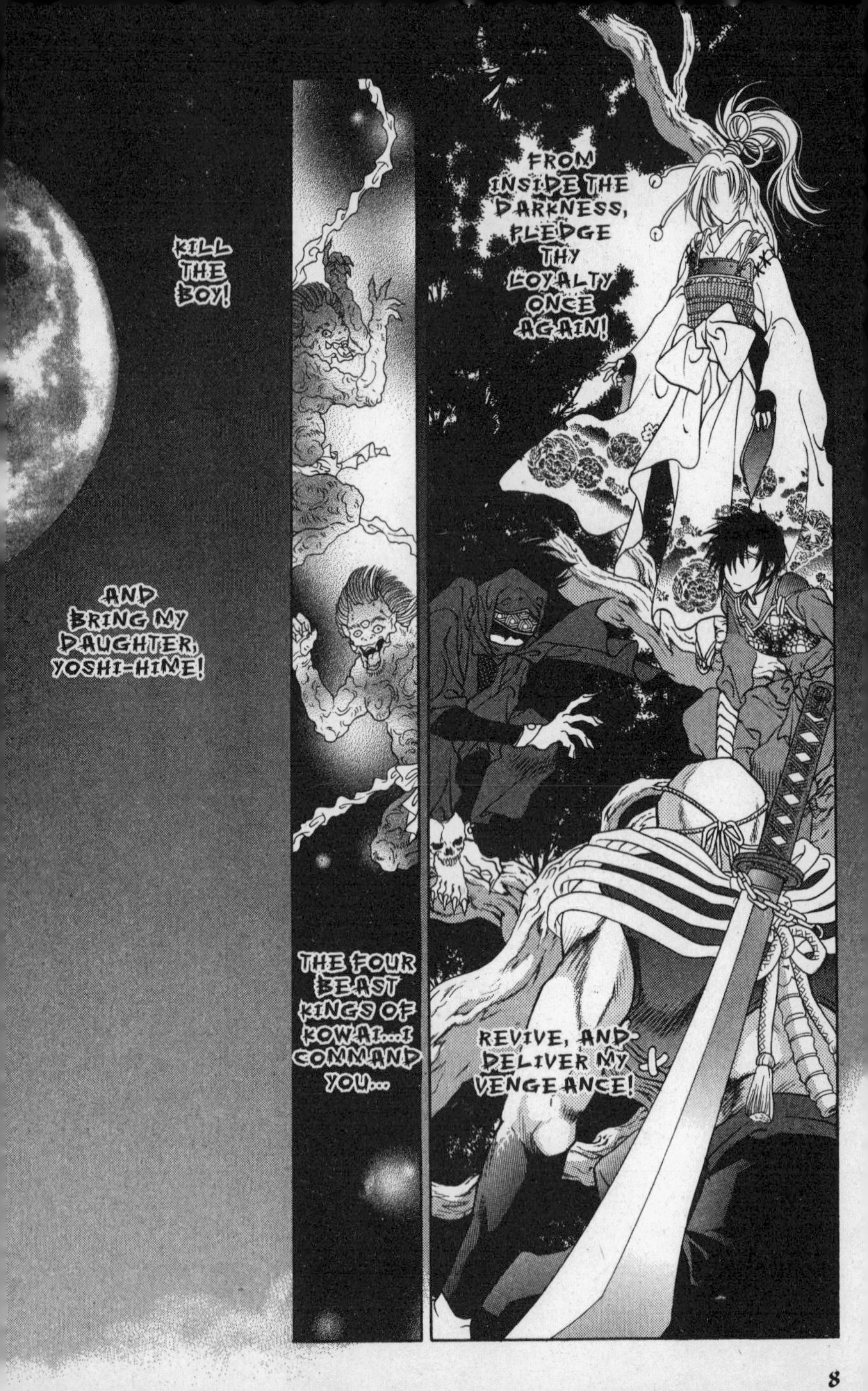
FROM INSIDE THE DARKNESS, PLEDGE THY LOYALTY ONCE AGAIN!
REVIVE, AND DELIVER MY VENGEANCE!
THE FOUR BEAST KINGS OF KOWAI...I COMMAND YOU...
KILL THE BOY!
AND BRING MY DAUGHTER, YOSHI-HIME!

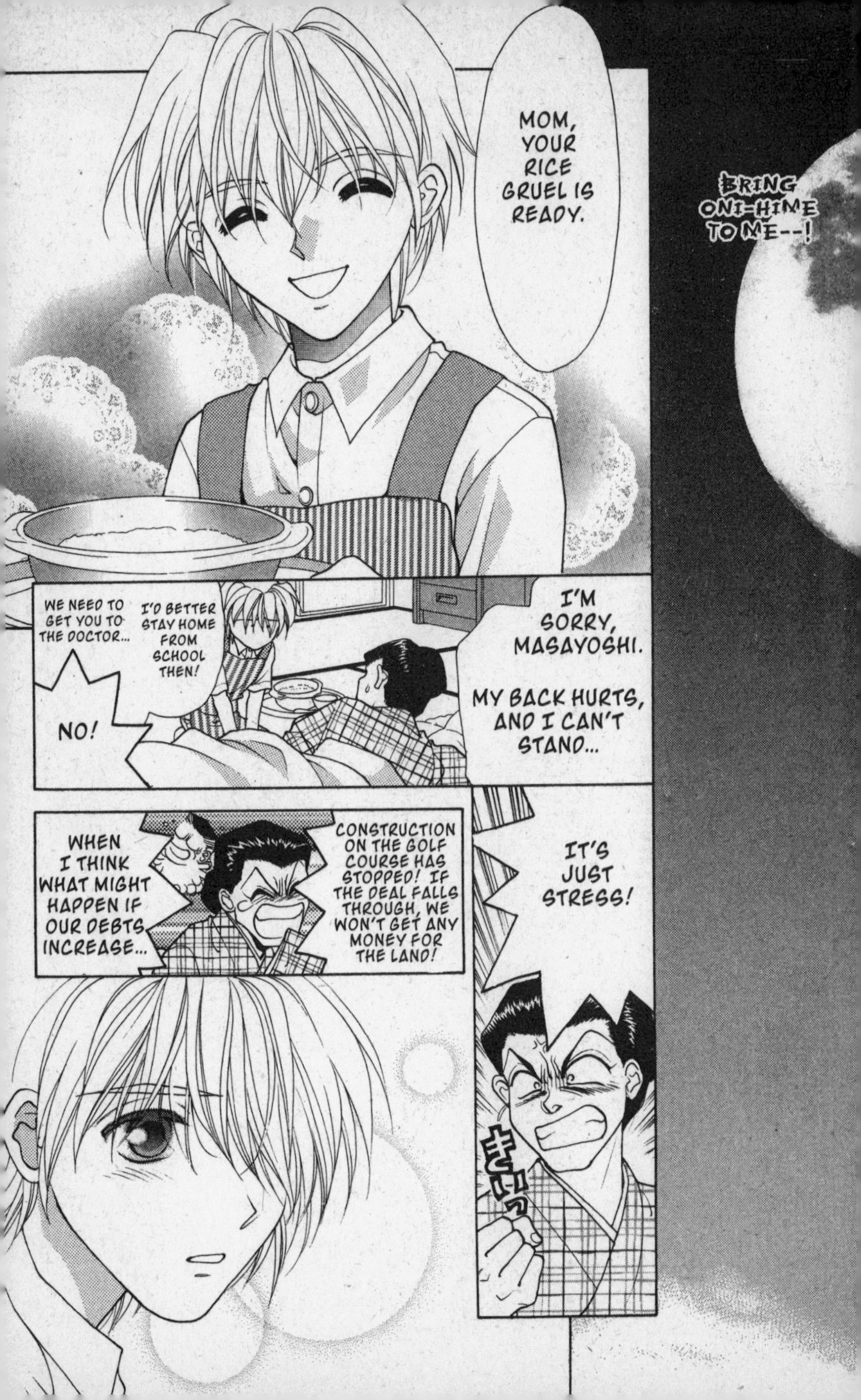
BRING ONI-HIME TO ME--!
MOM, YOUR RICE GRUEL IS READY.
I'M SORRY, MASAYOSHI.
MY BACK HURTS, AND I CAN'T STAND...
I'D BETTER STAY HOME FROM SCHOOL THEN!
WE NEED TO GET YOU TO THE DOCTOR...
NO!
IT'S JUST STRESS!
CONSTRUCTION ON THE GOLF COURSE HAS STOPPED! IF THE DEAL FALLS THROUGH, WE WON'T GET ANY MONEY FOR THE LAND!
WHEN I THINK WHAT MIGHT HAPPEN IF OUR DEBTS INCREASE...

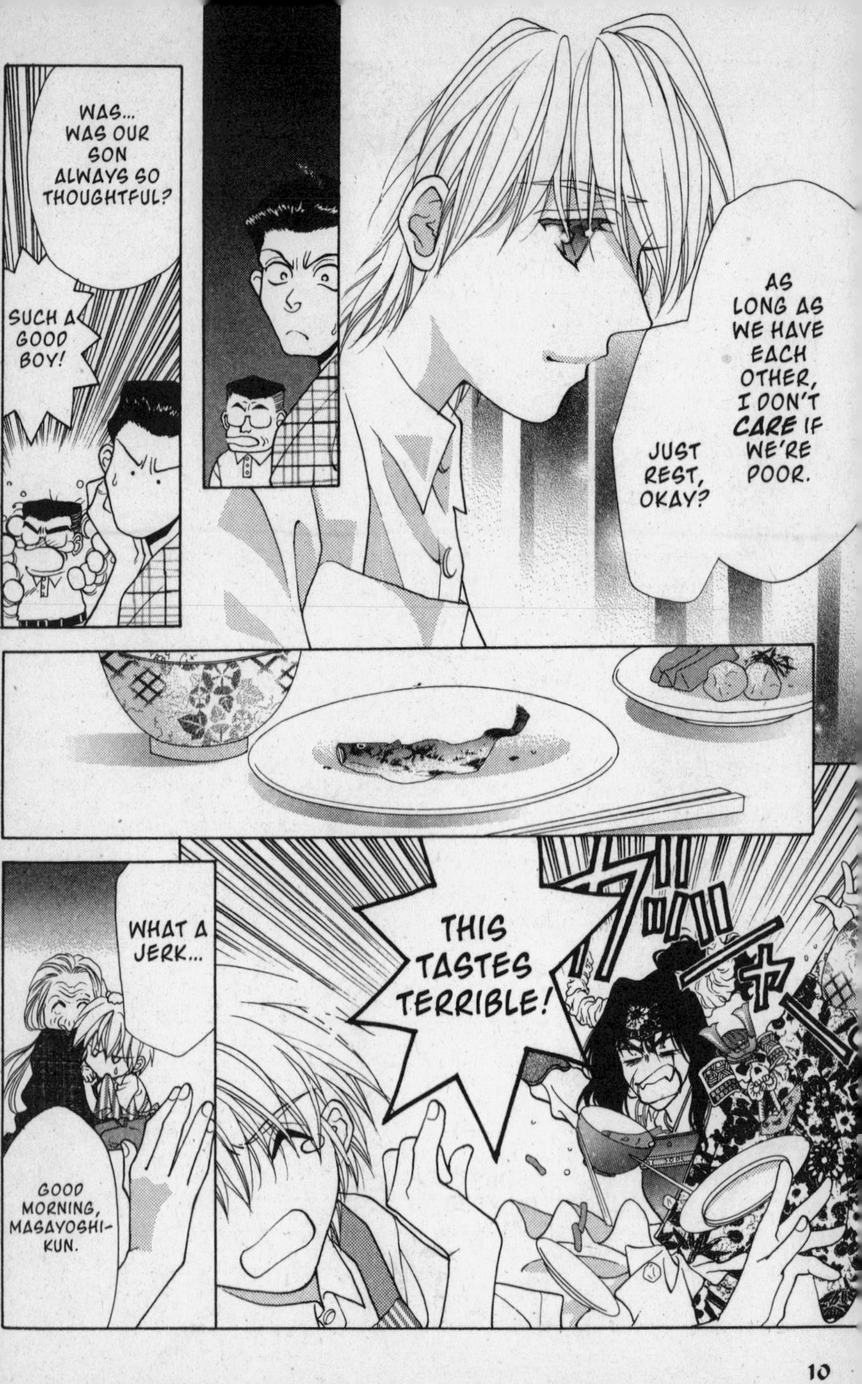
AS LONG AS WE HAVE EACH OTHER, I DON'T CARE IF WE'RE POOR.
JUST REST, OKAY?
WAS... WAS OUR SON ALWAYS SO THOUGHTFUL?
SUCH A GOOD BOY!
THIS TASTES TERRIBLE!
WHAT A JERK...
GOOD MORNING, MASAYOSHI-KUN.

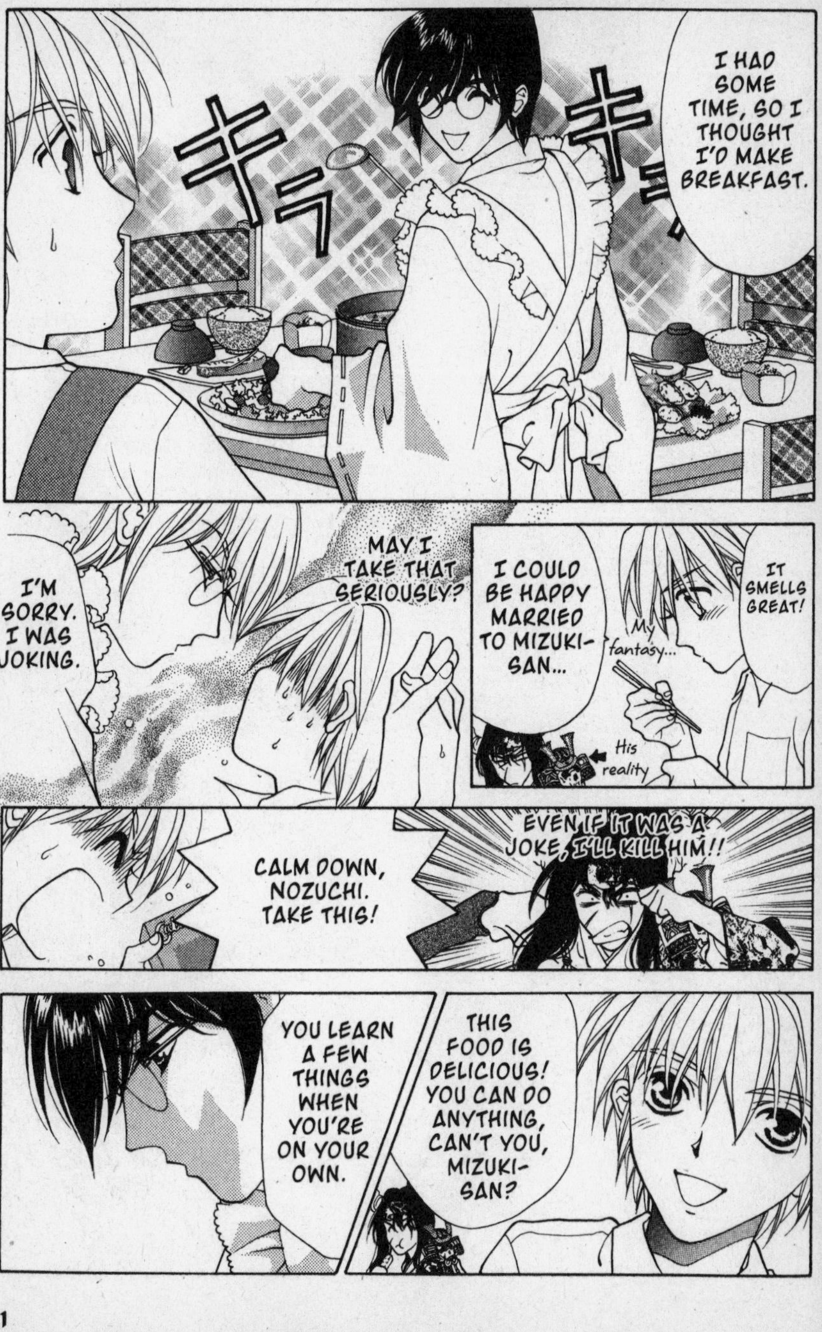
I HAD SOME TIME, SO I THOUGHT I'D MAKE BREAKFAST.
キラ
キラ
IT SMELLS GREAT!
I COULD BE HAPPY MARRIED TO MIZUKI-SAN...
My fantasy...
His reality
MAY I TAKE THAT SERIOUSLY?
I'M SORRY. I WAS JOKING.
EVEN IF IT WAS A JOKE, I'LL KILL HIM!!
CALM DOWN, NOZUCHI. TAKE THIS!
THIS FOOD IS DELICIOUS! YOU CAN DO ANYTHING, CAN'T YOU, MIZUKI-SAN?
YOU LEARN A FEW THINGS WHEN YOU'RE ON YOUR OWN.

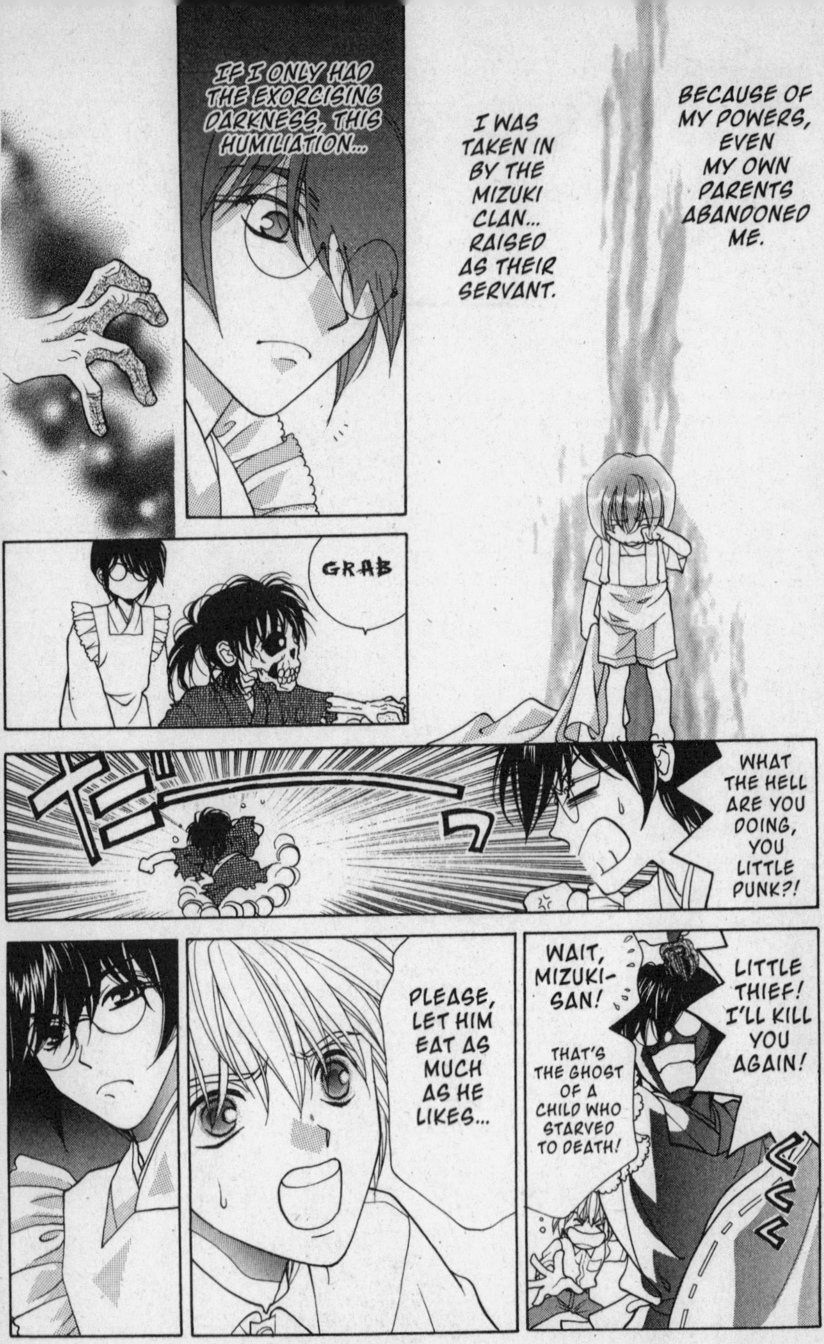
BECAUSE OF MY POWERS, EVEN MY OWN PARENTS ABANDONED ME.
I WAS TAKEN IN BY THE MIZUKI CLAN... RAISED AS THEIR SERVANT.
IF I ONLY HAD THE EXORCISING DARKNESS, THIS HUMILIATION...
GRAB
WHAT THE HELL ARE YOU DOING, YOU LITTLE PUNK?!
LITTLE THIEF! I'LL KILL YOU AGAIN!
WAIT, MIZUKI-SAN!
THAT'S THE GHOST OF A CHILD WHO STARVED TO DEATH!
PLEASE, LET HIM EAT AS MUCH AS HE LIKES...

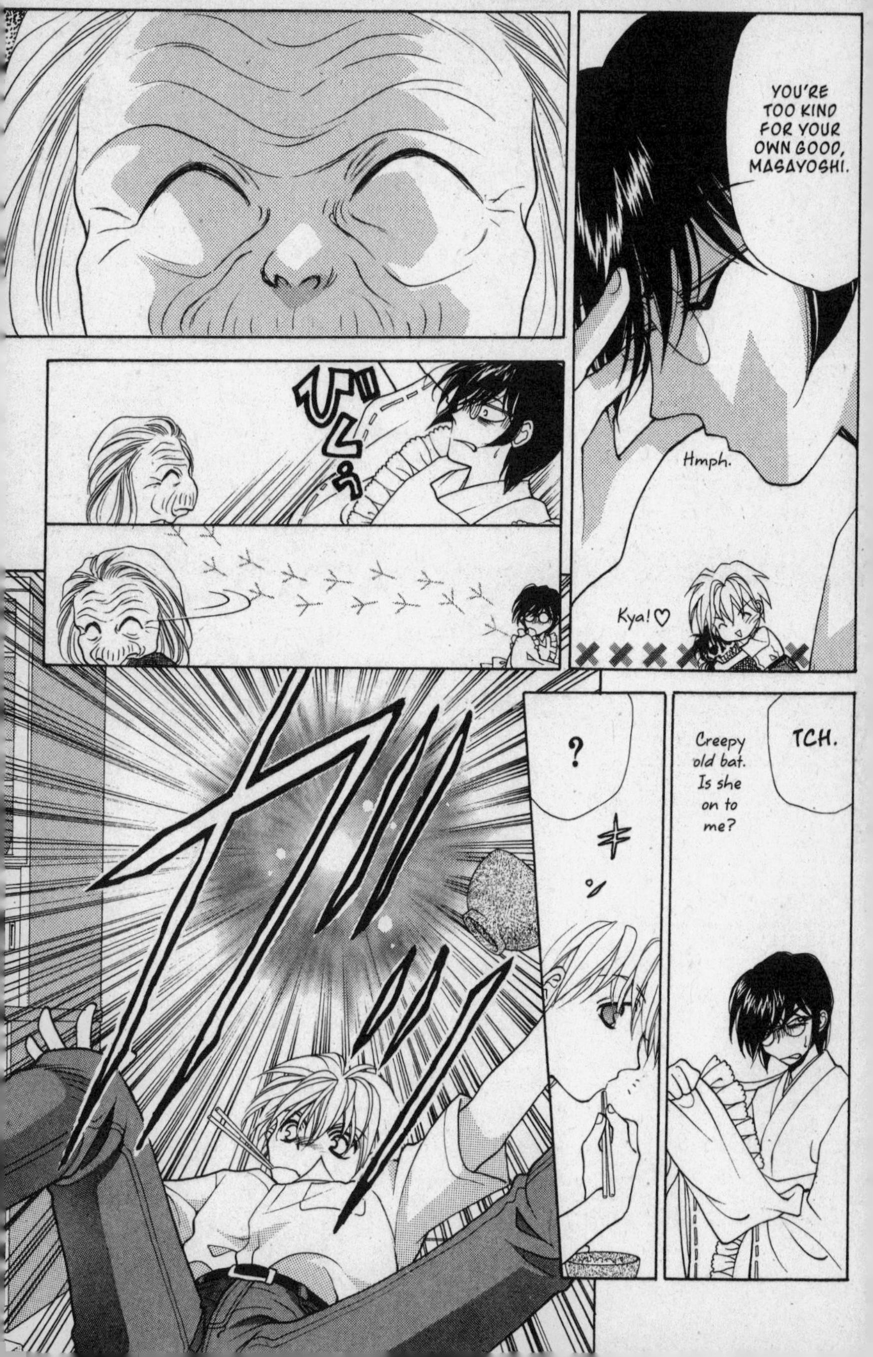
YOU'RE TOO KIND FOR YOUR OWN GOOD, MASAYOSHI.
Hmph.
Kya! ♡
TCH.
Creepy old bat. Is she on to me?
?

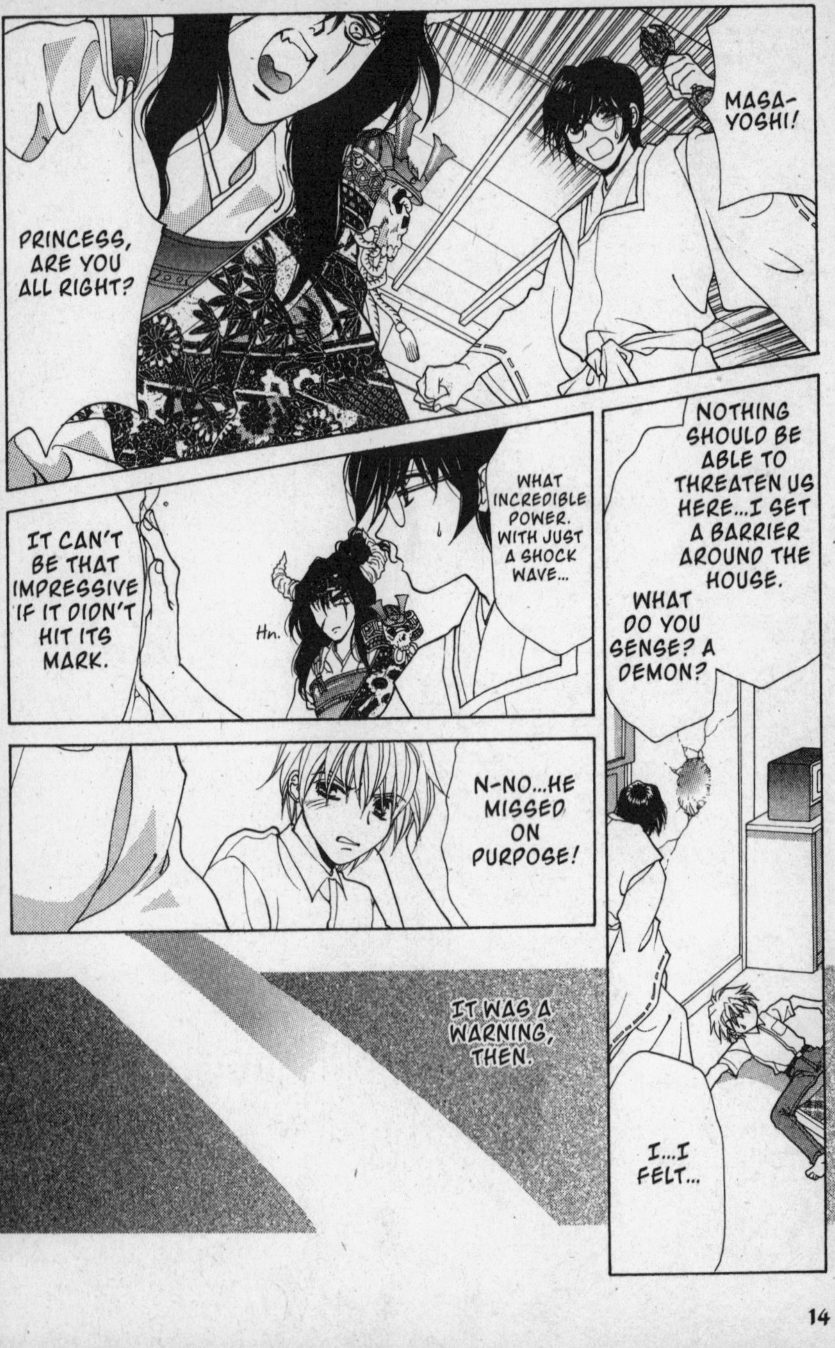
MASA-YOSHI!
PRINCESS, ARE YOU ALL RIGHT?
NOTHING SHOULD BE ABLE TO THREATEN US HERE...I SET A BARRIER AROUND THE HOUSE.
WHAT DO YOU SENSE? A DEMON?
I...I FELT...
WHAT INCREDIBLE POWER. WITH JUST A SHOCK WAVE...
Hn.
IT CAN'T BE THAT IMPRESSIVE IF IT DIDN'T HIT ITS MARK.
N-NO...HE MISSED ON PURPOSE!
IT WAS A WARNING, THEN.

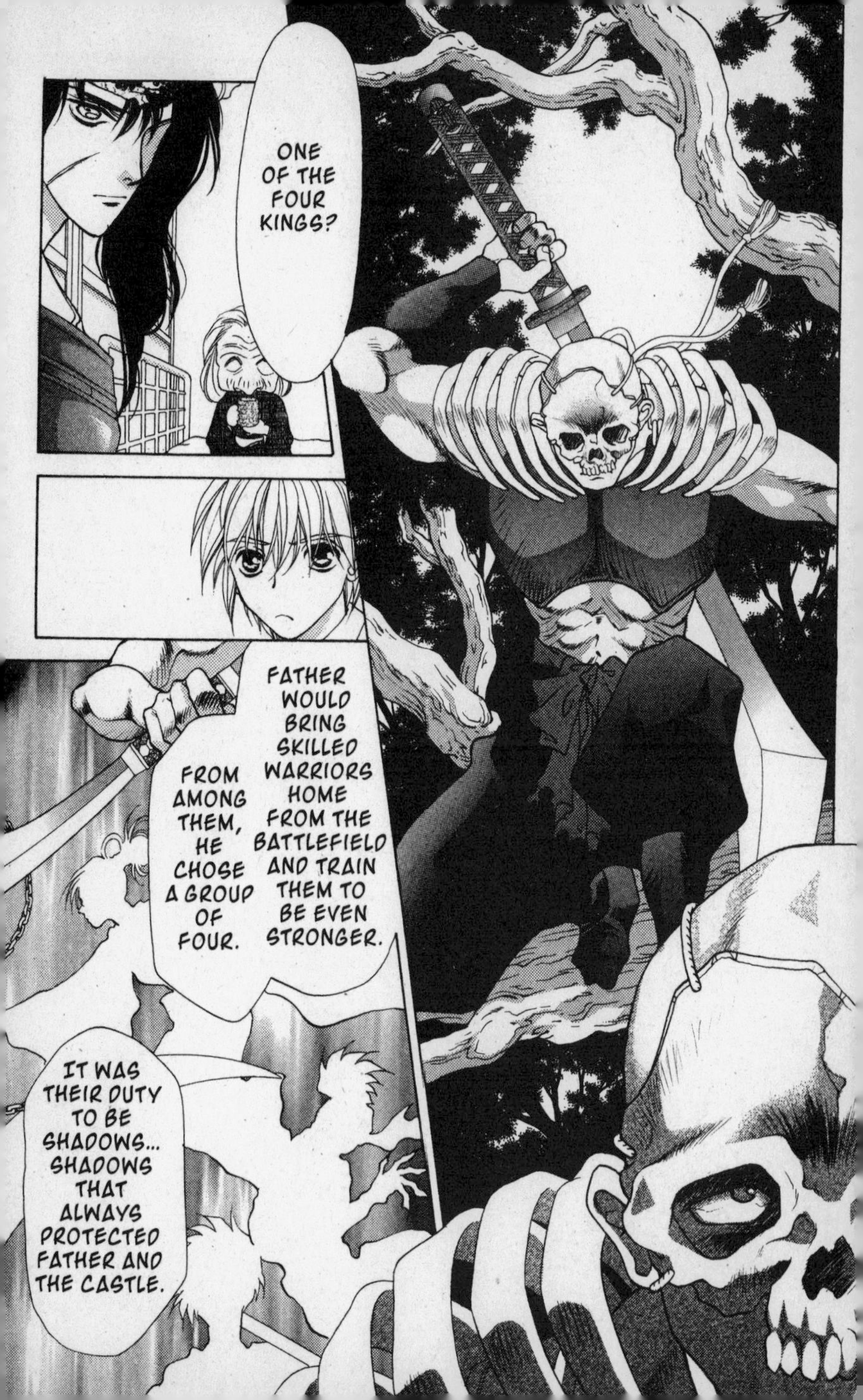
ONE OF THE FOUR KINGS?
FATHER WOULD BRING SKILLED WARRIORS HOME FROM THE BATTLEFIELD AND TRAIN THEM TO BE EVEN STRONGER.
FROM AMONG THEM, HE CHOSE A GROUP OF FOUR.
IT WAS THEIR DUTY TO BE SHADOWS... SHADOWS THAT ALWAYS PROTECTED FATHER AND THE CASTLE.

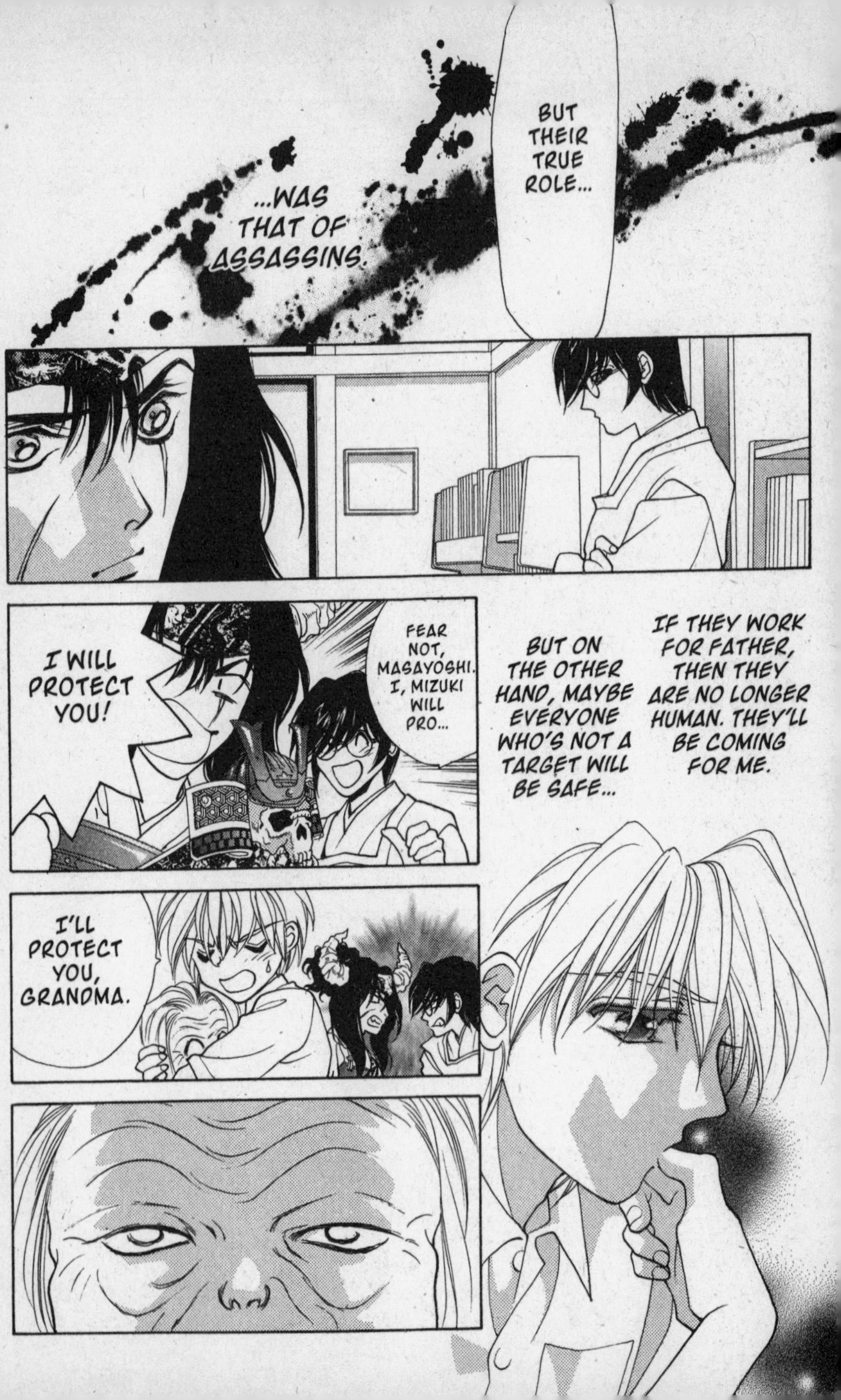
BUT THEIR TRUE ROLE...
...WAS THAT OF ASSASSINS.
IF THEY WORK FOR FATHER, THEN THEY ARE NO LONGER HUMAN. THEY'LL BE COMING FOR ME.
BUT ON THE OTHER HAND, MAYBE EVERYONE WHO'S NOT A TARGET WILL BE SAFE...
FEAR NOT, MASAYOSHI. I, MIZUKI WILL PRO...
I WILL PROTECT YOU!
I'LL PROTECT YOU, GRANDMA.

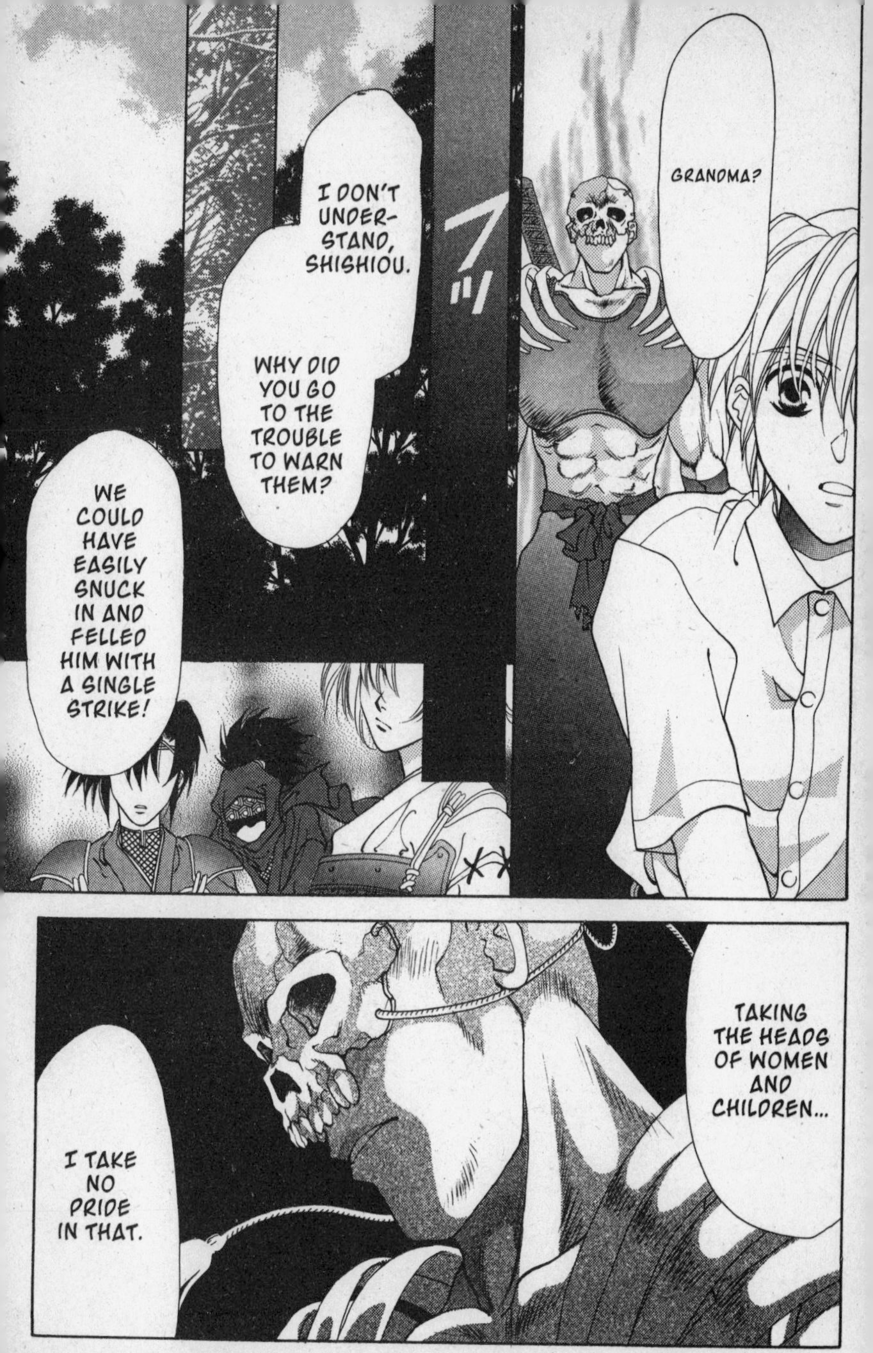
GRANDMA?
I DON'T UNDER-STAND, SHISHIOU.
WHY DID YOU GO TO THE TROUBLE TO WARN THEM?
WE COULD HAVE EASILY SNUCK IN AND FELLED HIM WITH A SINGLE STRIKE!
TAKING THE HEADS OF WOMEN AND CHILDREN...
I TAKE NO PRIDE IN THAT.

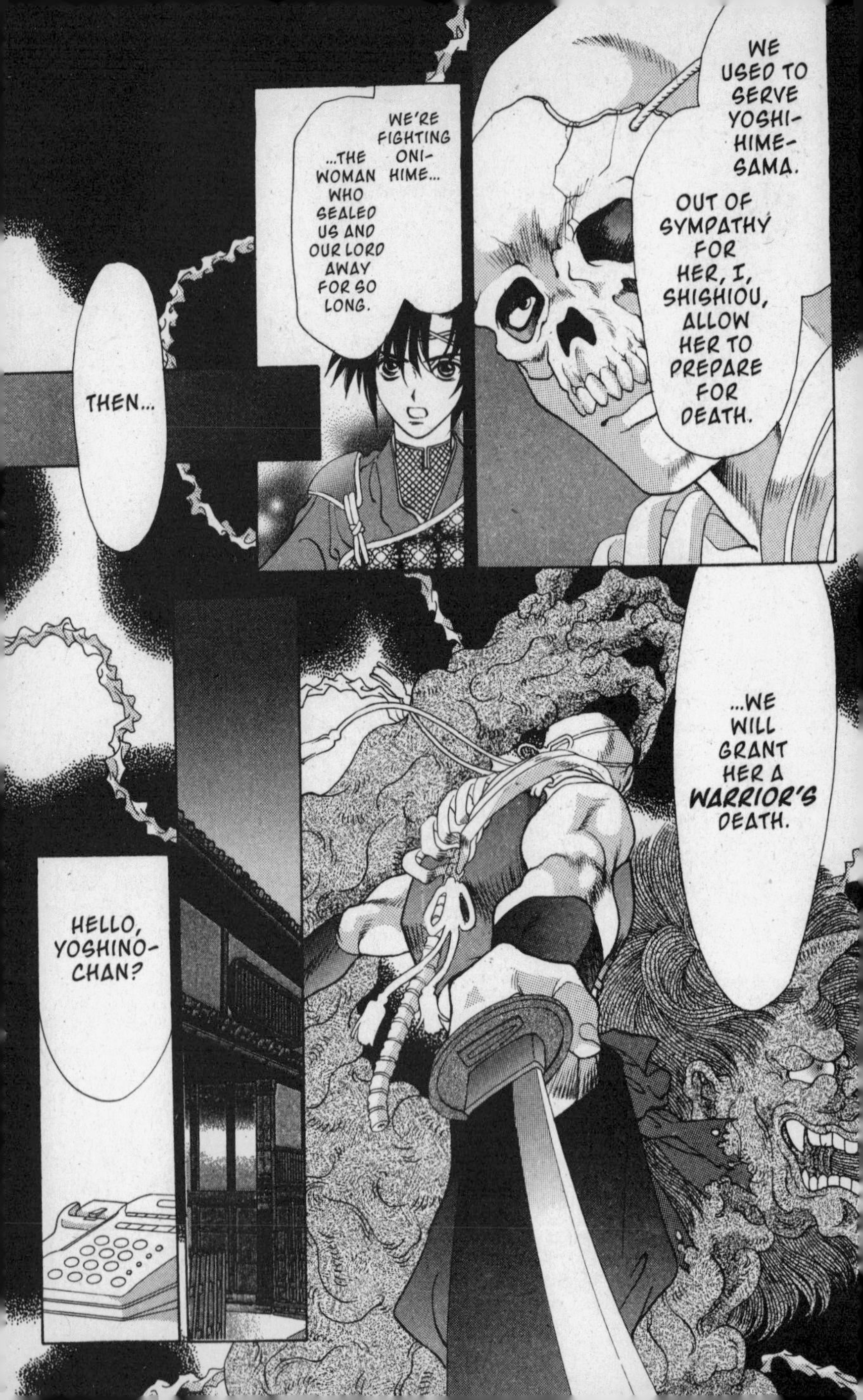
WE USED TO SERVE YOSHI-HIME-SAMA.
OUT OF SYMPATHY FOR HER, I, SHISHIOU, ALLOW HER TO PREPARE FOR DEATH.
WE'RE FIGHTING ONI-HIME...
...THE WOMAN WHO SEALED US AND OUR LORD AWAY FOR SO LONG.
THEN...
...WE WILL GRANT HER A WARRIOR'S DEATH.
HELLO, YOSHINO-CHAN?

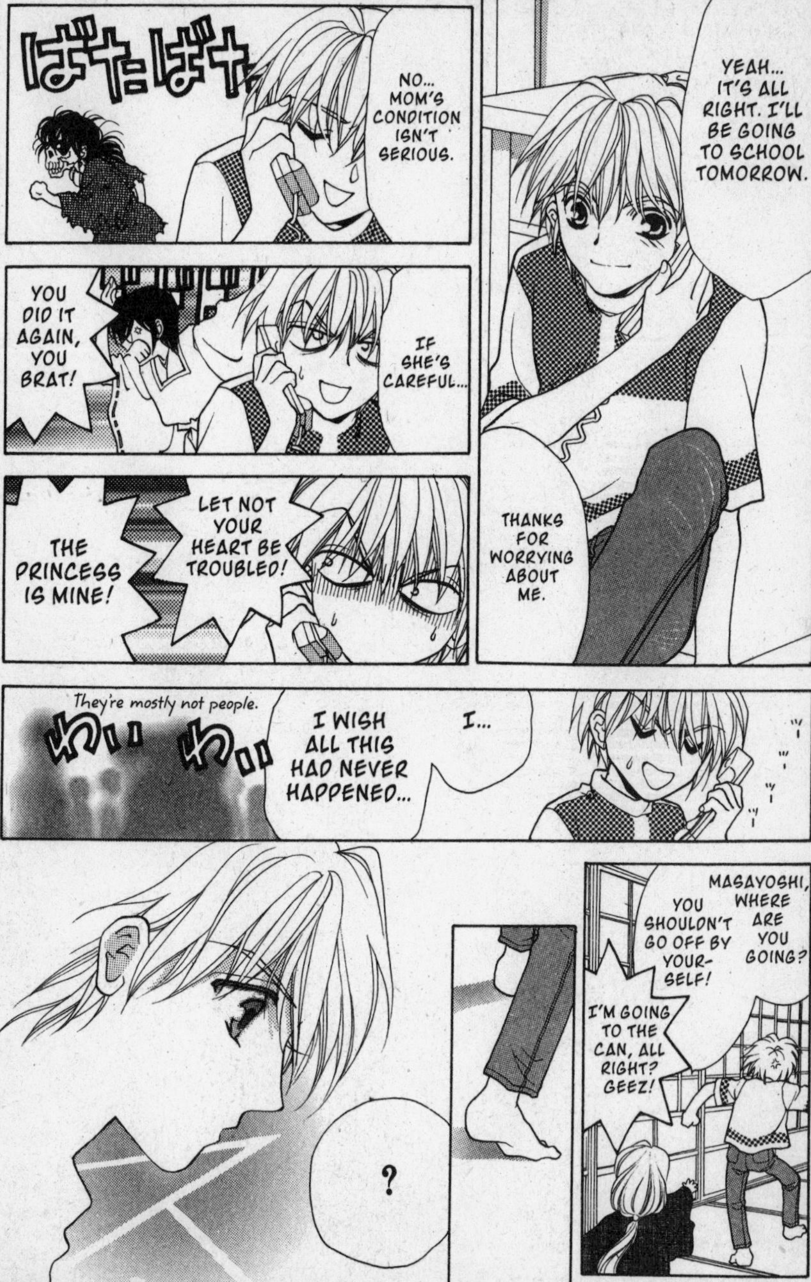
YEAH... IT'S ALL RIGHT. I'LL BE GOING TO SCHOOL TOMORROW.
THANKS FOR WORRYING ABOUT ME.
ばたばた
NO... MOM'S CONDITION ISN'T SERIOUS.
IF SHE'S CAREFUL...
YOU DID IT AGAIN, YOU BRAT!
LET NOT YOUR HEART BE TROUBLED!
THE PRINCESS IS MINE!
I...
I WISH ALL THIS HAD NEVER HAPPENED...
They're mostly not people.
わい わい
MASAYOSHI, WHERE ARE YOU GOING?
YOU SHOULDN'T GO OFF BY YOURSELF!
I'M GOING TO THE CAN, ALL RIGHT? GEEZ!
?

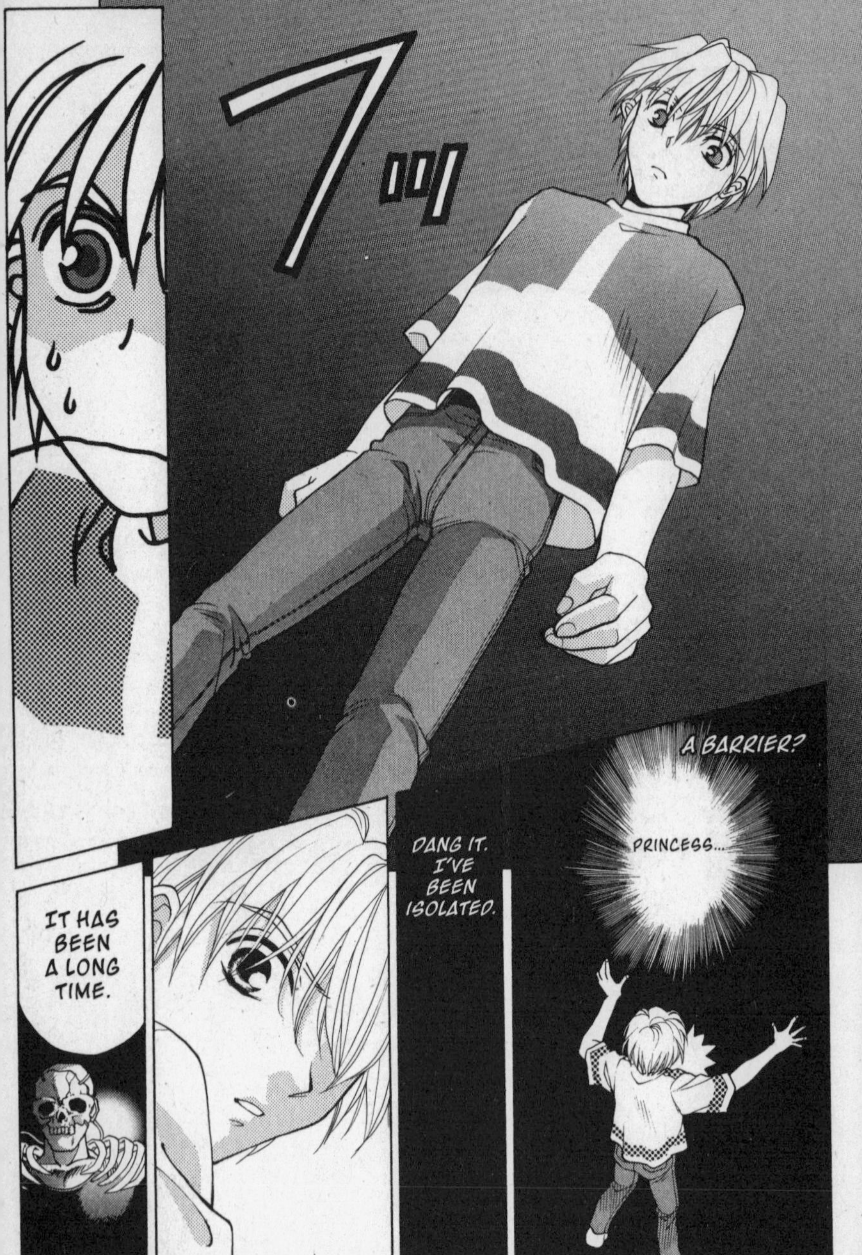
A BARRIER?
PRINCESS...
DANG IT. I'VE BEEN ISOLATED.
IT HAS BEEN A LONG TIME.

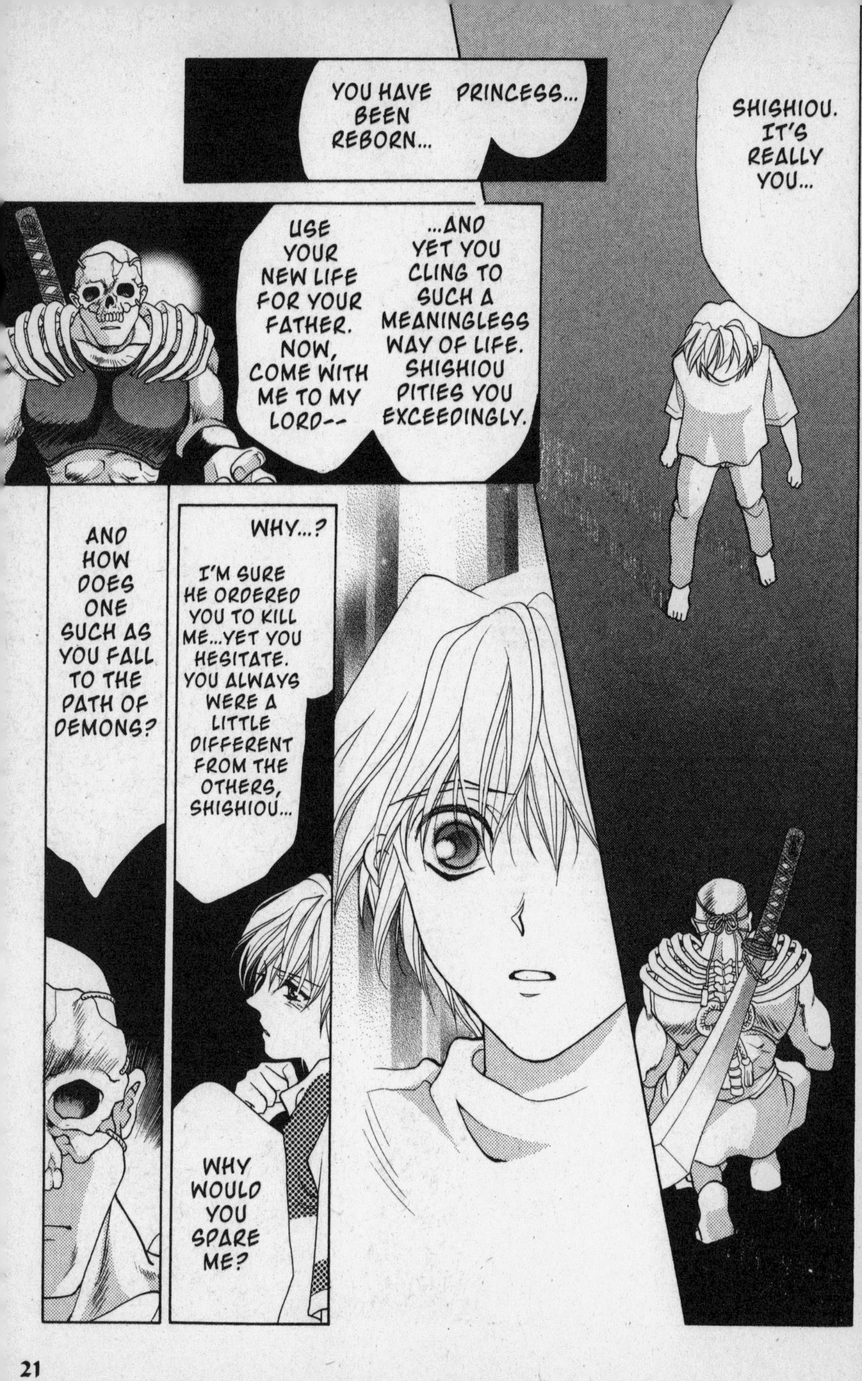
SHISHIOU. IT'S REALLY YOU...
PRINCESS...
YOU HAVE BEEN REBORN...
...AND YET YOU CLING TO SUCH A MEANINGLESS WAY OF LIFE. SHISHIOU PITIES YOU EXCEEDINGLY.
USE YOUR NEW LIFE FOR YOUR FATHER. NOW, COME WITH ME TO MY LORD--
WHY...?
I'M SURE HE ORDERED YOU TO KILL ME...YET YOU HESITATE. YOU ALWAYS WERE A LITTLE DIFFERENT FROM THE OTHERS, SHISHIOU...
WHY WOULD YOU SPARE ME?
AND HOW DOES ONE SUCH AS YOU FALL TO THE PATH OF DEMONS?

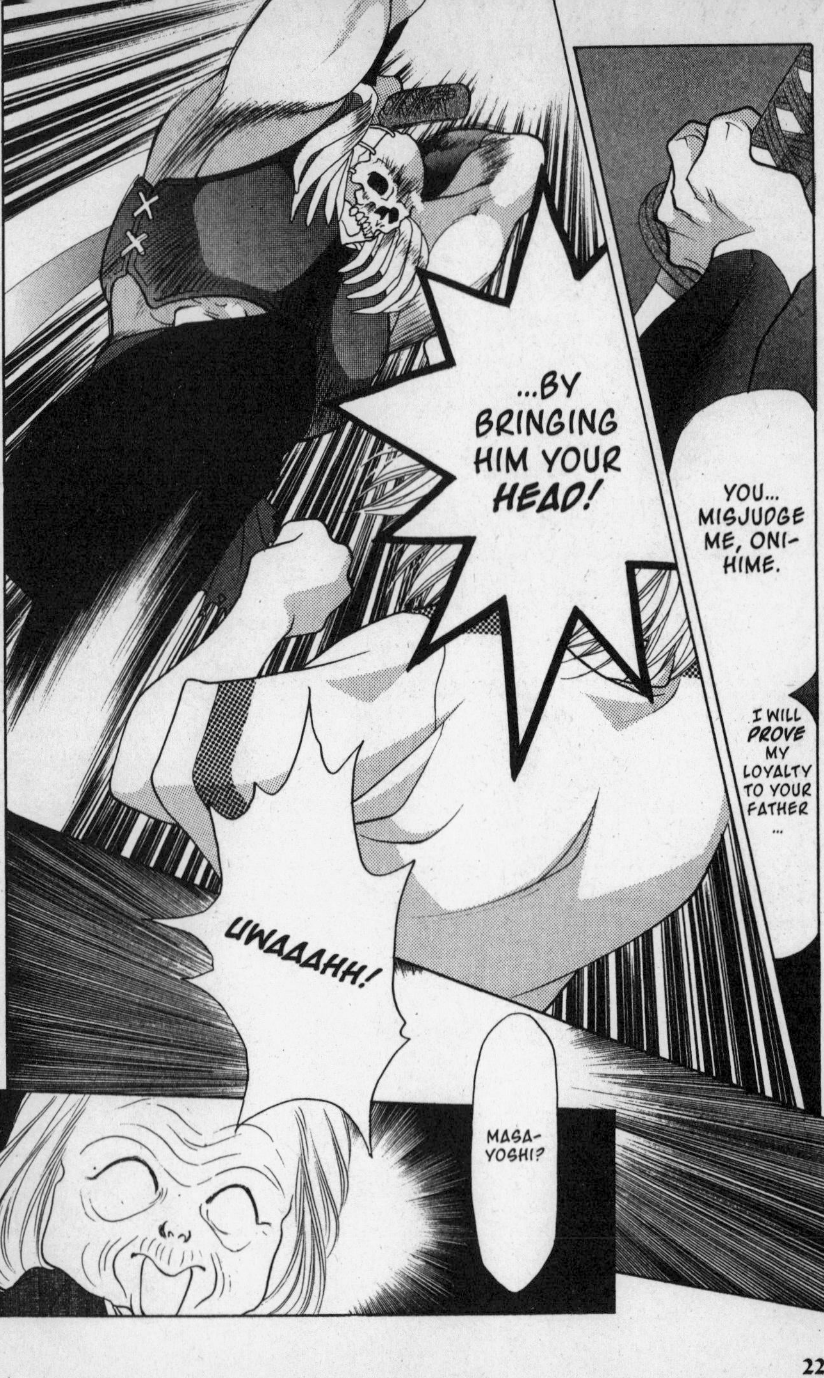
YOU... MISJUDGE ME, ONI-HIME.
I WILL PROVE MY LOYALTY TO YOUR FATHER ...
...BY BRINGING HIM YOUR HEAD!
UWAAAHH!
MASA-YOSHI?

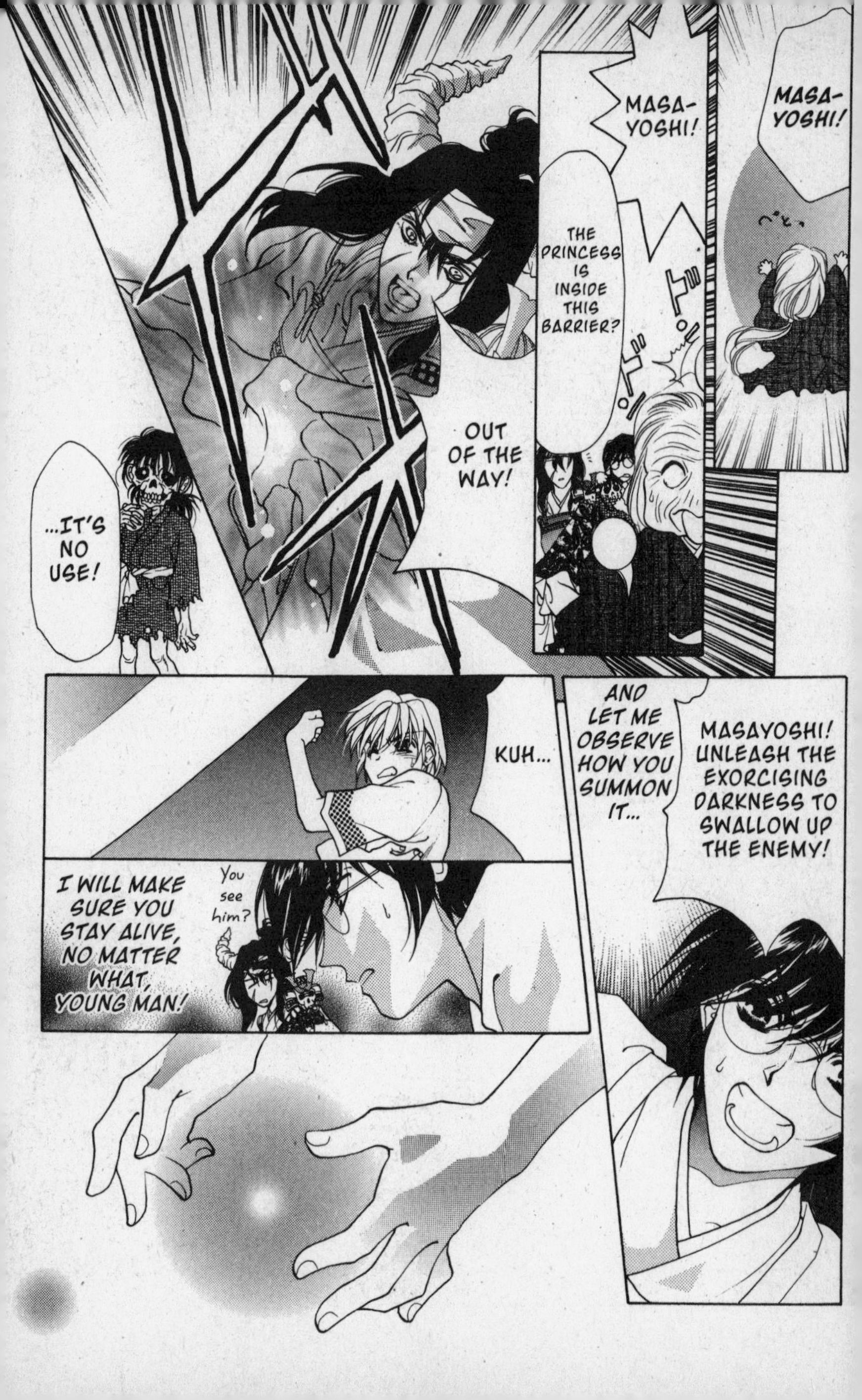
MASA-YOSHI!
MASA-YOSHI!
THE PRINCESS IS INSIDE THIS BARRIER?
OUT OF THE WAY!
...IT'S NO USE!
MASAYOSHI! UNLEASH THE EXORCISING DARKNESS TO SWALLOW UP THE ENEMY!
AND LET ME OBSERVE HOW YOU SUMMON IT...
KUH...
You see him?
I WILL MAKE SURE YOU STAY ALIVE, NO MATTER WHAT, YOUNG MAN!

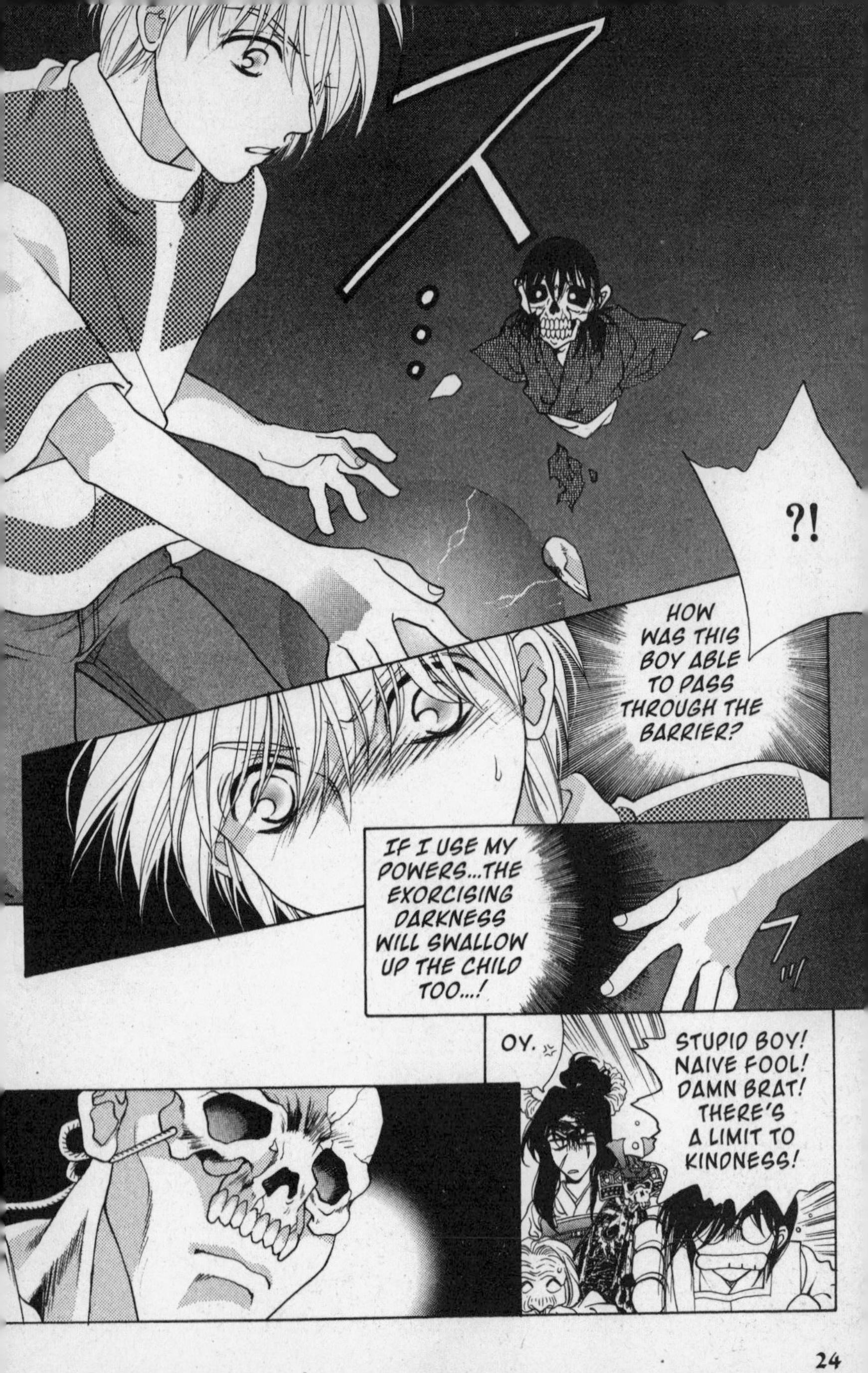
?!
HOW WAS THIS BOY ABLE TO PASS THROUGH THE BARRIER?
IF I USE MY POWERS...THE EXORCISING DARKNESS WILL SWALLOW UP THE CHILD TOO...!
STUPID BOY! NAIVE FOOL! DAMN BRAT! THERE'S A LIMIT TO KINDNESS!
OY.

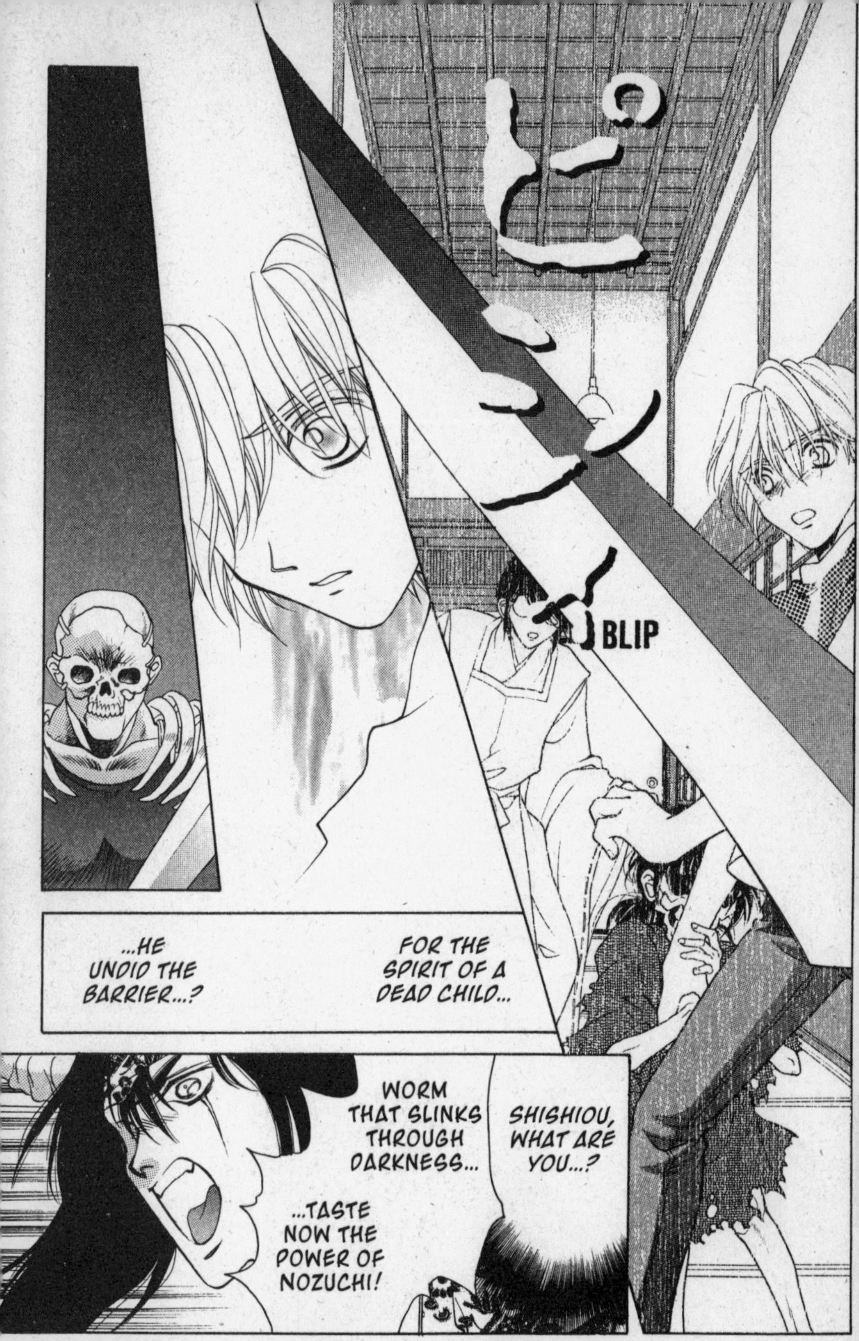
BLIP
FOR THE SPIRIT OF A DEAD CHILD...
...HE UNDID THE BARRIER...?
SHISHIOU, WHAT ARE YOU...?
WORM THAT SLINKS THROUGH DARKNESS...
...TASTE NOW THE POWER OF NOZUCHI!

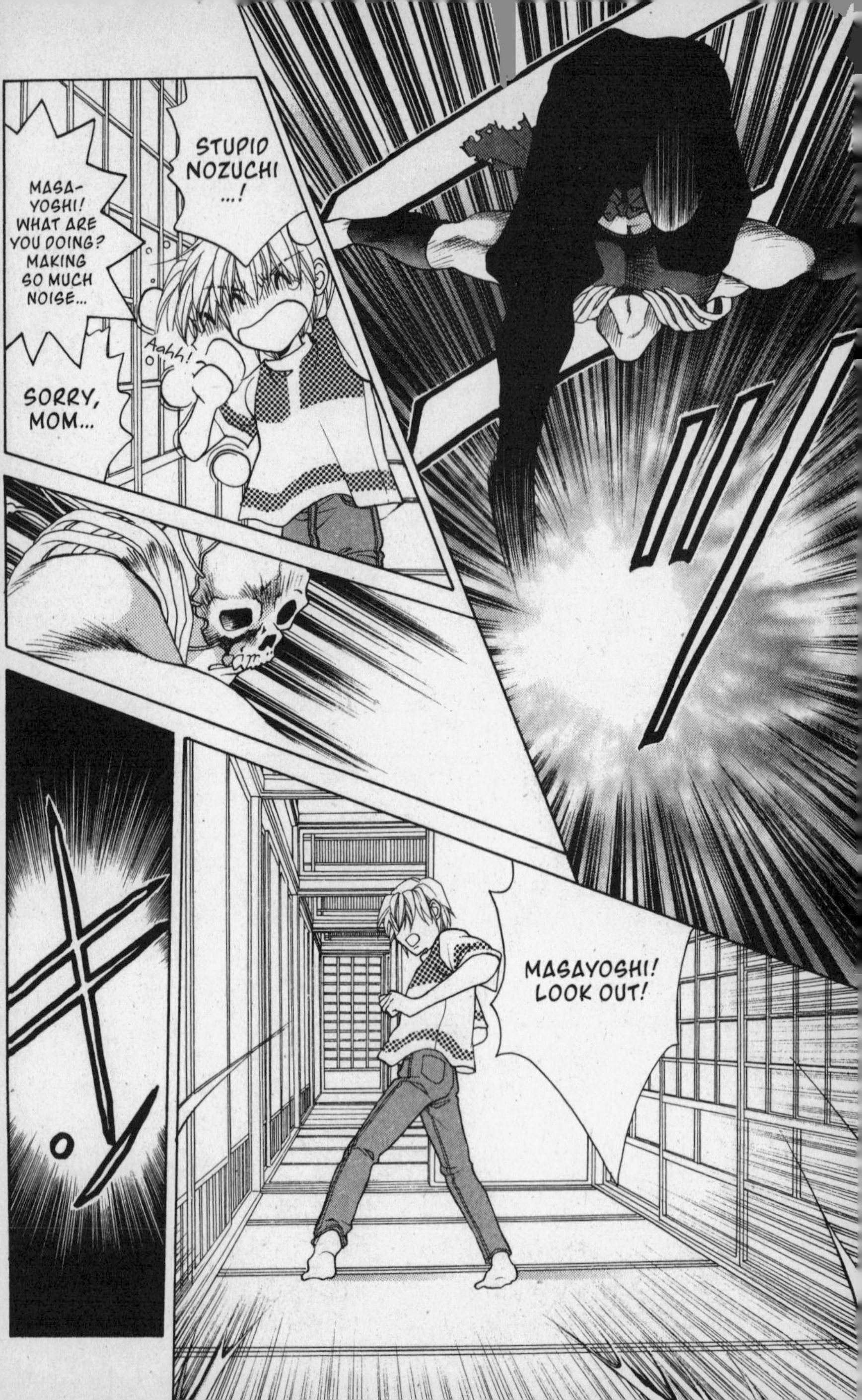
STUPID NOZUCHI ...!
MASA-YOSHI! WHAT ARE YOU DOING? MAKING SO MUCH NOISE...
Aahh!
SORRY, MOM...
MASAYOSHI! LOOK OUT!

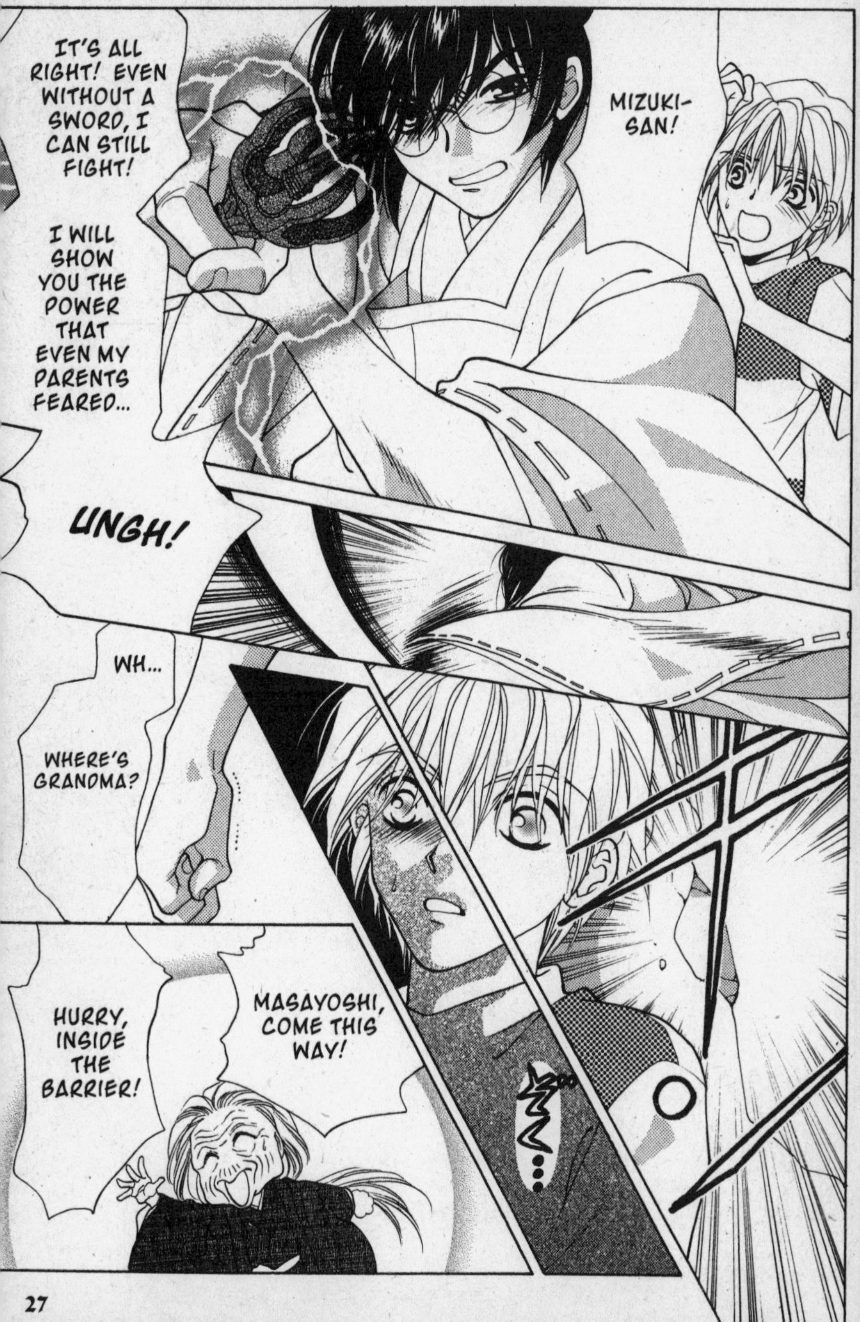
MIZUKI-SAN!
IT'S ALL RIGHT! EVEN WITHOUT A SWORD, I CAN STILL FIGHT!
I WILL SHOW YOU THE POWER THAT EVEN MY PARENTS FEARED...
UNGH!
WH...
WHERE'S GRANDMA?
MASAYOSHI, COME THIS WAY!
HURRY, INSIDE THE BARRIER!

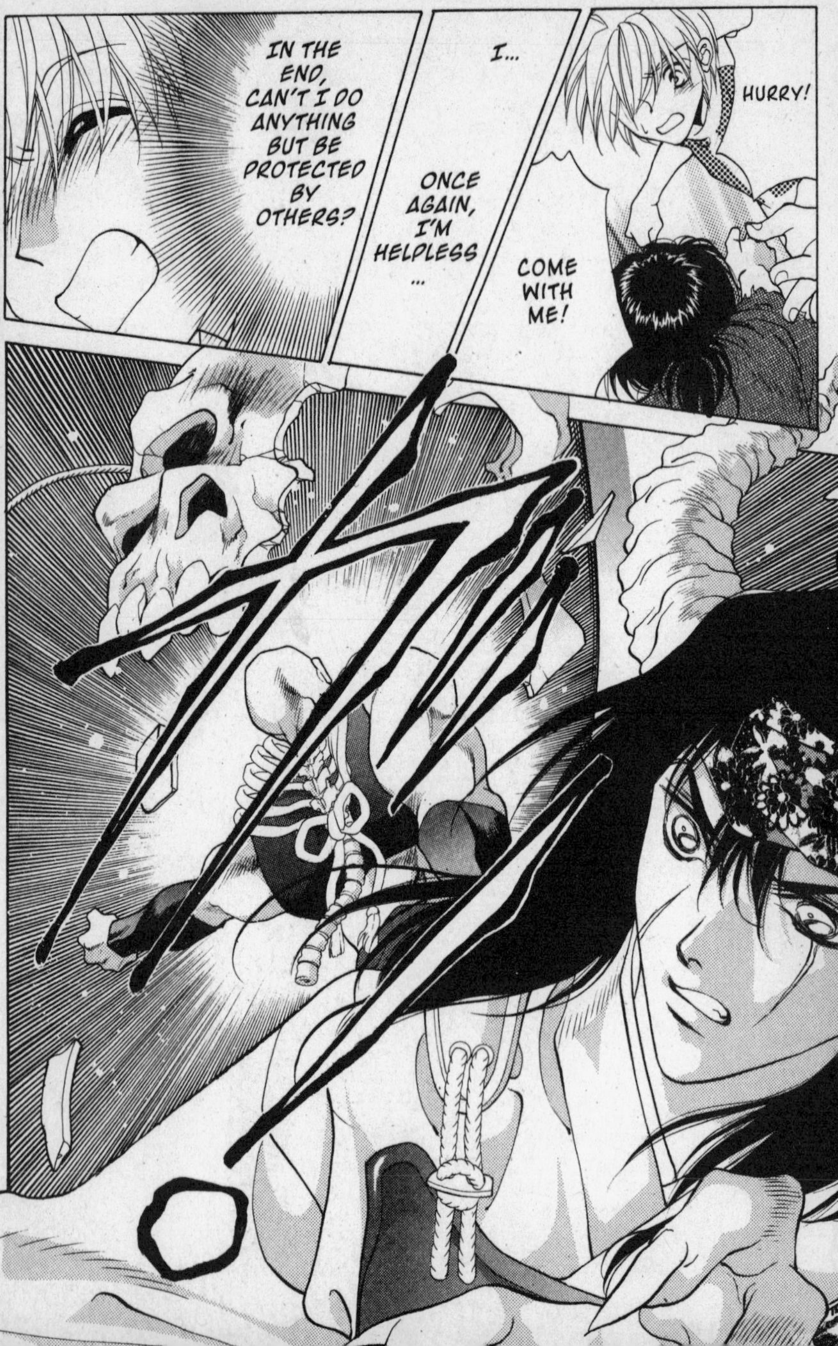
HURRY!
COME WITH ME!
I...
ONCE AGAIN, I'M HELPLESS ...
IN THE END, CAN'T I DO ANYTHING BUT BE PROTECTED BY OTHERS?

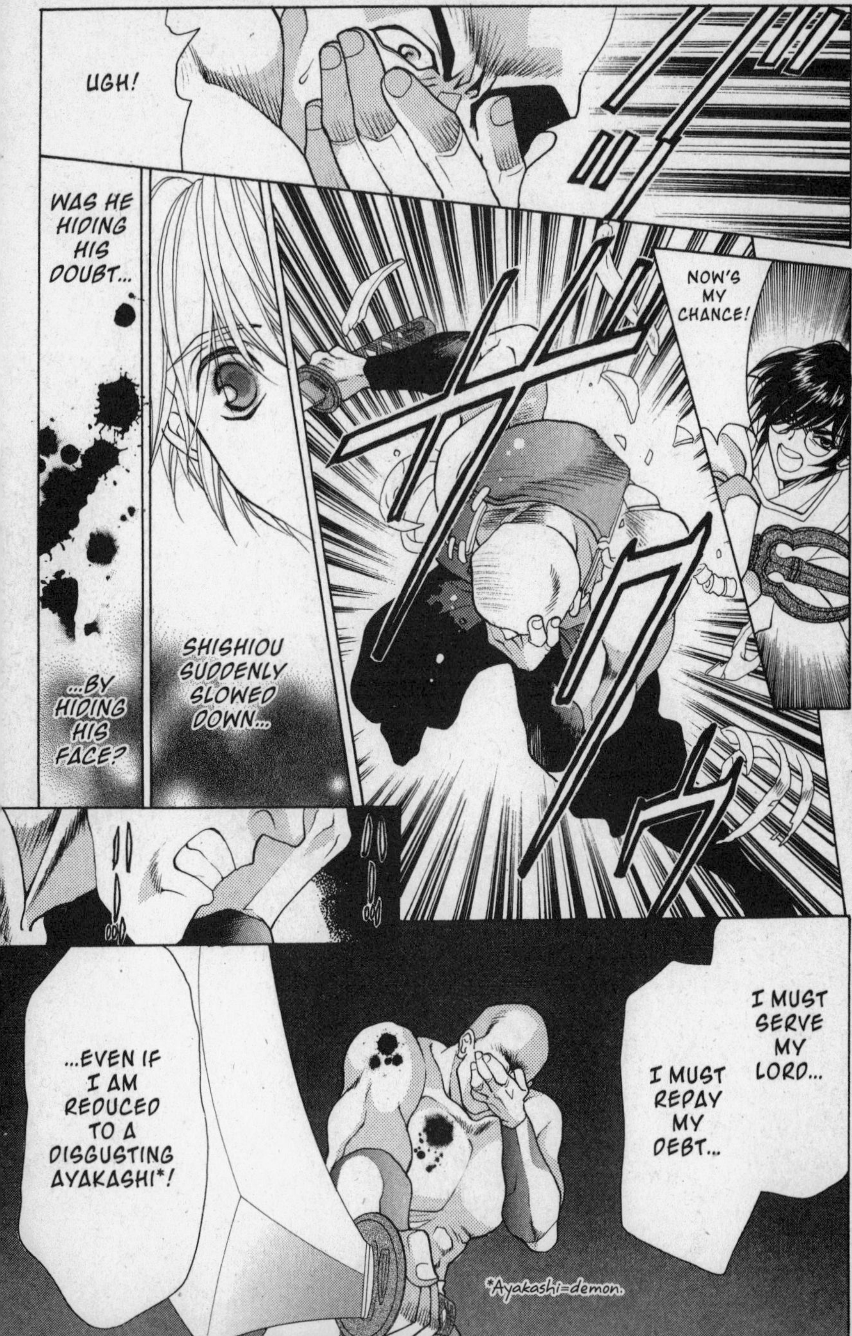
UGH!
NOW'S MY CHANCE!
SHISHIOU SUDDENLY SLOWED DOWN...
WAS HE HIDING HIS DOUBT...
...BY HIDING HIS FACE?
I MUST SERVE MY LORD...
I MUST REPAY MY DEBT...
...EVEN IF I AM REDUCED TO A DISGUSTING AYAKASHI*!
*Ayakashi=demon.

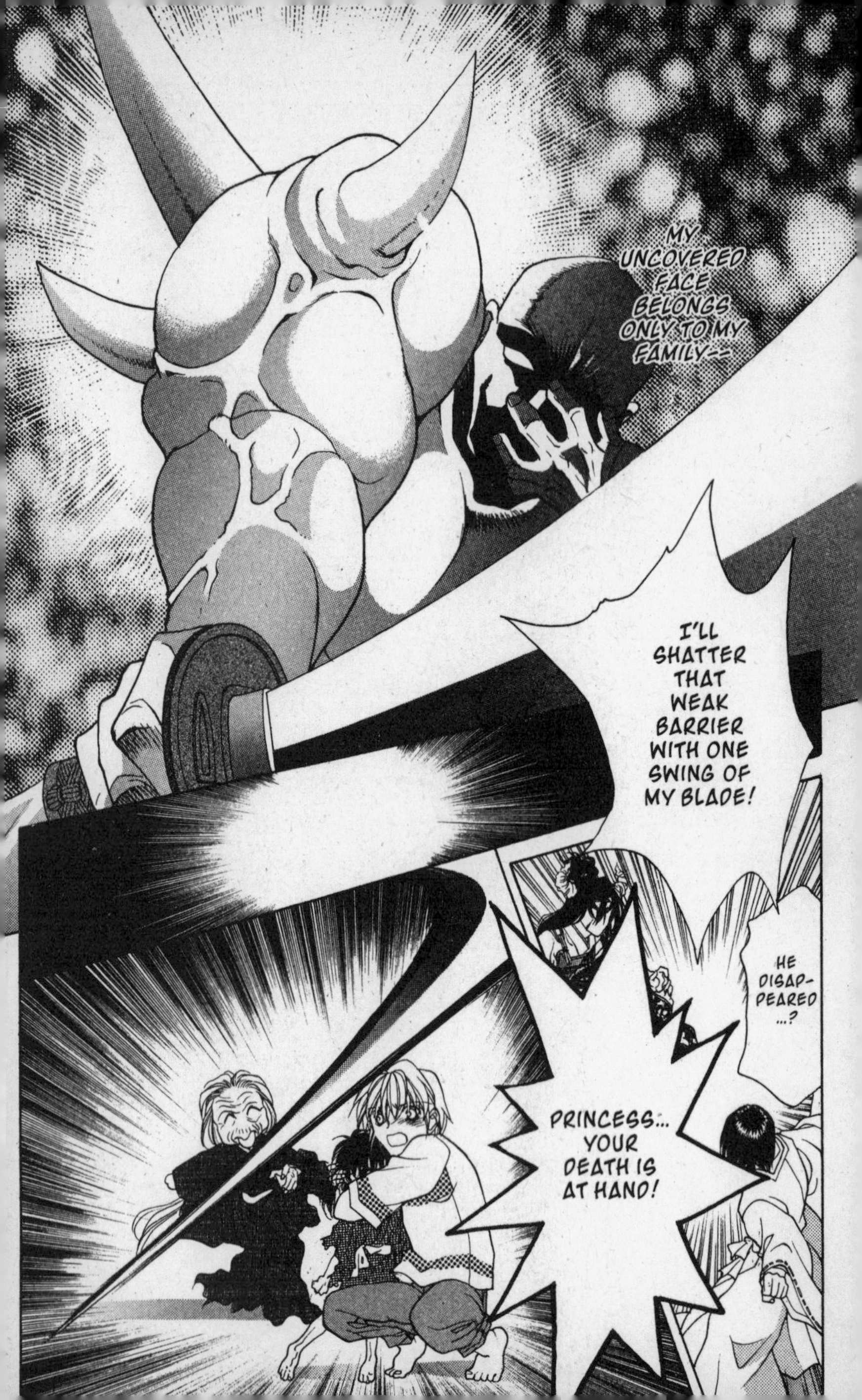
MY UNCOVERED FACE BELONGS ONLY TO MY FAMILY--
I'LL SHATTER THAT WEAK BARRIER WITH ONE SWING OF MY BLADE!
HE DISAP-PEARED ...?
PRINCESS... YOUR DEATH IS AT HAND!

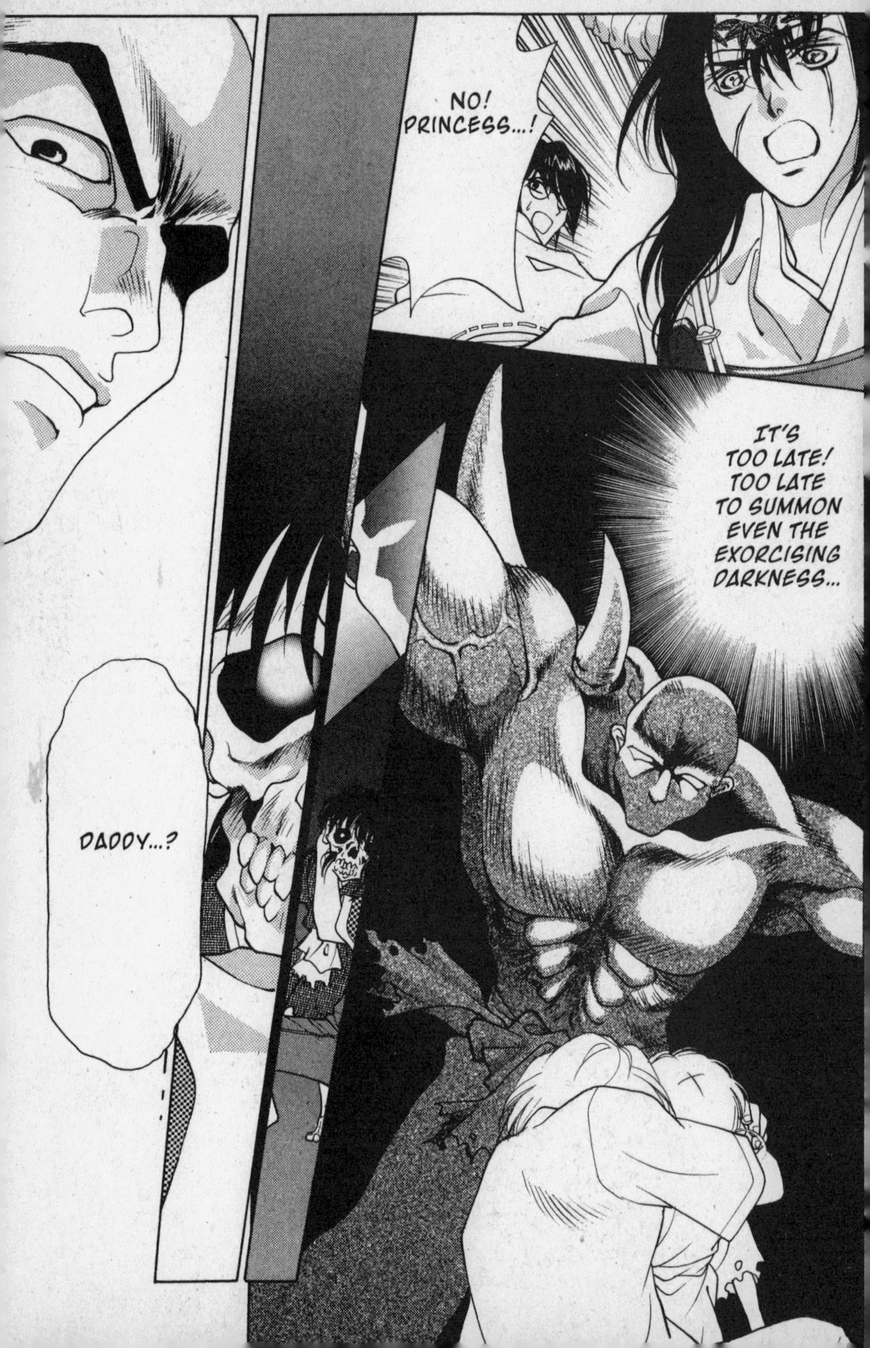
NO! PRINCESS...!
IT'S TOO LATE! TOO LATE TO SUMMON EVEN THE EXORCISING DARKNESS...
DADDY...?

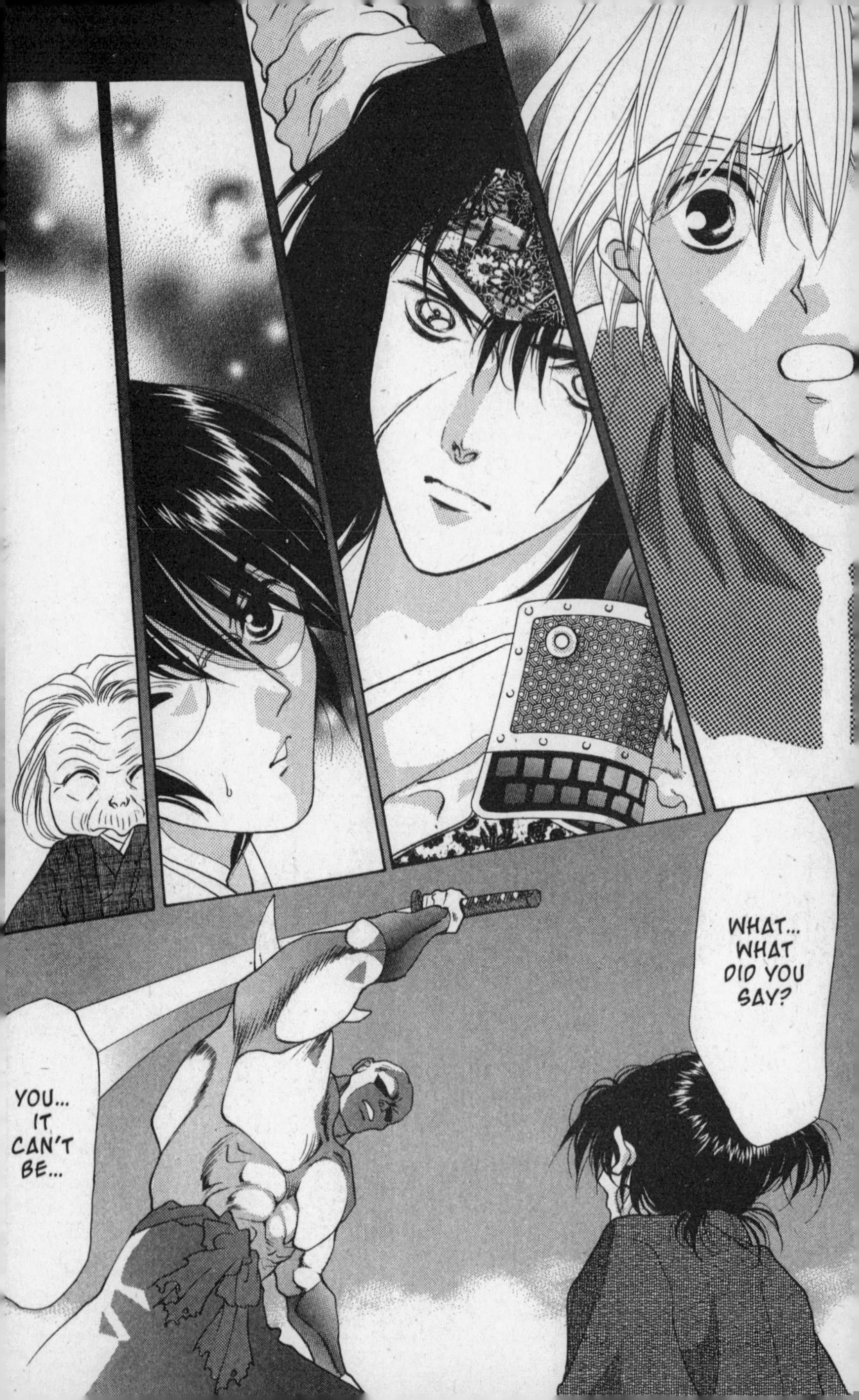
WHAT... WHAT DID YOU SAY?
YOU... IT CAN'T BE...

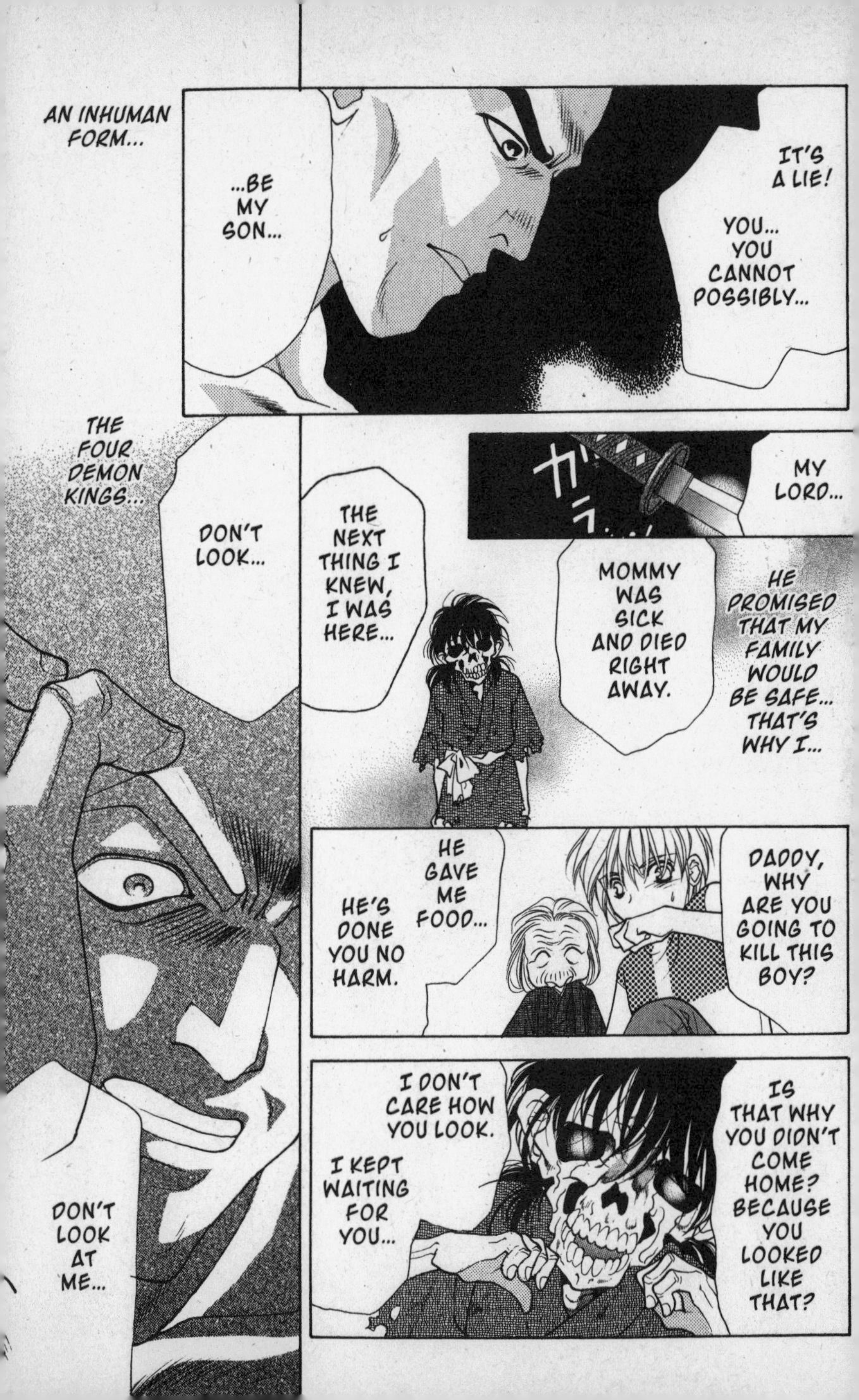
IT'S A LIE!
YOU... YOU CANNOT POSSIBLY...
...BE MY SON...
AN INHUMAN FORM...
MY LORD...
HE PROMISED THAT MY FAMILY WOULD BE SAFE... THAT'S WHY I...
MOMMY WAS SICK AND DIED RIGHT AWAY.
THE NEXT THING I KNEW, I WAS HERE...
DADDY, WHY ARE YOU GOING TO KILL THIS BOY?
HE GAVE ME FOOD...
HE'S DONE YOU NO HARM.
IS THAT WHY YOU DIDN'T COME HOME? BECAUSE YOU LOOKED LIKE THAT?
I DON'T CARE HOW YOU LOOK.
I KEPT WAITING FOR YOU...
THE FOUR DEMON KINGS...
DON'T LOOK...
DON'T LOOK AT ME...

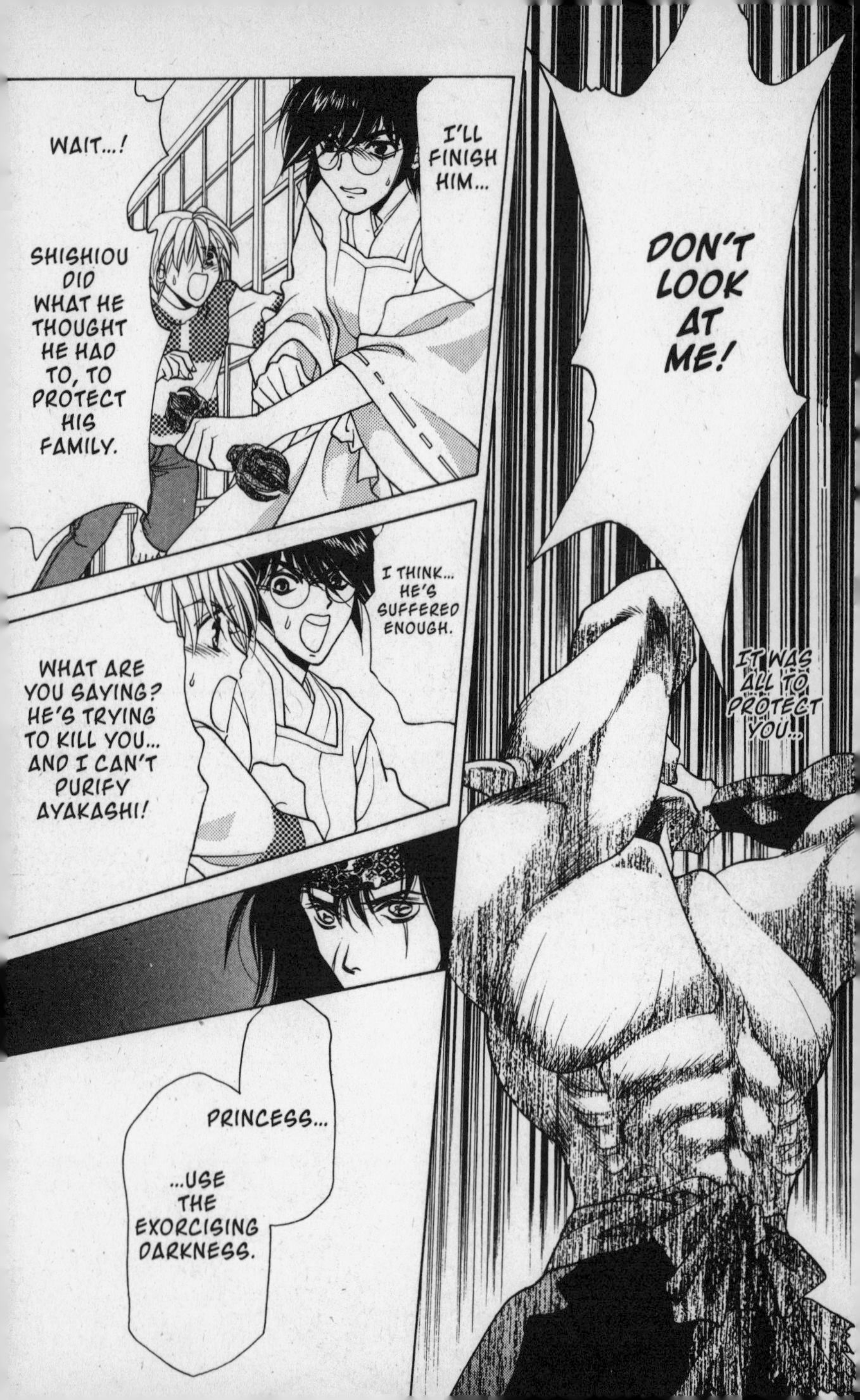
DON'T LOOK AT ME!
IT WAS ALL TO PROTECT YOU...
I'LL FINISH HIM...
WAIT...!
SHISHIOU DID WHAT HE THOUGHT HE HAD TO, TO PROTECT HIS FAMILY.
I THINK... HE'S SUFFERED ENOUGH.
WHAT ARE YOU SAYING? HE'S TRYING TO KILL YOU... AND I CAN'T PURIFY AYAKASHI!
PRINCESS...
...USE THE EXORCISING DARKNESS.

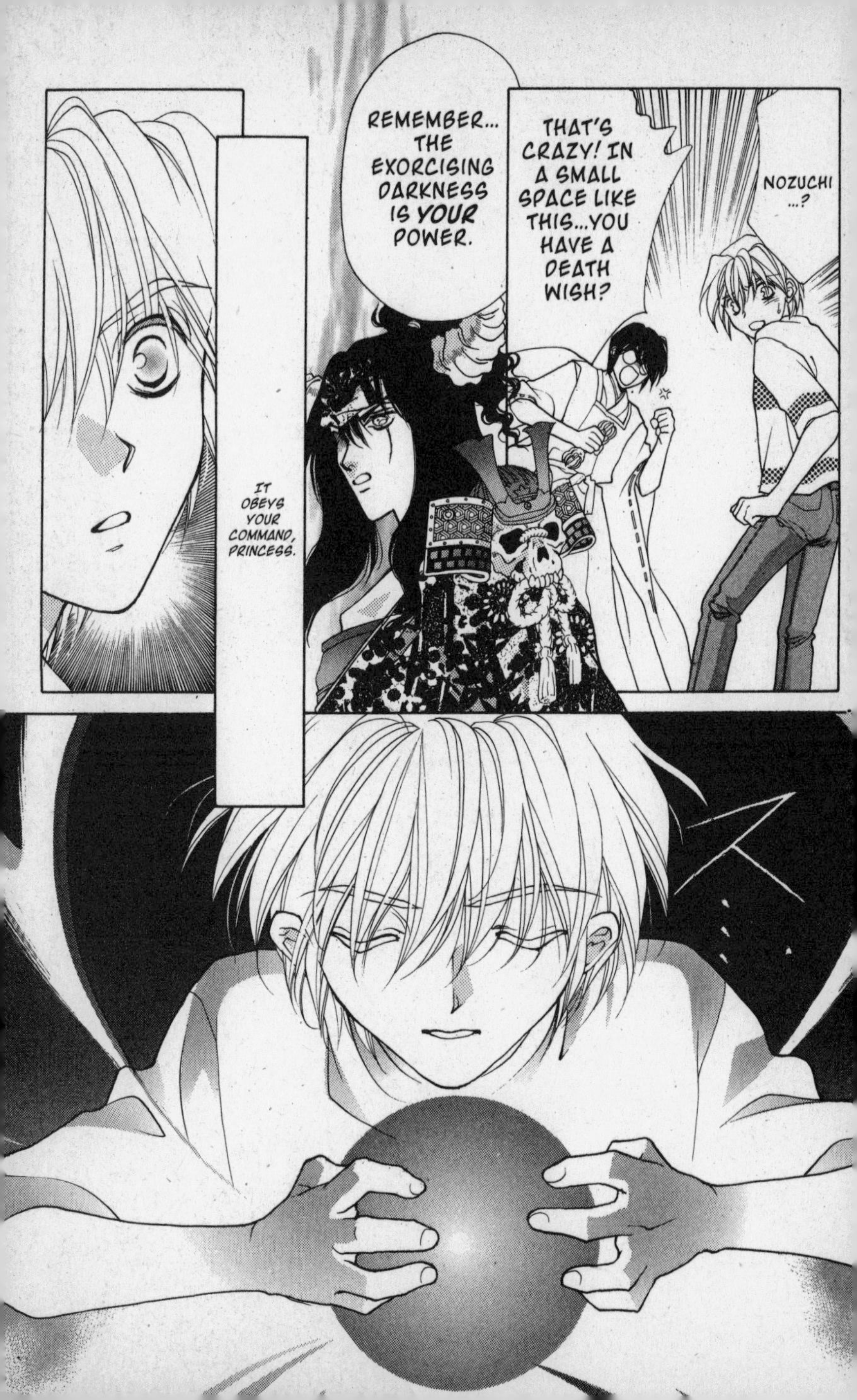
NOZUCHI ...?
THAT'S CRAZY! IN A SMALL SPACE LIKE THIS...YOU HAVE A DEATH WISH?
REMEMBER... THE EXORCISING DARKNESS IS *YOUR* POWER.
IT OBEYS YOUR COMMAND, PRINCESS.

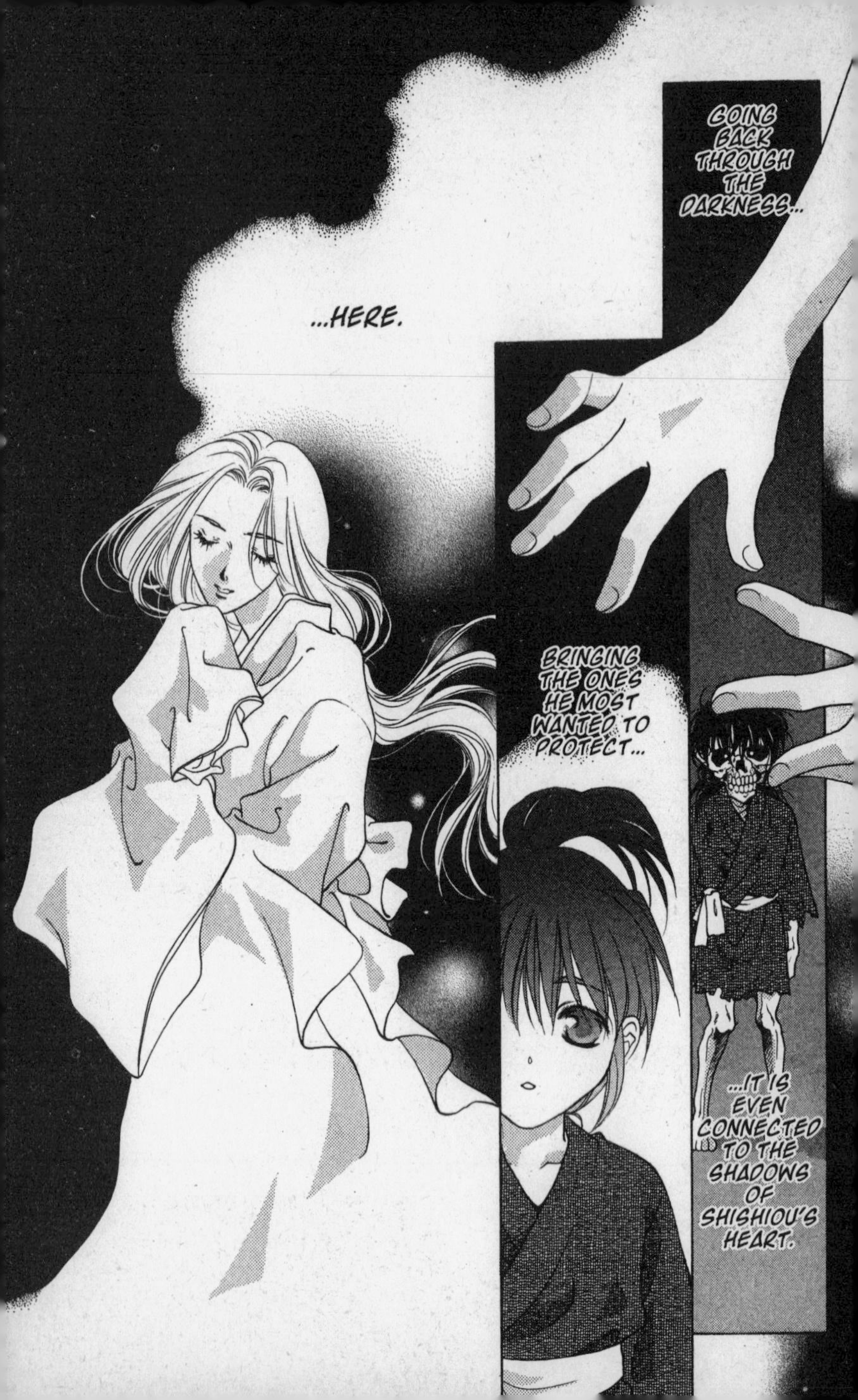
GOING BACK THROUGH THE DARKNESS...
BRINGING THE ONES HE MOST WANTED TO PROTECT...
...IT IS EVEN CONNECTED TO THE SHADOWS OF SHISHIOU'S HEART.
...HERE.

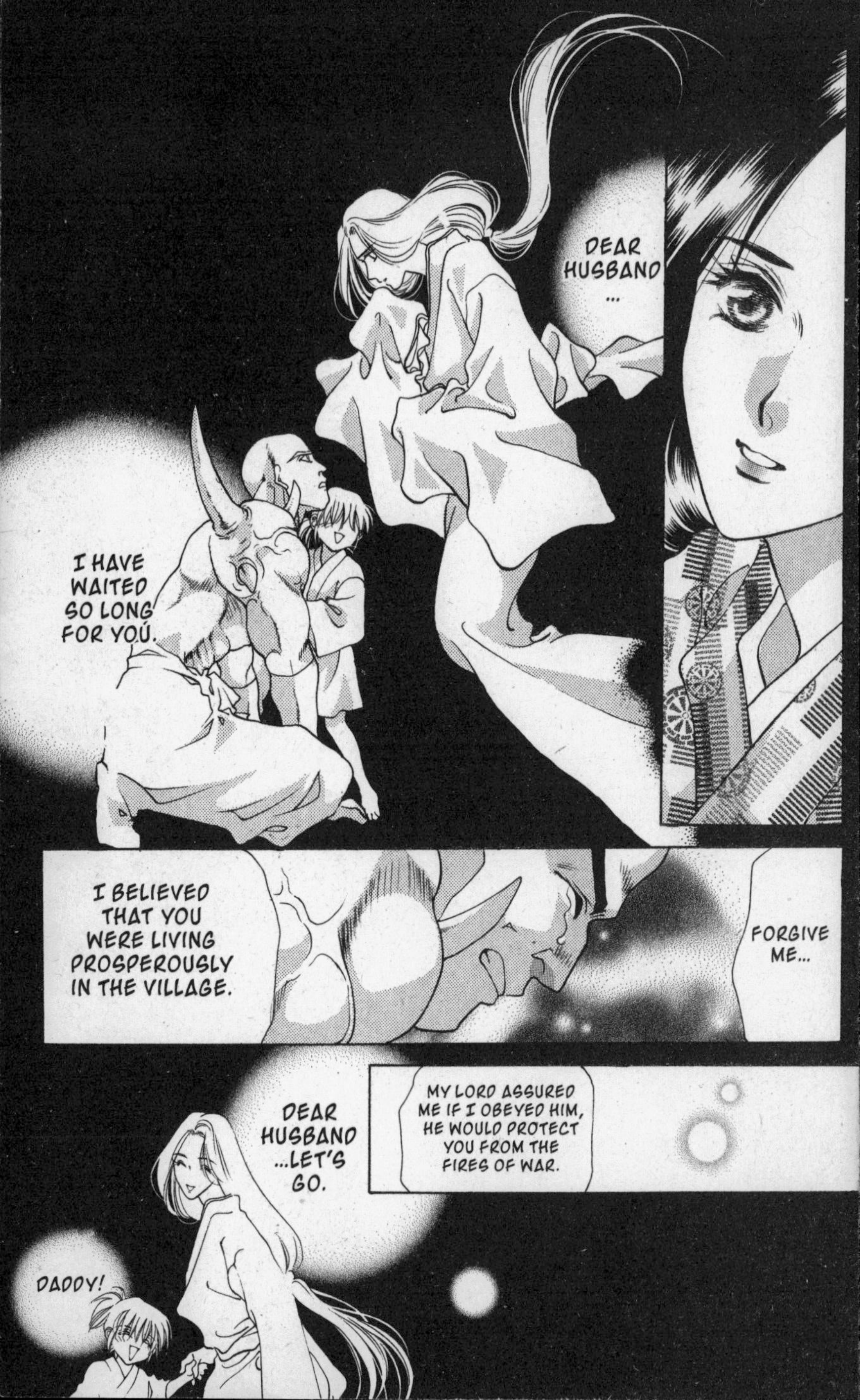
DEAR HUSBAND ...
I HAVE WAITED SO LONG FOR YOU.
FORGIVE ME...
I BELIEVED THAT YOU WERE LIVING PROSPEROUSLY IN THE VILLAGE.
MY LORD ASSURED ME IF I OBEYED HIM, HE WOULD PROTECT YOU FROM THE FIRES OF WAR.
DEAR HUSBAND ...LET'S GO.
DADDY!

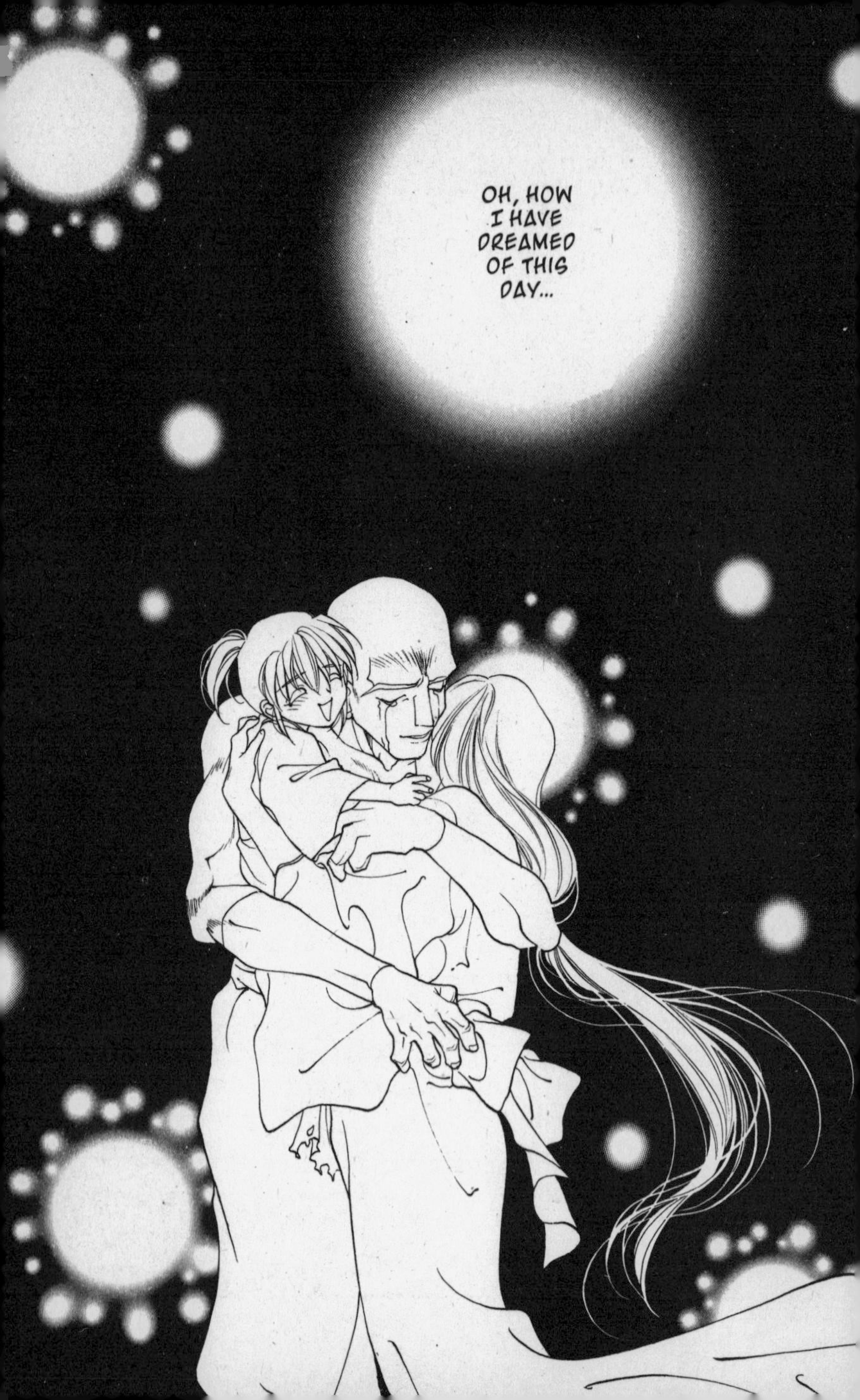
OH, HOW I HAVE DREAMED OF THIS DAY...

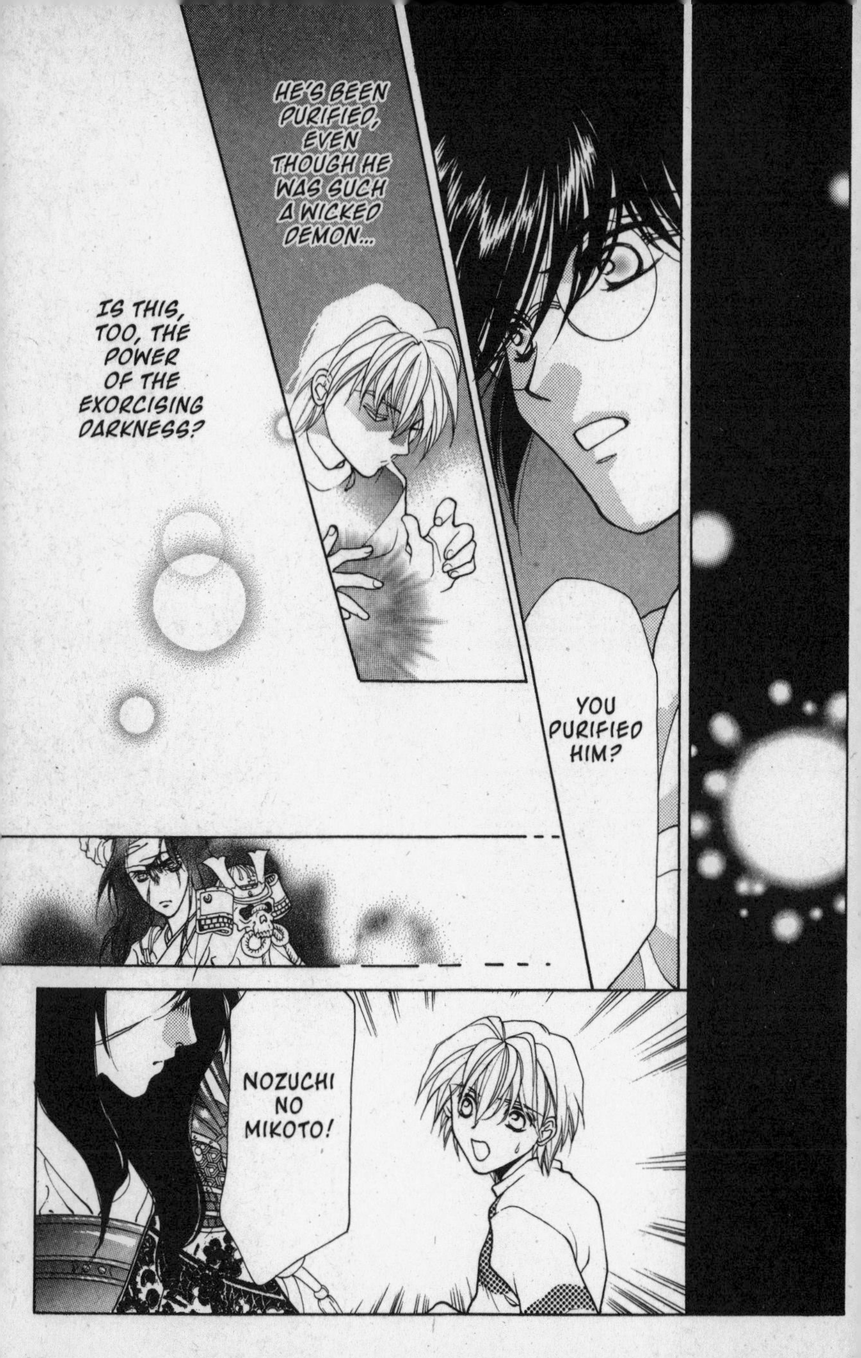
YOU PURIFIED HIM?
HE'S BEEN PURIFIED, EVEN THOUGH HE WAS SUCH A WICKED DEMON...
IS THIS, TOO, THE POWER OF THE EXORCISING DARKNESS?
NOZUCHI NO MIKOTO!

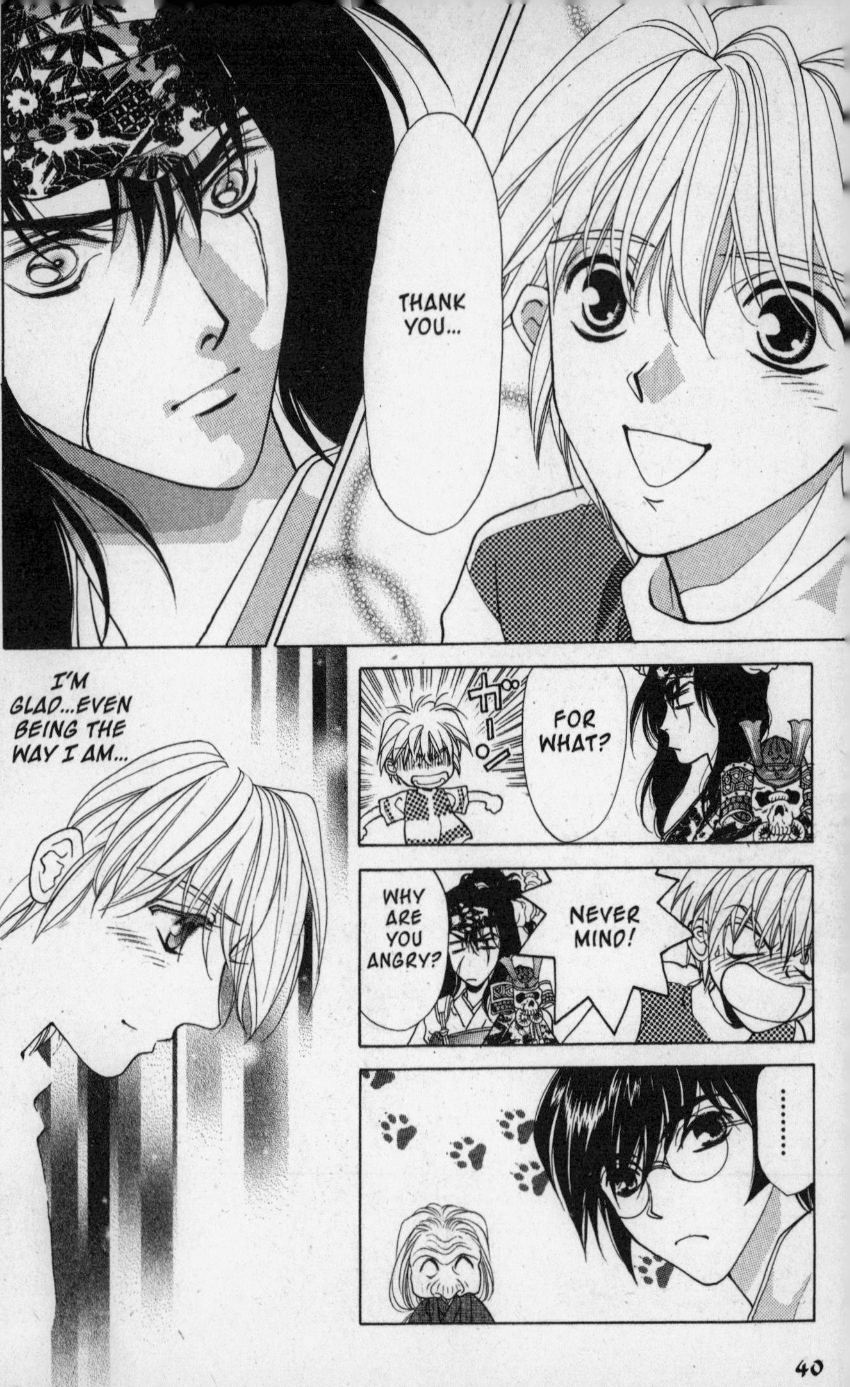
THANK YOU...
FOR WHAT?
NEVER MIND!
WHY ARE YOU ANGRY?
......
I'M GLAD...EVEN BEING THE WAY I AM...

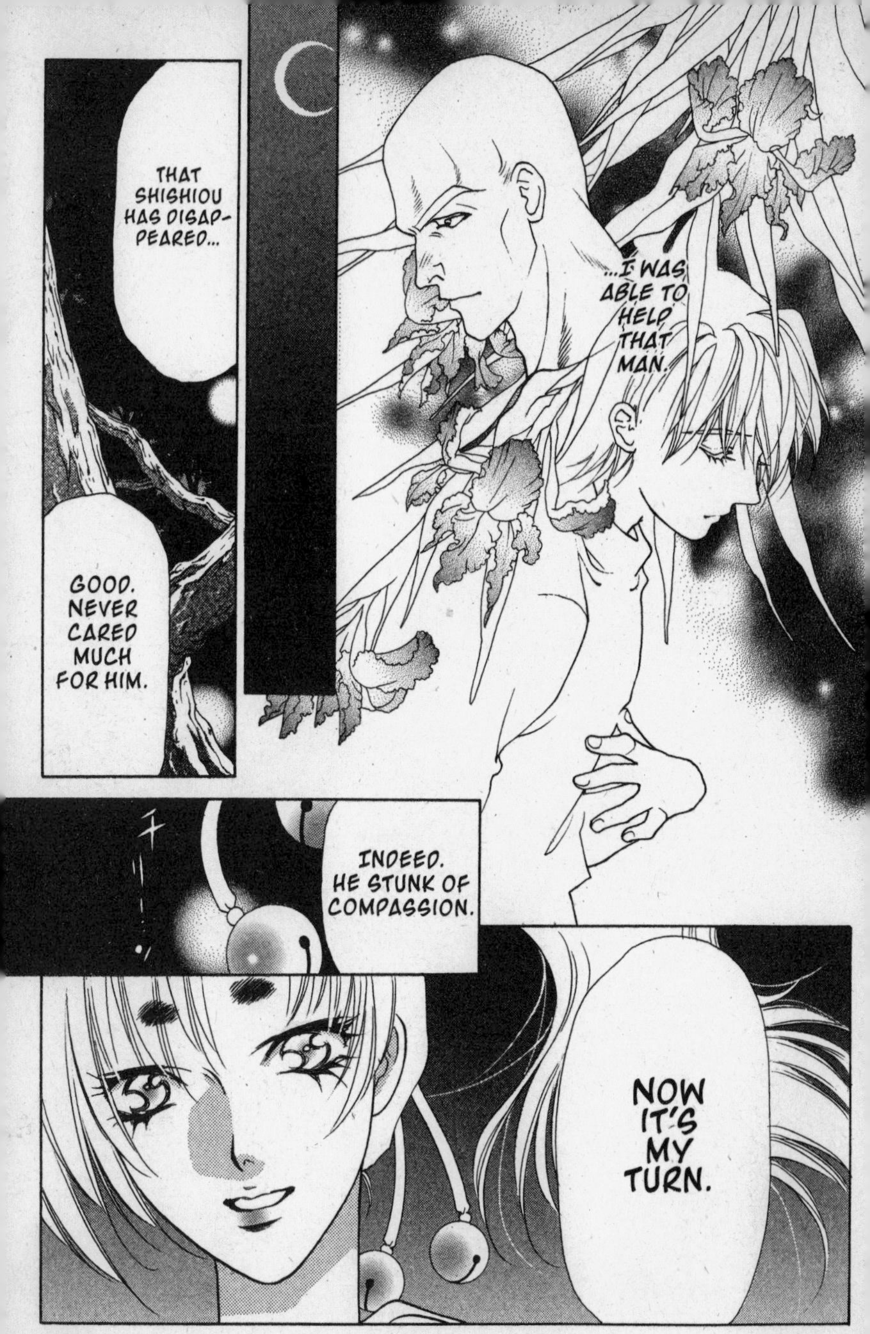
...I WAS ABLE TO HELP THAT MAN.
THAT SHISHIOU HAS DISAP-PEARED...
GOOD. NEVER CARED MUCH FOR HIM.
INDEED. HE STUNK OF COMPASSION.
NOW IT'S MY TURN.

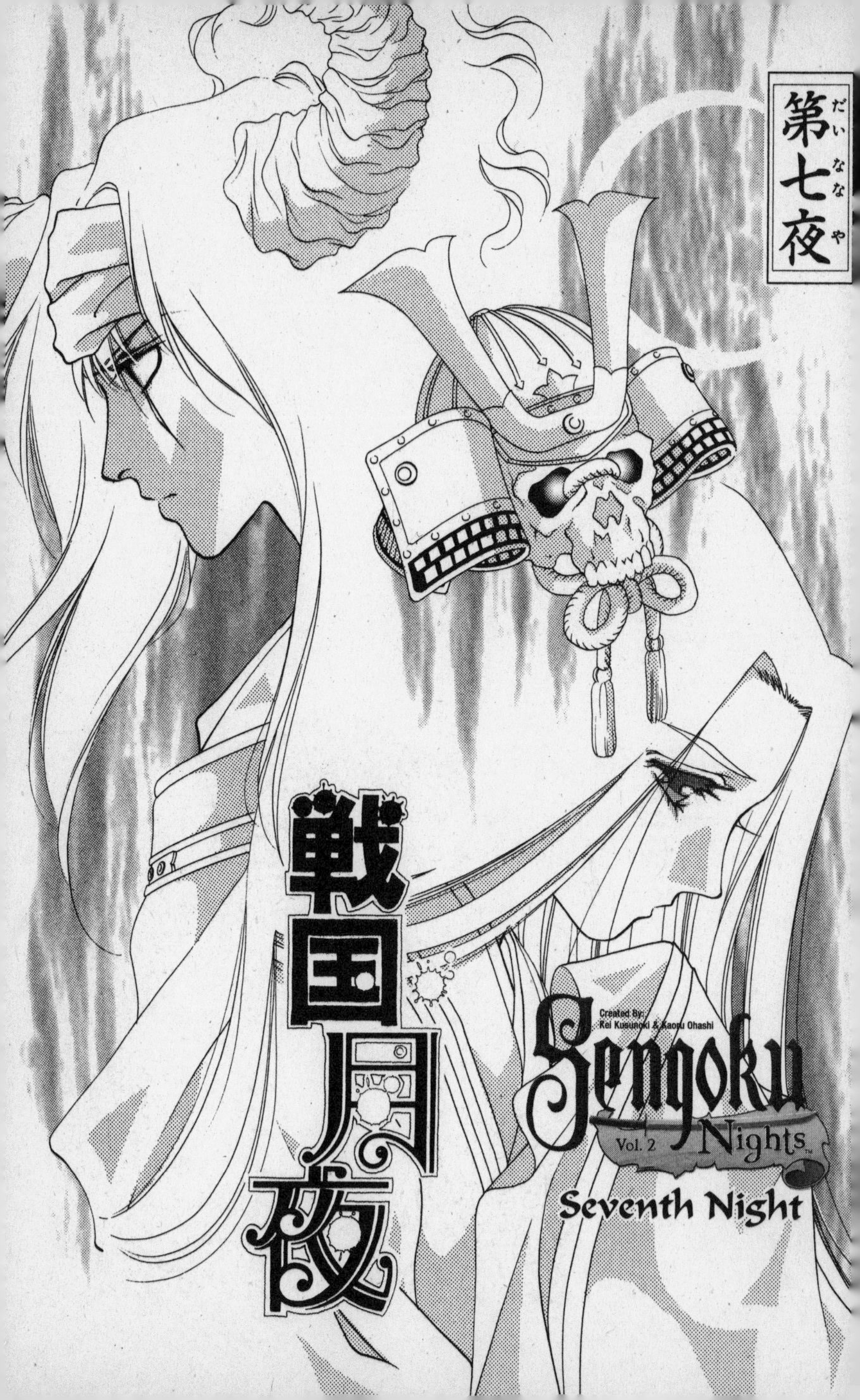
第七夜
だいななや
戦国月夜
Created By:
Kei Kusunoki & Kaoru Ohashi
Sengoku
Vol. 2 Nights
Seventh Night

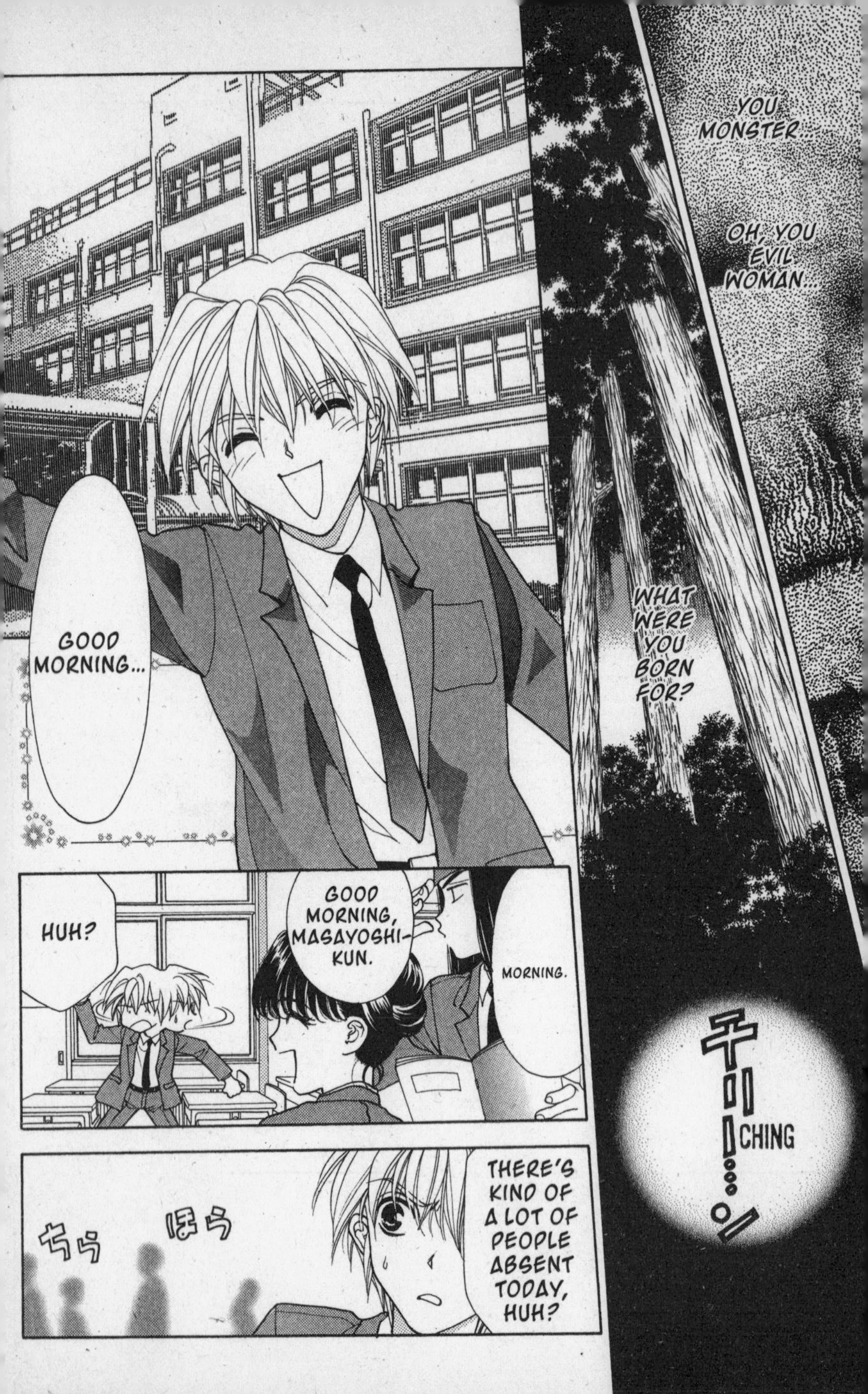
YOU MONSTER...
OH, YOU EVIL WOMAN...
WHAT WERE YOU BORN FOR?
CHING
GOOD MORNING...
MORNING.
GOOD MORNING, MASAYOSHI-KUN.
HUH?
THERE'S KIND OF A LOT OF PEOPLE ABSENT TODAY, HUH?
ほら
ちら

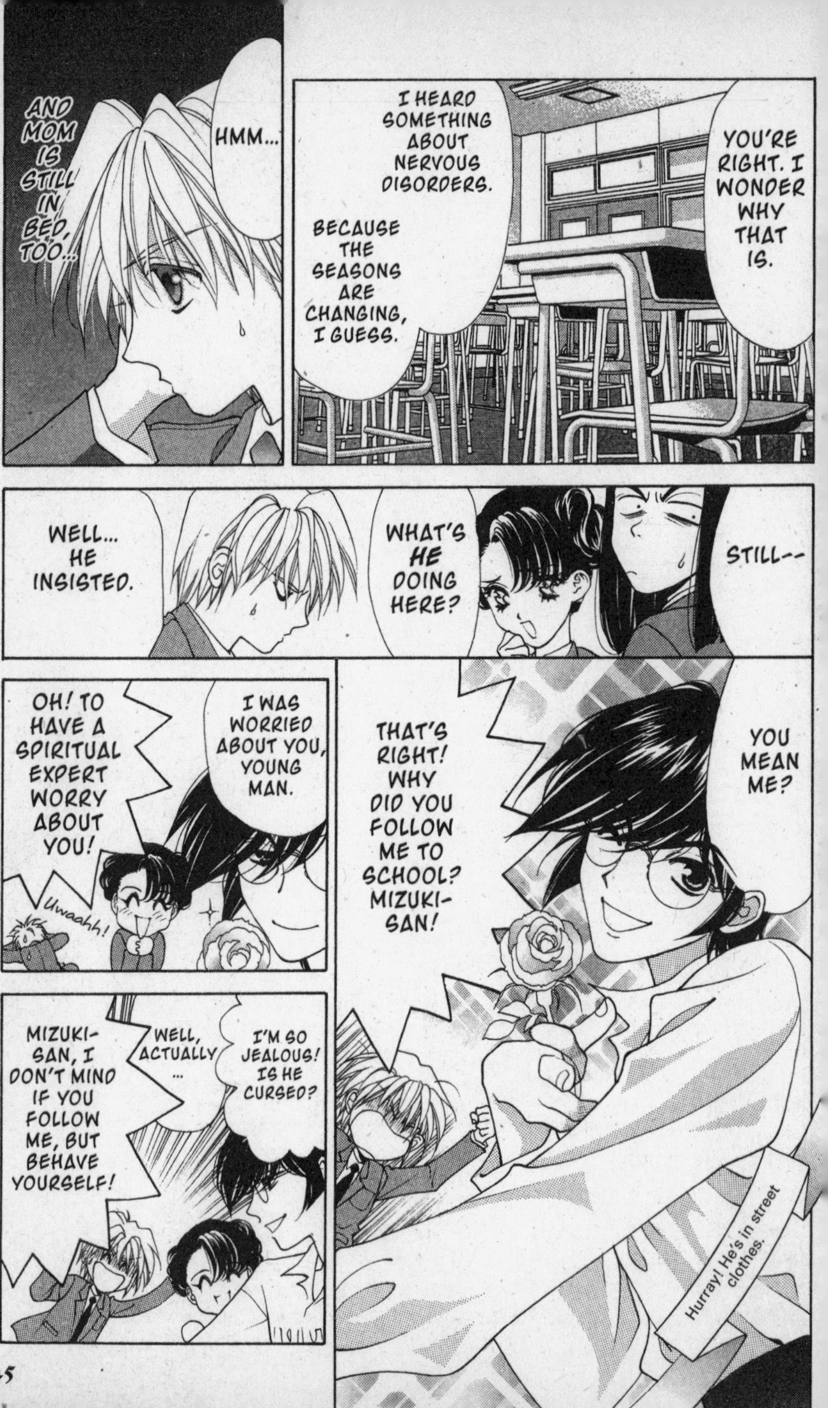
YOU'RE RIGHT. I WONDER WHY THAT IS.
I HEARD SOMETHING ABOUT NERVOUS DISORDERS.
BECAUSE THE SEASONS ARE CHANGING, I GUESS.
HMM...
AND MOM IS STILL IN BED, TOO...
STILL--
WHAT'S *HE* DOING HERE?
WELL... HE INSISTED.
YOU MEAN ME?
THAT'S RIGHT! WHY DID YOU FOLLOW ME TO SCHOOL? MIZUKI-SAN!
Hurray! He's in street clothes.
I WAS WORRIED ABOUT YOU, YOUNG MAN.
OH! TO HAVE A SPIRITUAL EXPERT WORRY ABOUT YOU!
Uwaahh!
I'M SO JEALOUS! IS HE CURSED?
WELL, ACTUALLY...
MIZUKI-SAN, I DON'T MIND IF YOU FOLLOW ME, BUT BEHAVE YOURSELF!

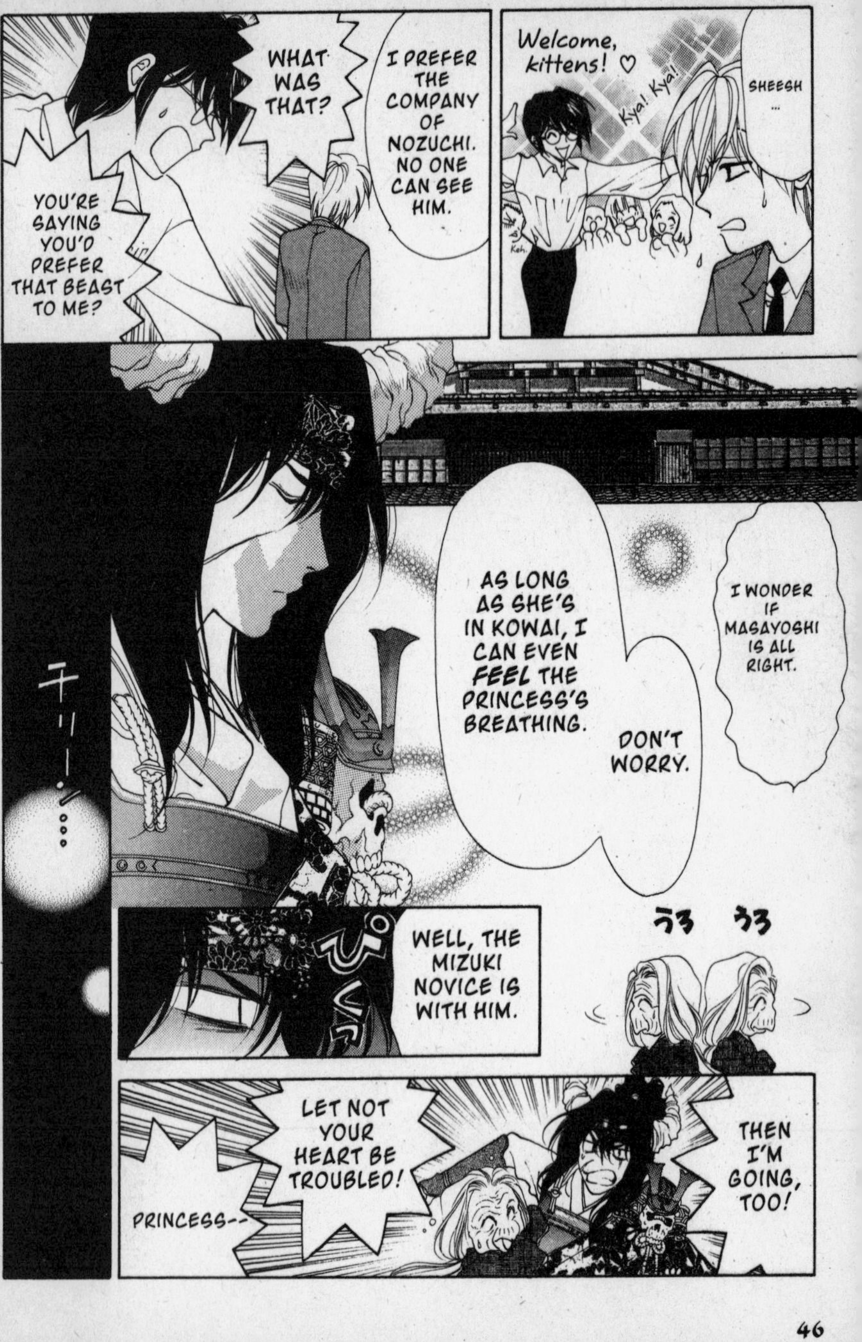
Welcome, kittens! ♡
Kya! Kya!
SHEESH ...
Keh.
I PREFER THE COMPANY OF NOZUCHI. NO ONE CAN SEE HIM.
WHAT WAS THAT?
YOU'RE SAYING YOU'D PREFER THAT BEAST TO ME?
I WONDER IF MASAYOSHI IS ALL RIGHT.
AS LONG AS SHE'S IN KOWAI, I CAN EVEN *FEEL* THE PRINCESS'S BREATHING.
DON'T WORRY.
チリ…
うろ うろ
WELL, THE MIZUKI NOVICE IS WITH HIM.
THEN I'M GOING, TOO!
LET NOT YOUR HEART BE TROUBLED!
PRINCESS--

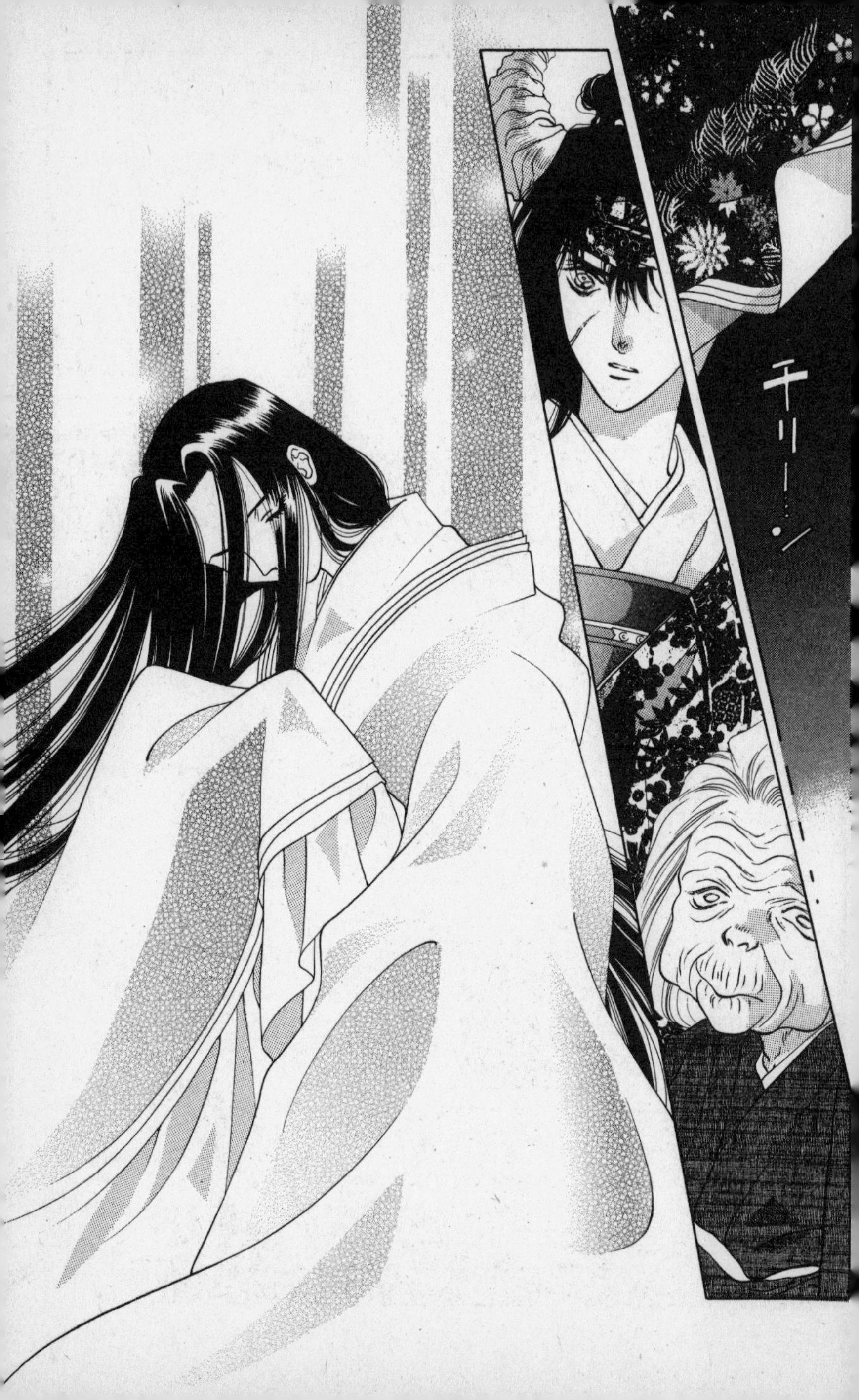
チリー…!

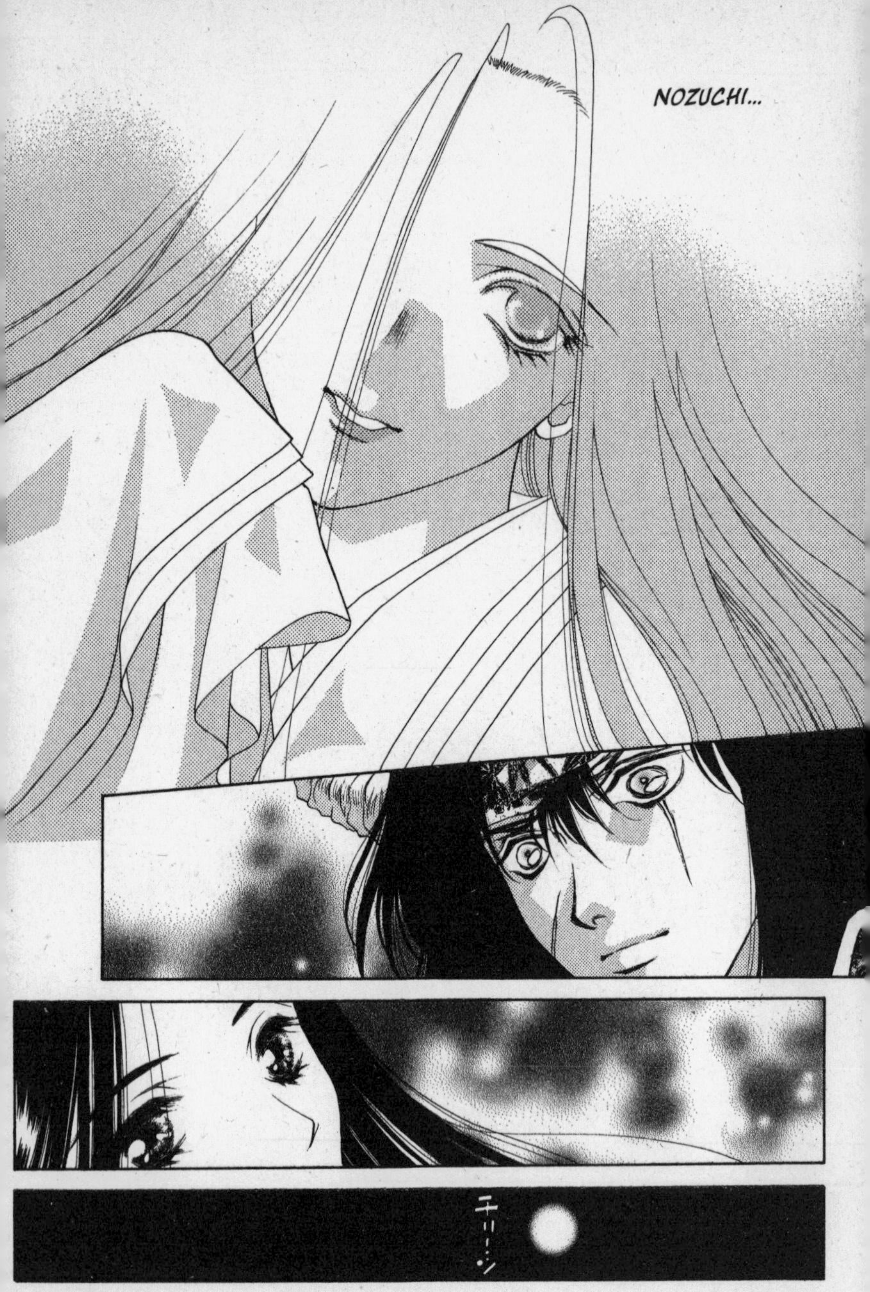
NOZUCHI...
チリーン

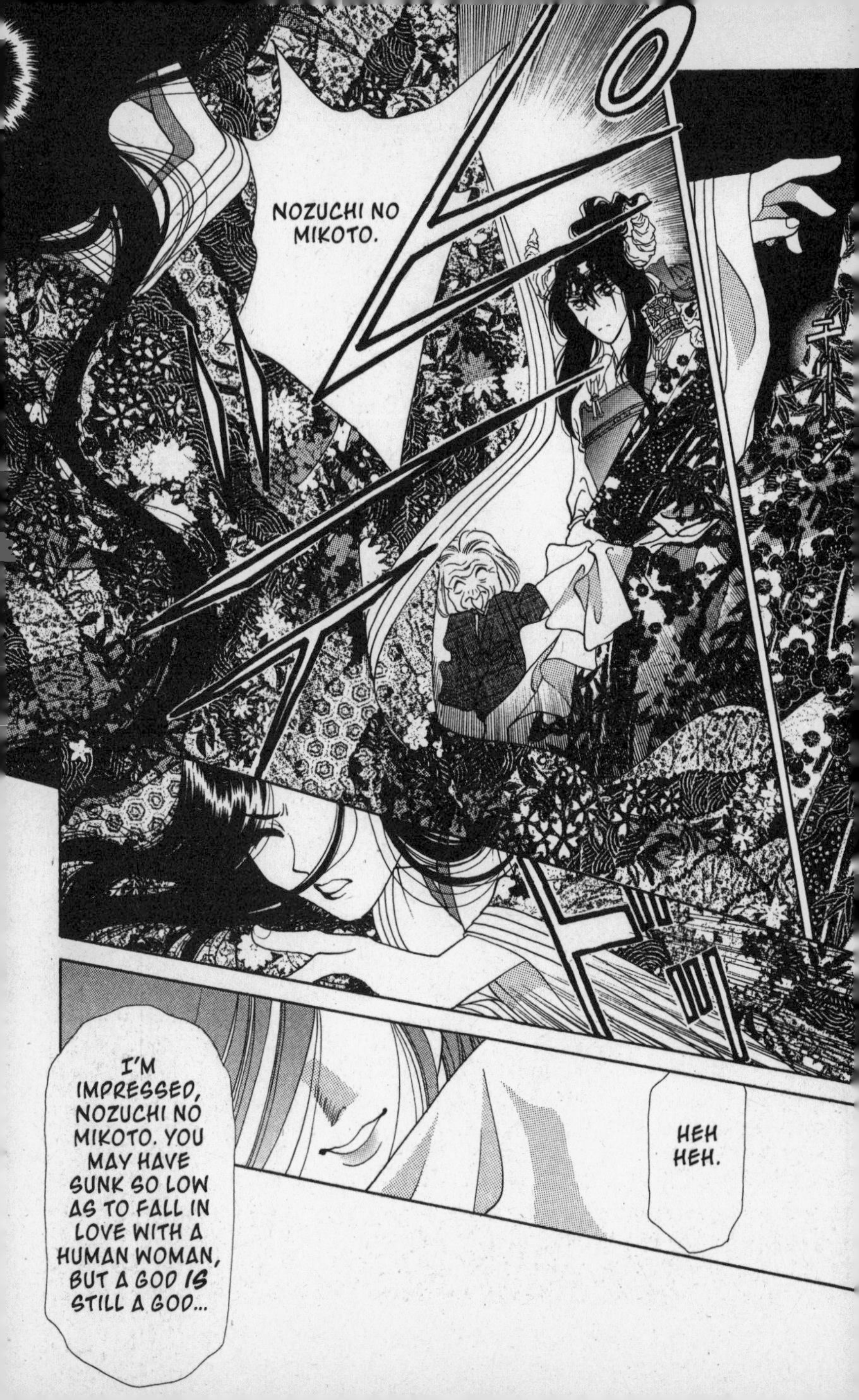
NOZUCHI NO MIKOTO.
HEH HEH.
I'M IMPRESSED, NOZUCHI NO MIKOTO. YOU MAY HAVE SUNK SO LOW AS TO FALL IN LOVE WITH A HUMAN WOMAN, BUT A GOD IS STILL A GOD...

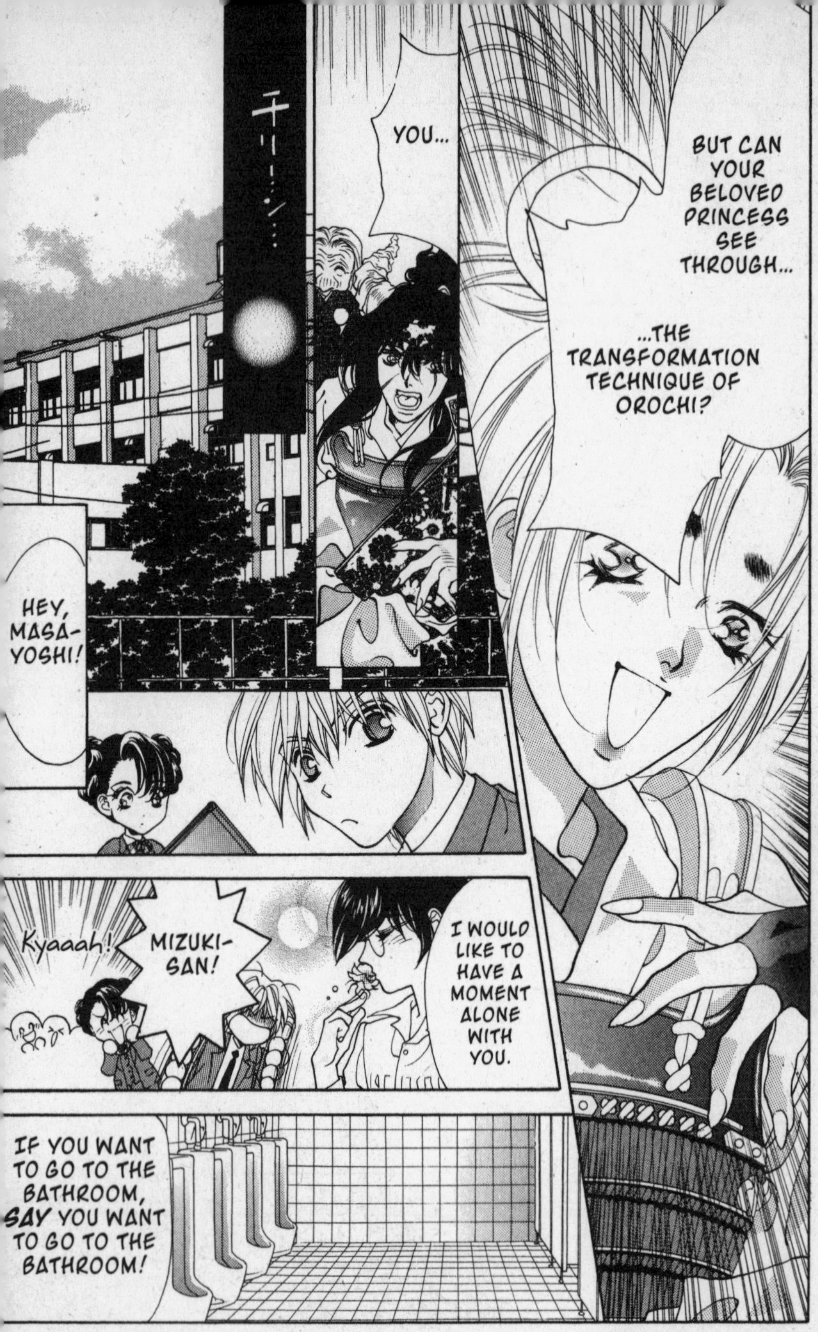
YOU...
BUT CAN YOUR BELOVED PRINCESS SEE THROUGH...
...THE TRANSFORMATION TECHNIQUE OF OROCHI?
チリ…ン…
HEY, MASA-YOSHI!
I WOULD LIKE TO HAVE A MOMENT ALONE WITH YOU.
MIZUKI-SAN!
Kyaaah!
IF YOU WANT TO GO TO THE BATHROOM, **SAY** YOU WANT TO GO TO THE BATHROOM!

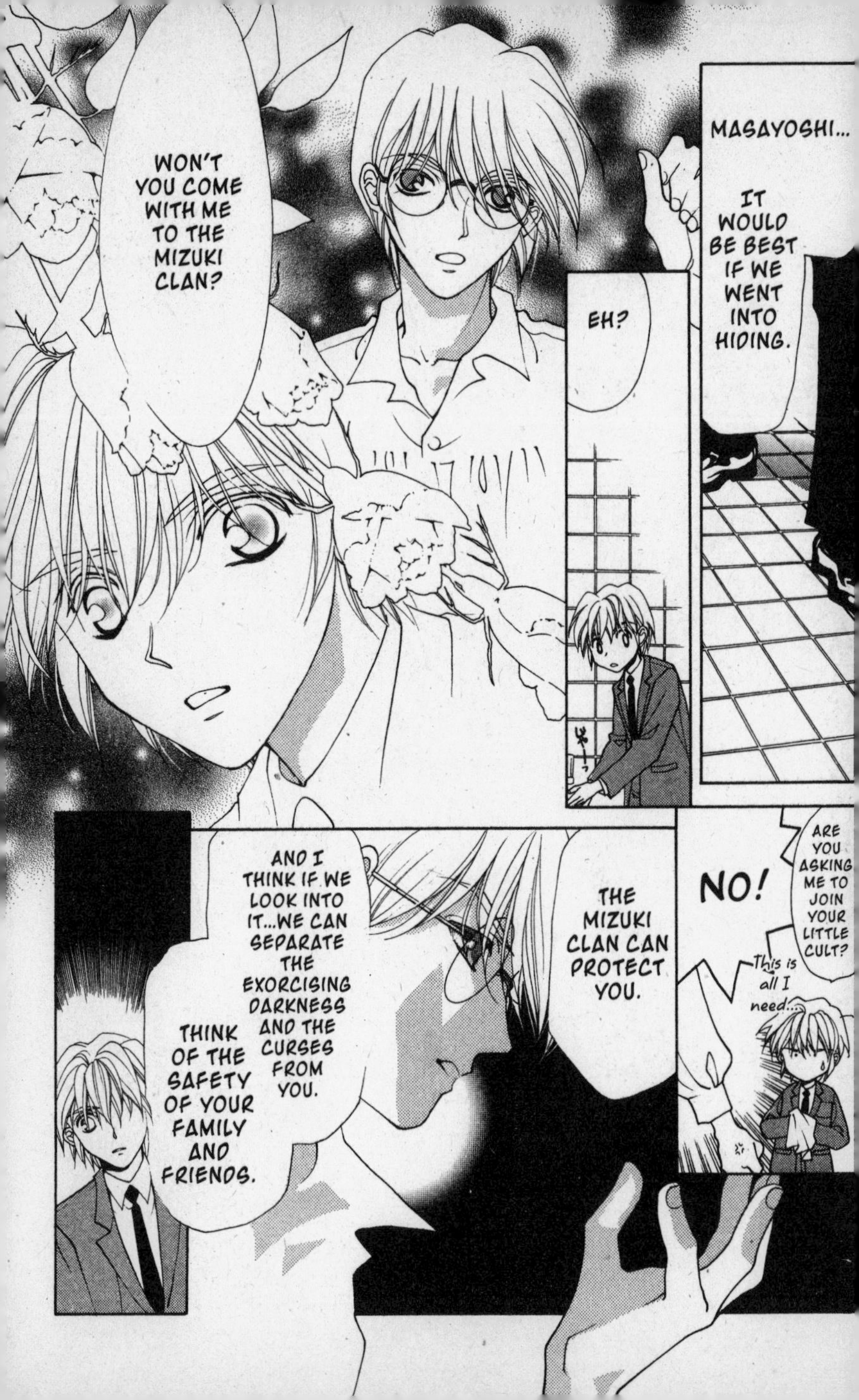
MASAYOSHI...
IT WOULD BE BEST IF WE WENT INTO HIDING.
EH?
WON'T YOU COME WITH ME TO THE MIZUKI CLAN?
ARE YOU ASKING ME TO JOIN YOUR LITTLE CULT?
NO!
This is all I need...
THE MIZUKI CLAN CAN PROTECT YOU.
AND I THINK IF WE LOOK INTO IT...WE CAN SEPARATE THE EXORCISING DARKNESS AND THE CURSES FROM YOU.
THINK OF THE SAFETY OF YOUR FAMILY AND FRIENDS.

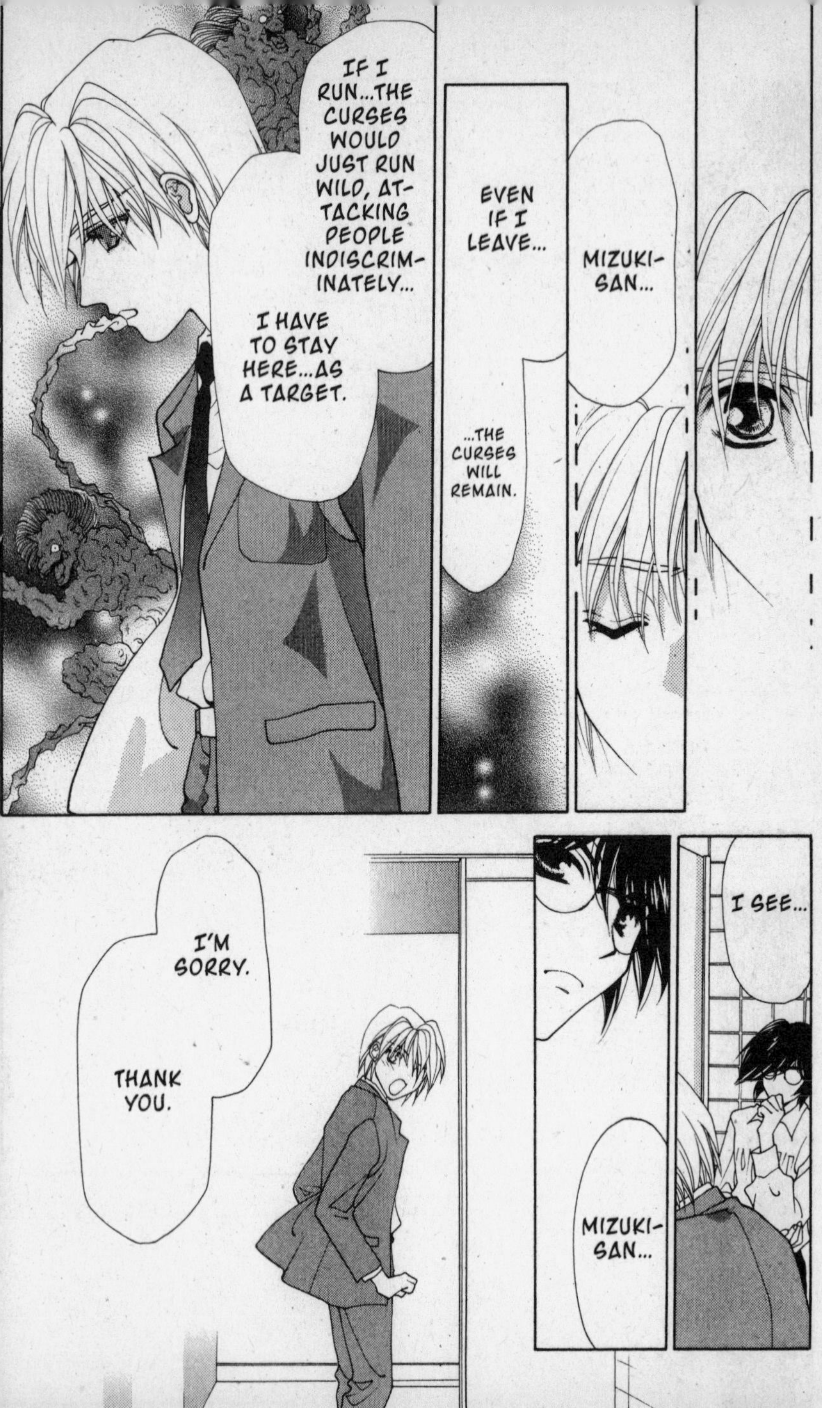
MIZUKI-SAN...
EVEN IF I LEAVE...
...THE CURSES WILL REMAIN.
IF I RUN...THE CURSES WOULD JUST RUN WILD, ATTACKING PEOPLE INDISCRIMINATELY...
I HAVE TO STAY HERE...AS A TARGET.
I SEE...
MIZUKI-SAN...
I'M SORRY.
THANK YOU.

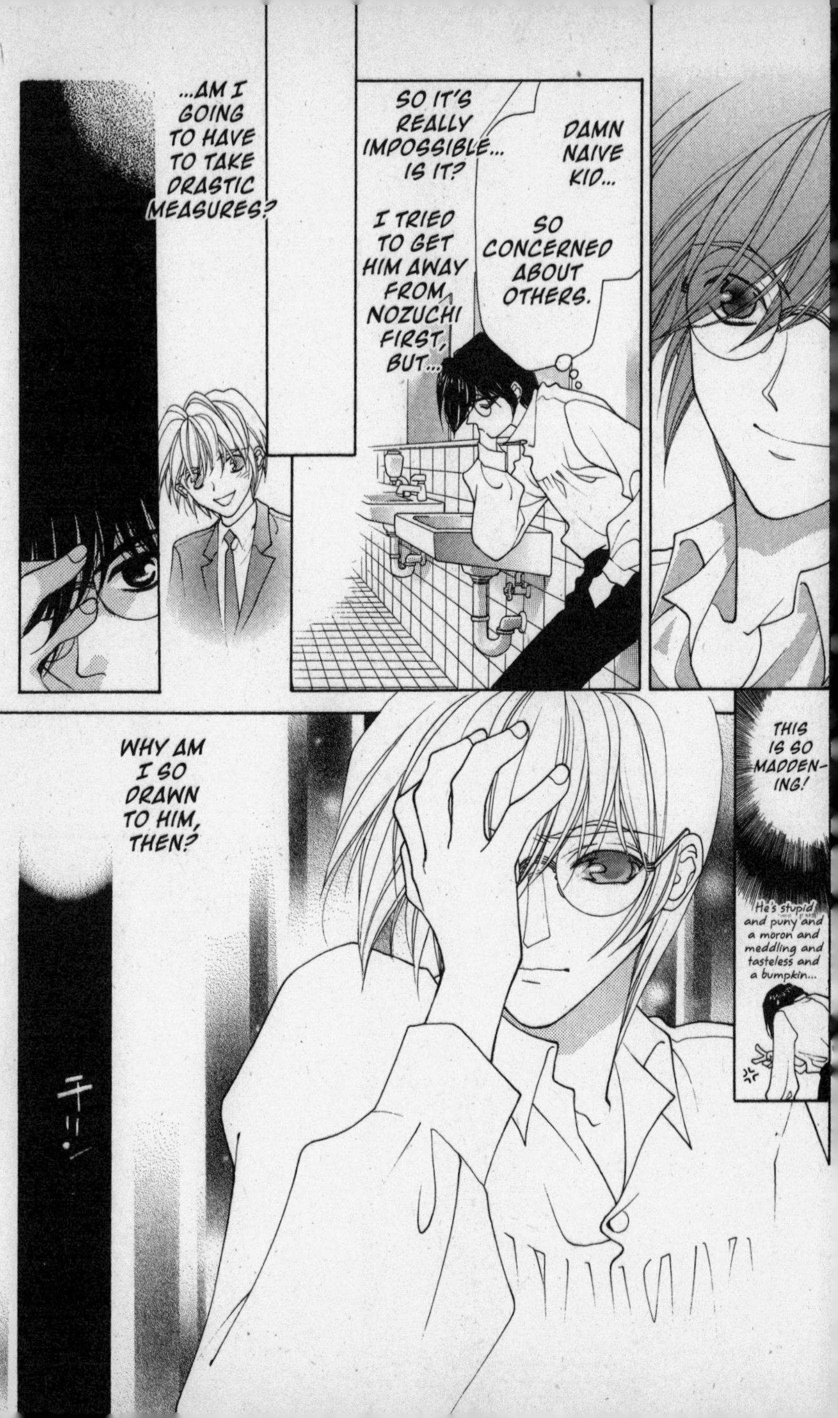
DAMN NAIVE KID...
SO CONCERNED ABOUT OTHERS.
SO IT'S REALLY IMPOSSIBLE... IS IT?
I TRIED TO GET HIM AWAY FROM NOZUCHI FIRST, BUT...
...AM I GOING TO HAVE TO TAKE DRASTIC MEASURES?
THIS IS SO MADDENING!
He's stupid and puny and a moron and meddling and tasteless and a bumpkin...
WHY AM I SO DRAWN TO HIM, THEN?

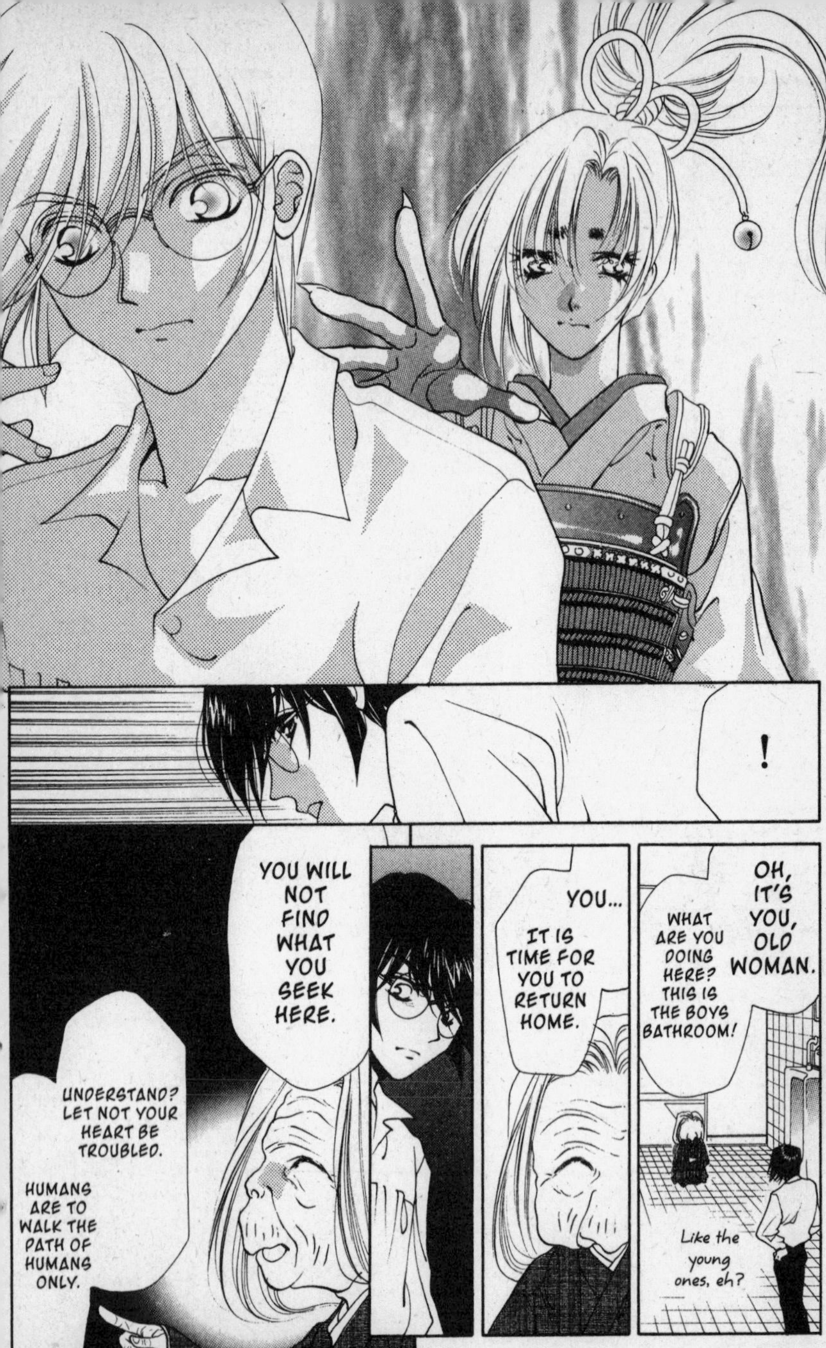
!
OH, IT'S YOU, OLD WOMAN.
WHAT ARE YOU DOING HERE? THIS IS THE BOYS BATHROOM!
Like the young ones, eh?
YOU...
IT IS TIME FOR YOU TO RETURN HOME.
YOU WILL NOT FIND WHAT YOU SEEK HERE.
UNDERSTAND? LET NOT YOUR HEART BE TROUBLED.
HUMANS ARE TO WALK THE PATH OF HUMANS ONLY.

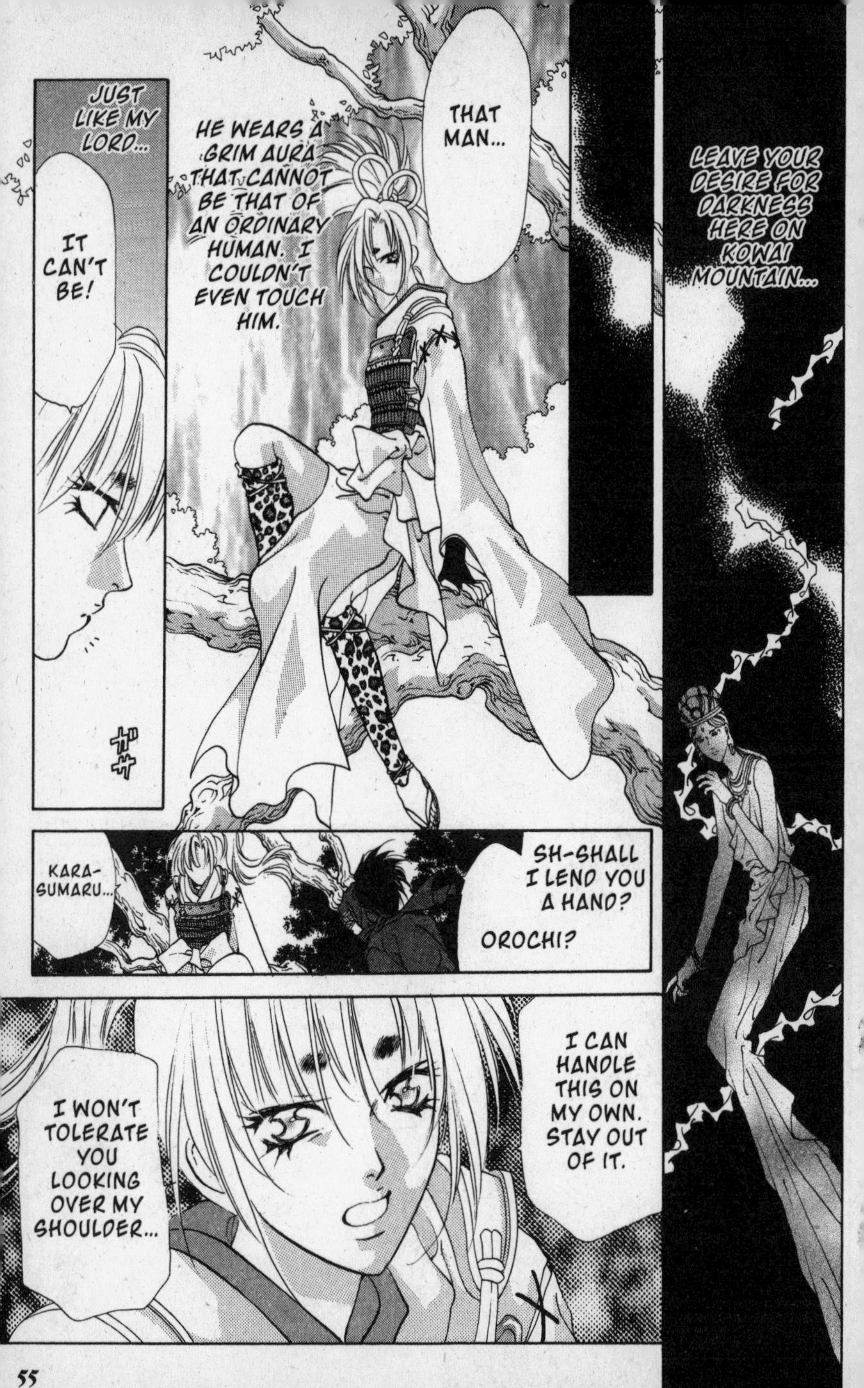
LEAVE YOUR DESIRE FOR DARKNESS HERE ON KOWAI MOUNTAIN...
THAT MAN...
HE WEARS A GRIM AURA THAT CANNOT BE THAT OF AN ORDINARY HUMAN. I COULDN'T EVEN TOUCH HIM.
JUST LIKE MY LORD...
IT CAN'T BE!
ガッ
SH-SHALL I LEND YOU A HAND?
OROCHI?
KARA-SUMARU...
I CAN HANDLE THIS ON MY OWN. STAY OUT OF IT.
I WON'T TOLERATE YOU LOOKING OVER MY SHOULDER...

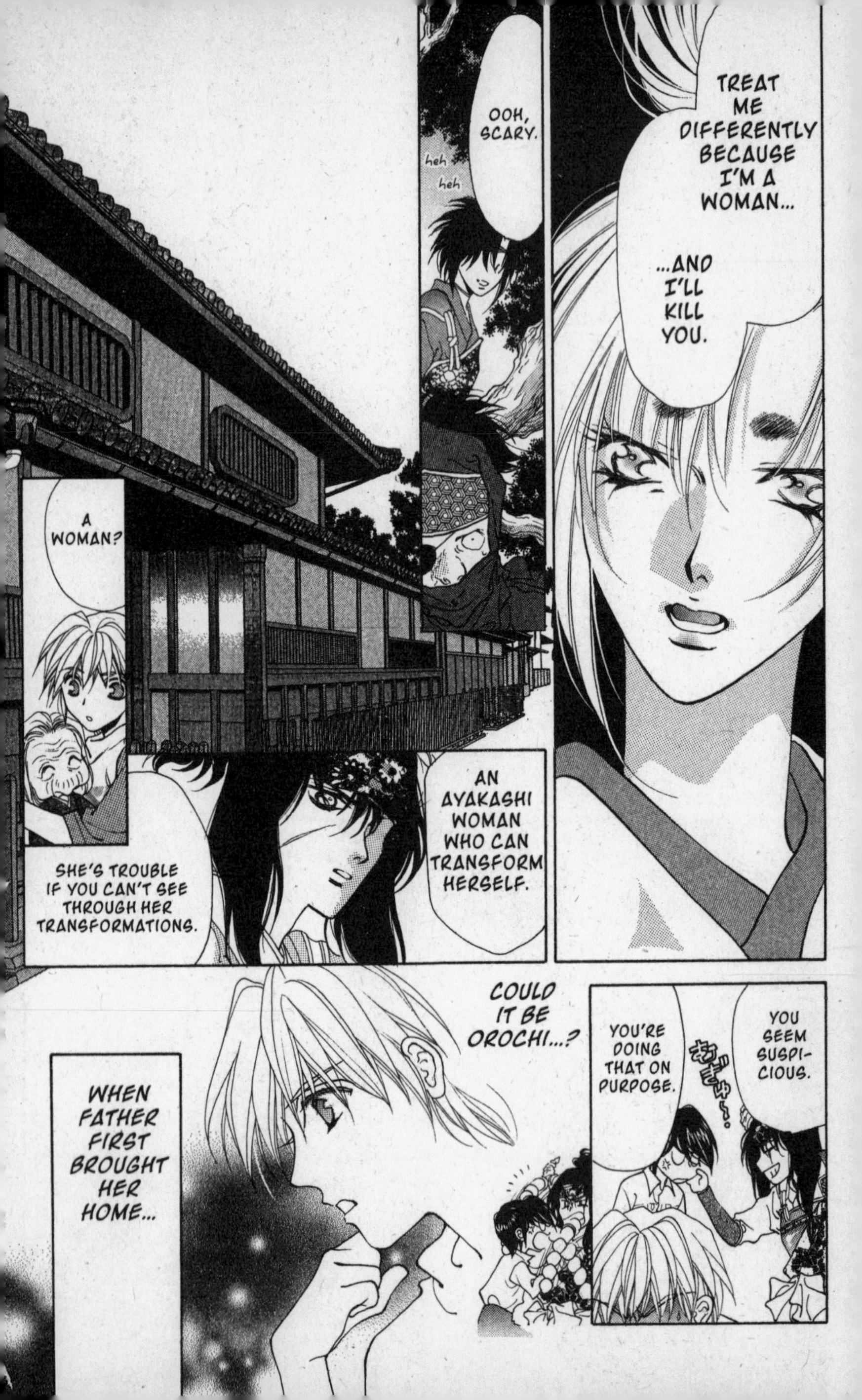
TREAT ME DIFFERENTLY BECAUSE I'M A WOMAN...
...AND I'LL KILL YOU.
OOH, SCARY.
heh heh
A WOMAN?
AN AYAKASHI WOMAN WHO CAN TRANSFORM HERSELF.
SHE'S TROUBLE IF YOU CAN'T SEE THROUGH HER TRANSFORMATIONS.
YOU SEEM SUSPICIOUS.
YOU'RE DOING THAT ON PURPOSE.
COULD IT BE OROCHI...?
WHEN FATHER FIRST BROUGHT HER HOME...

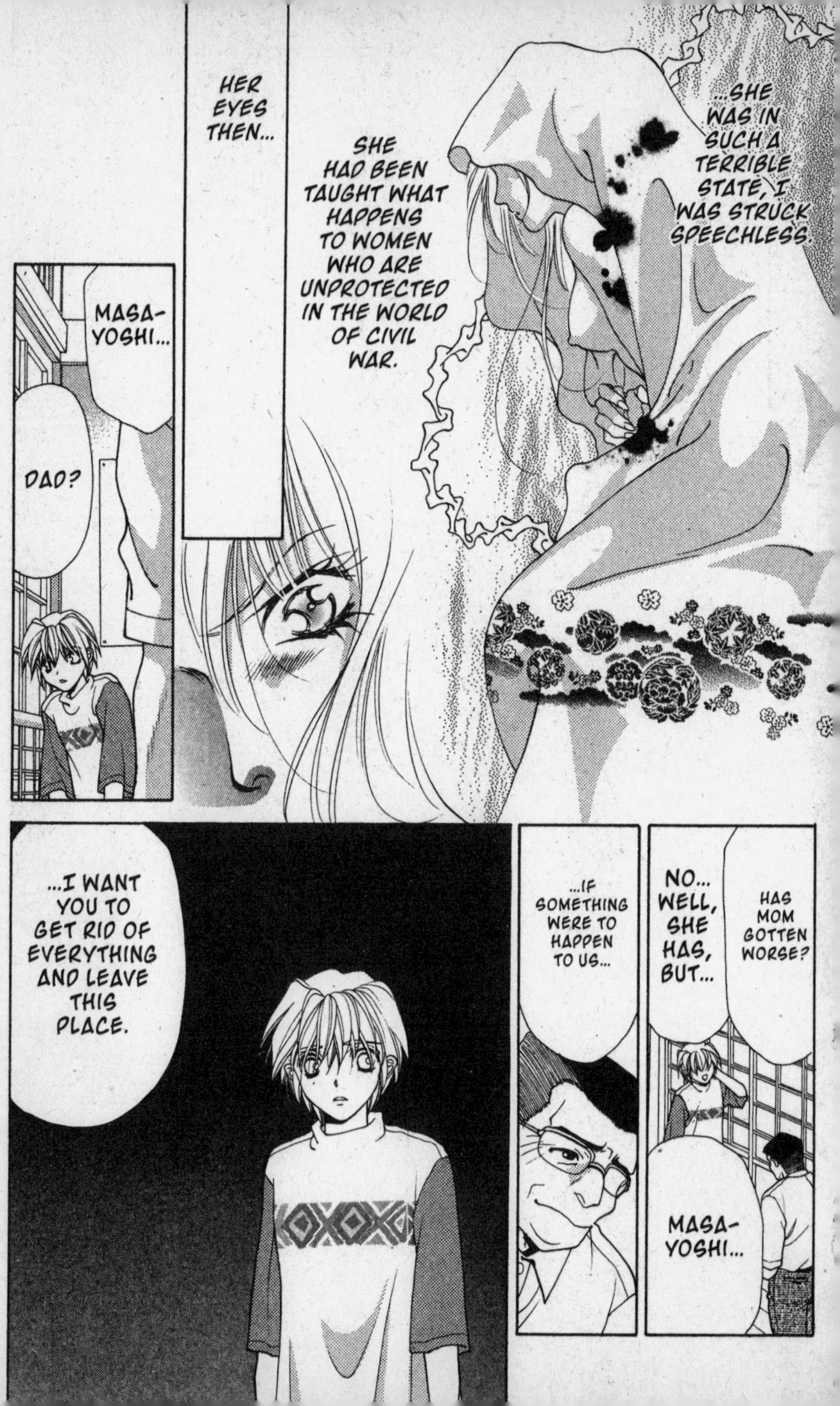
...SHE WAS IN SUCH A TERRIBLE STATE, I WAS STRUCK SPEECHLESS.
SHE HAD BEEN TAUGHT WHAT HAPPENS TO WOMEN WHO ARE UNPROTECTED IN THE WORLD OF CIVIL WAR.
HER EYES THEN...
MASA-YOSHI...
DAD?
HAS MOM GOTTEN WORSE?
NO... WELL, SHE HAS, BUT...
MASA-YOSHI...
...IF SOMETHING WERE TO HAPPEN TO US...
...I WANT YOU TO GET RID OF EVERYTHING AND LEAVE THIS PLACE.

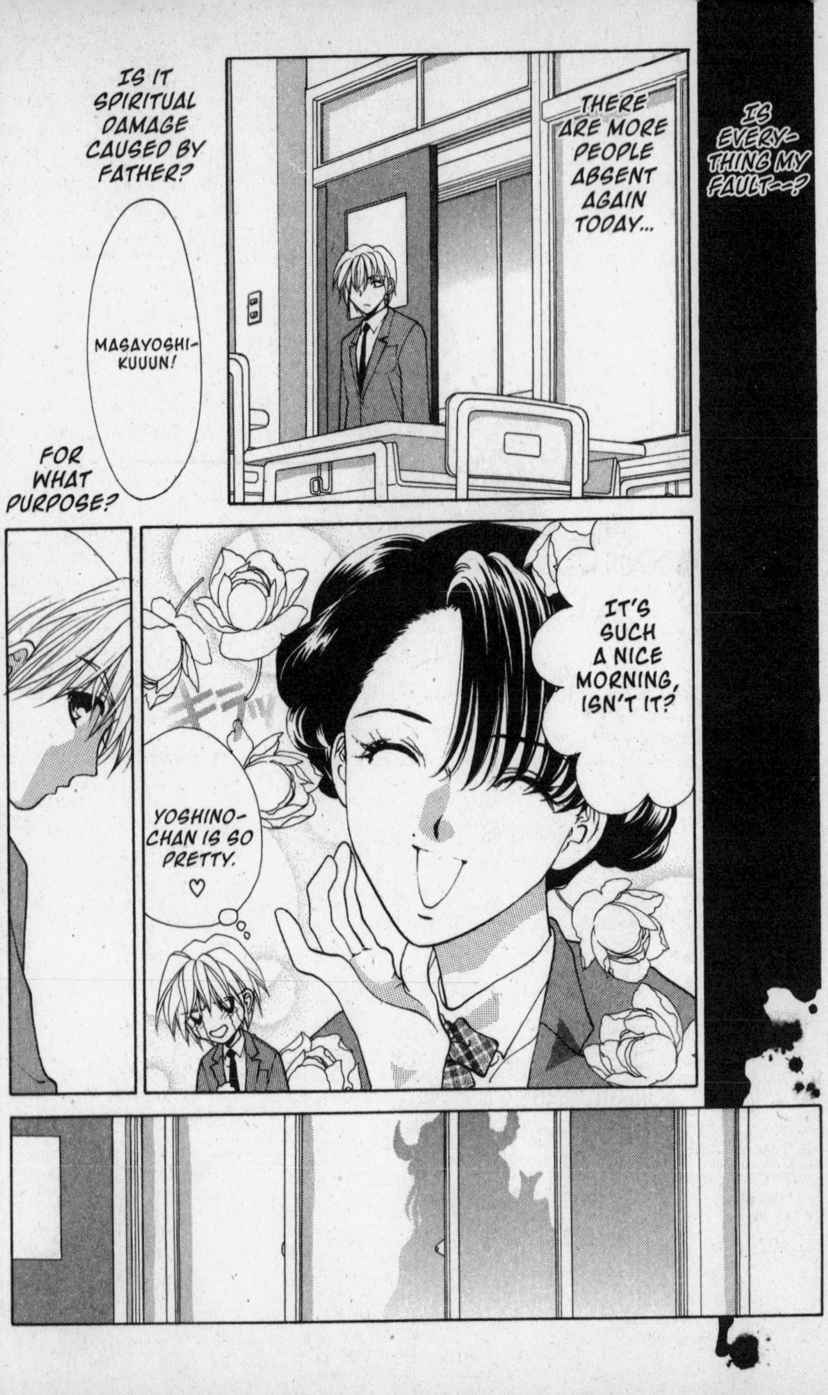
IS EVERY-THING MY FAULT--?
THERE ARE MORE PEOPLE ABSENT AGAIN TODAY...
IS IT SPIRITUAL DAMAGE CAUSED BY FATHER?
MASAYOSHI-KUUUN!
FOR WHAT PURPOSE?
IT'S SUCH A NICE MORNING, ISN'T IT?
YOSHINO-CHAN IS SO PRETTY. ♡

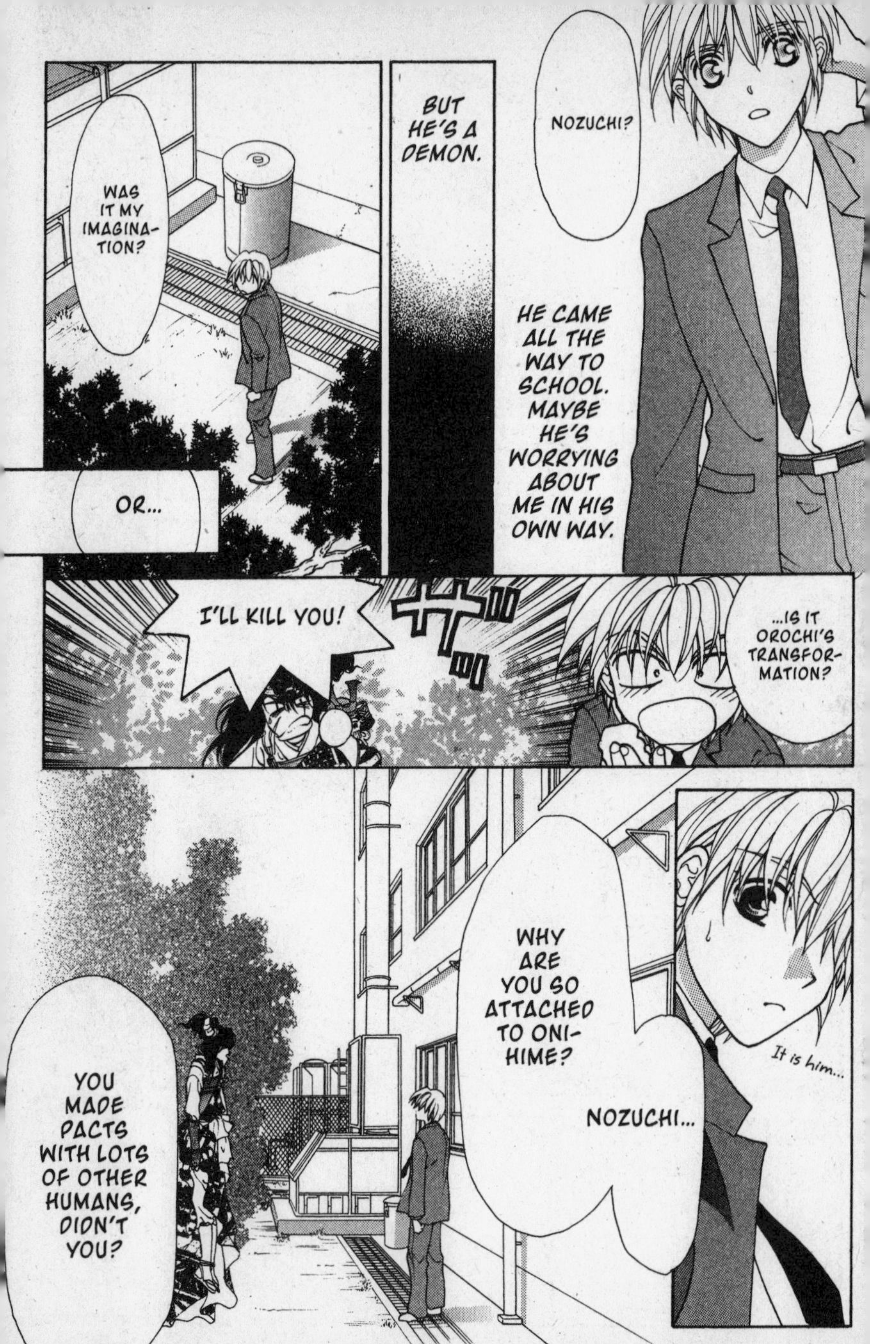
NOZUCHI?
HE CAME ALL THE WAY TO SCHOOL. MAYBE HE'S WORRYING ABOUT ME IN HIS OWN WAY.
BUT HE'S A DEMON.
WAS IT MY IMAGINATION?
OR...
...IS IT OROCHI'S TRANSFORMATION?
I'LL KILL YOU!
It is him...
WHY ARE YOU SO ATTACHED TO ONI-HIME?
NOZUCHI...
YOU MADE PACTS WITH LOTS OF OTHER HUMANS, DIDN'T YOU?

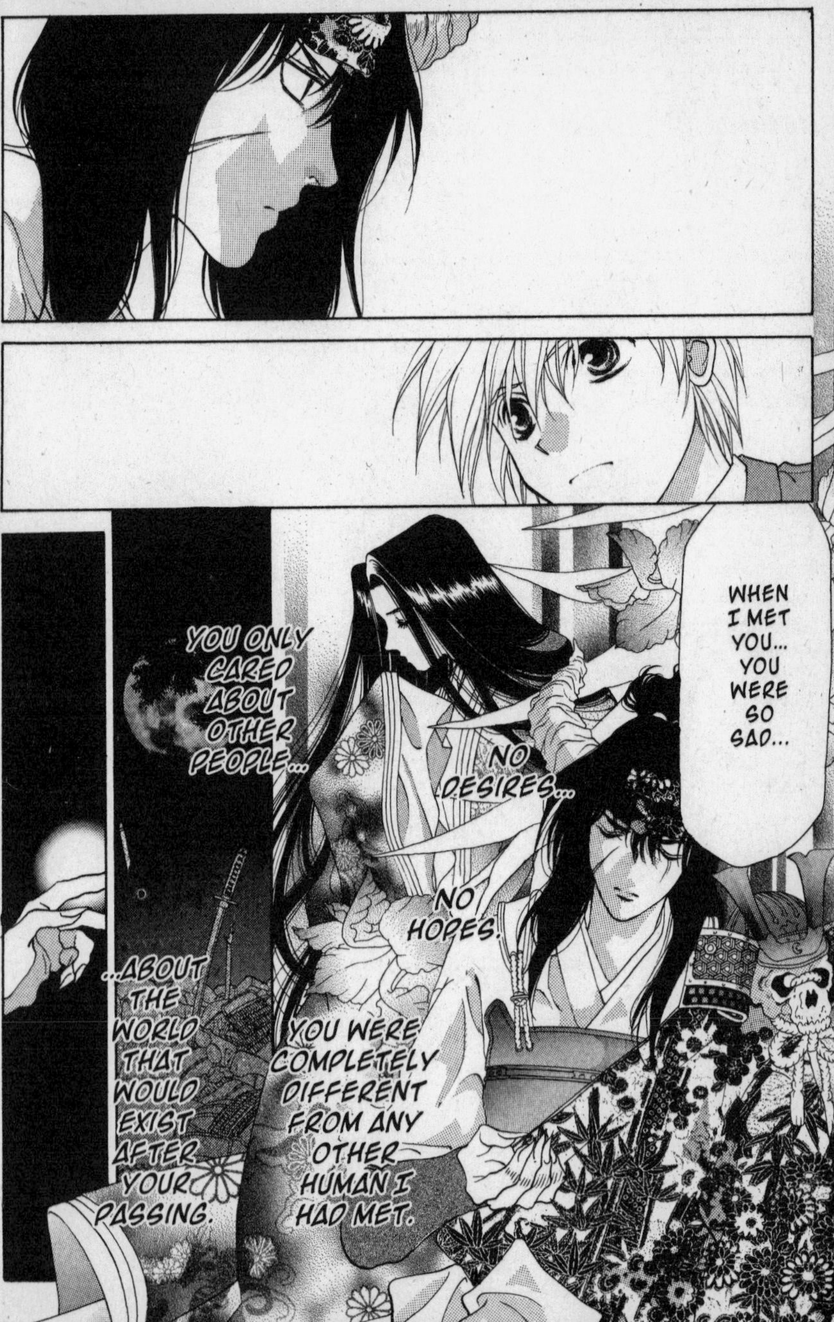
WHEN I MET YOU... YOU WERE SO SAD...
NO DESIRES...
NO HOPES.
YOU WERE COMPLETELY DIFFERENT FROM ANY OTHER HUMAN I HAD MET.
YOU ONLY CARED ABOUT OTHER PEOPLE...
...ABOUT THE WORLD THAT WOULD EXIST AFTER YOUR PASSING.

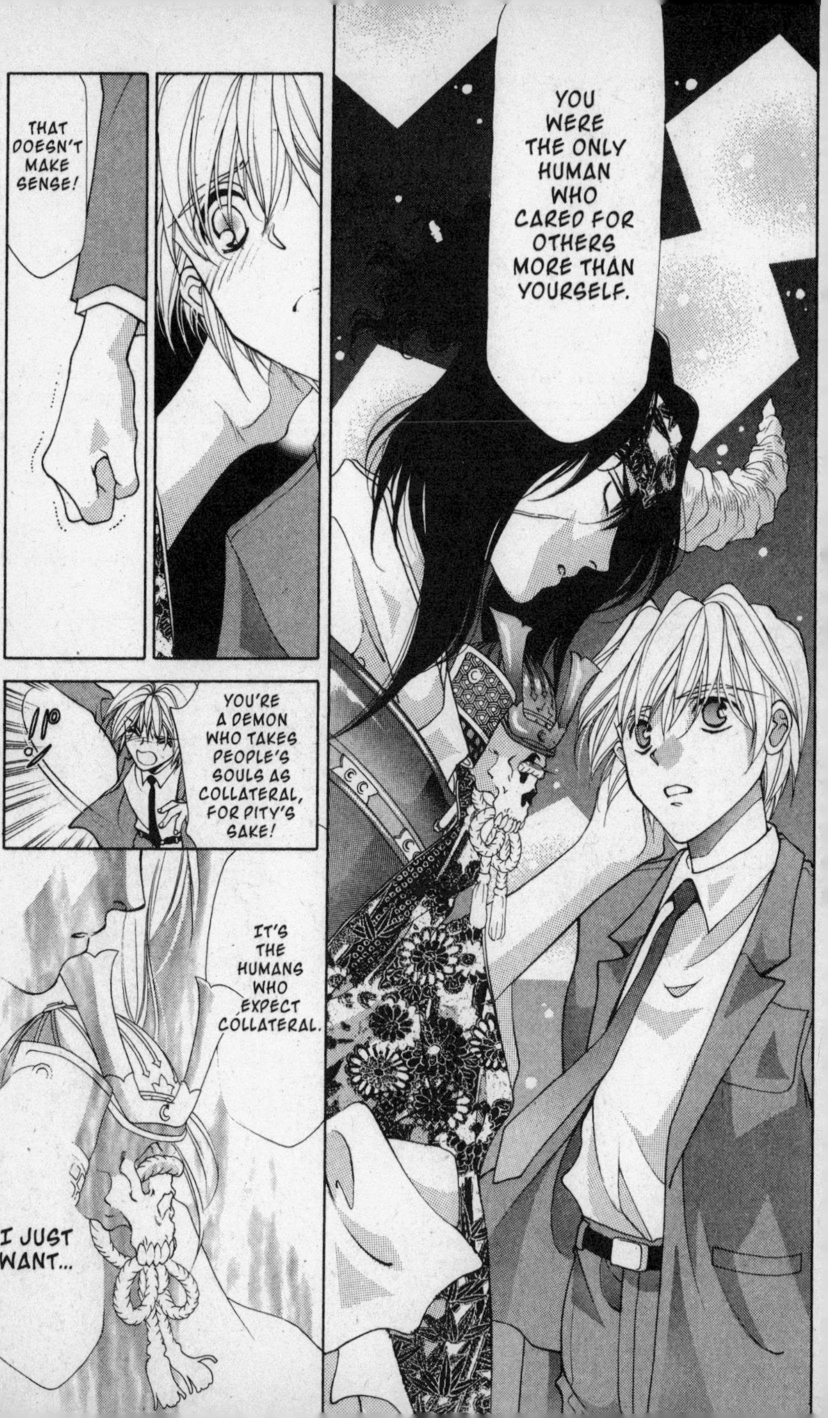
YOU WERE THE ONLY HUMAN WHO CARED FOR OTHERS MORE THAN YOURSELF.
THAT DOESN'T MAKE SENSE!
YOU'RE A DEMON WHO TAKES PEOPLE'S SOULS AS COLLATERAL, FOR PITY'S SAKE!
IT'S THE HUMANS WHO EXPECT COLLATERAL.
I JUST WANT...

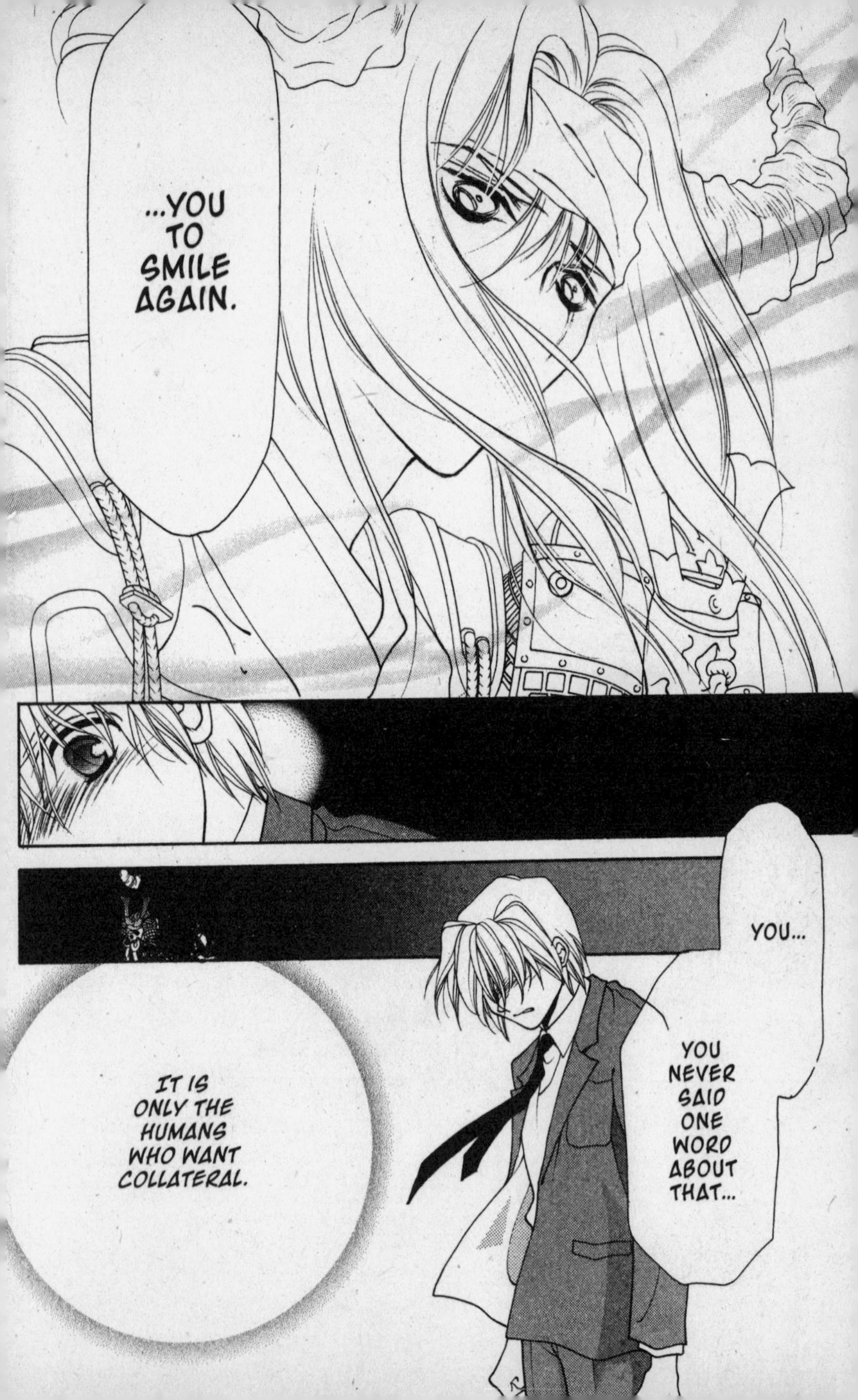
...YOU TO SMILE AGAIN.
YOU...
YOU NEVER SAID ONE WORD ABOUT THAT...
IT IS ONLY THE HUMANS WHO WANT COLLATERAL.

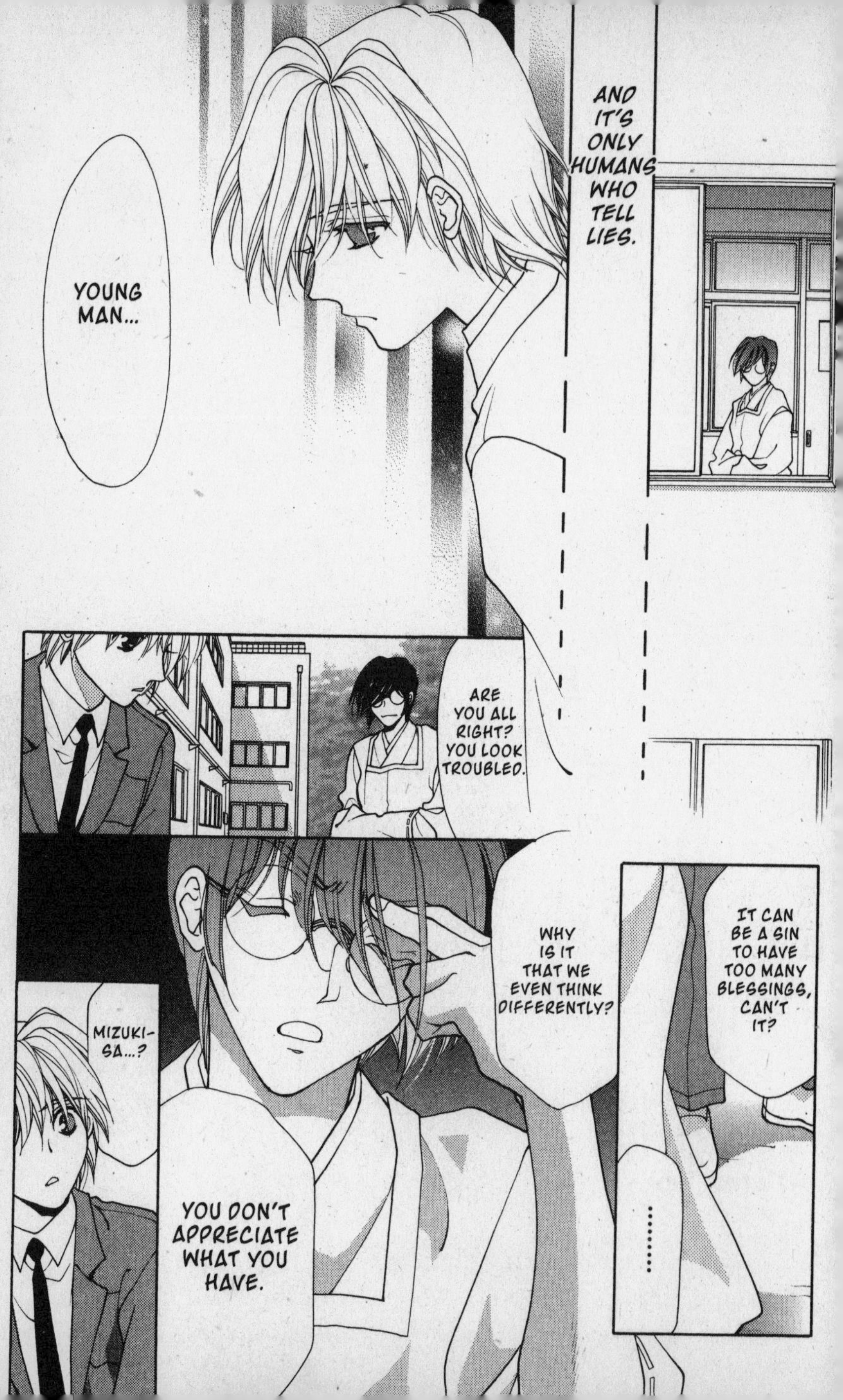
AND IT'S ONLY HUMANS WHO TELL LIES.
YOUNG MAN...
ARE YOU ALL RIGHT? YOU LOOK TROUBLED.
IT CAN BE A SIN TO HAVE TOO MANY BLESSINGS, CAN'T IT?
......
WHY IS IT THAT WE EVEN THINK DIFFERENTLY?
YOU DON'T APPRECIATE WHAT YOU HAVE.
MIZUKI-SA...?

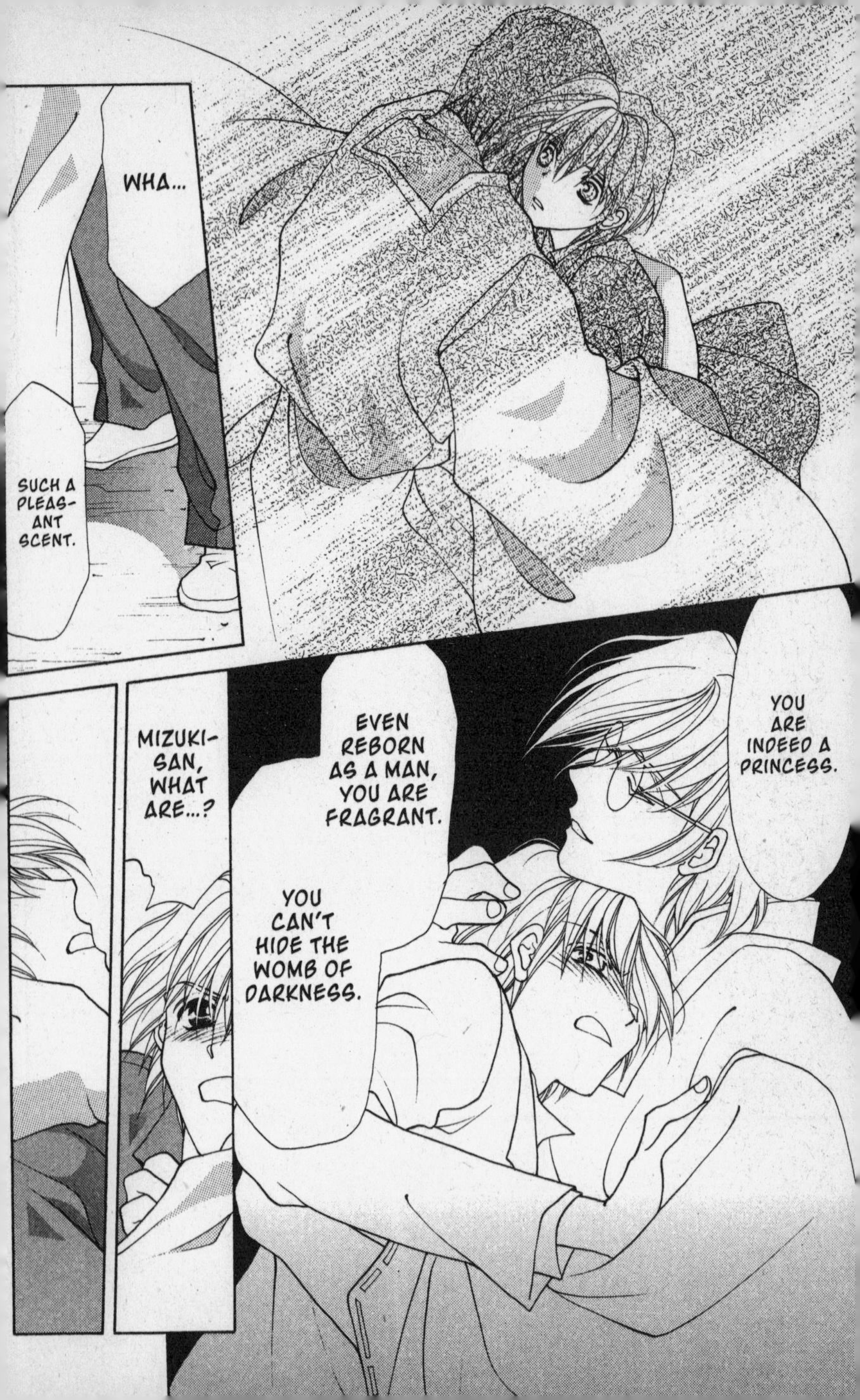
WHA...
SUCH A PLEASANT SCENT.
YOU ARE INDEED A PRINCESS.
EVEN REBORN AS A MAN, YOU ARE FRAGRANT.
YOU CAN'T HIDE THE WOMB OF DARKNESS.
MIZUKI-SAN, WHAT ARE...?

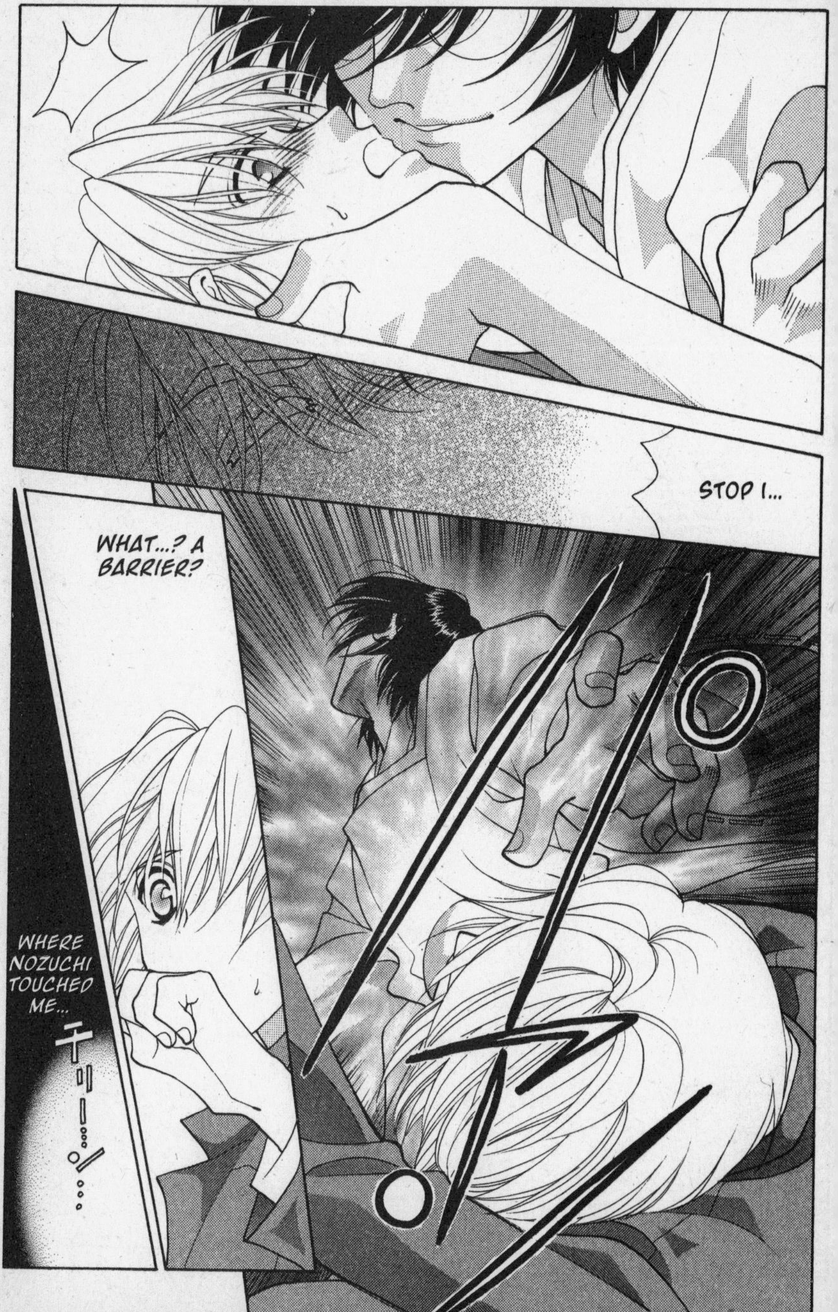
STOP I...
WHAT...? A BARRIER?
WHERE NOZUCHI TOUCHED ME...

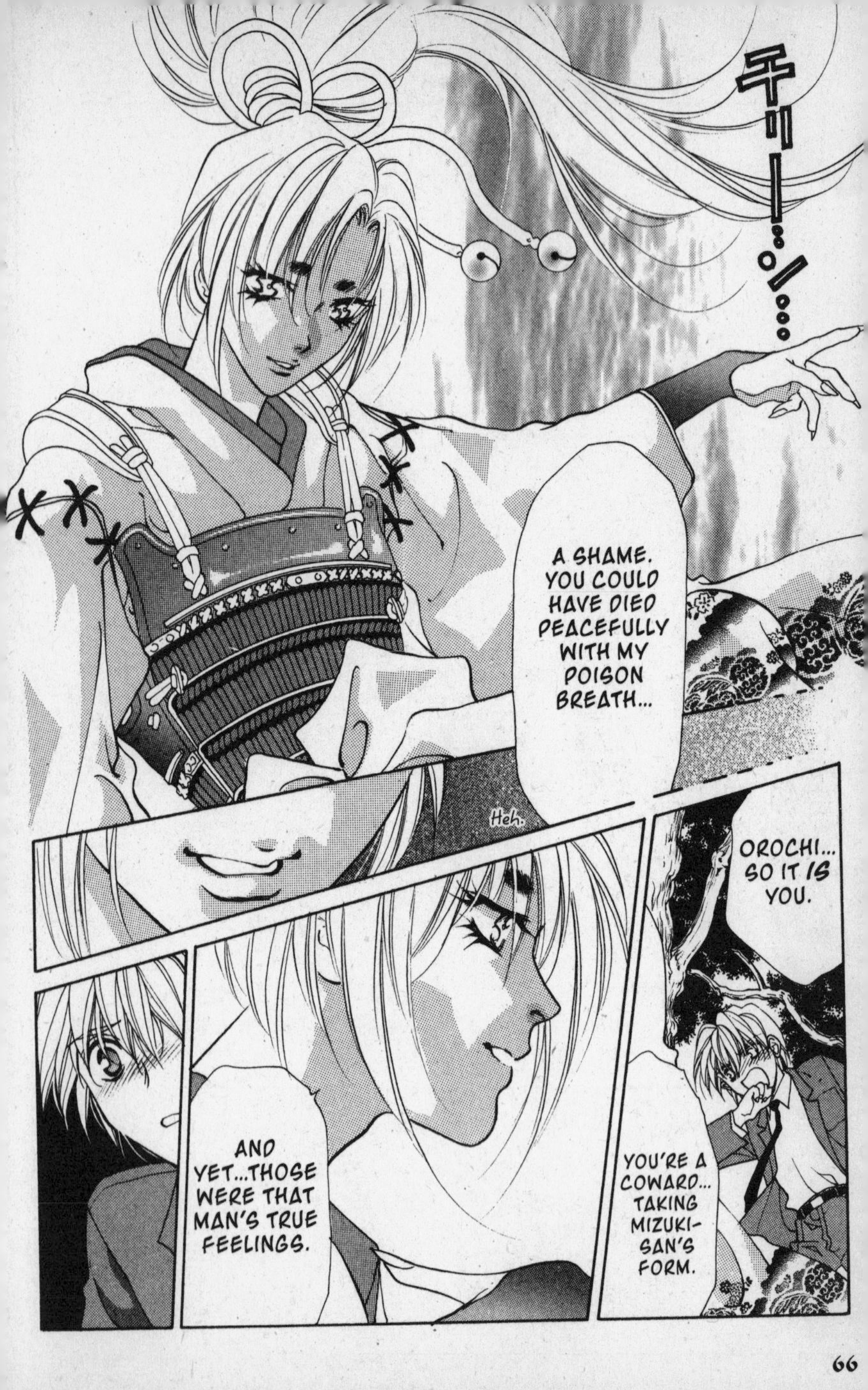
A SHAME. YOU COULD HAVE DIED PEACEFULLY WITH MY POISON BREATH...
OROCHI... SO IT IS YOU.
YOU'RE A COWARD... TAKING MIZUKI-SAN'S FORM.
Heh.
AND YET...THOSE WERE THAT MAN'S TRUE FEELINGS.

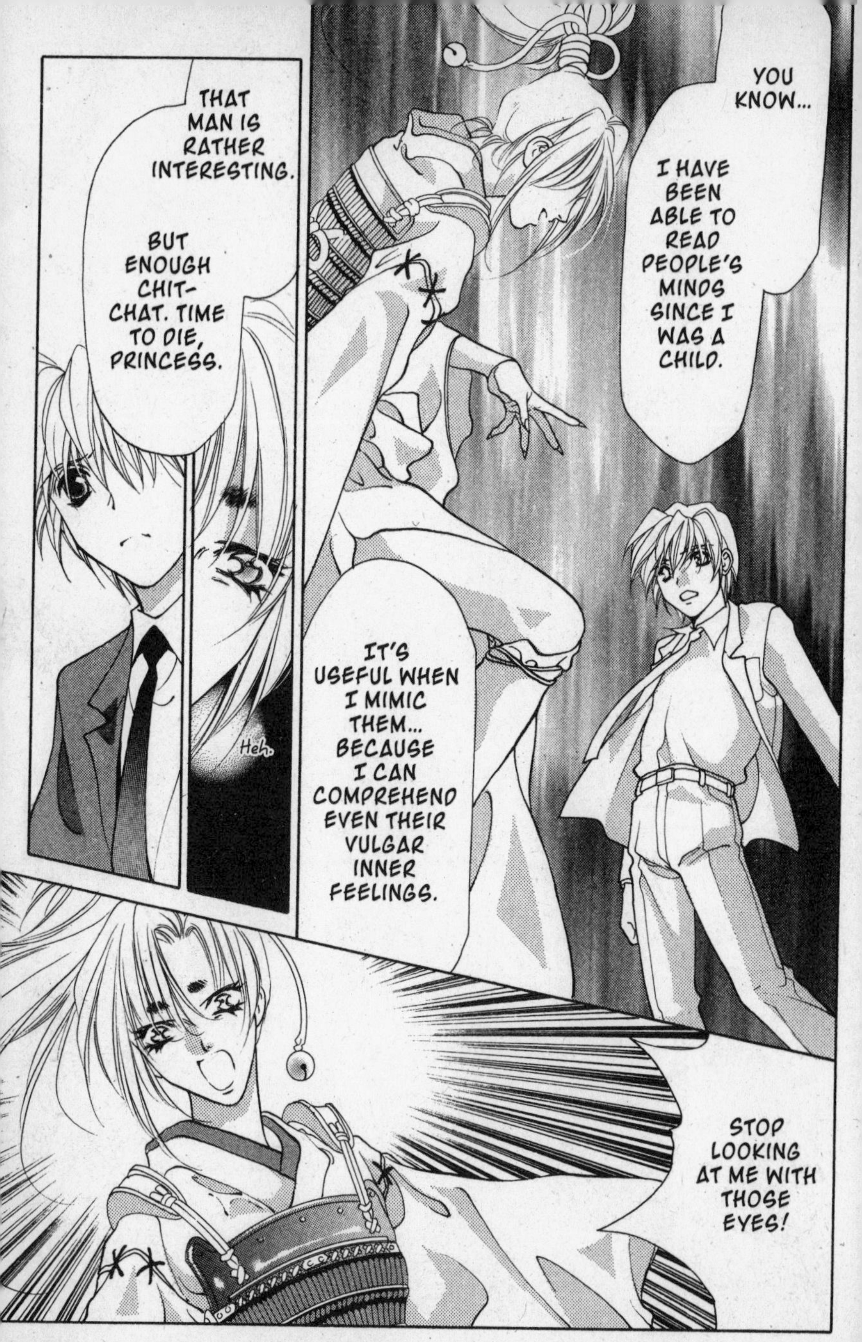
YOU KNOW...
I HAVE BEEN ABLE TO READ PEOPLE'S MINDS SINCE I WAS A CHILD.
IT'S USEFUL WHEN I MIMIC THEM... BECAUSE I CAN COMPREHEND EVEN THEIR VULGAR INNER FEELINGS.
THAT MAN IS RATHER INTERESTING.
BUT ENOUGH CHIT-CHAT. TIME TO DIE, PRINCESS.
Heh.
STOP LOOKING AT ME WITH THOSE EYES!

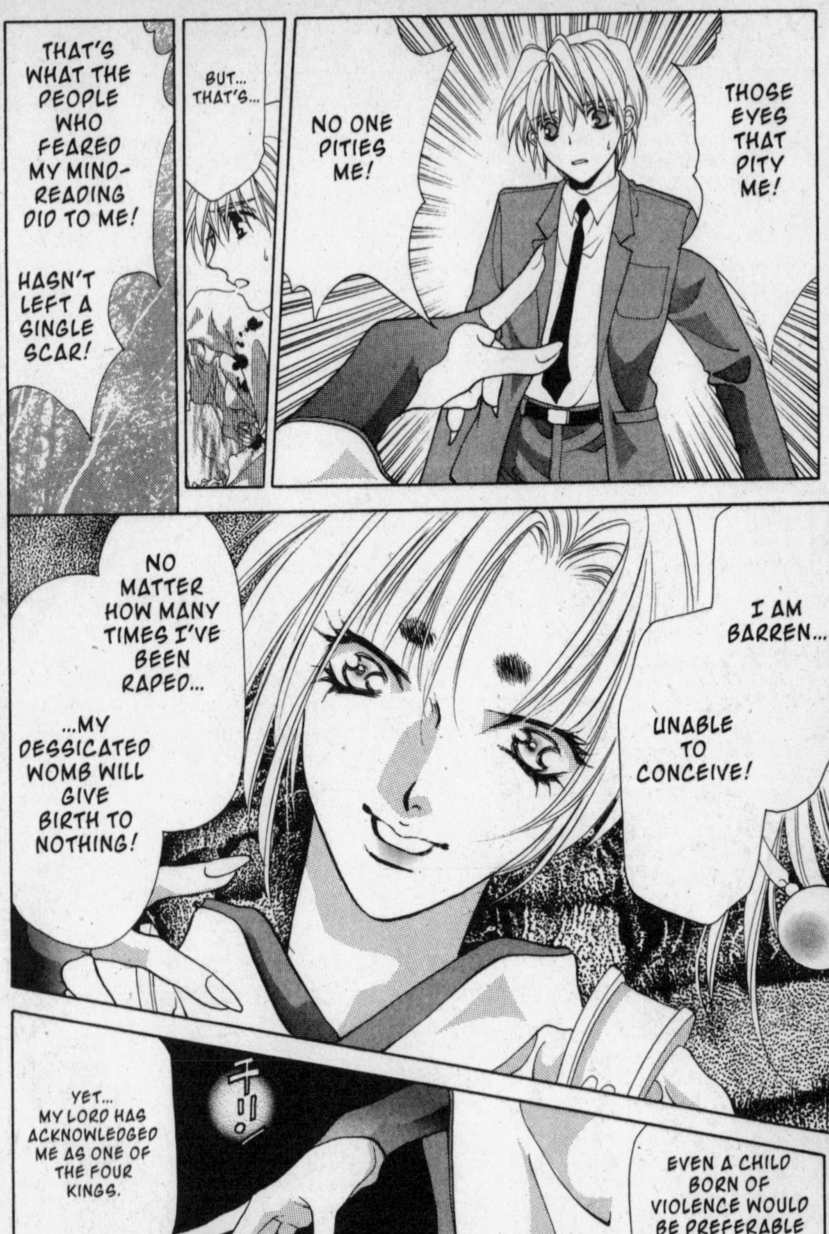
THOSE EYES THAT PITY ME!
NO ONE PITIES ME!
BUT... THAT'S...
THAT'S WHAT THE PEOPLE WHO FEARED MY MIND-READING DID TO ME!
HASN'T LEFT A SINGLE SCAR!
I AM BARREN...
UNABLE TO CONCEIVE!
NO MATTER HOW MANY TIMES I'VE BEEN RAPED...
...MY DESSICATED WOMB WILL GIVE BIRTH TO NOTHING!
EVEN A CHILD BORN OF VIOLENCE WOULD BE PREFERABLE TO NOTHING!
YET... MY LORD HAS ACKNOWLEDGED ME AS ONE OF THE FOUR KINGS.

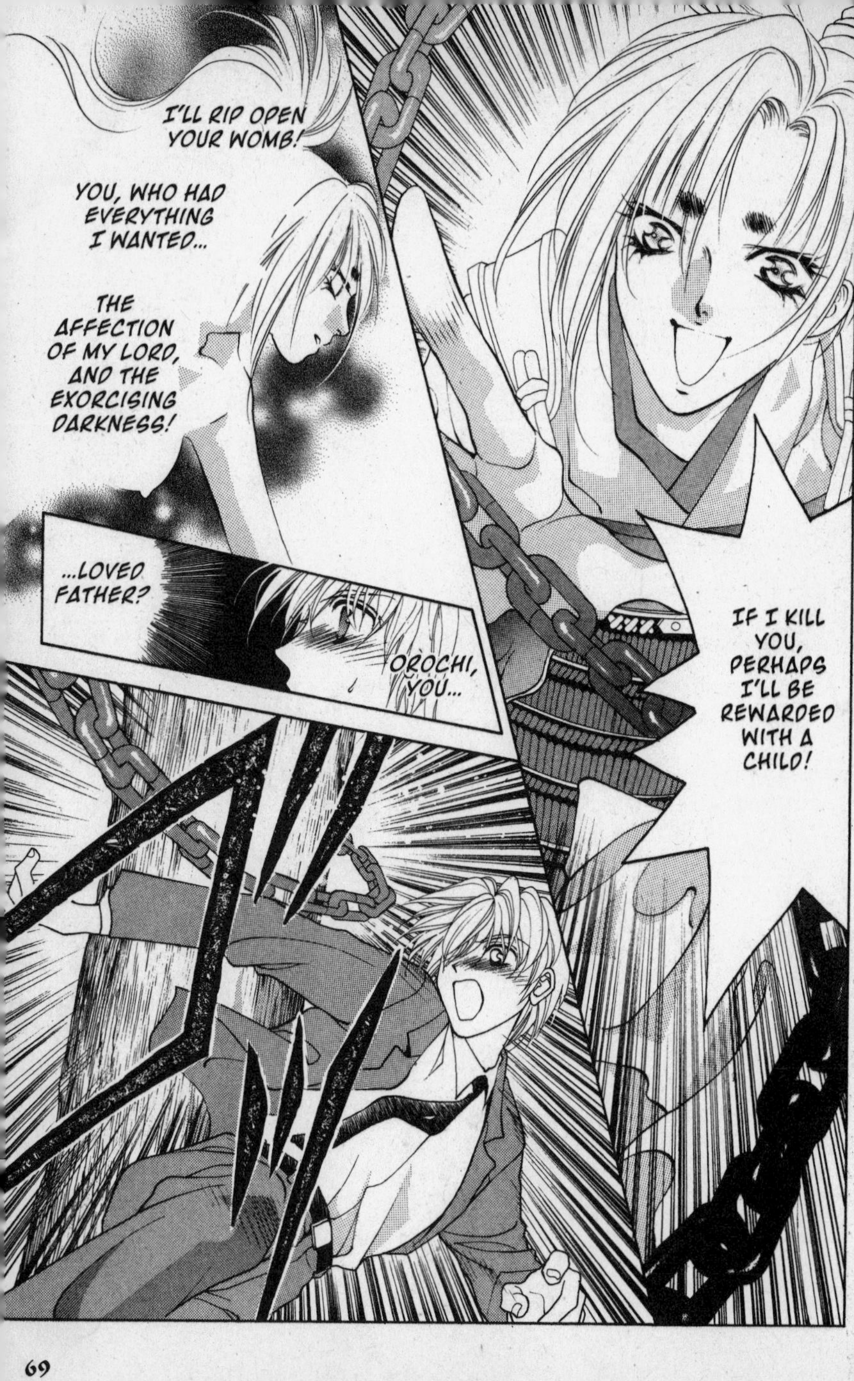

I'LL RIP OPEN YOUR WOMB!
YOU, WHO HAD EVERYTHING I WANTED...
THE AFFECTION OF MY LORD, AND THE EXORCISING DARKNESS!
IF I KILL YOU, PERHAPS I'LL BE REWARDED WITH A CHILD!
OROCHI, YOU...
...LOVED FATHER?

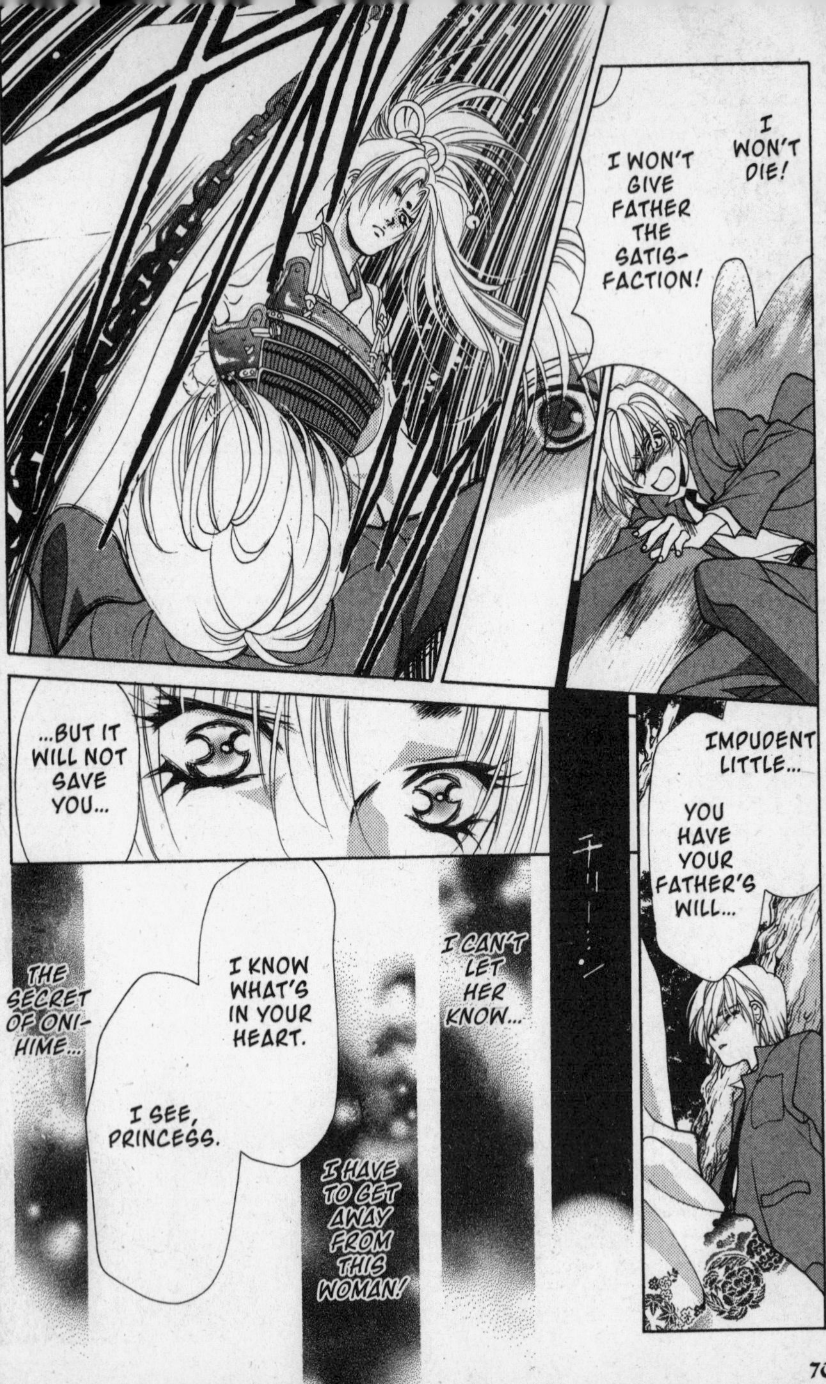
I WON'T DIE!
I WON'T GIVE FATHER THE SATIS-FACTION!
IMPUDENT LITTLE...
YOU HAVE YOUR FATHER'S WILL...
チリー…ン
...BUT IT WILL NOT SAVE YOU...
I CAN'T LET HER KNOW...
I KNOW WHAT'S IN YOUR HEART.
I SEE, PRINCESS.
THE SECRET OF ONI-HIME...
I HAVE TO GET AWAY FROM THIS WOMAN!

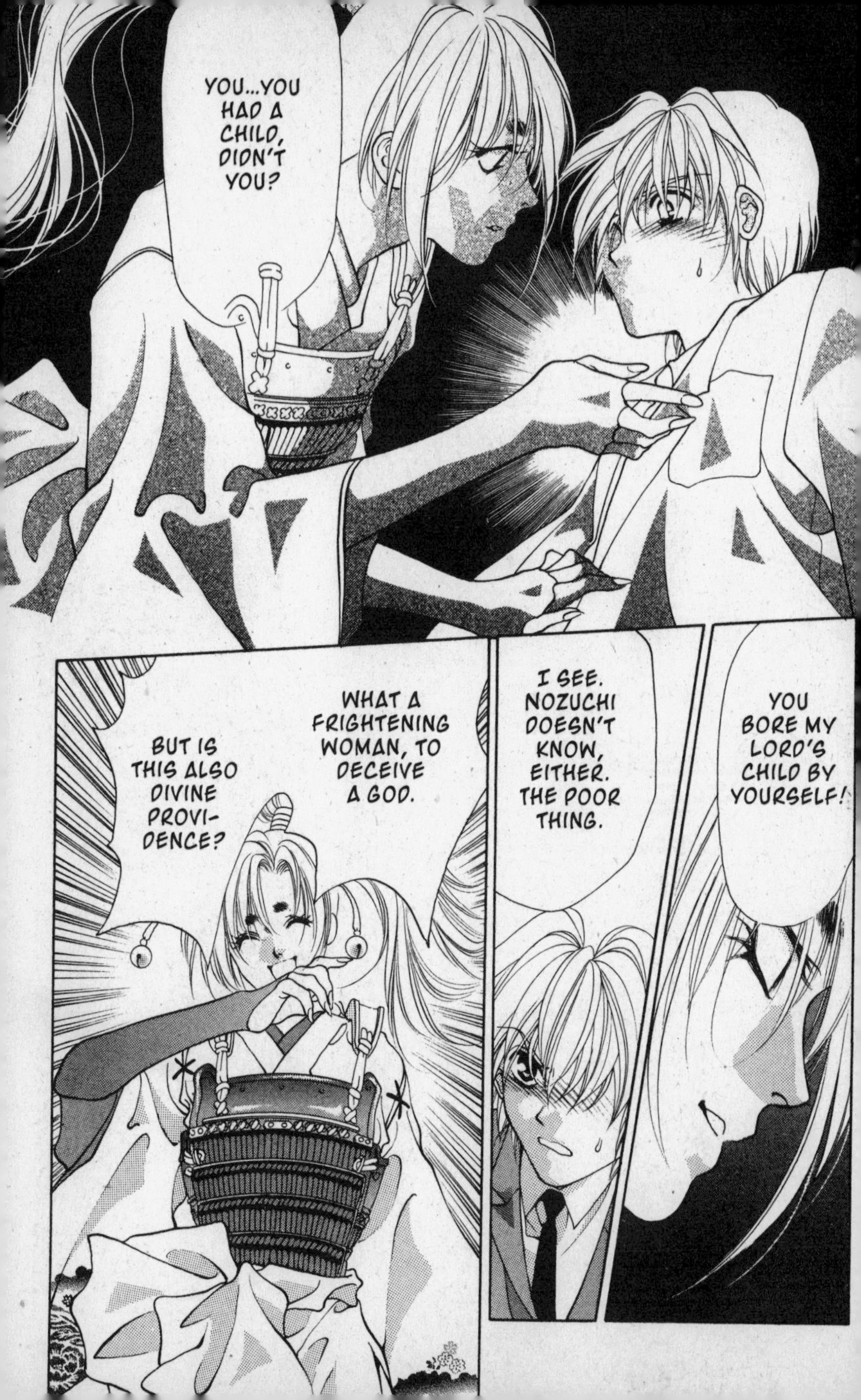
YOU...YOU HAD A CHILD, DIDN'T YOU?
YOU BORE MY LORD'S CHILD BY YOURSELF!
I SEE. NOZUCHI DOESN'T KNOW, EITHER. THE POOR THING.
WHAT A FRIGHTENING WOMAN, TO DECEIVE A GOD.
BUT IS THIS ALSO DIVINE PROVI-DENCE?

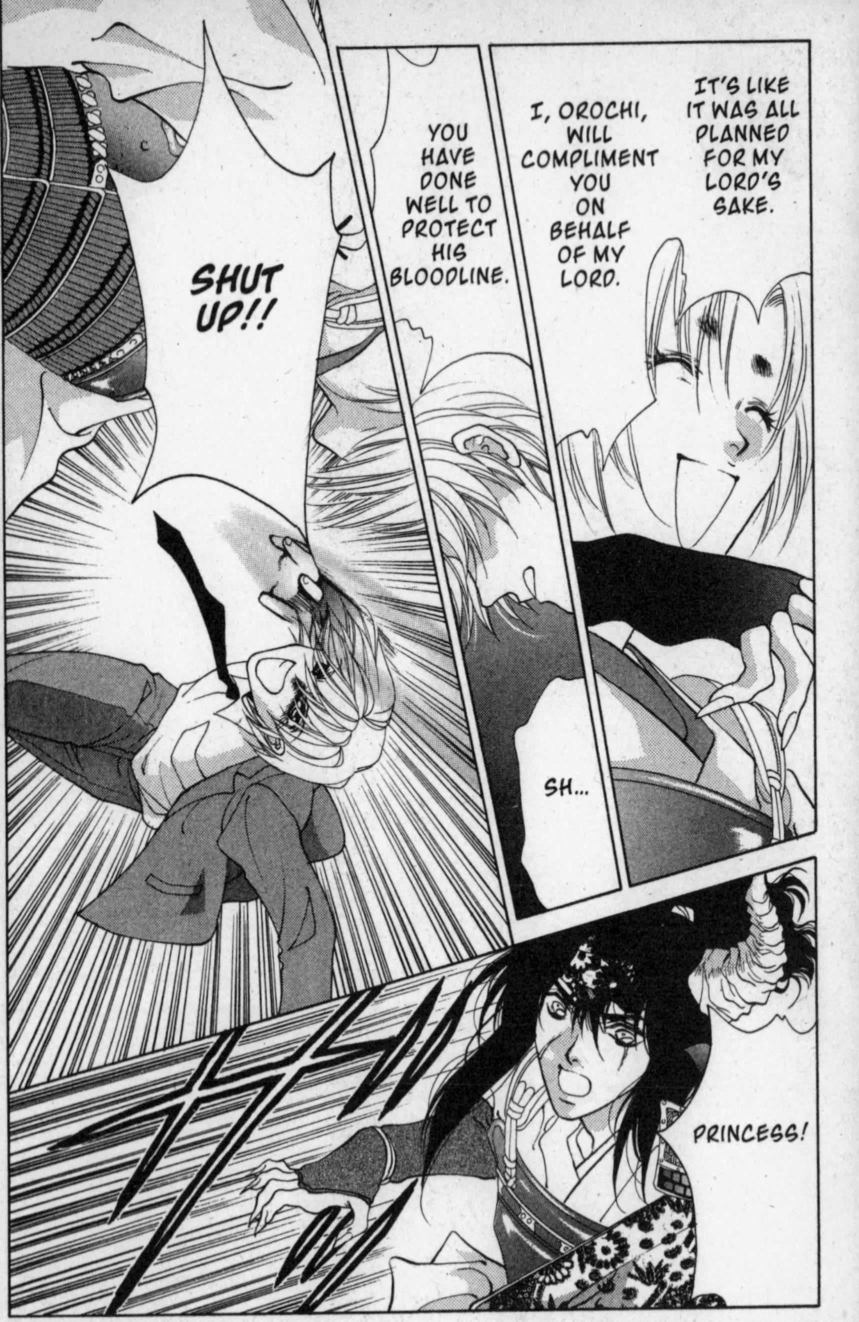
IT'S LIKE IT WAS ALL PLANNED FOR MY LORD'S SAKE.
I, OROCHI, WILL COMPLIMENT YOU ON BEHALF OF MY LORD.
SH...
YOU HAVE DONE WELL TO PROTECT HIS BLOODLINE.
SHUT UP!!
PRINCESS!

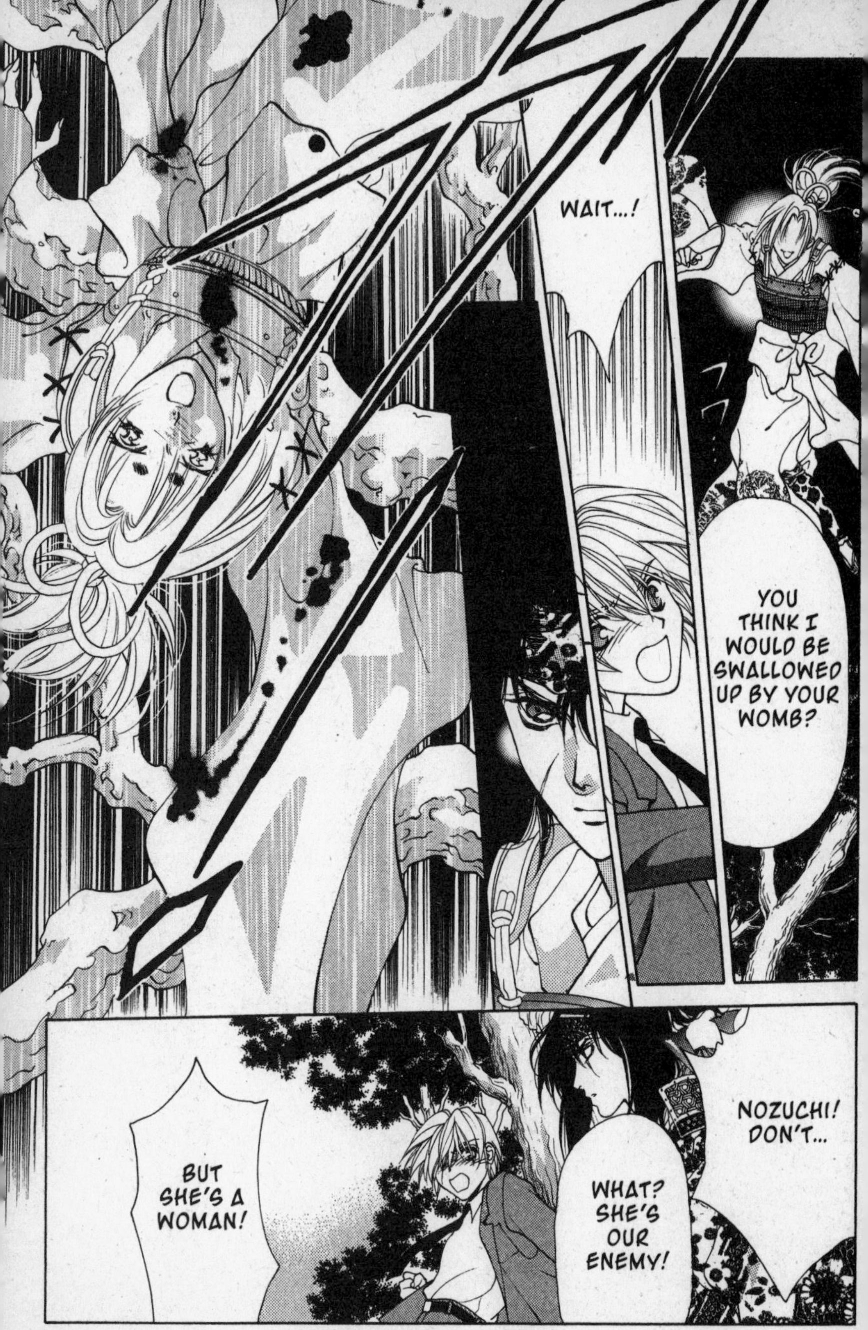
YOU THINK I WOULD BE SWALLOWED UP BY YOUR WOMB?
WAIT...!
NOZUCHI! DON'T...
WHAT? SHE'S OUR ENEMY!
BUT SHE'S A WOMAN!

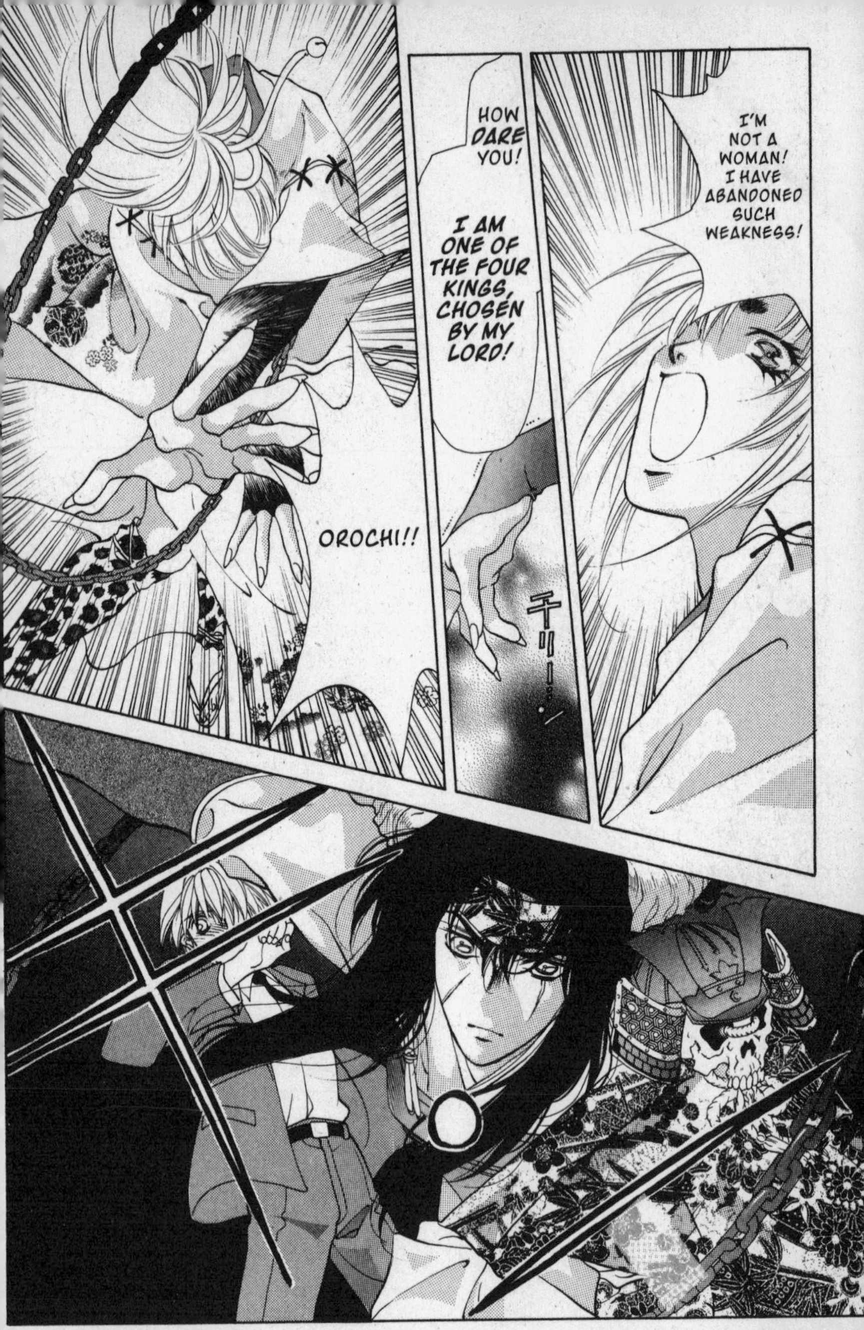
I'M NOT A WOMAN! I HAVE ABANDONED SUCH WEAKNESS!
HOW DARE YOU!
I AM ONE OF THE FOUR KINGS, CHOSEN BY MY LORD!
チリー…
OROCHI!!

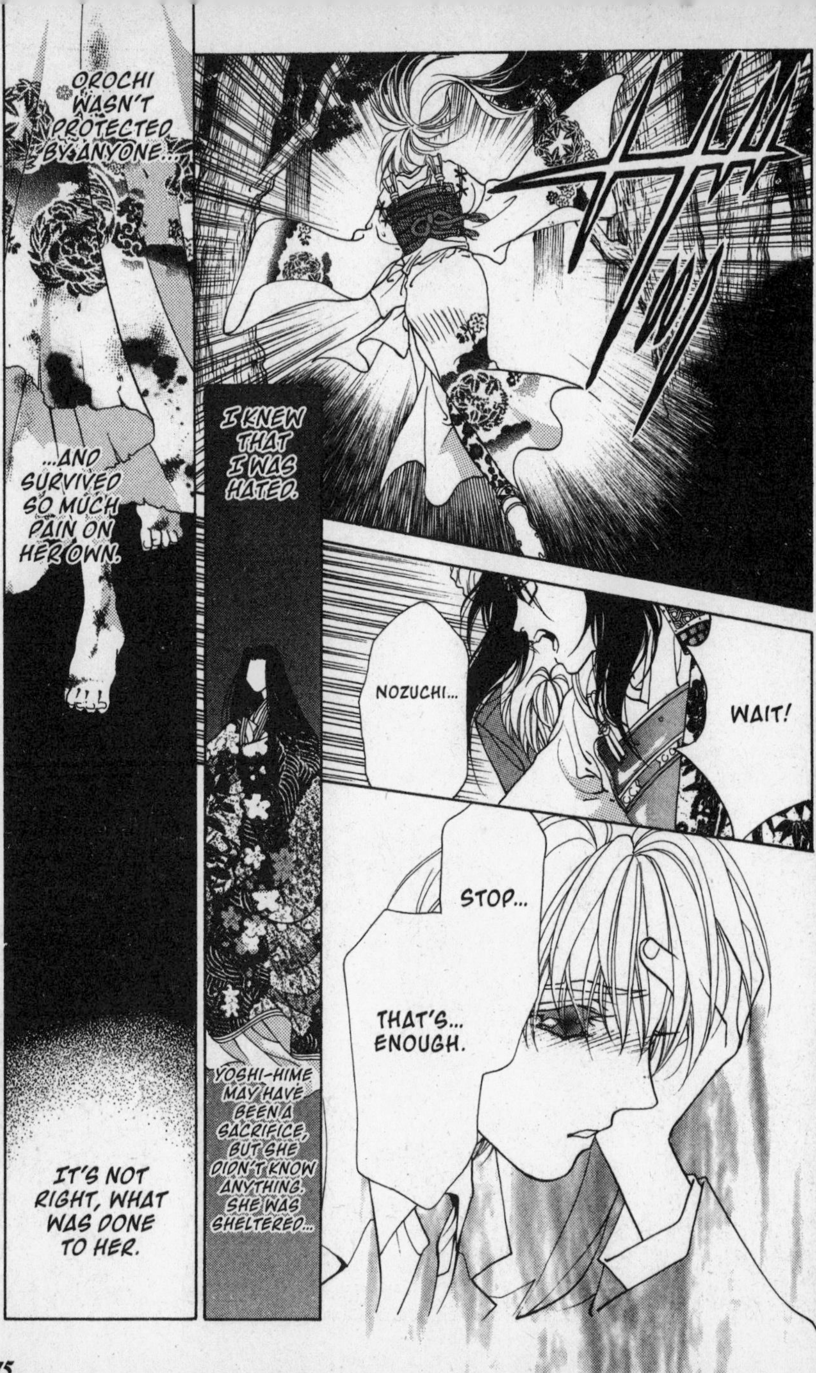
WAIT!
NOZUCHI...
STOP...
THAT'S... ENOUGH.
I KNEW THAT I WAS HATED.
YOSHI-HIME MAY HAVE BEEN A SACRIFICE, BUT SHE DIDN'T KNOW ANYTHING. SHE WAS SHELTERED...
OROCHI WASN'T PROTECTED BY ANYONE...
...AND SURVIVED SO MUCH PAIN ON HER OWN.
IT'S NOT RIGHT, WHAT WAS DONE TO HER.

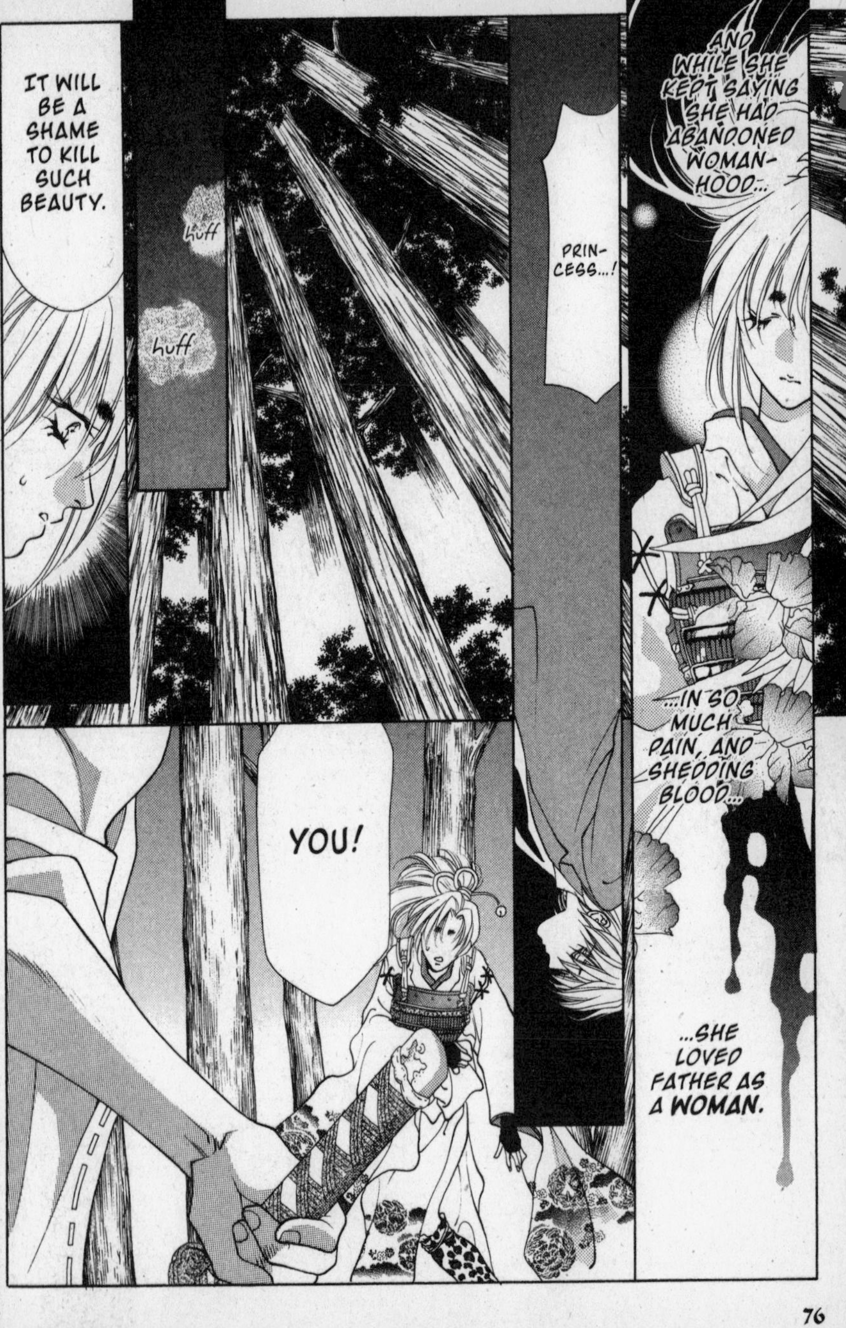
AND WHILE SHE KEPT SAYING SHE HAD ABANDONED WOMAN-HOOD...
...IN SO MUCH PAIN, AND SHEDDING BLOOD...
...SHE LOVED FATHER AS A WOMAN.
PRIN-CESS...!
huff
huff
IT WILL BE A SHAME TO KILL SUCH BEAUTY.
YOU!

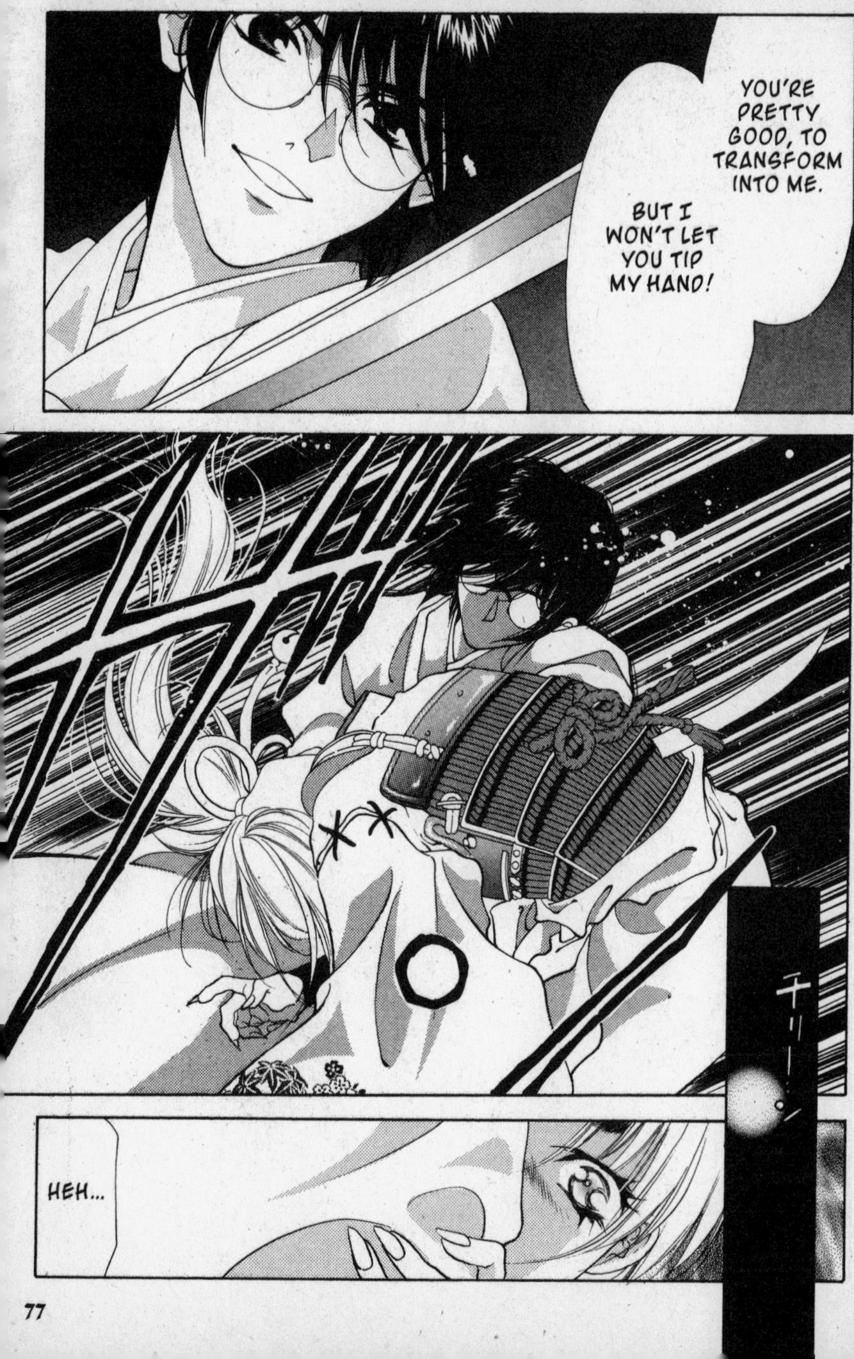
YOU'RE PRETTY GOOD, TO TRANSFORM INTO ME.
BUT I WON'T LET YOU TIP MY HAND!
チリーン
HEH...

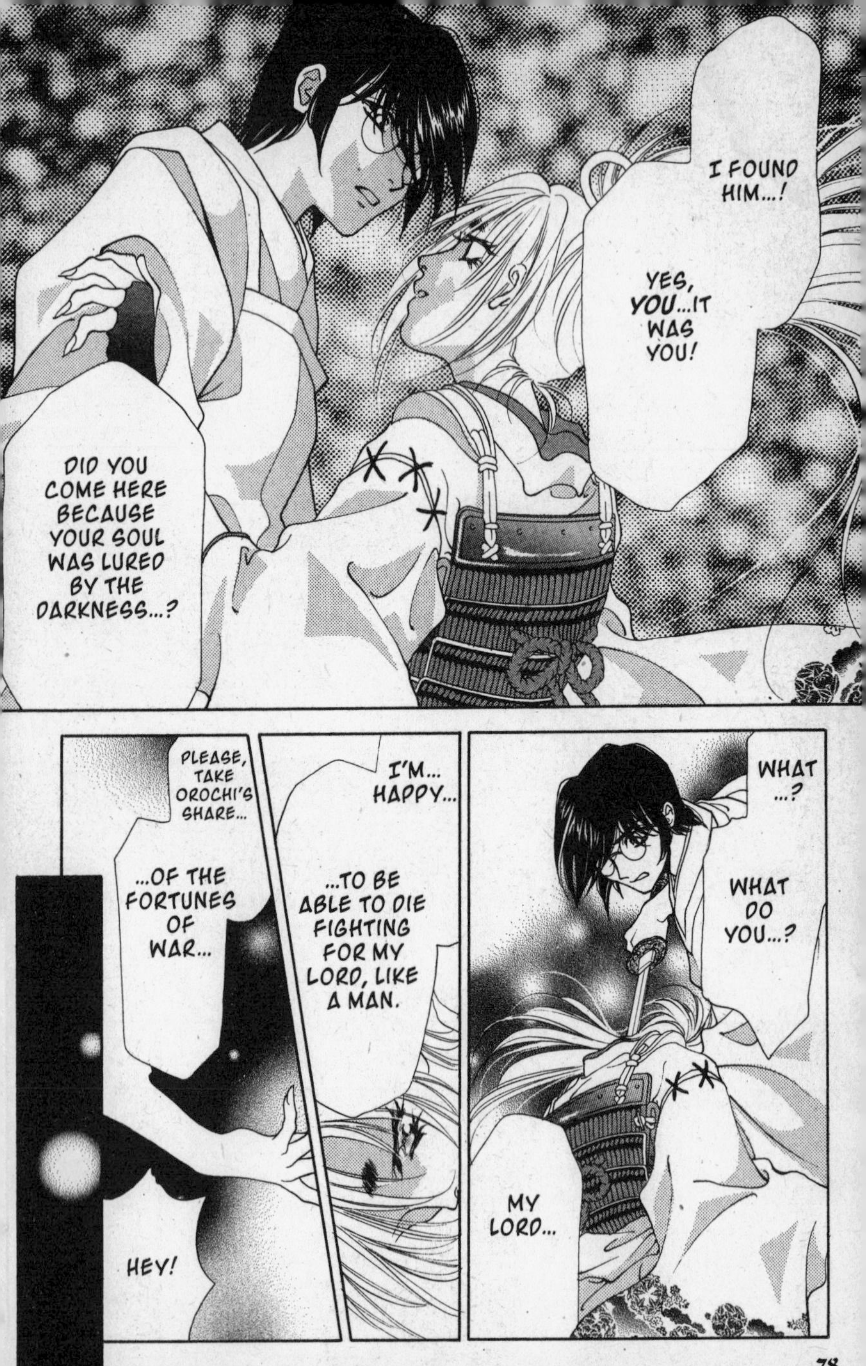
I FOUND HIM...!
YES, YOU...IT WAS YOU!
DID YOU COME HERE BECAUSE YOUR SOUL WAS LURED BY THE DARKNESS...?
WHAT ...?
WHAT DO YOU...?
MY LORD...
I'M... HAPPY...
...TO BE ABLE TO DIE FIGHTING FOR MY LORD, LIKE A MAN.
PLEASE, TAKE OROCHI'S SHARE...
...OF THE FORTUNES OF WAR...
HEY!

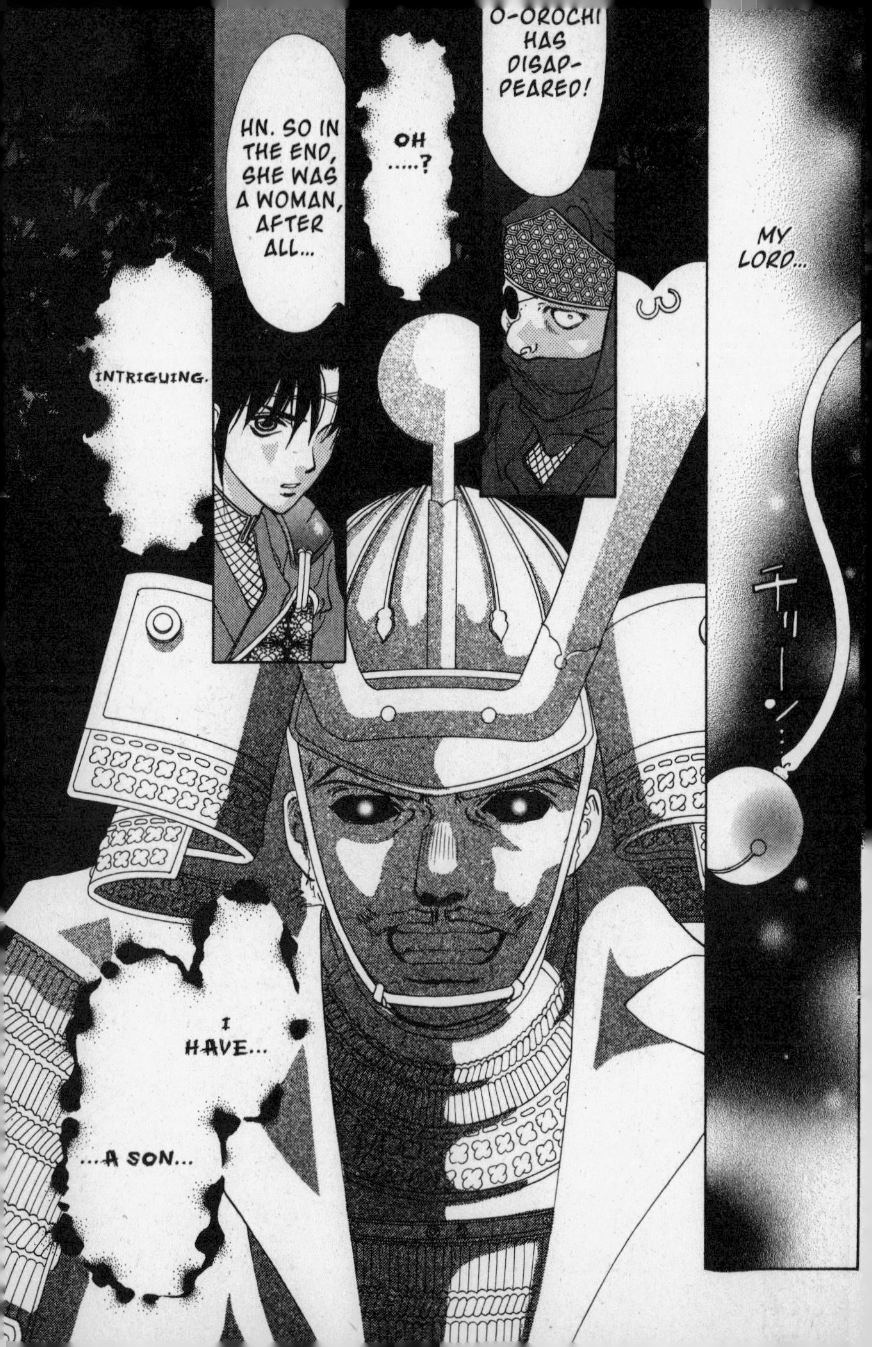
MY LORD...
チリーン…
O-OROCHI HAS DISAPPEARED!
OH .....?
HN. SO IN THE END, SHE WAS A WOMAN, AFTER ALL...
INTRIGUING.
I HAVE...
...A SON...

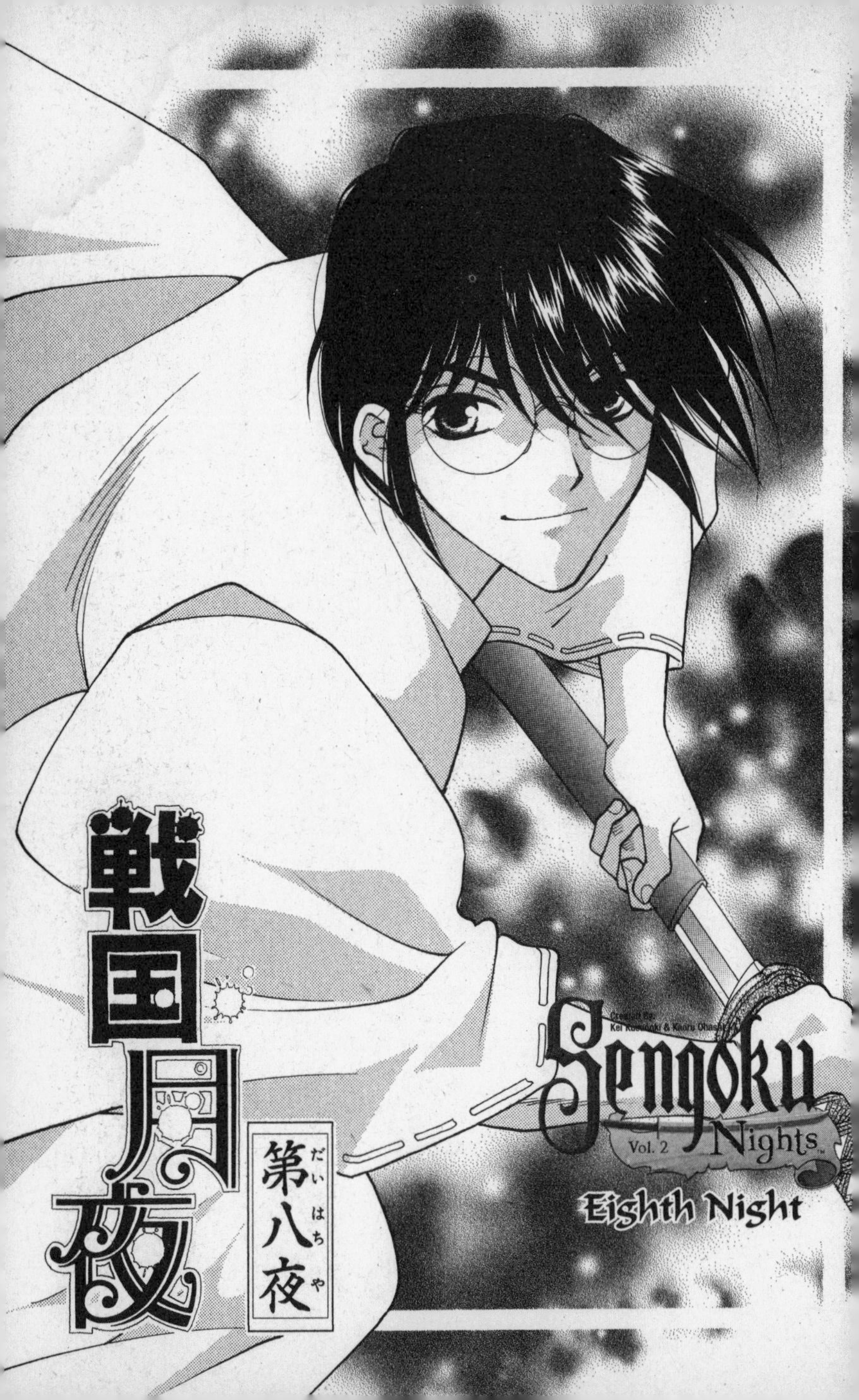
Sengoku Nights
Vol. 2
Eighth Night
第八夜
戦国月夜

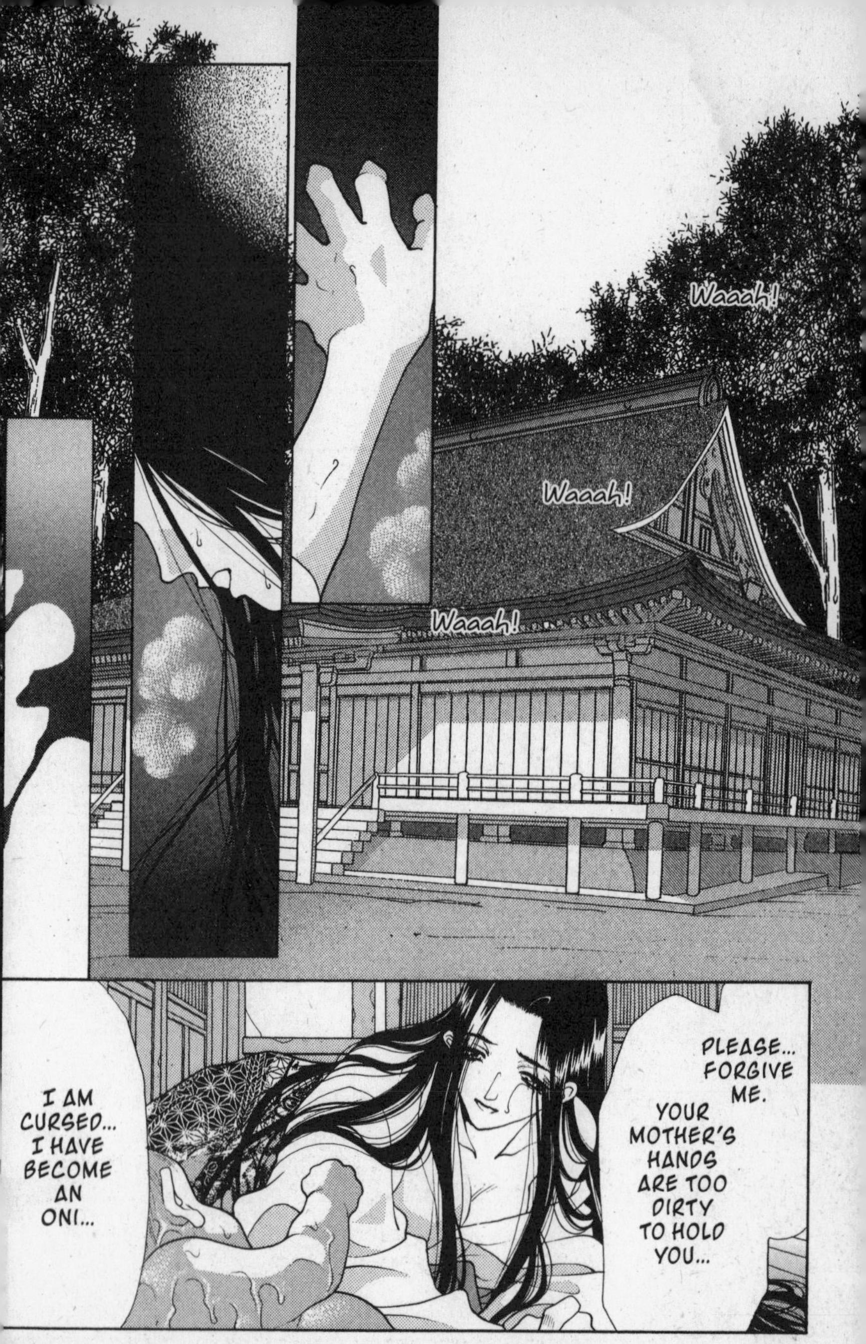
Waaah!
Waaah!
Waaah!
PLEASE... FORGIVE ME.
YOUR MOTHER'S HANDS ARE TOO DIRTY TO HOLD YOU...
I AM CURSED... I HAVE BECOME AN ONI...

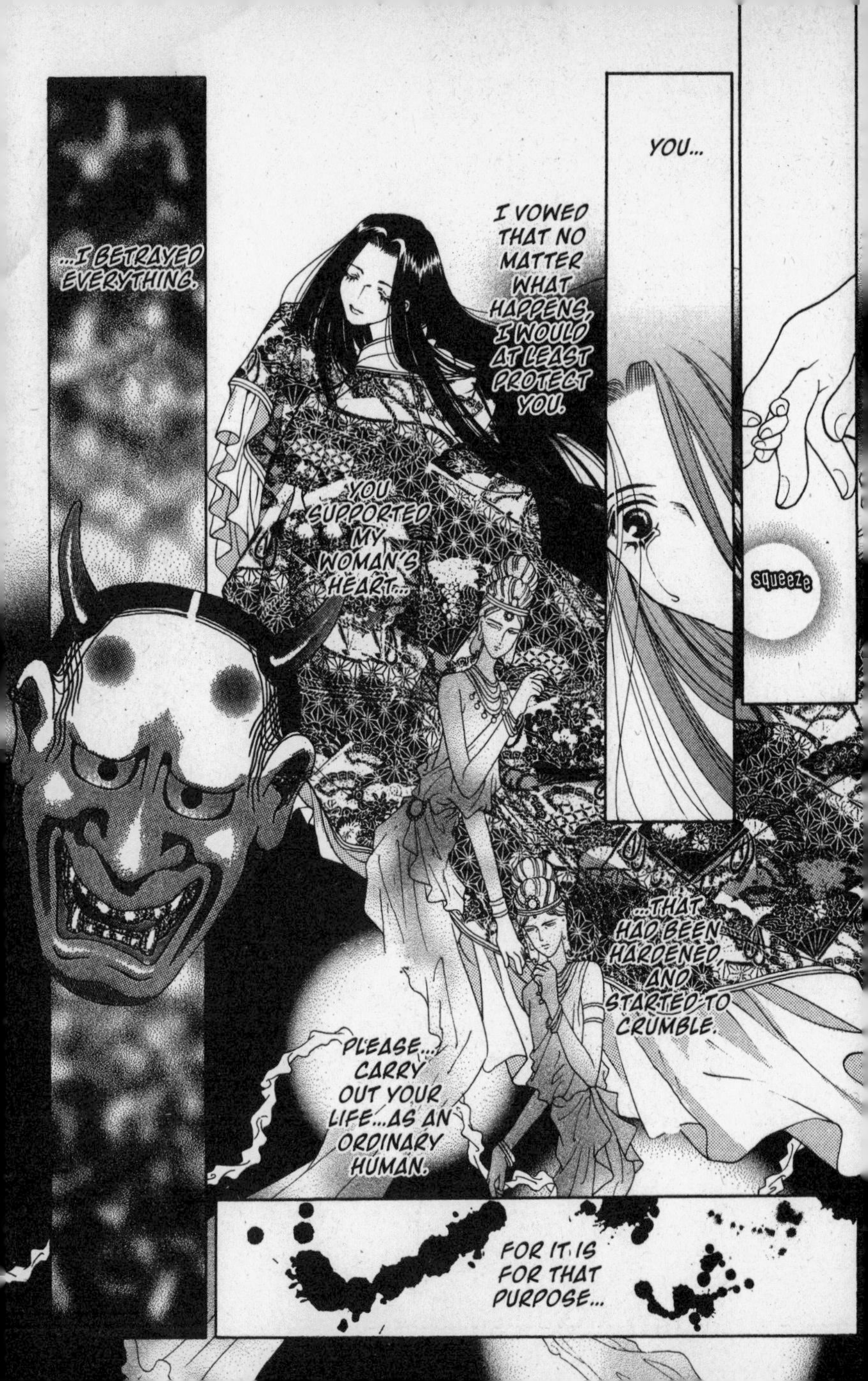
YOU...
squeeze
I VOWED THAT NO MATTER WHAT HAPPENS, I WOULD AT LEAST PROTECT YOU.
...I BETRAYED EVERYTHING.
YOU SUPPORTED MY WOMAN'S HEART...
...THAT HAD BEEN HARDENED, AND STARTED TO CRUMBLE.
PLEASE... CARRY OUT YOUR LIFE...AS AN ORDINARY HUMAN.
FOR IT IS FOR THAT PURPOSE...

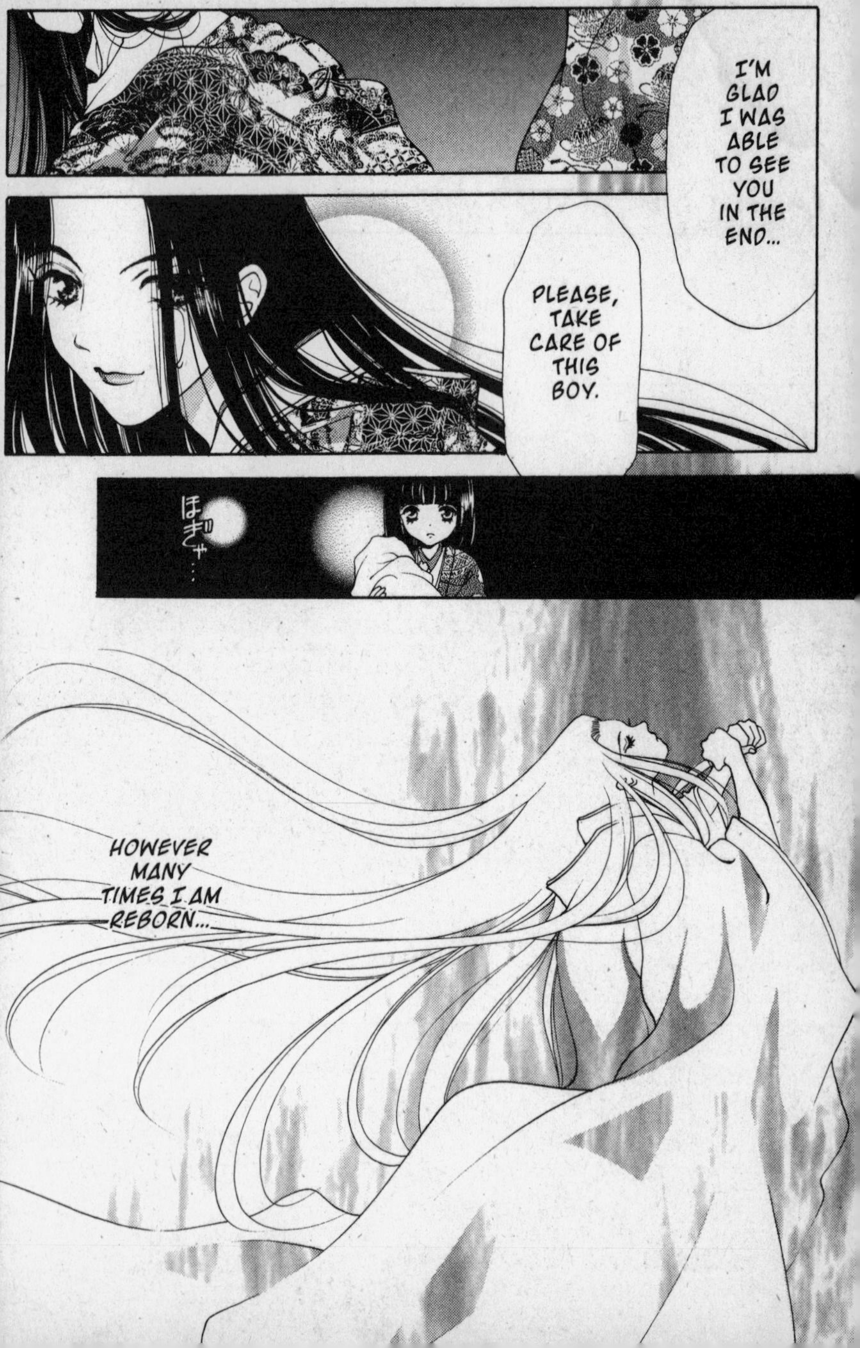
I'M GLAD I WAS ABLE TO SEE YOU IN THE END...
PLEASE, TAKE CARE OF THIS BOY.
ほぎゃ…
HOWEVER MANY TIMES I AM REBORN...

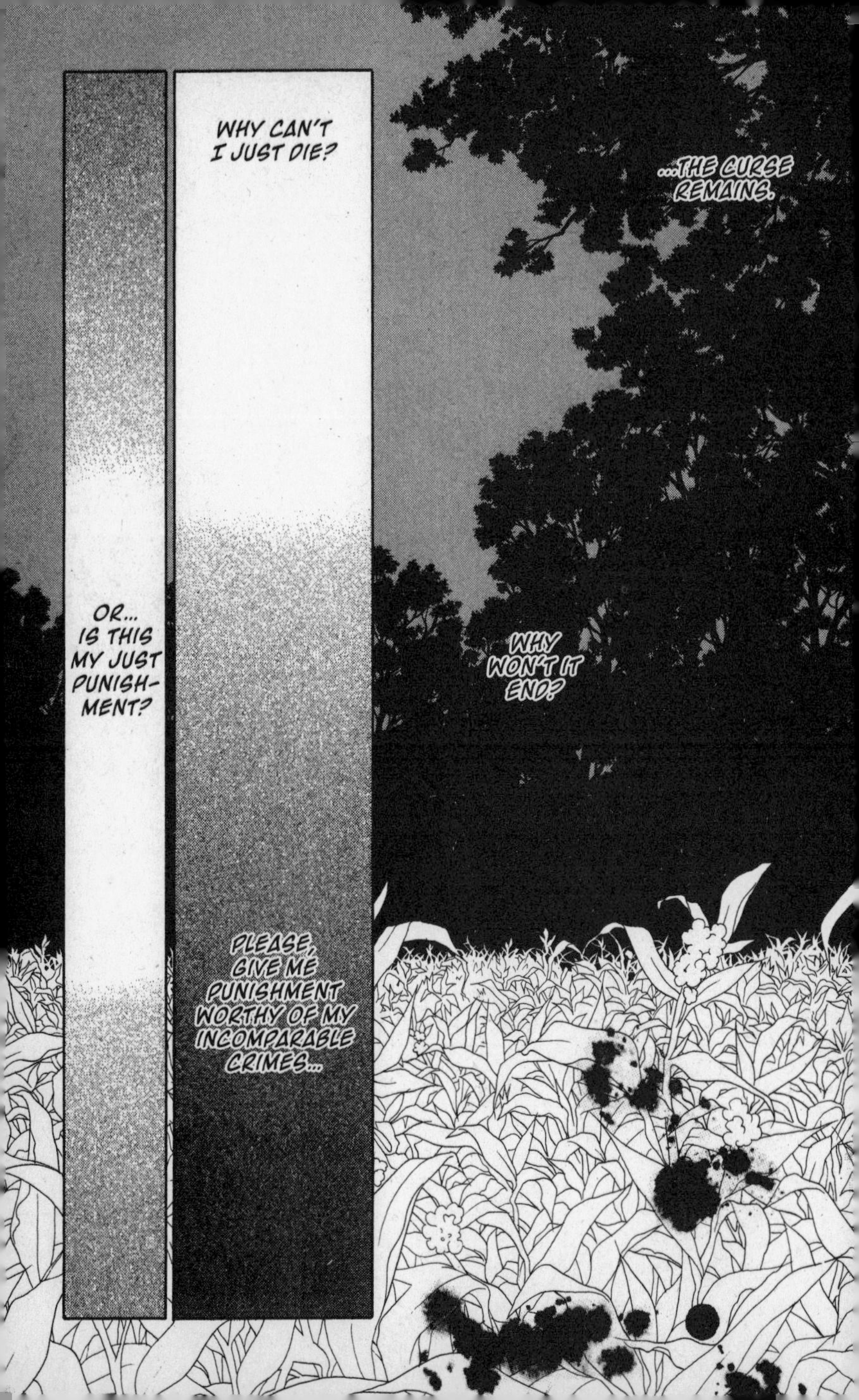
...THE CURSE REMAINS.
WHY WON'T IT END?
WHY CAN'T I JUST DIE?
PLEASE, GIVE ME PUNISHMENT WORTHY OF MY INCOMPARABLE CRIMES...
OR... IS THIS MY JUST PUNISHMENT?

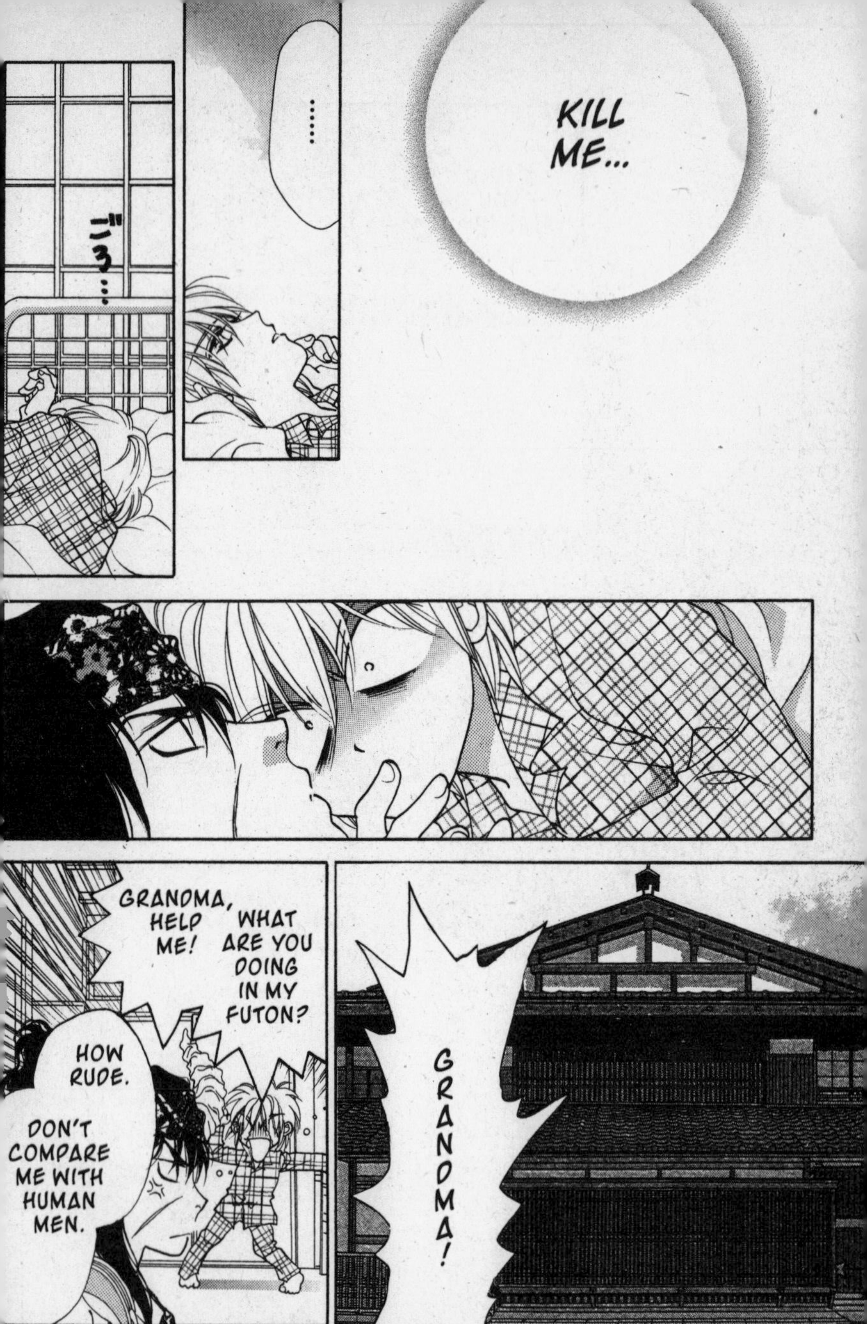
KILL ME...
......
ごろ…
GRANDMA!
GRANDMA, HELP ME! WHAT ARE YOU DOING IN MY FUTON?
HOW RUDE.
DON'T COMPARE ME WITH HUMAN MEN.

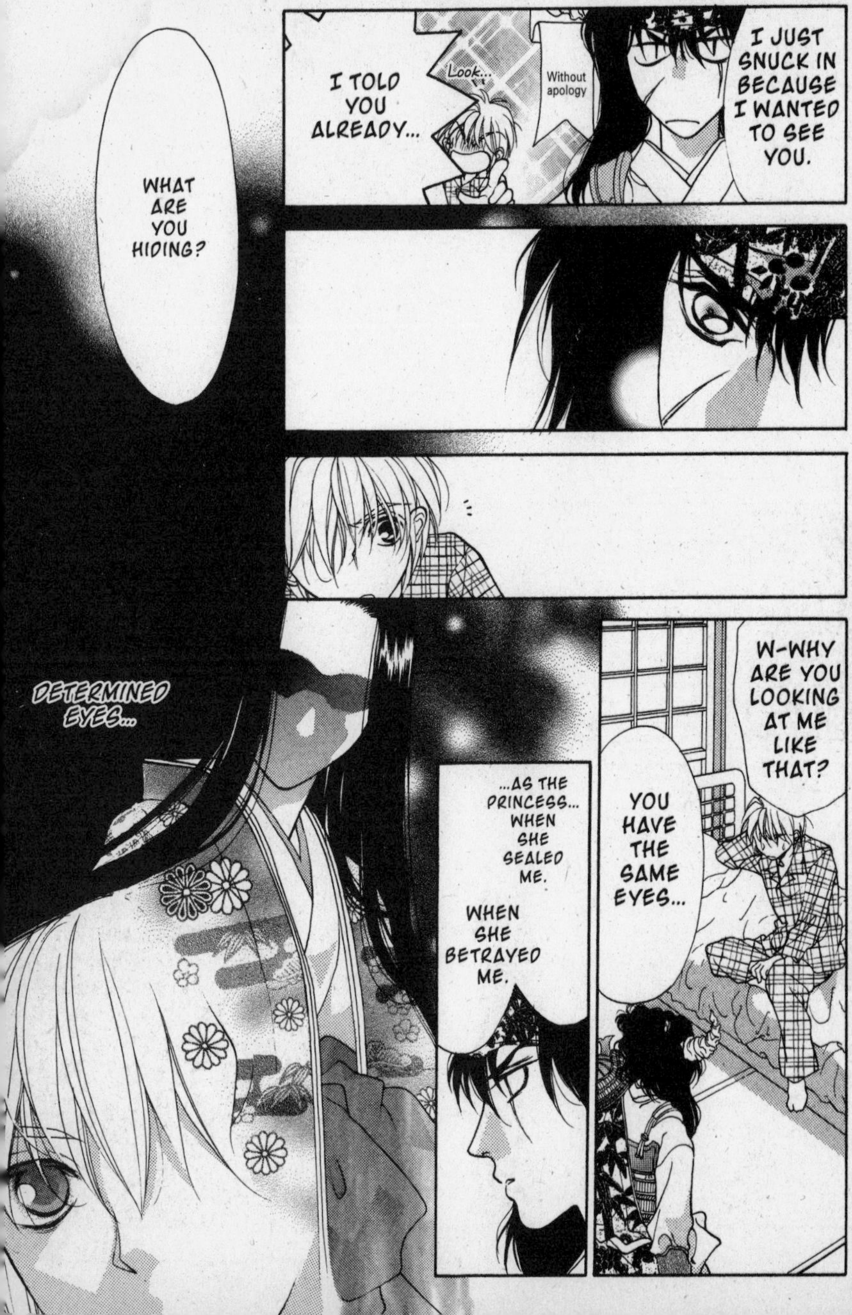
I JUST SNUCK IN BECAUSE I WANTED TO SEE YOU.
Without apology
Look...
I TOLD YOU ALREADY...
WHAT ARE YOU HIDING?
W-WHY ARE YOU LOOKING AT ME LIKE THAT?
YOU HAVE THE SAME EYES...
...AS THE PRINCESS... WHEN SHE SEALED ME.
WHEN SHE BETRAYED ME.
DETERMINED EYES...

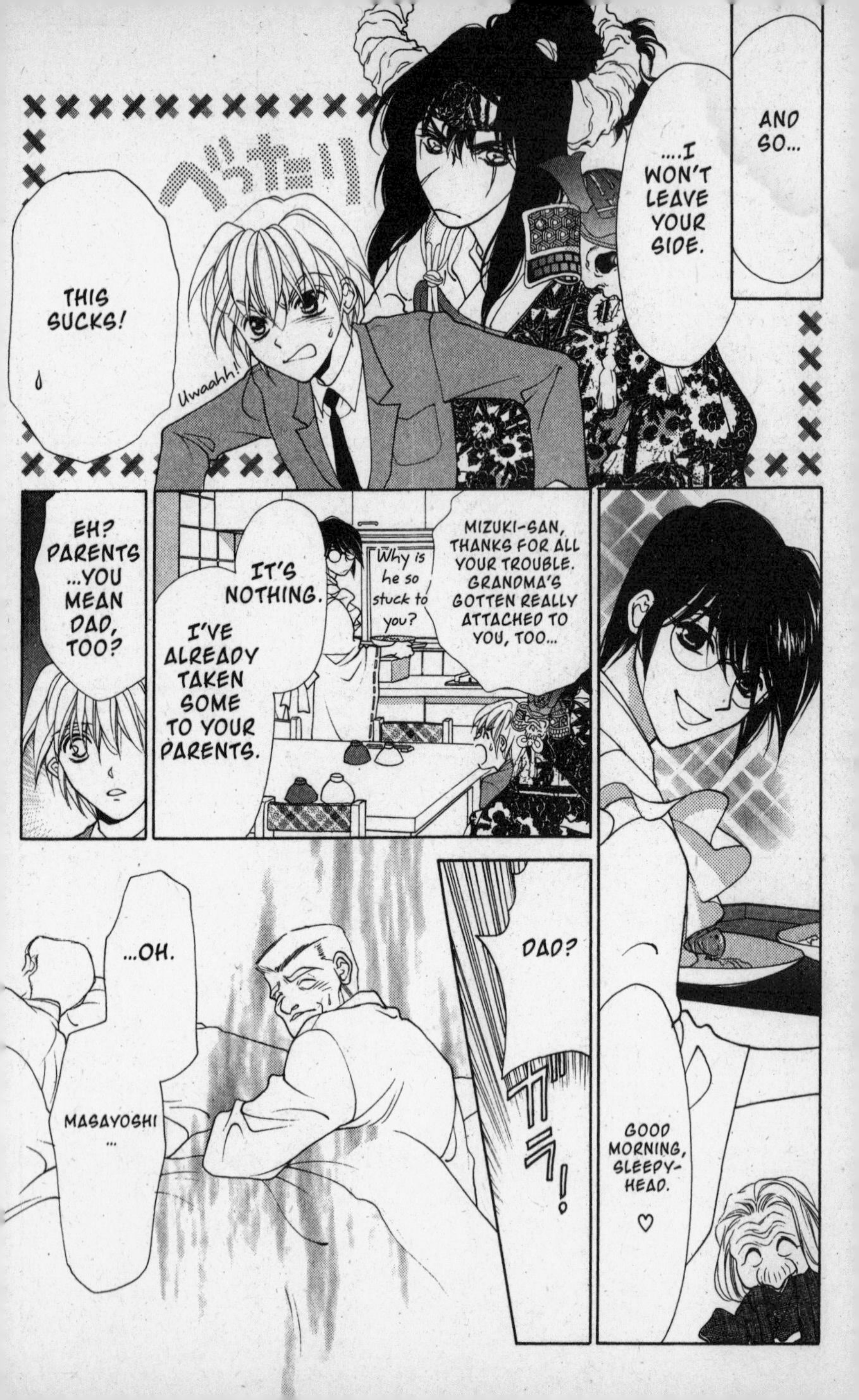
AND SO...
....I WON'T LEAVE YOUR SIDE.
べったり
Uwaahh!
THIS SUCKS!
MIZUKI-SAN, THANKS FOR ALL YOUR TROUBLE. GRANDMA'S GOTTEN REALLY ATTACHED TO YOU, TOO...
Why is he so stuck to you?
IT'S NOTHING.
I'VE ALREADY TAKEN SOME TO YOUR PARENTS.
EH? PARENTS ...YOU MEAN DAD, TOO?
GOOD MORNING, SLEEPY-HEAD. ♡
DAD?
ガラ!
...OH.
MASAYOSHI ...

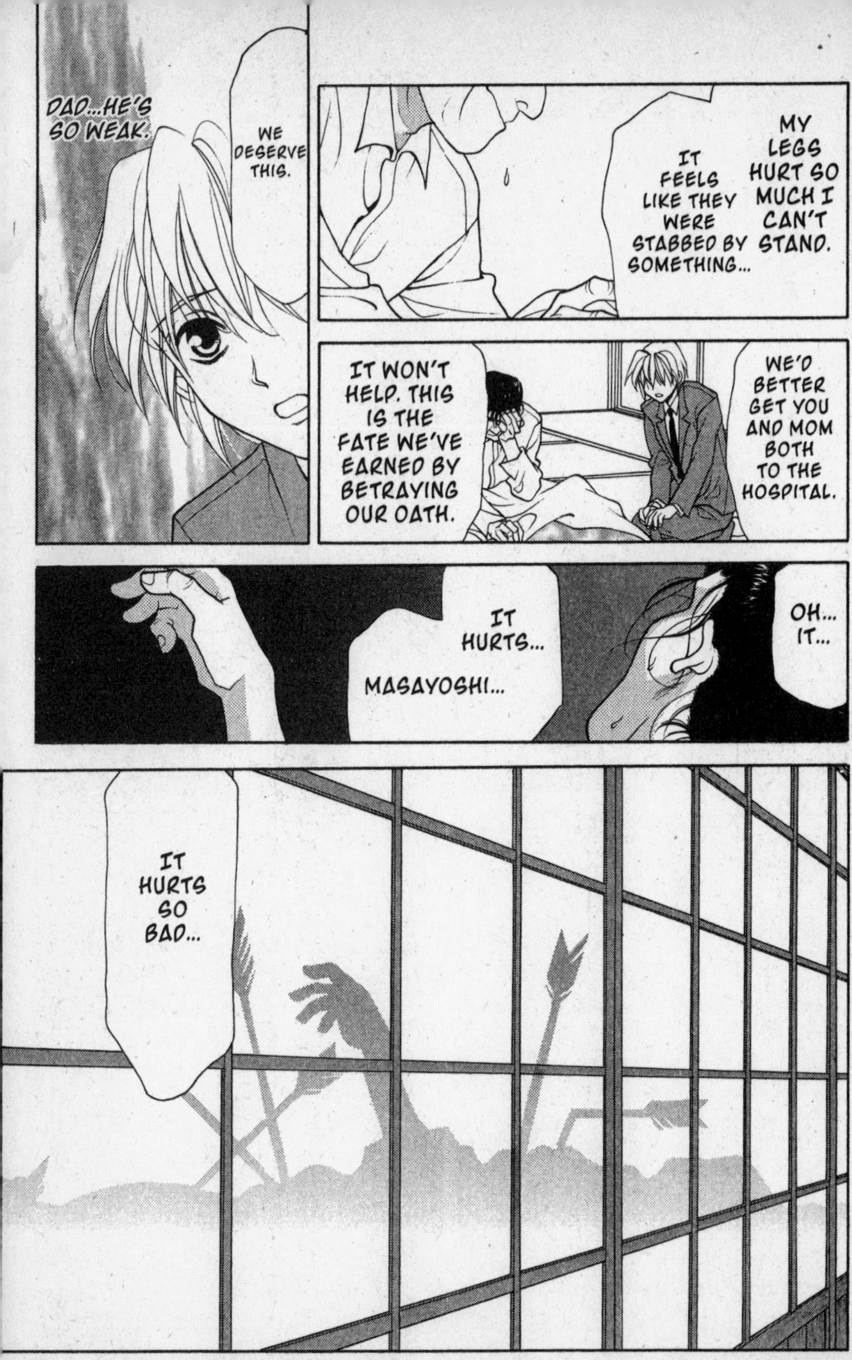
MY LEGS HURT SO MUCH I CAN'T STAND.
IT FEELS LIKE THEY WERE STABBED BY SOMETHING...
WE'D BETTER GET YOU AND MOM BOTH TO THE HOSPITAL.
IT WON'T HELP. THIS IS THE FATE WE'VE EARNED BY BETRAYING OUR OATH.
WE DESERVE THIS.
DAD...HE'S SO WEAK.
OH... IT...
IT HURTS...
MASAYOSHI...
IT HURTS SO BAD...

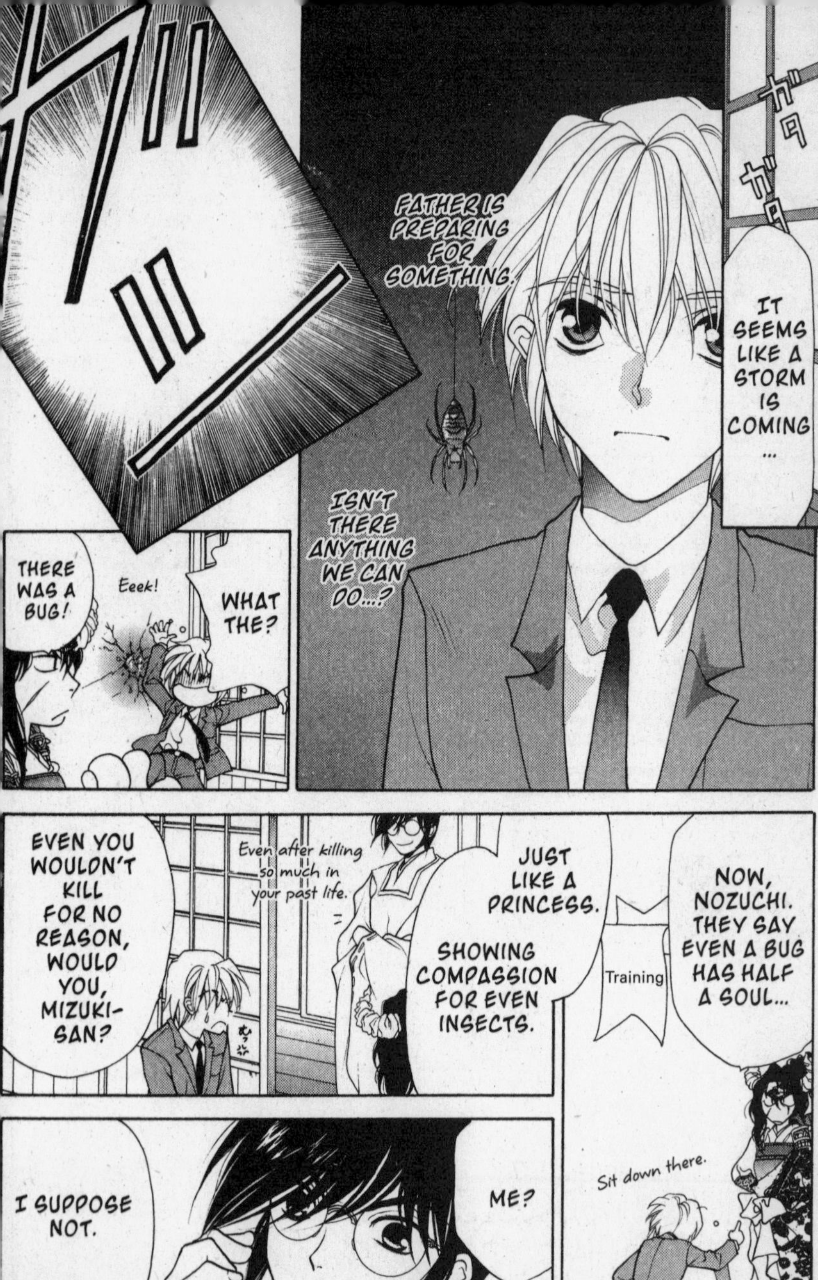

ガタ
ガタ
IT SEEMS LIKE A STORM IS COMING ...
FATHER IS PREPARING FOR SOMETHING.
ISN'T THERE ANYTHING WE CAN DO...?
WHAT THE?
Eeek!
THERE WAS A BUG!
NOW, NOZUCHI. THEY SAY EVEN A BUG HAS HALF A SOUL...
Training
Sit down there.
JUST LIKE A PRINCESS.
SHOWING COMPASSION FOR EVEN INSECTS.
Even after killing so much in your past life.
EVEN YOU WOULDN'T KILL FOR NO REASON, WOULD YOU, MIZUKI-SAN?
ME?
I SUPPOSE NOT.

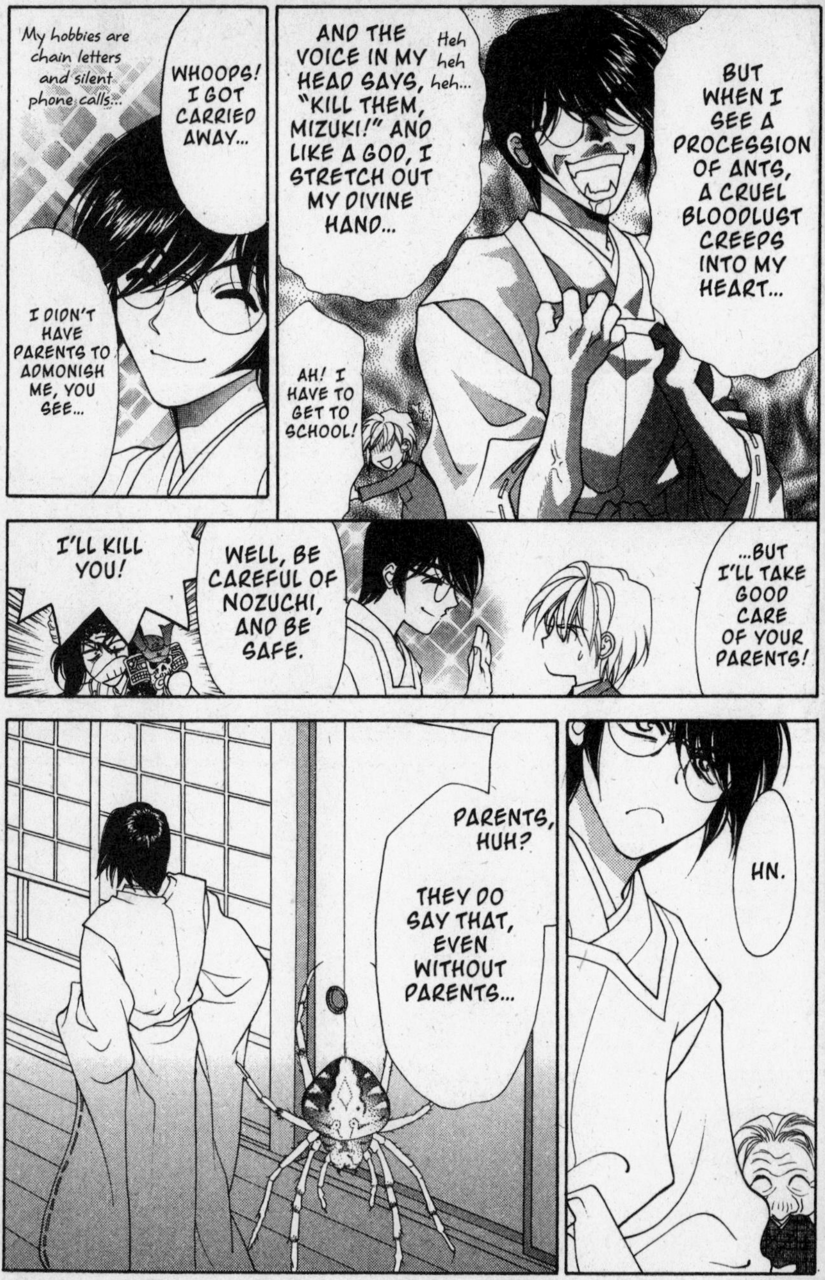
BUT WHEN I SEE A PROCESSION OF ANTS, A CRUEL BLOODLUST CREEPS INTO MY HEART...
AND THE VOICE IN MY HEAD SAYS, "KILL THEM, MIZUKI!" AND LIKE A GOD, I STRETCH OUT MY DIVINE HAND...
Heh heh heh...
AH! I HAVE TO GET TO SCHOOL!
WHOOPS! I GOT CARRIED AWAY...
My hobbies are chain letters and silent phone calls...
I DIDN'T HAVE PARENTS TO ADMONISH ME, YOU SEE...
...BUT I'LL TAKE GOOD CARE OF YOUR PARENTS!
WELL, BE CAREFUL OF NOZUCHI, AND BE SAFE.
I'LL KILL YOU!
HN.
PARENTS, HUH?
THEY DO SAY THAT, EVEN WITHOUT PARENTS...

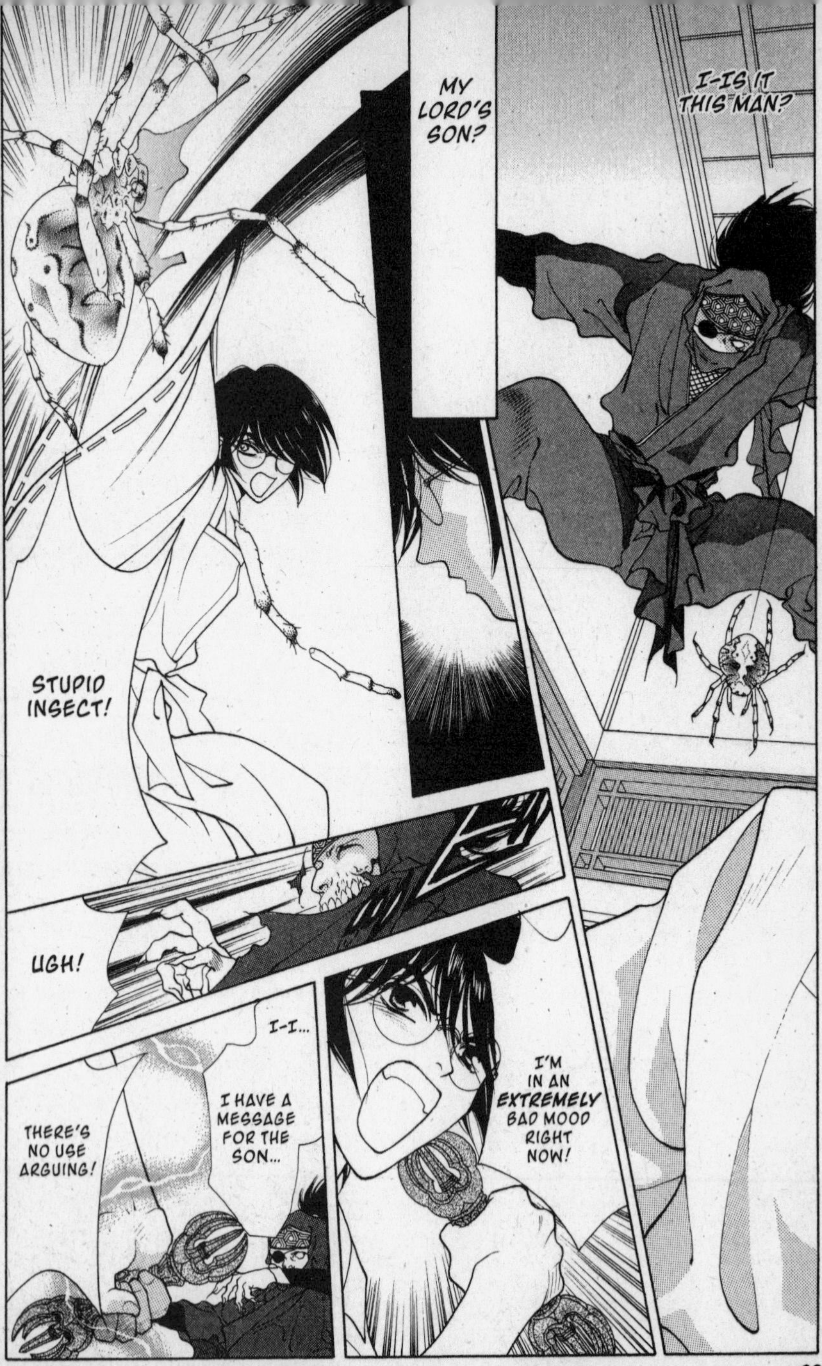
I-IS IT THIS MAN?
MY LORD'S SON?
STUPID INSECT!
UGH!
I'M IN AN **EXTREMELY** BAD MOOD RIGHT NOW!
I-I...
I HAVE A MESSAGE FOR THE SON...
THERE'S NO USE ARGUING!

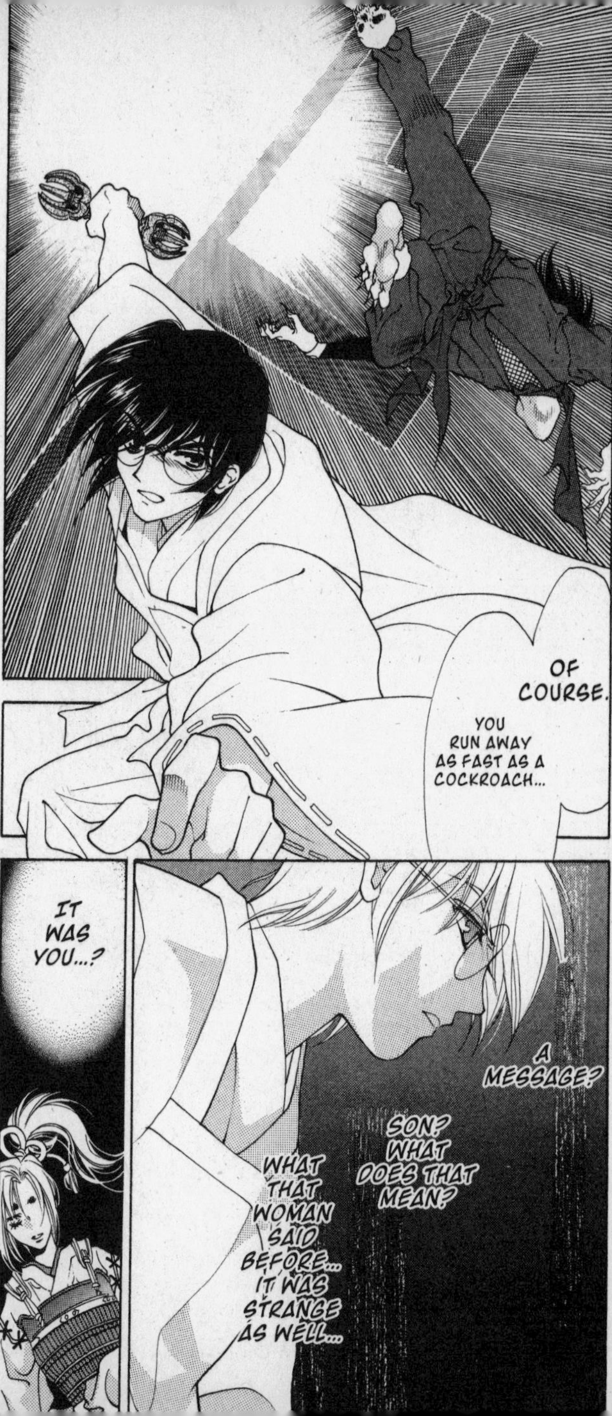
OF COURSE.
YOU RUN AWAY AS FAST AS A COCKROACH...
A MESSAGE?
SON? WHAT DOES THAT MEAN?
WHAT THAT WOMAN SAID BEFORE... IT WAS STRANGE AS WELL...
IT WAS YOU...?

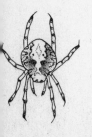

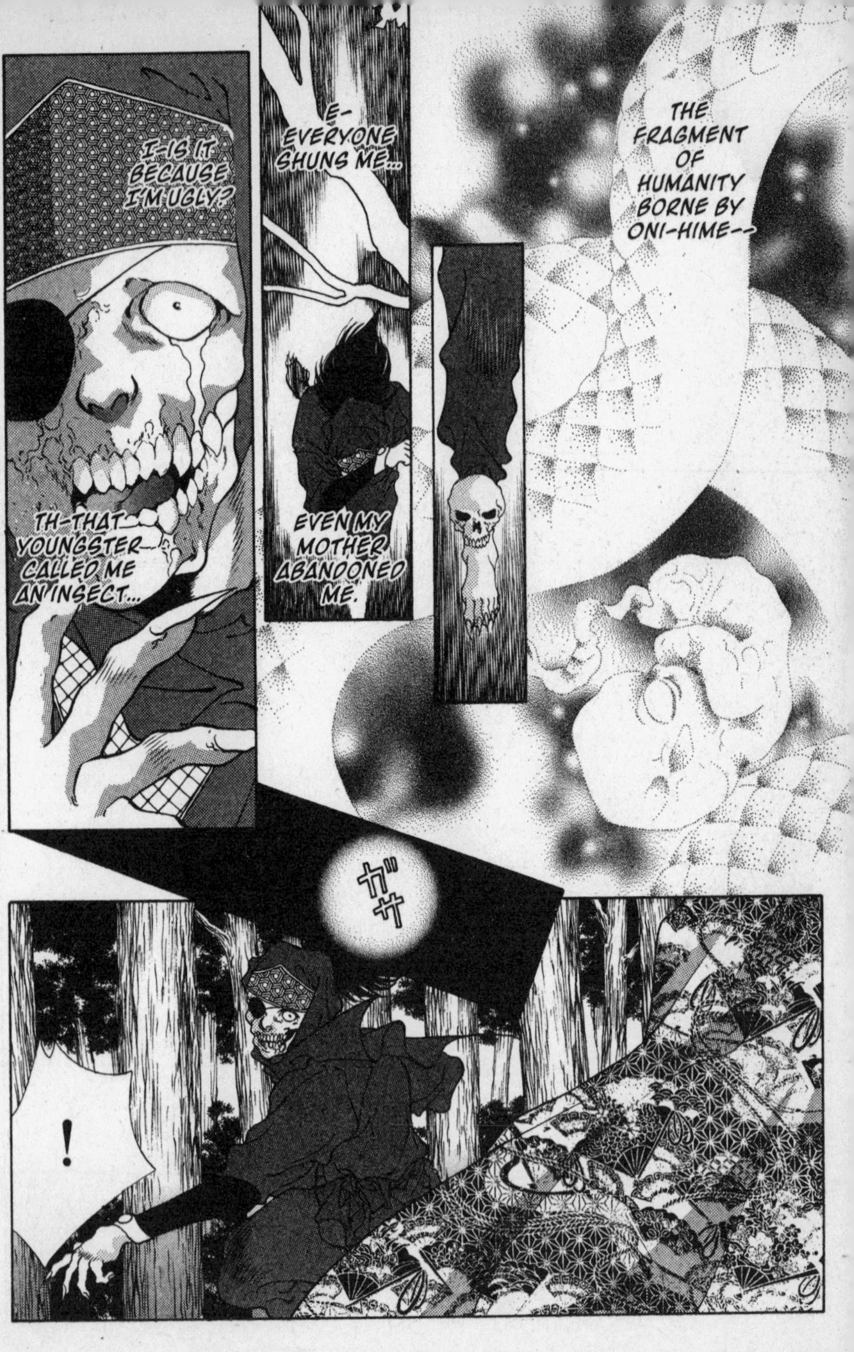
THE FRAGMENT OF HUMANITY BORNE BY ONI-HIME--
E-EVERYONE SHUNS ME...
EVEN MY MOTHER ABANDONED ME.
I-IS IT BECAUSE I'M UGLY?
TH-THAT YOUNGSTER CALLED ME AN INSECT...
ガサ
!

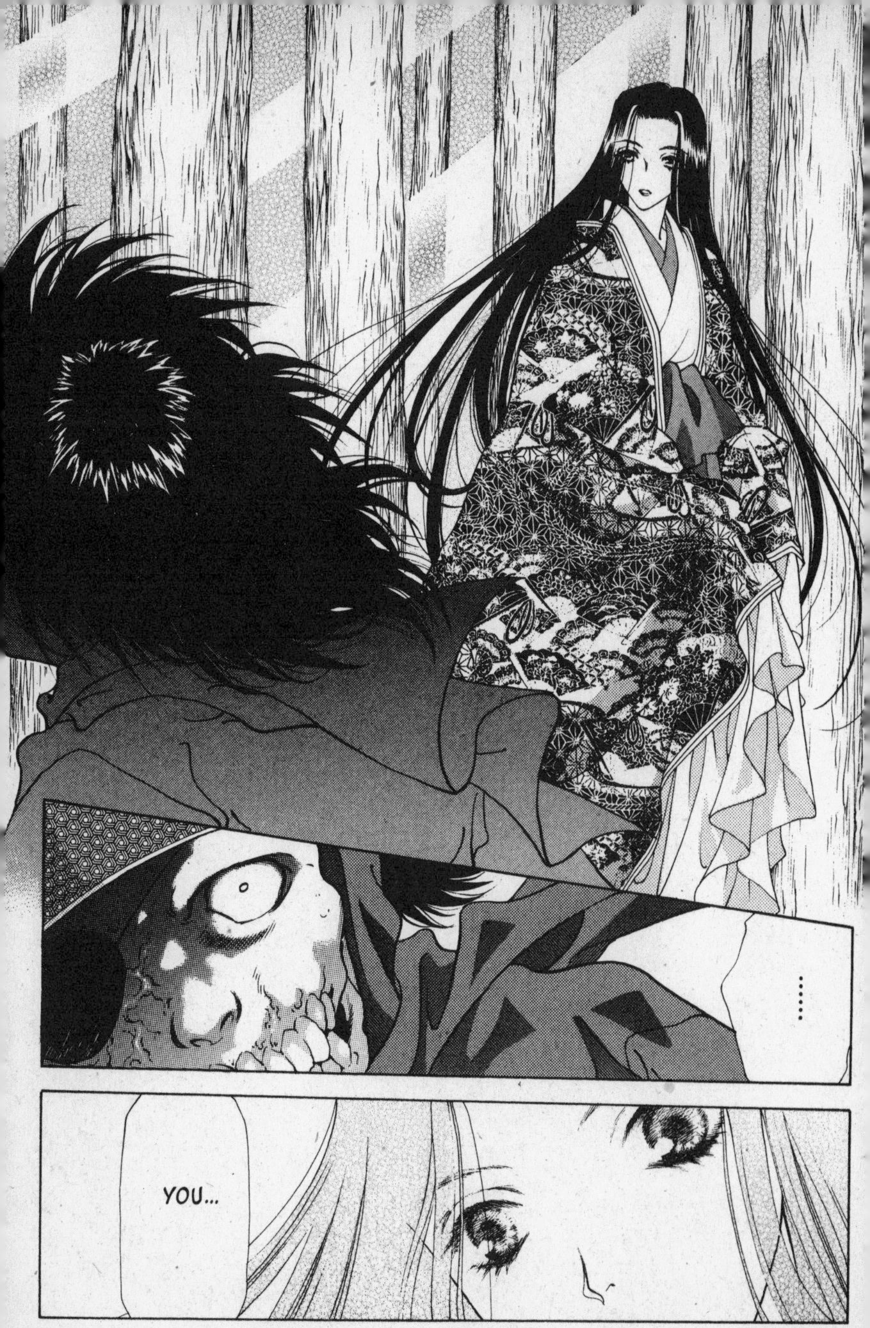
......
YOU...

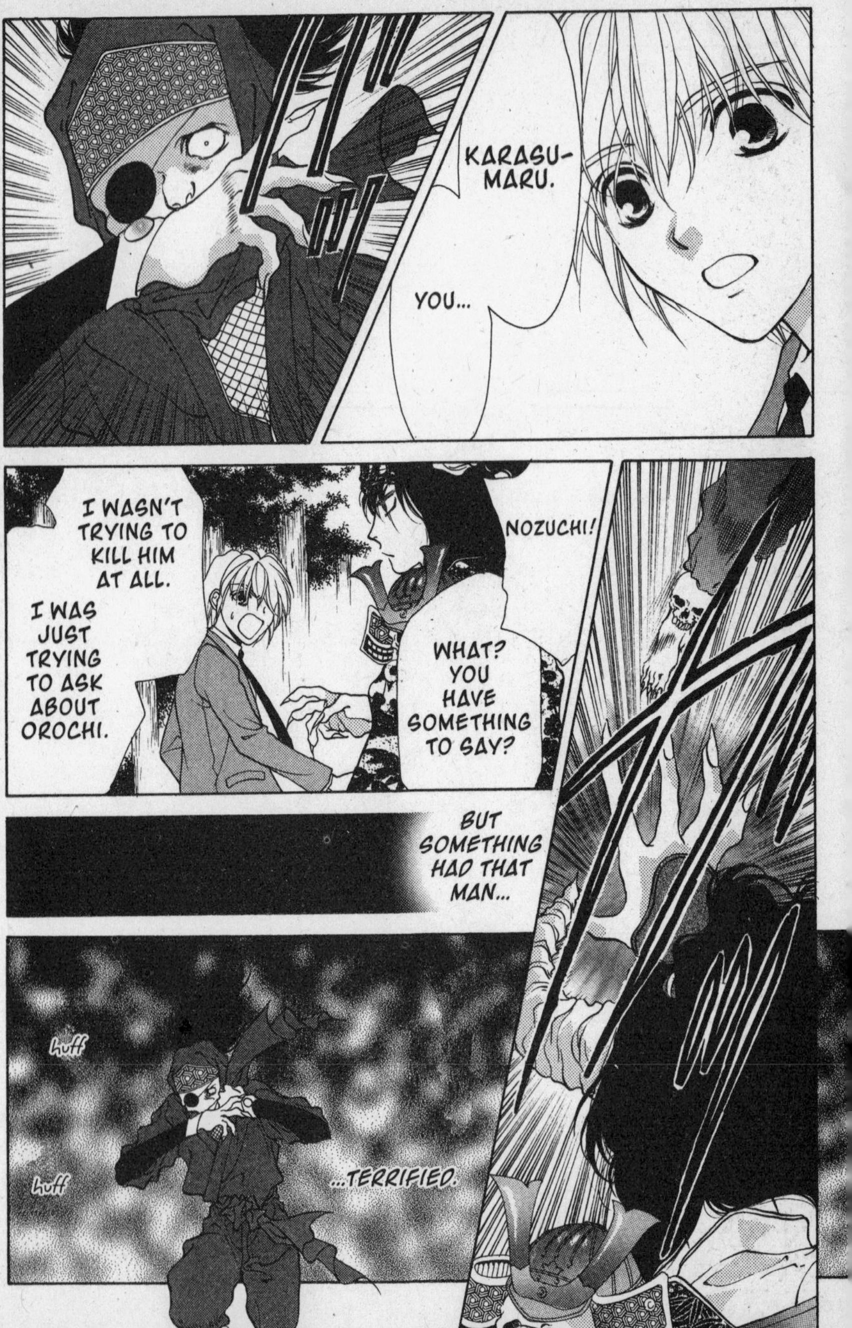
KARASU-
MARU.
YOU...
NOZUCHI!
WHAT? YOU HAVE SOMETHING TO SAY?
I WASN'T TRYING TO KILL HIM AT ALL.
I WAS JUST TRYING TO ASK ABOUT OROCHI.
BUT SOMETHING HAD THAT MAN...
huff
huff
...TERRIFIED.

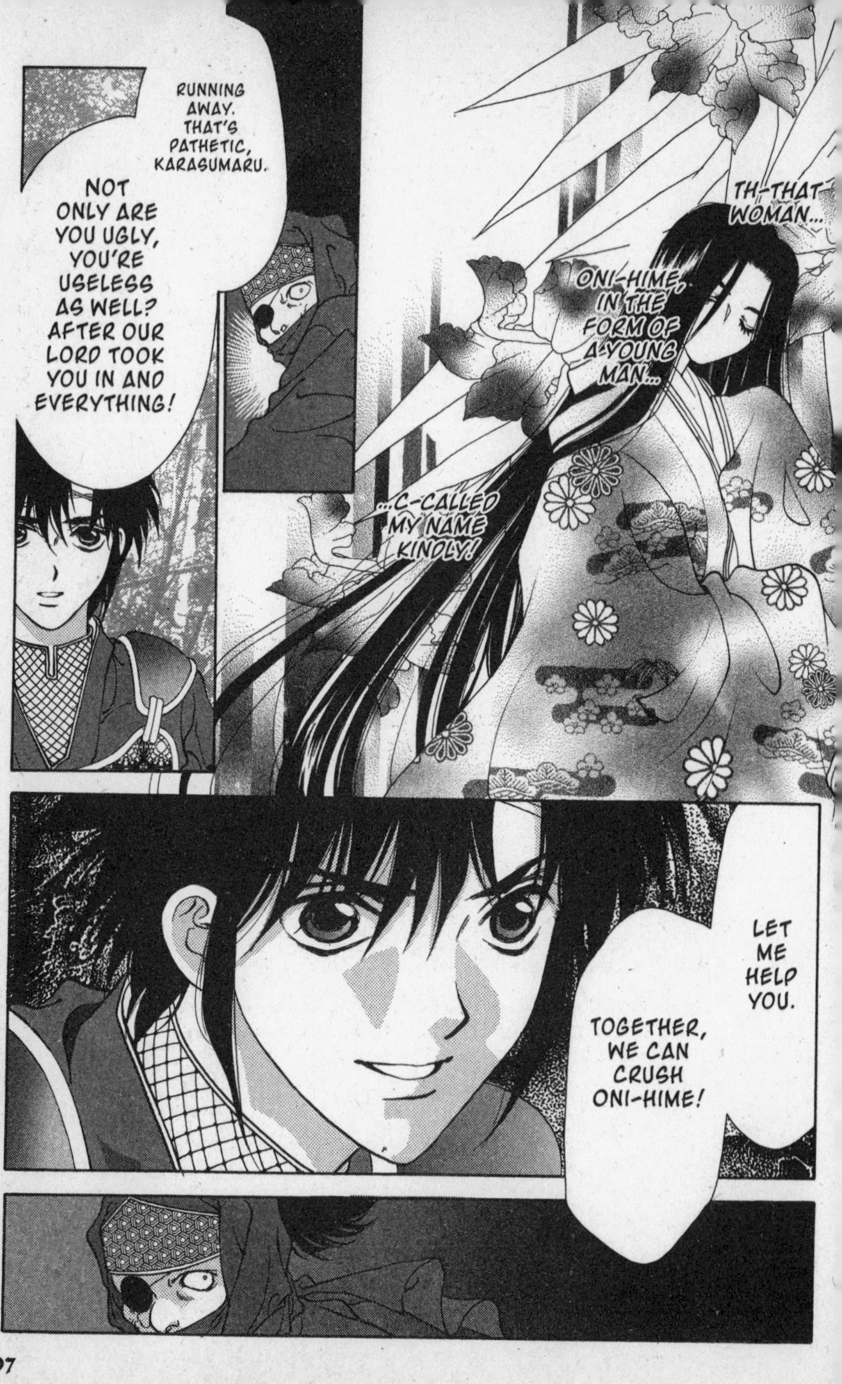
TH-THAT WOMAN...
ONI-HIME, IN THE FORM OF A YOUNG MAN...
...C-CALLED MY NAME KINDLY!
RUNNING AWAY. THAT'S PATHETIC, KARASUMARU.
NOT ONLY ARE YOU UGLY, YOU'RE USELESS AS WELL? AFTER OUR LORD TOOK YOU IN AND EVERYTHING!
LET ME HELP YOU.
TOGETHER, WE CAN CRUSH ONI-HIME!

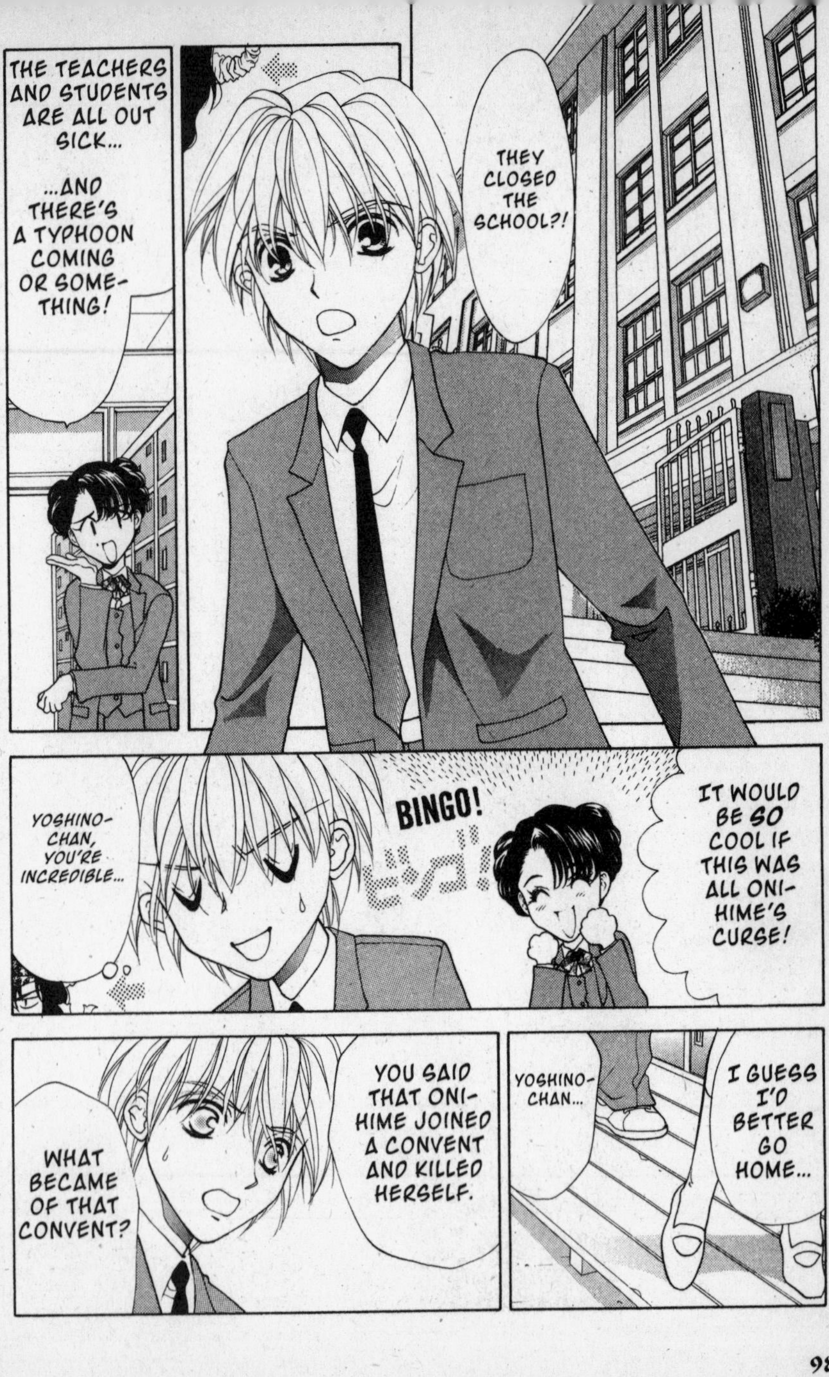
THEY CLOSED THE SCHOOL?!
THE TEACHERS AND STUDENTS ARE ALL OUT SICK...
...AND THERE'S A TYPHOON COMING OR SOME-THING!
IT WOULD BE SO COOL IF THIS WAS ALL ONI-HIME'S CURSE!
BINGO!
ビンゴ!
YOSHINO-CHAN, YOU'RE INCREDIBLE...
I GUESS I'D BETTER GO HOME...
YOSHINO-CHAN...
YOU SAID THAT ONI-HIME JOINED A CONVENT AND KILLED HERSELF.
WHAT BECAME OF THAT CONVENT?

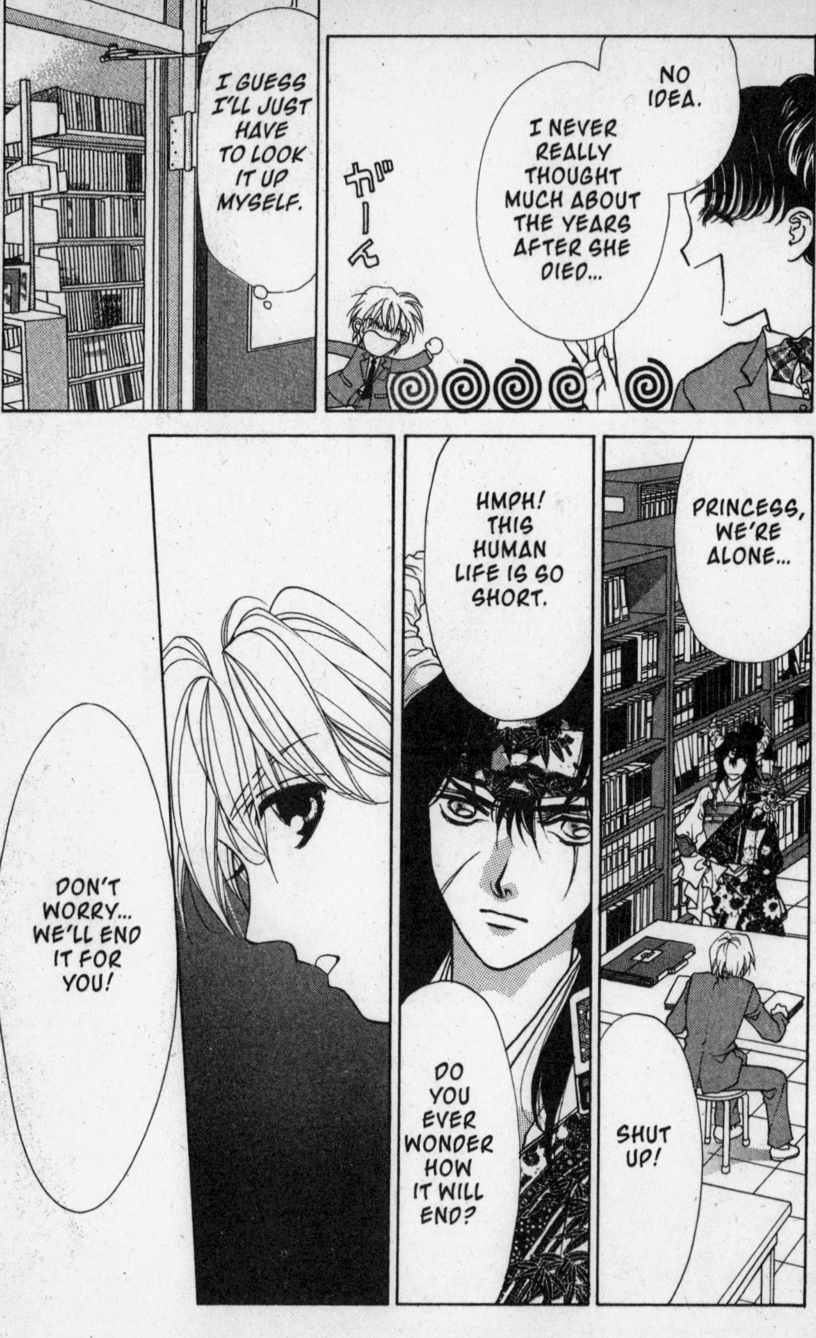
NO IDEA.
I NEVER REALLY THOUGHT MUCH ABOUT THE YEARS AFTER SHE DIED...
ガーん
I GUESS I'LL JUST HAVE TO LOOK IT UP MYSELF.
PRINCESS, WE'RE ALONE...
SHUT UP!
HMPH! THIS HUMAN LIFE IS SO SHORT.
DO YOU EVER WONDER HOW IT WILL END?
DON'T WORRY... WE'LL END IT FOR YOU!

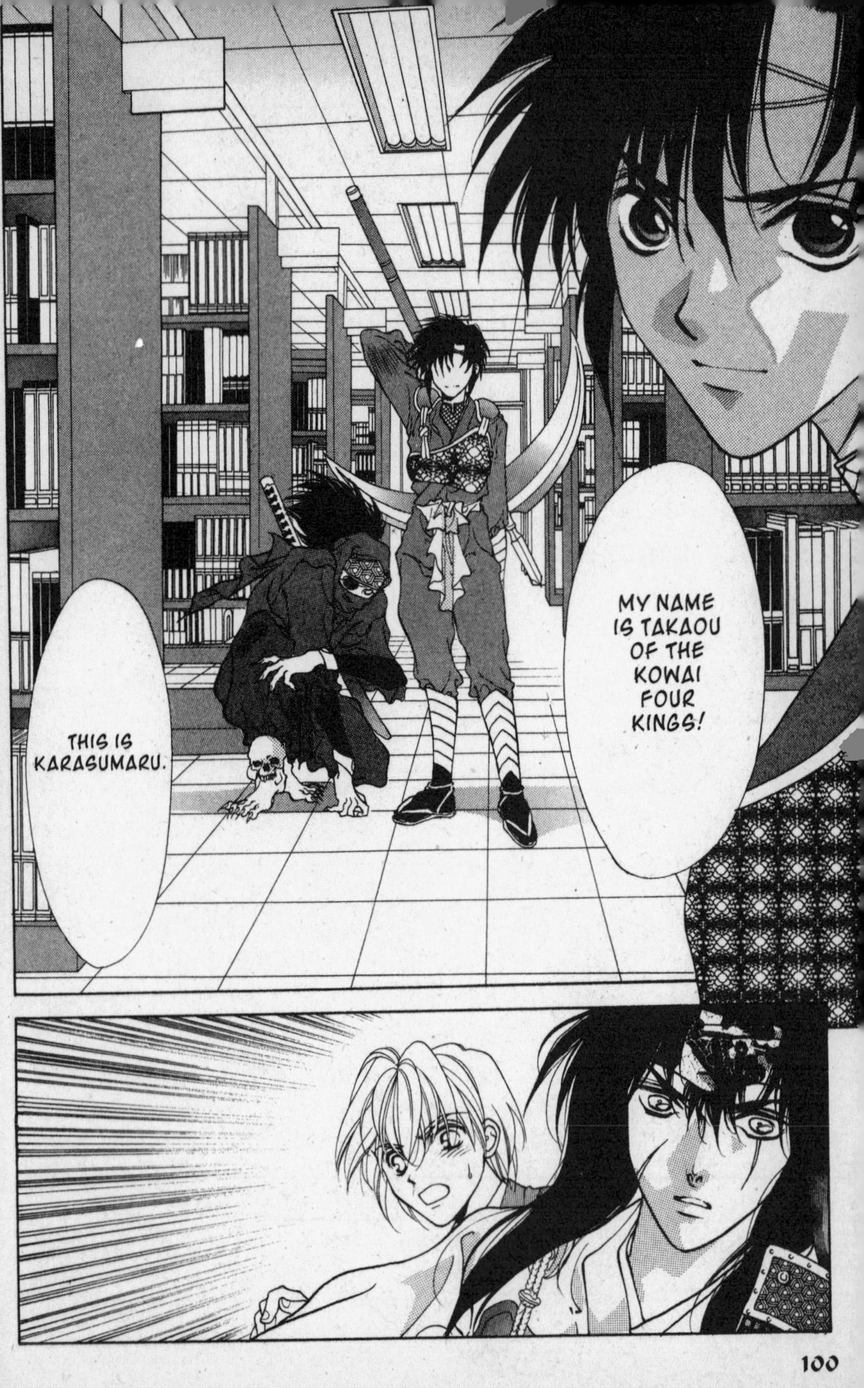
MY NAME IS TAKAOU OF THE KOWAI FOUR KINGS!
THIS IS KARASUMARU.

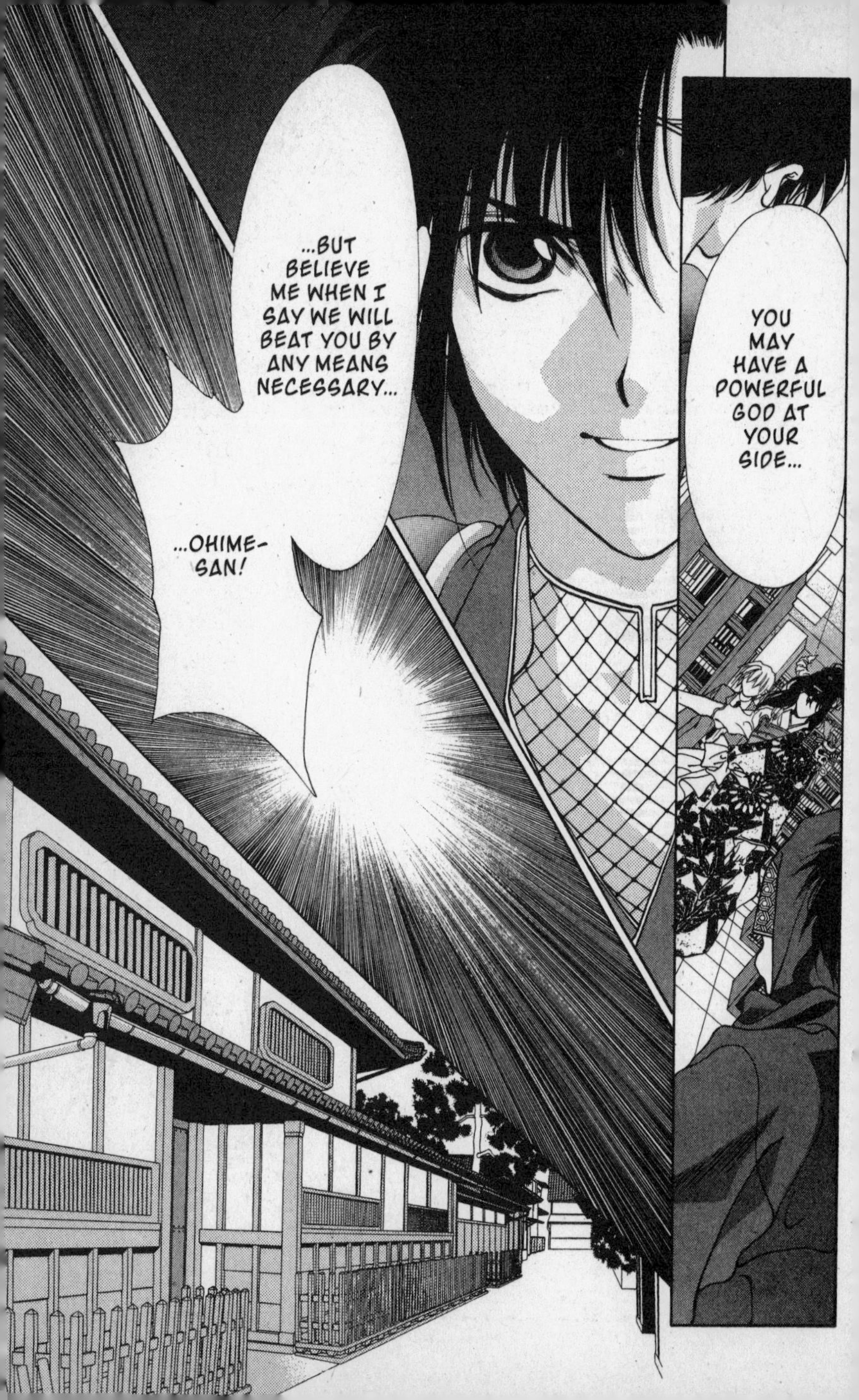
YOU MAY HAVE A POWERFUL GOD AT YOUR SIDE...
...BUT BELIEVE ME WHEN I SAY WE WILL BEAT YOU BY ANY MEANS NECESSARY...
...OHIME-SAN!

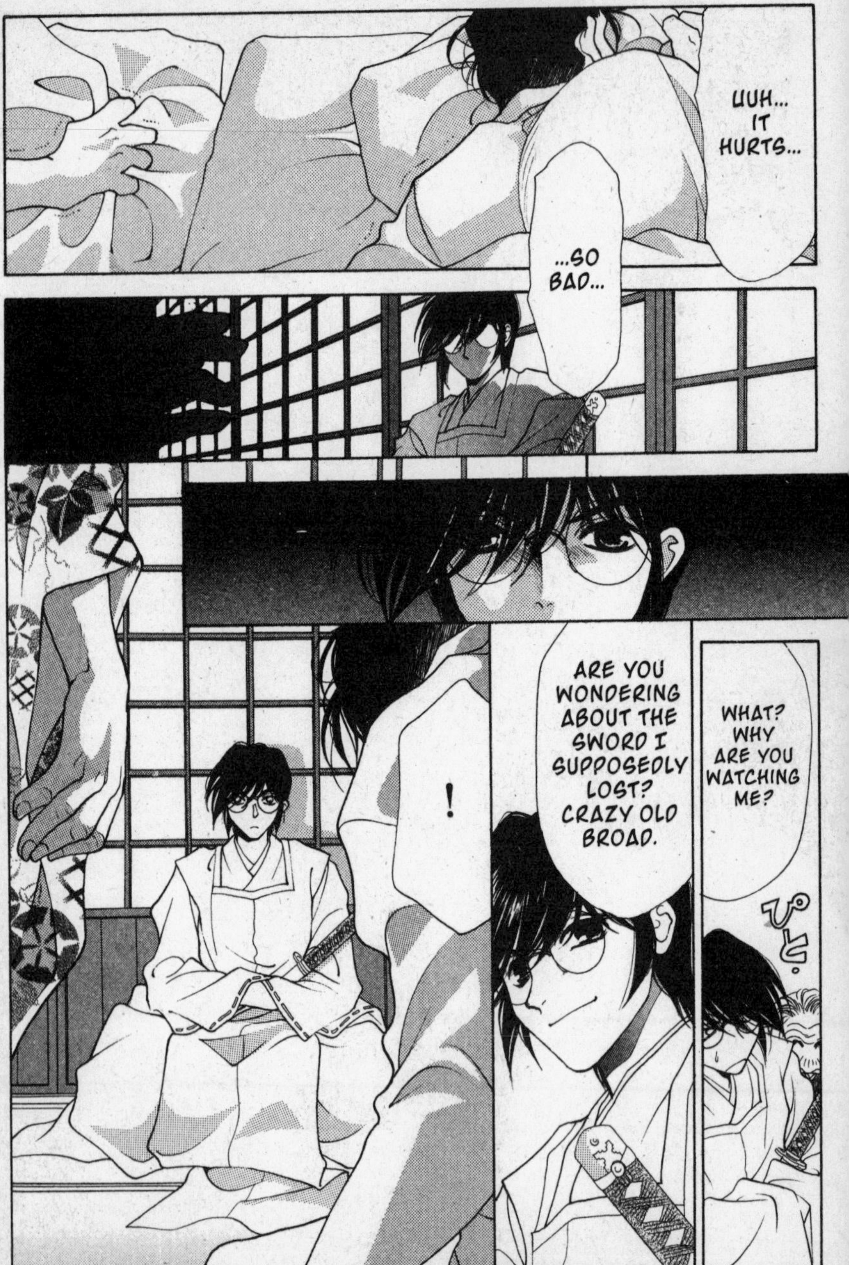
UUH... IT HURTS...
...SO BAD...
WHAT? WHY ARE YOU WATCHING ME?
ARE YOU WONDERING ABOUT THE SWORD I SUPPOSEDLY LOST? CRAZY OLD BROAD.
!

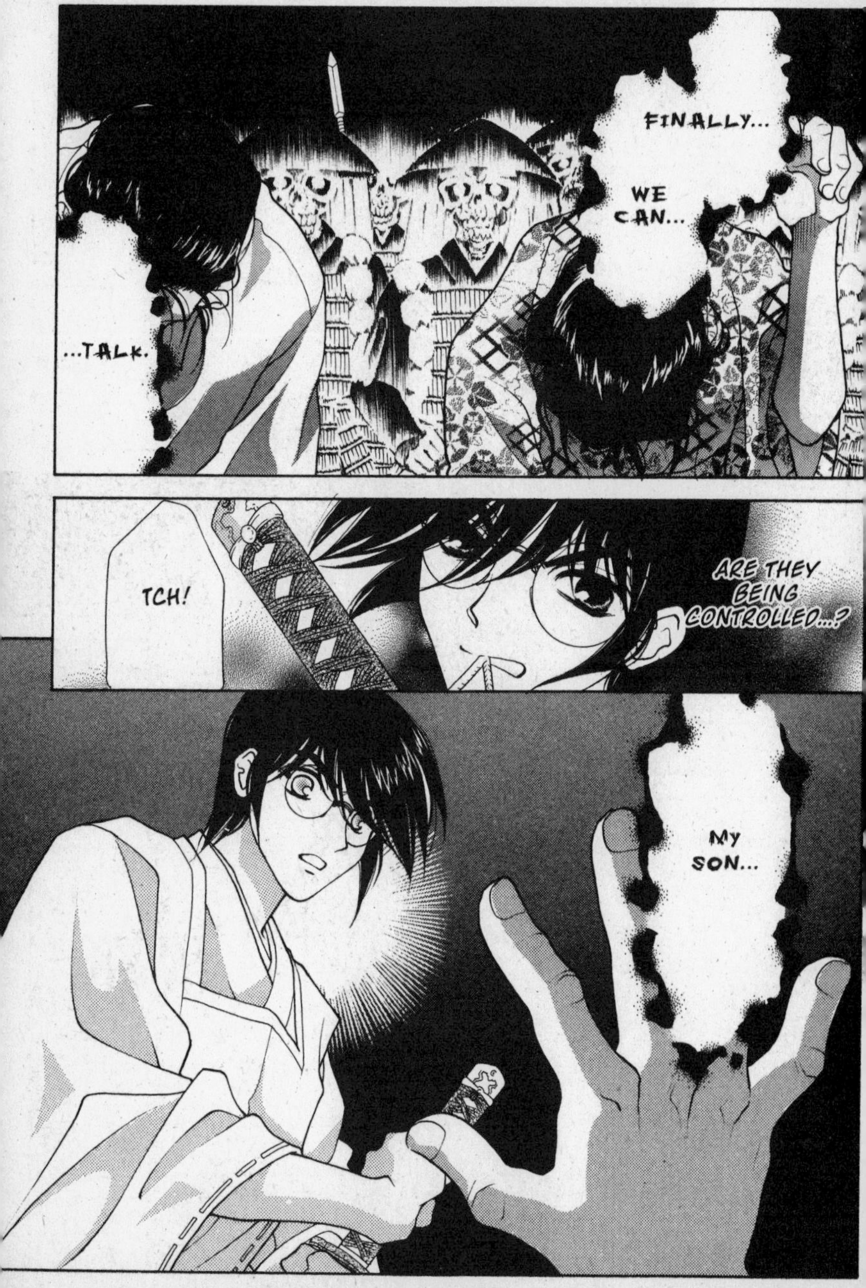
FINALLY...
WE CAN...
...TALK.
ARE THEY BEING CONTROLLED...?
TCH!
MY SON...

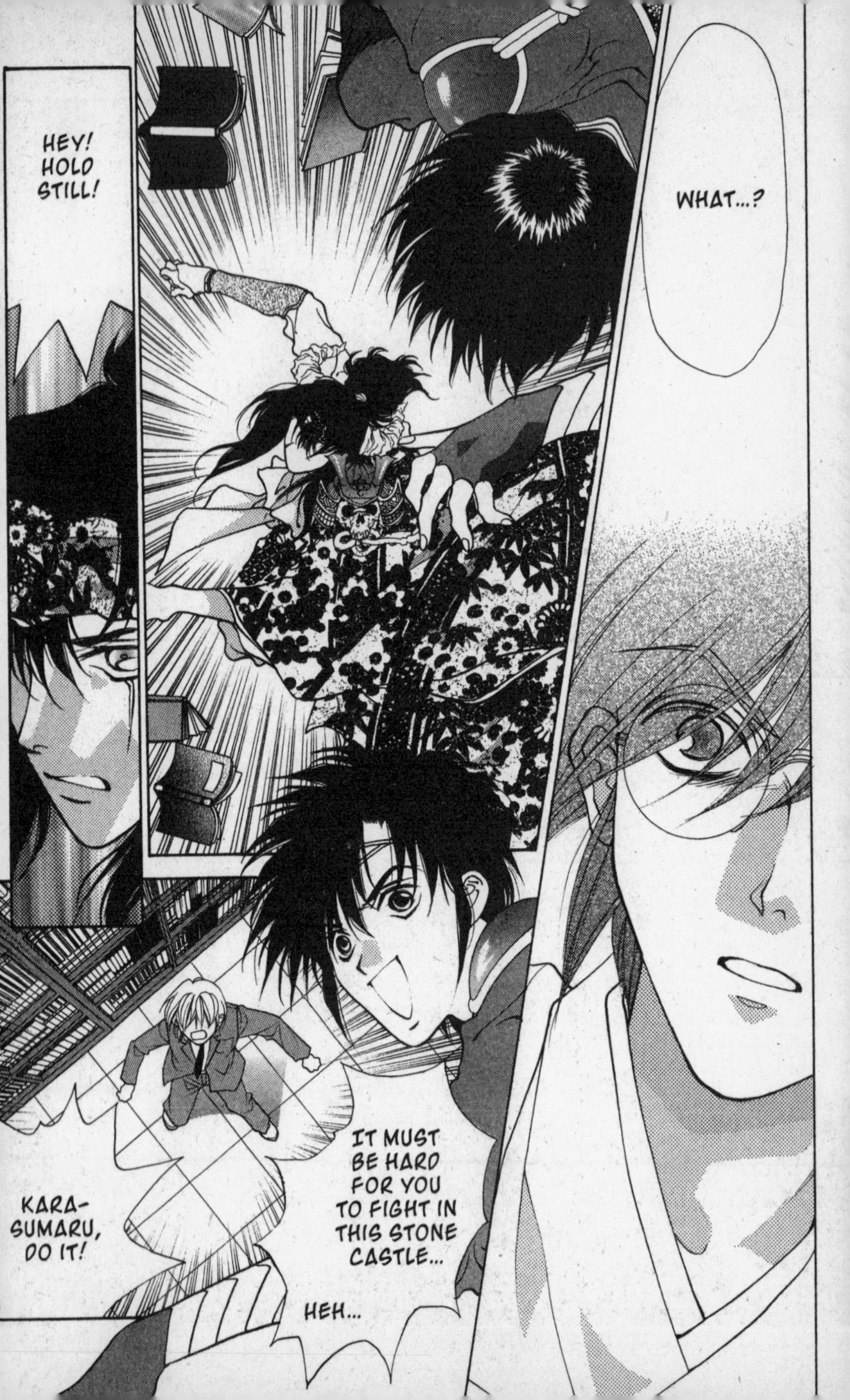
WHAT...?
HEY! HOLD STILL!
IT MUST BE HARD FOR YOU TO FIGHT IN THIS STONE CASTLE...
KARA-SUMARU, DO IT!
HEH...

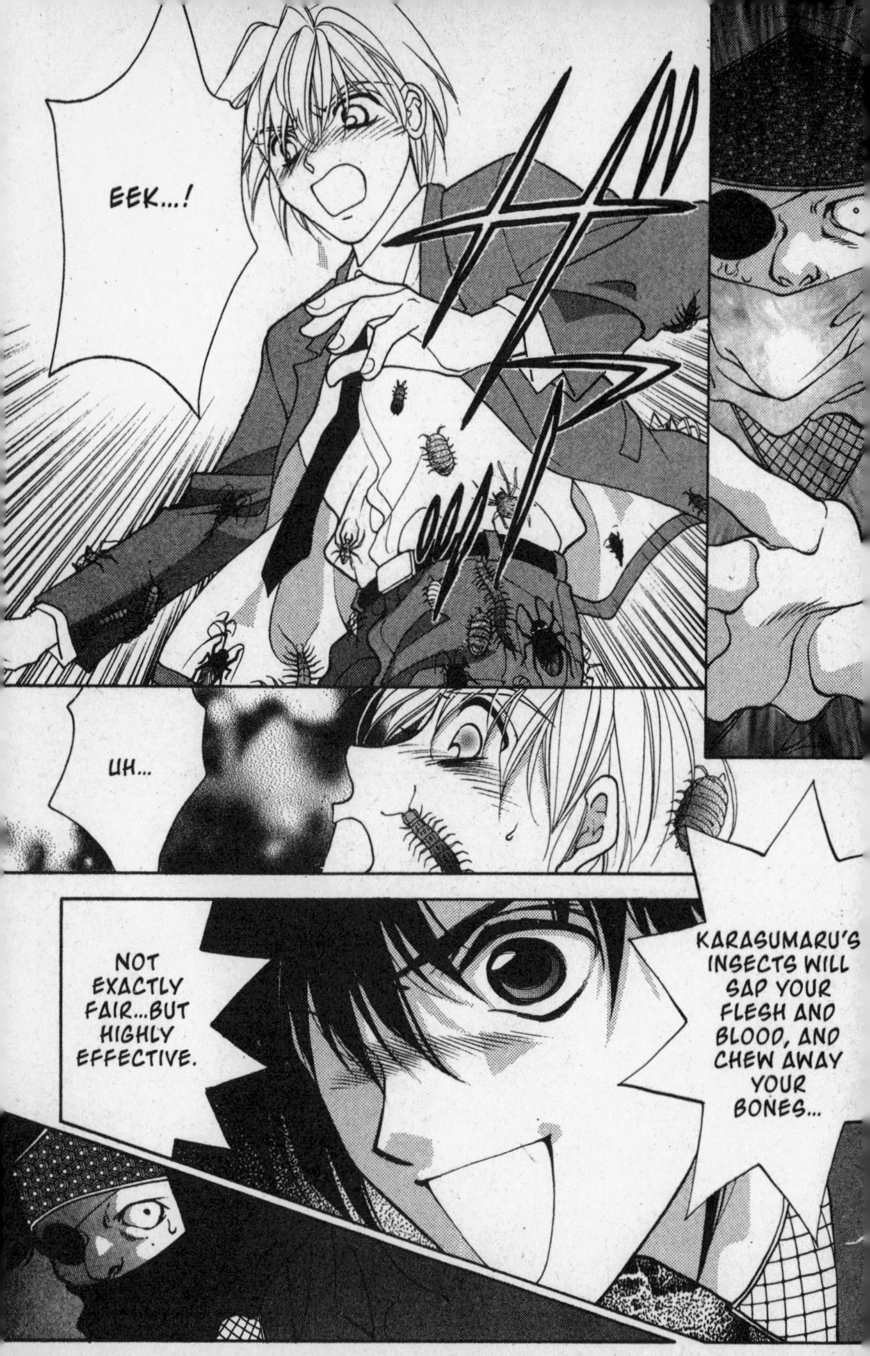
EEK...!
UH...
KARASUMARU'S INSECTS WILL SAP YOUR FLESH AND BLOOD, AND CHEW AWAY YOUR BONES...
NOT EXACTLY FAIR...BUT HIGHLY EFFECTIVE.

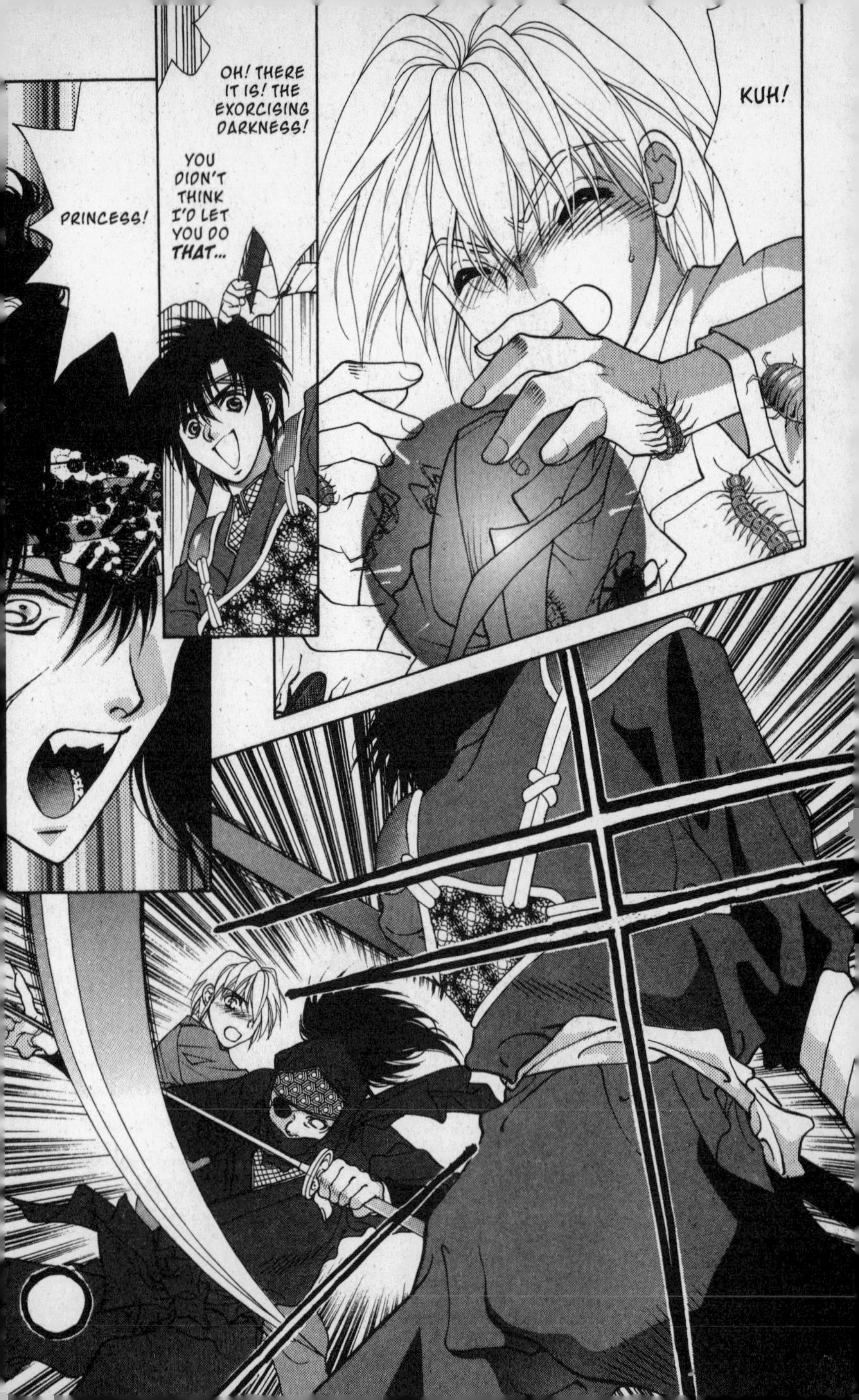
KUH!
OH! THERE IT IS! THE EXORCISING DARKNESS!
YOU DIDN'T THINK I'D LET YOU DO THAT...
PRINCESS!

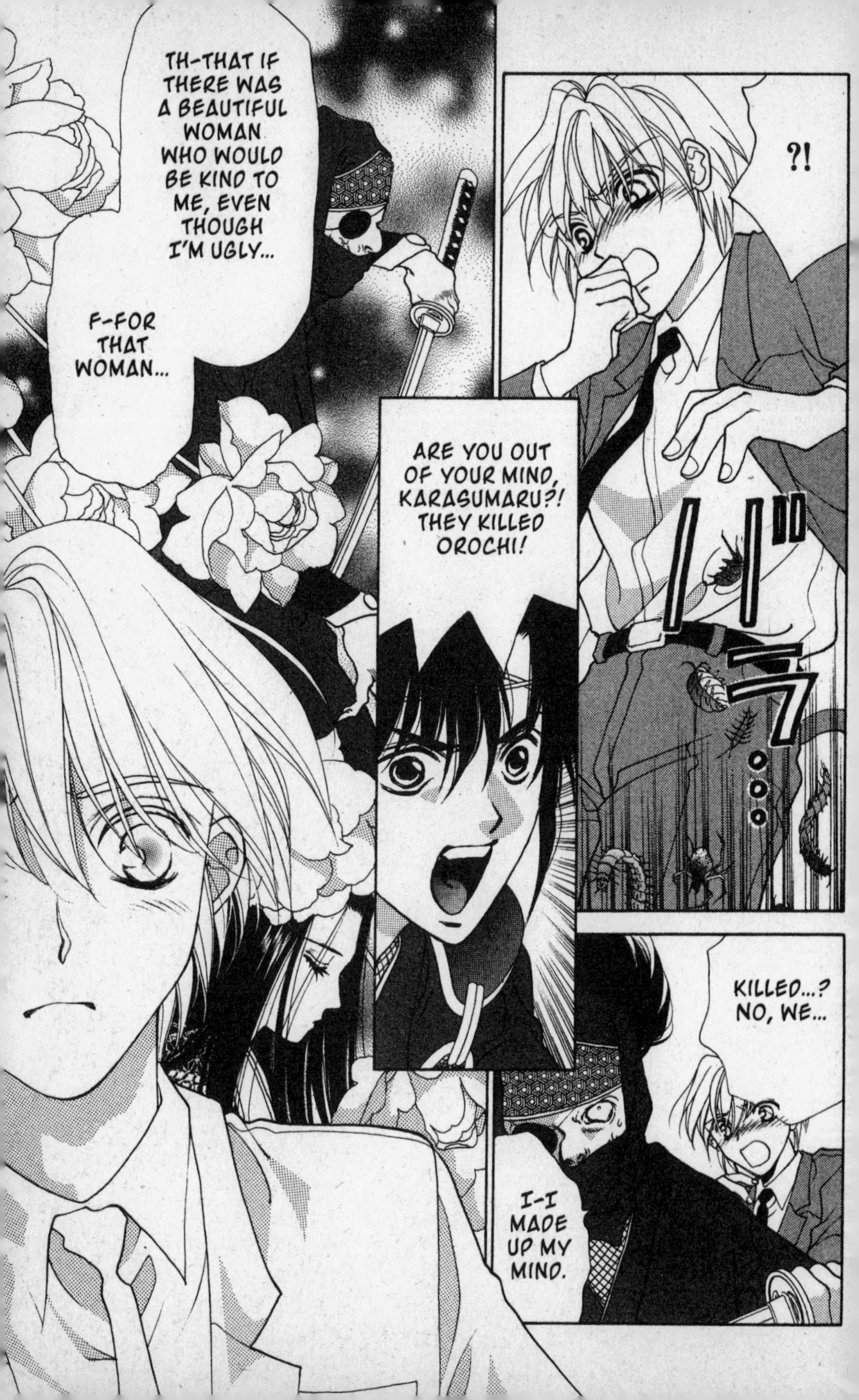
?!
ARE YOU OUT OF YOUR MIND, KARASUMARU?! THEY KILLED OROCHI!
バラ…
KILLED...? NO, WE...
I-I MADE UP MY MIND.
TH-THAT IF THERE WAS A BEAUTIFUL WOMAN WHO WOULD BE KIND TO ME, EVEN THOUGH I'M UGLY...
F-FOR THAT WOMAN...

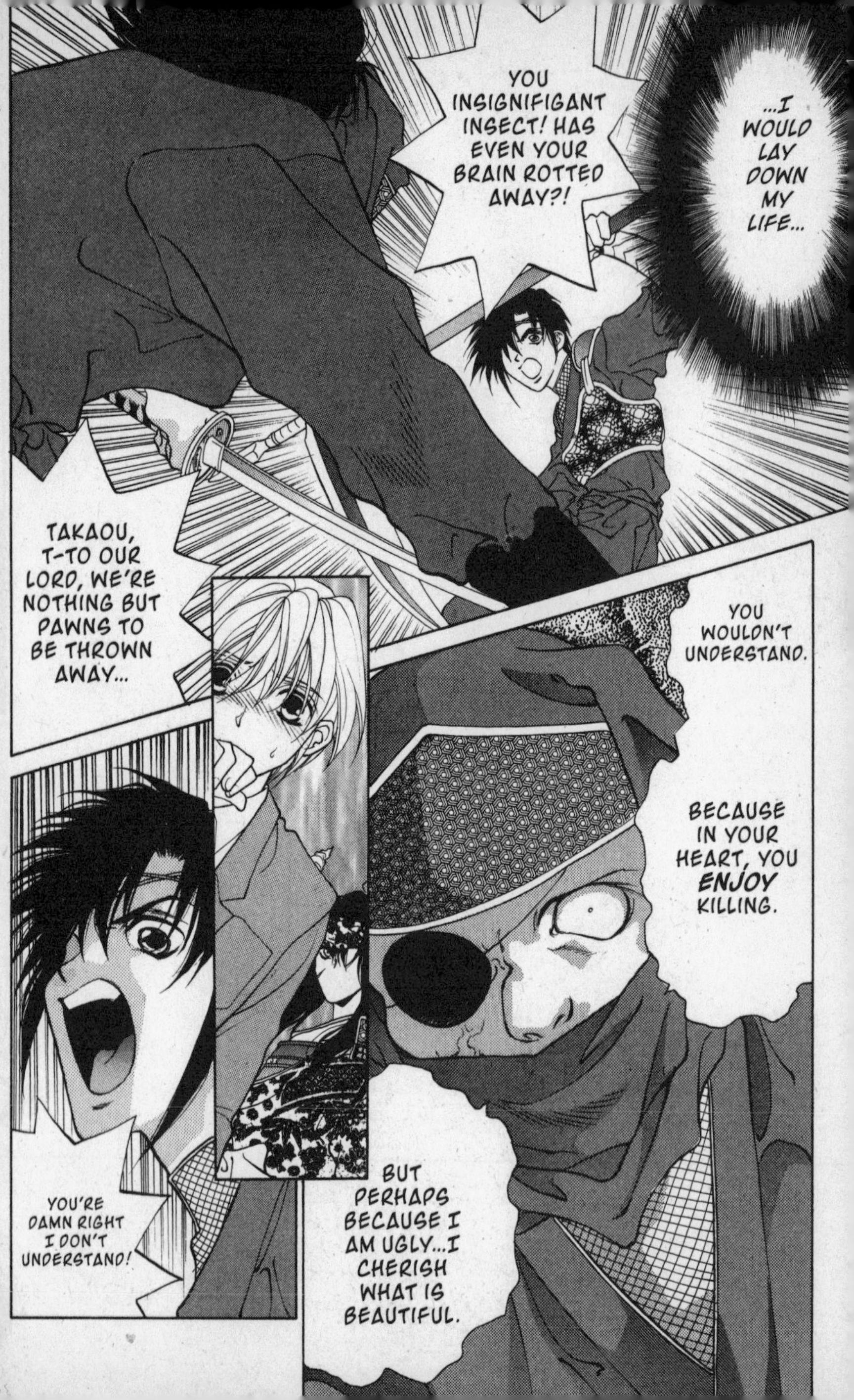
...I WOULD LAY DOWN MY LIFE...
YOU INSIGNIFIGANT INSECT! HAS EVEN YOUR BRAIN ROTTED AWAY?!
TAKAOU, T-TO OUR LORD, WE'RE NOTHING BUT PAWNS TO BE THROWN AWAY...
YOU WOULDN'T UNDERSTAND.
BECAUSE IN YOUR HEART, YOU ENJOY KILLING.
BUT PERHAPS BECAUSE I AM UGLY...I CHERISH WHAT IS BEAUTIFUL.
YOU'RE DAMN RIGHT I DON'T UNDERSTAND!

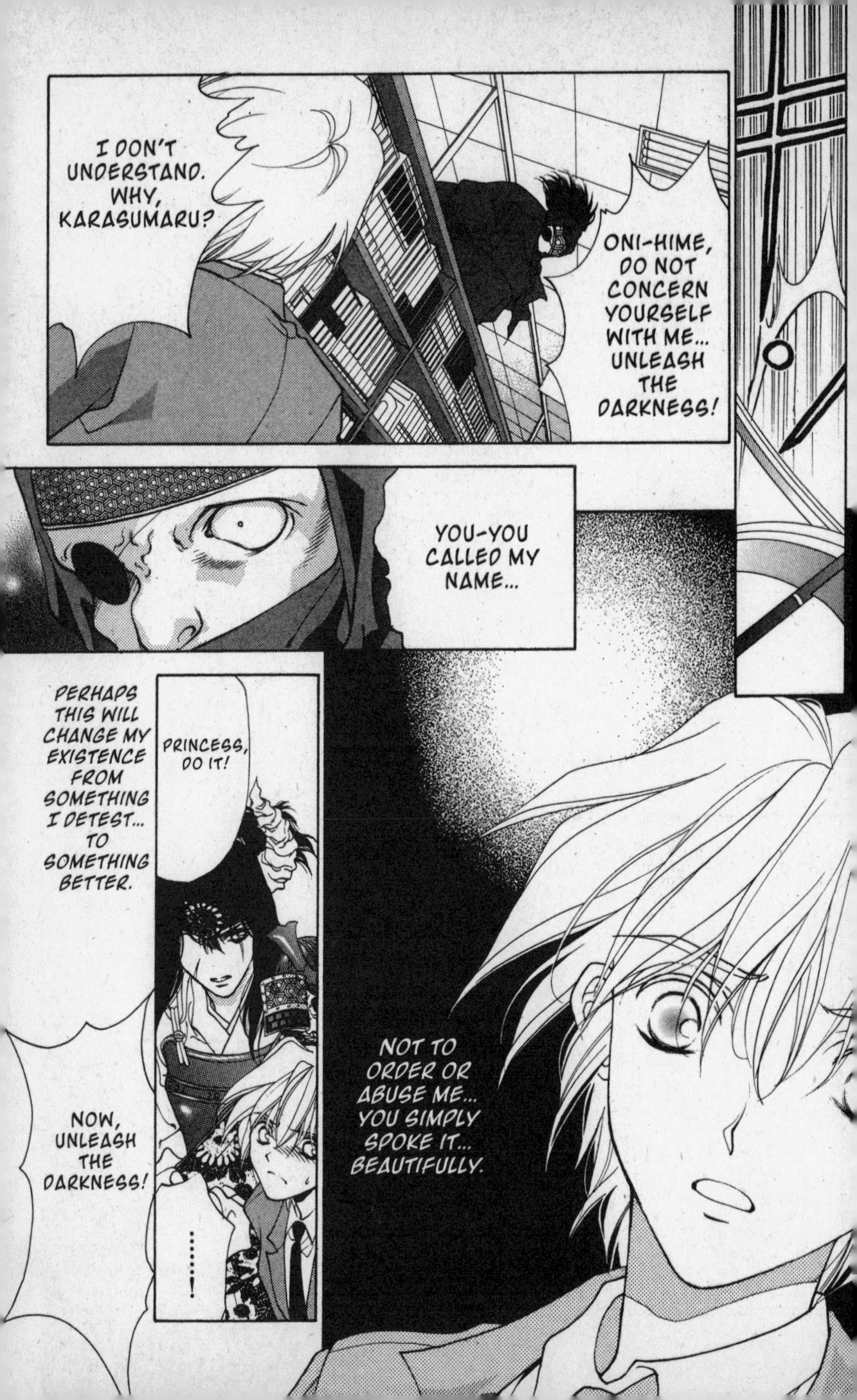

I DON'T UNDERSTAND. WHY, KARASUMARU?
ONI-HIME, DO NOT CONCERN YOURSELF WITH ME... UNLEASH THE DARKNESS!
YOU-YOU CALLED MY NAME...
NOT TO ORDER OR ABUSE ME... YOU SIMPLY SPOKE IT... BEAUTIFULLY.
PERHAPS THIS WILL CHANGE MY EXISTENCE FROM SOMETHING I DETEST... TO SOMETHING BETTER.
PRINCESS, DO IT!
NOW, UNLEASH THE DARKNESS!
......!

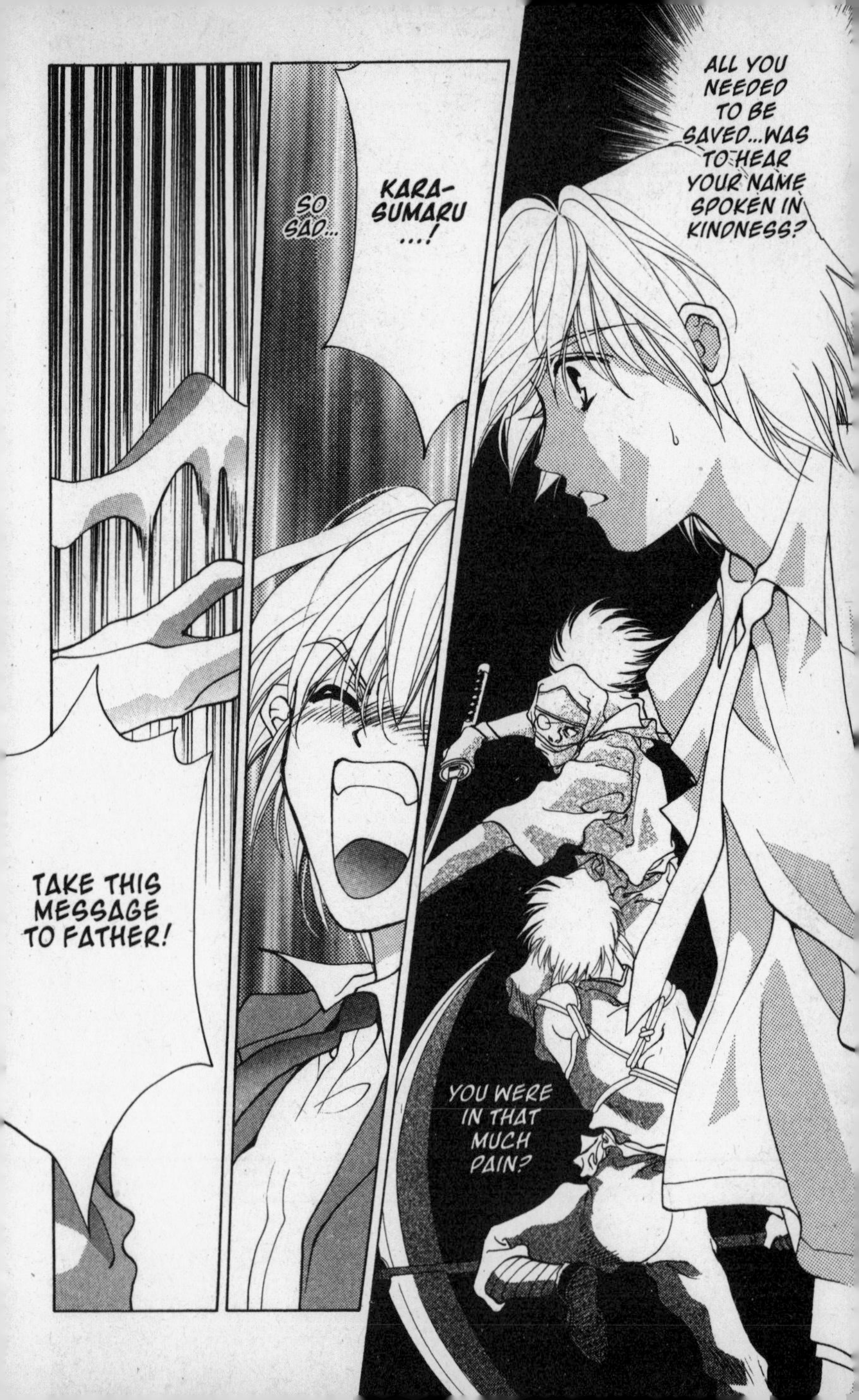
ALL YOU NEEDED TO BE SAVED...WAS TO HEAR YOUR NAME SPOKEN IN KINDNESS?
YOU WERE IN THAT MUCH PAIN?
KARA-SUMARU ...!
SO SAD...
TAKE THIS MESSAGE TO FATHER!

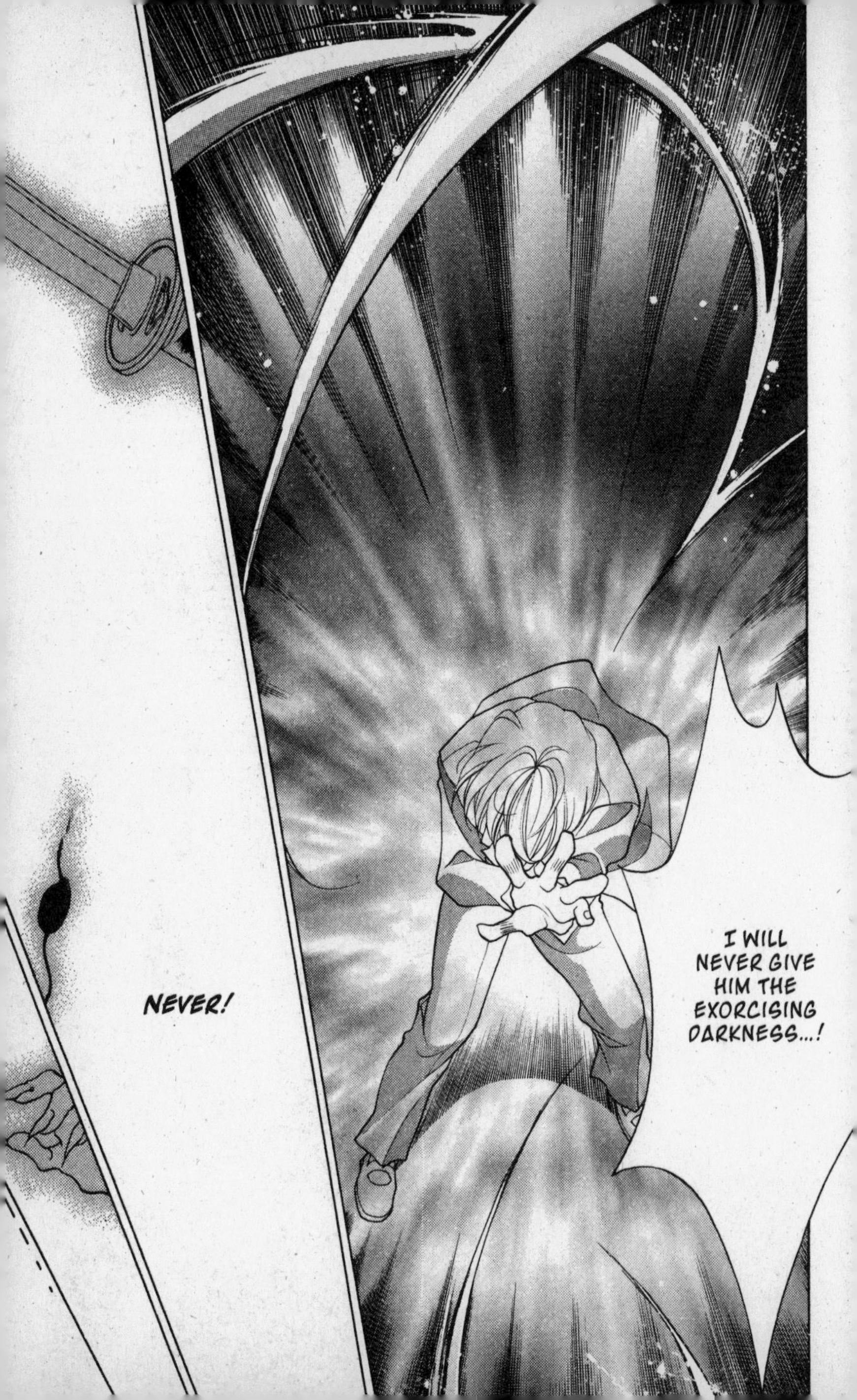
I WILL NEVER GIVE HIM THE EXORCISING DARKNESS...!
NEVER!

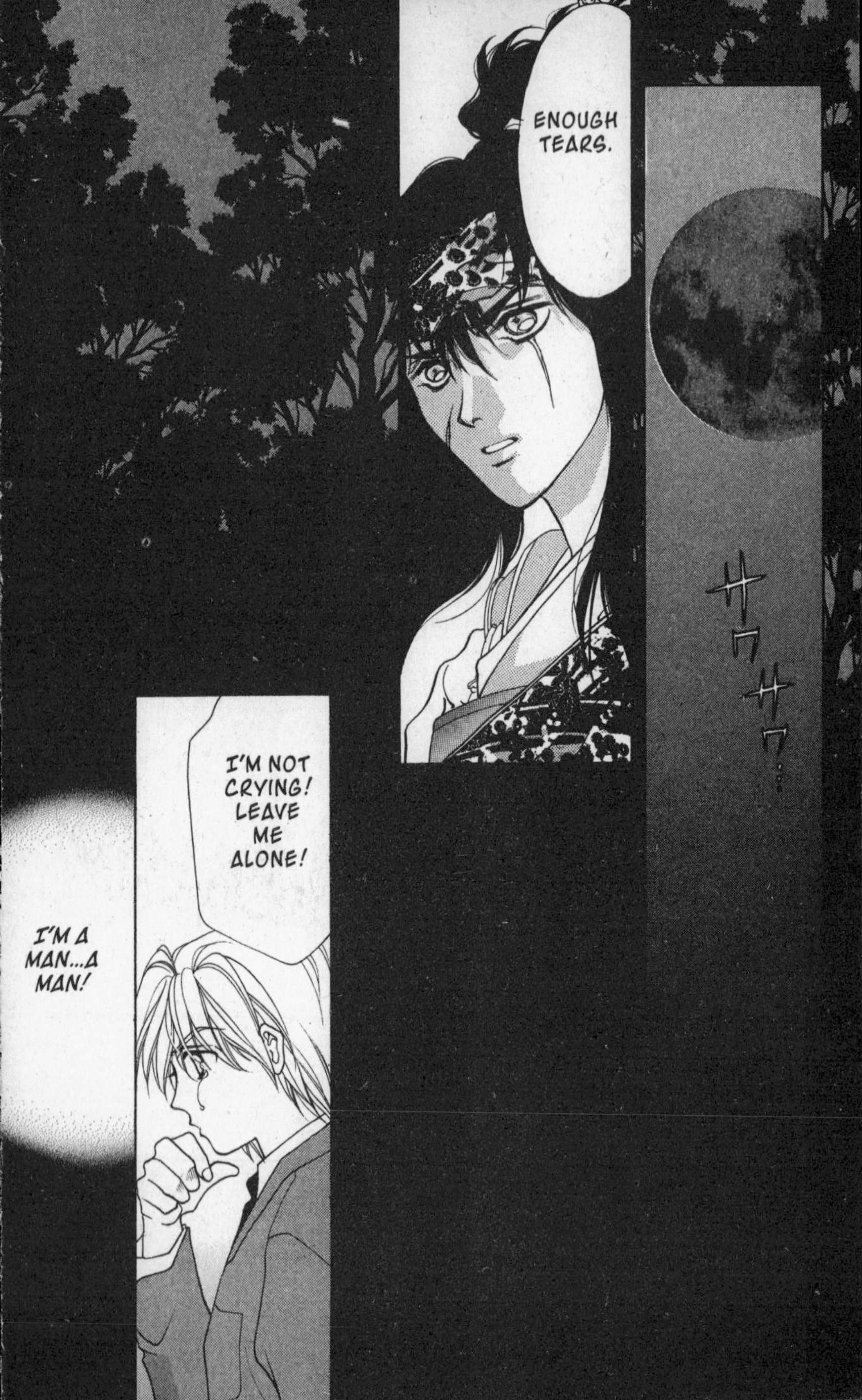
ENOUGH TEARS.
サワサワ…
I'M NOT CRYING! LEAVE ME ALONE!
I'M A MAN...A MAN!

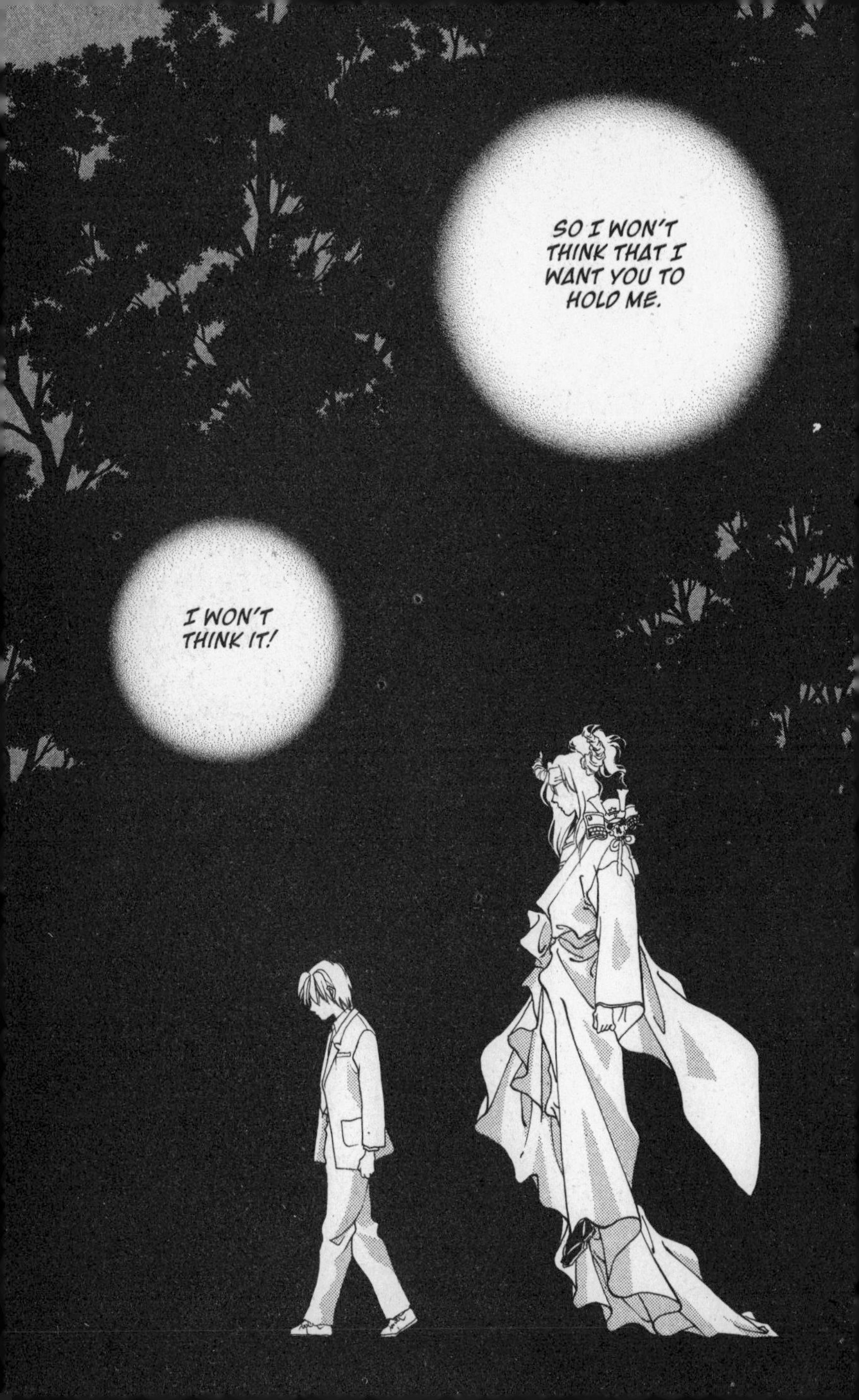
SO I WON'T THINK THAT I WANT YOU TO HOLD ME.
I WON'T THINK IT!

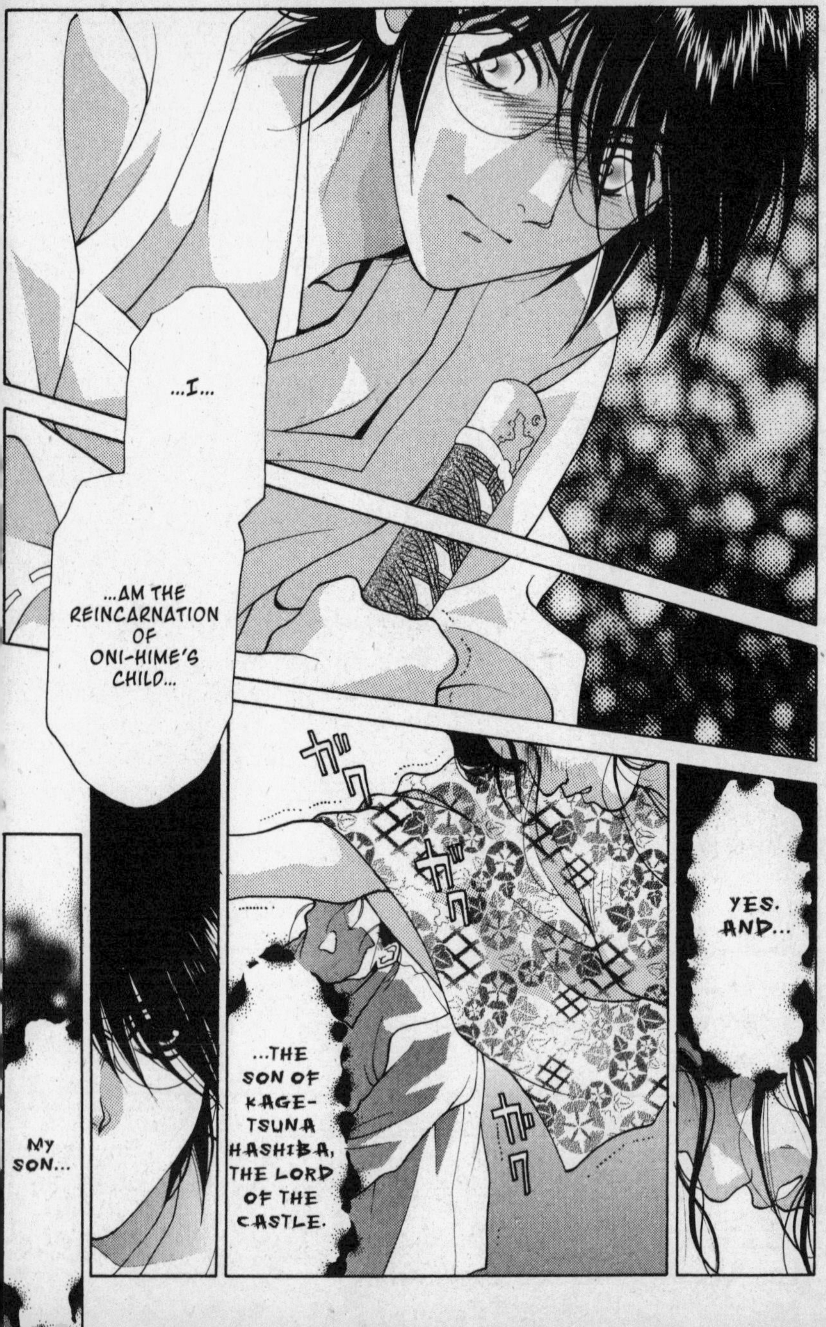
...I...
...AM THE REINCARNATION OF ONI-HIME'S CHILD...
YES. AND...
ガク
ガクガク
......
......
...THE SON OF KAGE-TSUNA HASHIBA, THE LORD OF THE CASTLE.
ガク
MY SON...

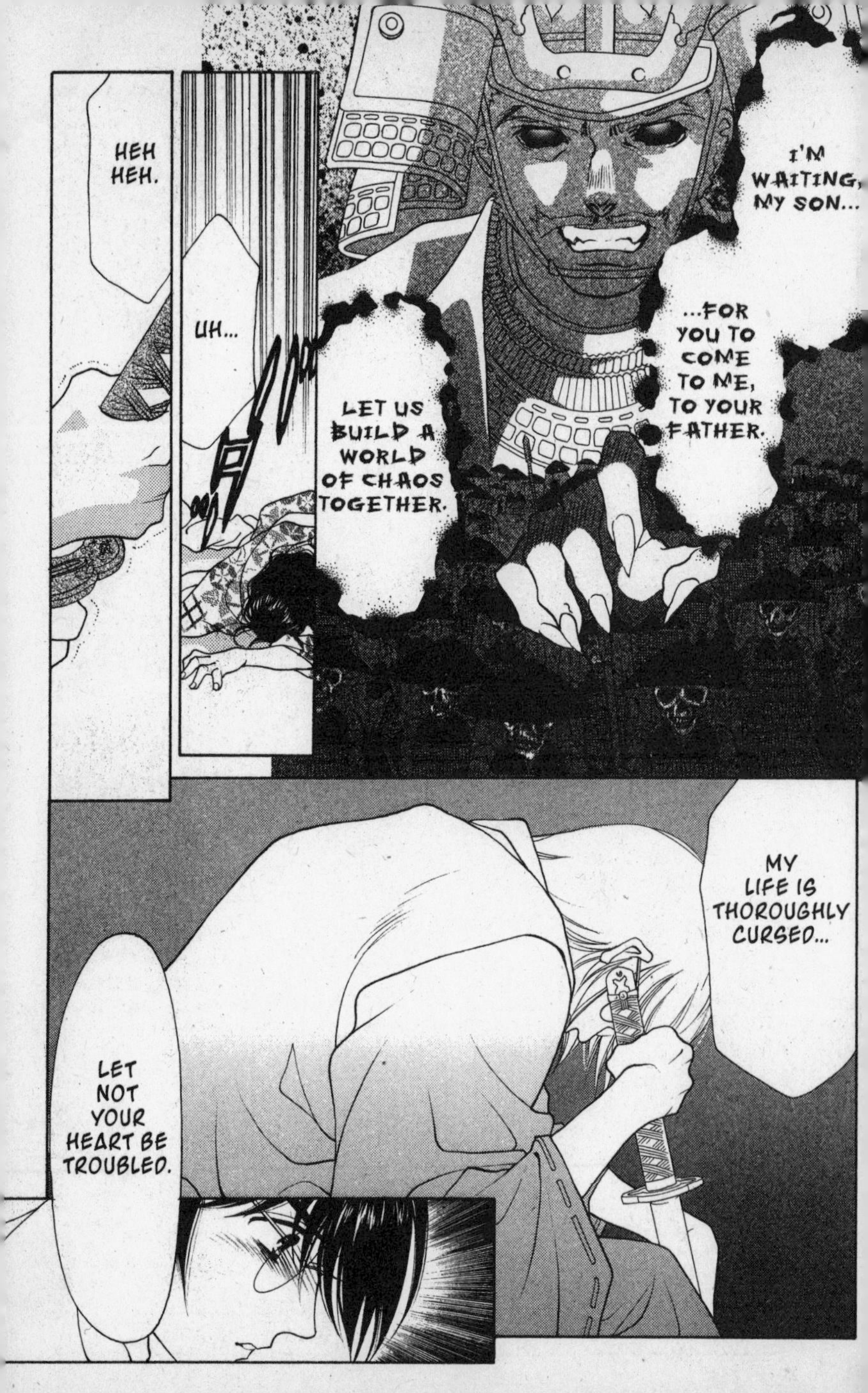
I'M WAITING, MY SON...
...FOR YOU TO COME TO ME, TO YOUR FATHER.
LET US BUILD A WORLD OF CHAOS TOGETHER.
UH...
HEH HEH.
MY LIFE IS THOROUGHLY CURSED...
LET NOT YOUR HEART BE TROUBLED.

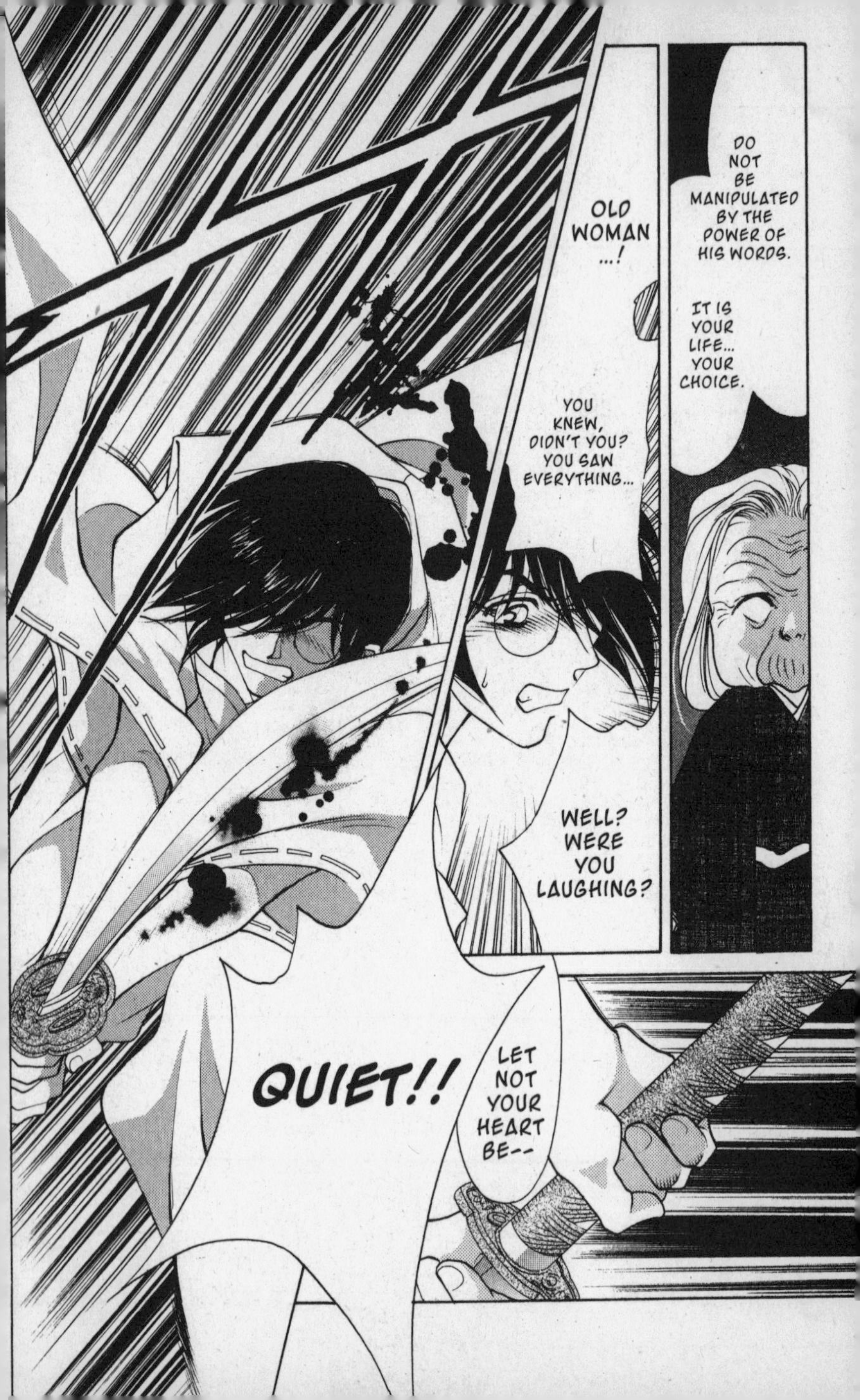
DO NOT BE MANIPULATED BY THE POWER OF HIS WORDS.
IT IS YOUR LIFE... YOUR CHOICE.
OLD WOMAN ...!
YOU KNEW, DIDN'T YOU? YOU SAW EVERYTHING...
WELL? WERE YOU LAUGHING?
LET NOT YOUR HEART BE--
QUIET!!

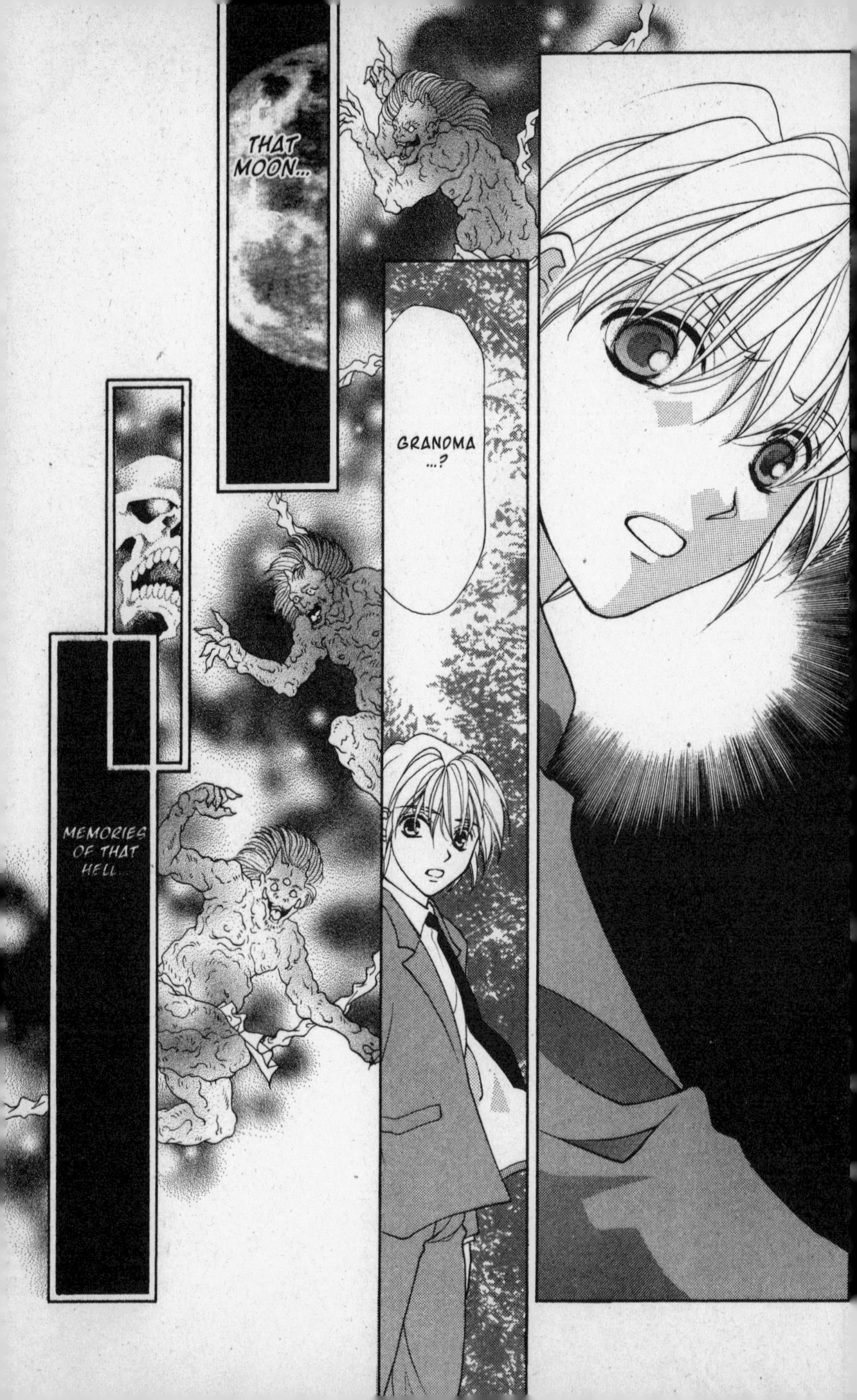
GRANDMA ...?
THAT MOON...
MEMORIES OF THAT HELL...

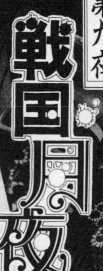

第九夜
だいきゅうや
戦国月夜

Created By:
Kei Kusunoki & Kaoru Ohashi

Sengoku Nights
Vol. 2
Ninth Night

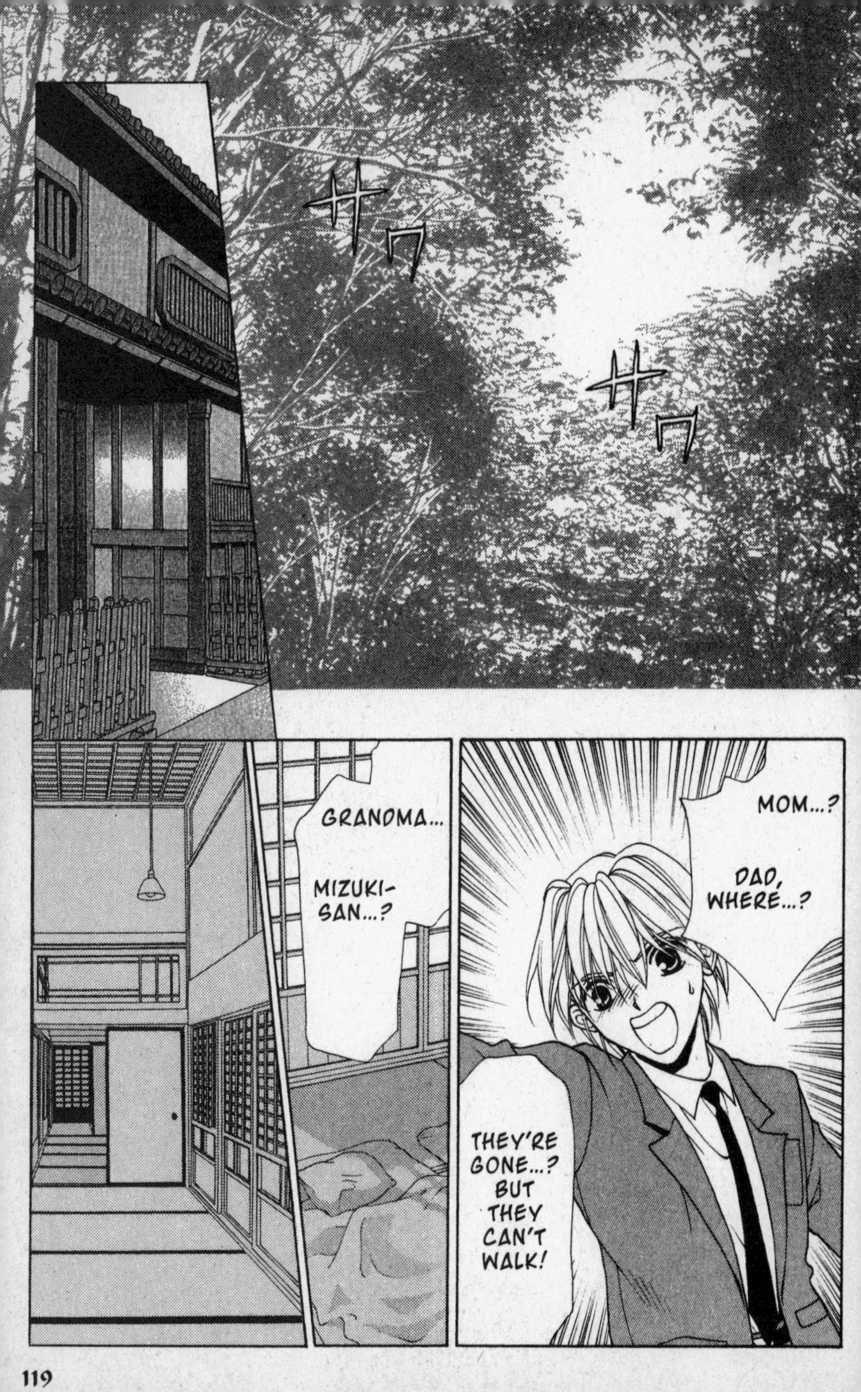

サワ
サワ
MOM...?
DAD, WHERE...?
THEY'RE GONE...? BUT THEY CAN'T WALK!
GRANDMA...
MIZUKI-SAN...?

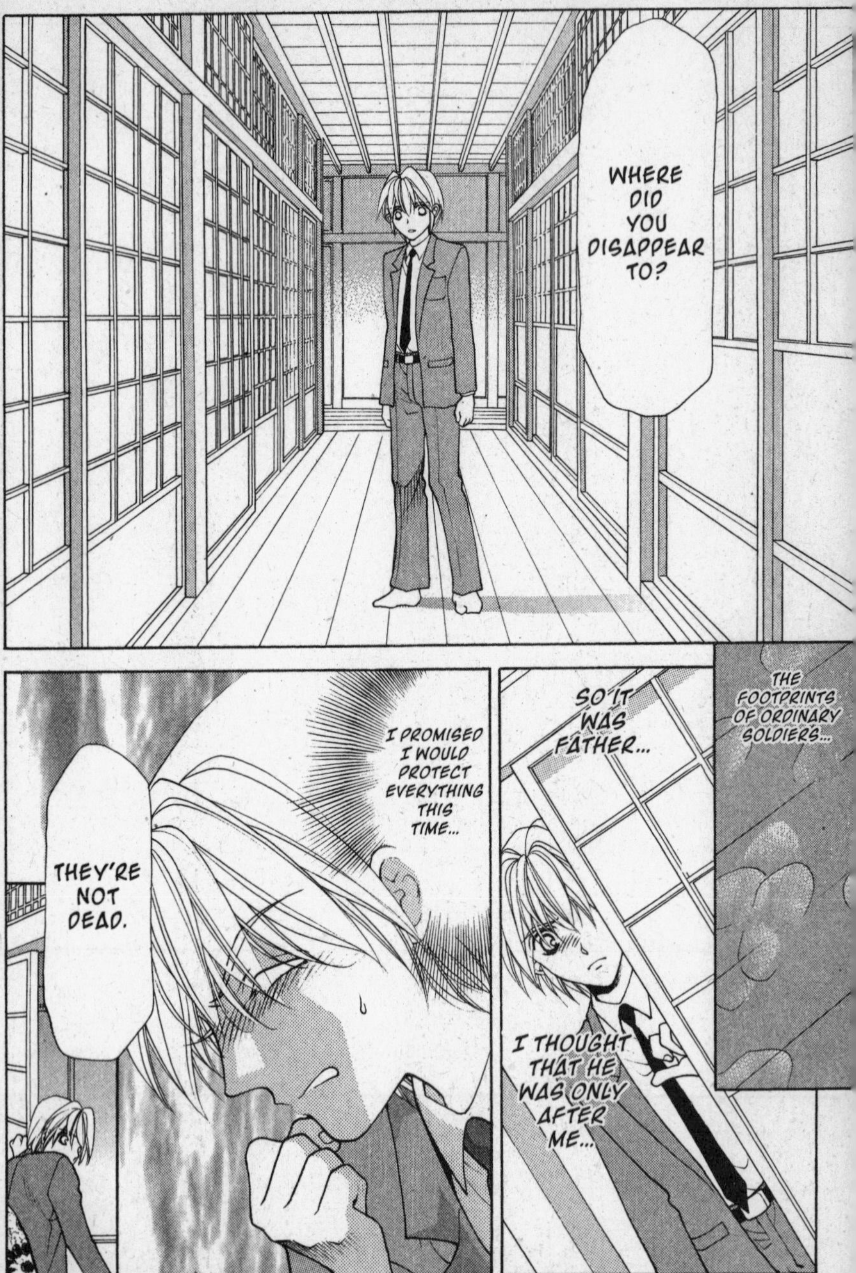
WHERE DID YOU DISAPPEAR TO?
THE FOOTPRINTS OF ORDINARY SOLDIERS...
SO IT WAS FATHER...
I THOUGHT THAT HE WAS ONLY AFTER ME...
I PROMISED I WOULD PROTECT EVERYTHING THIS TIME...
THEY'RE NOT DEAD.

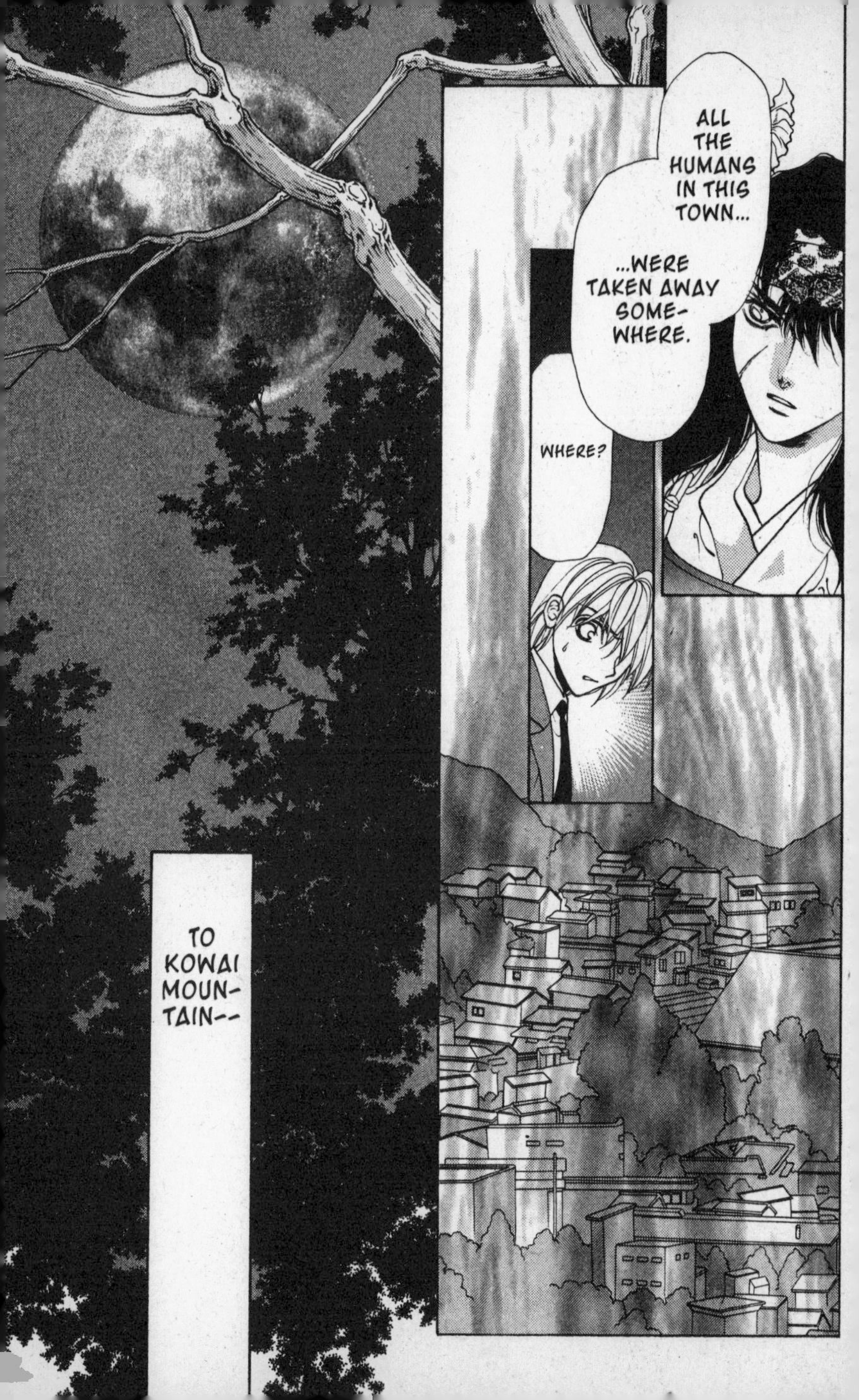
ALL THE HUMANS IN THIS TOWN...
...WERE TAKEN AWAY SOME-WHERE.
WHERE?
TO KOWAI MOUN-TAIN--

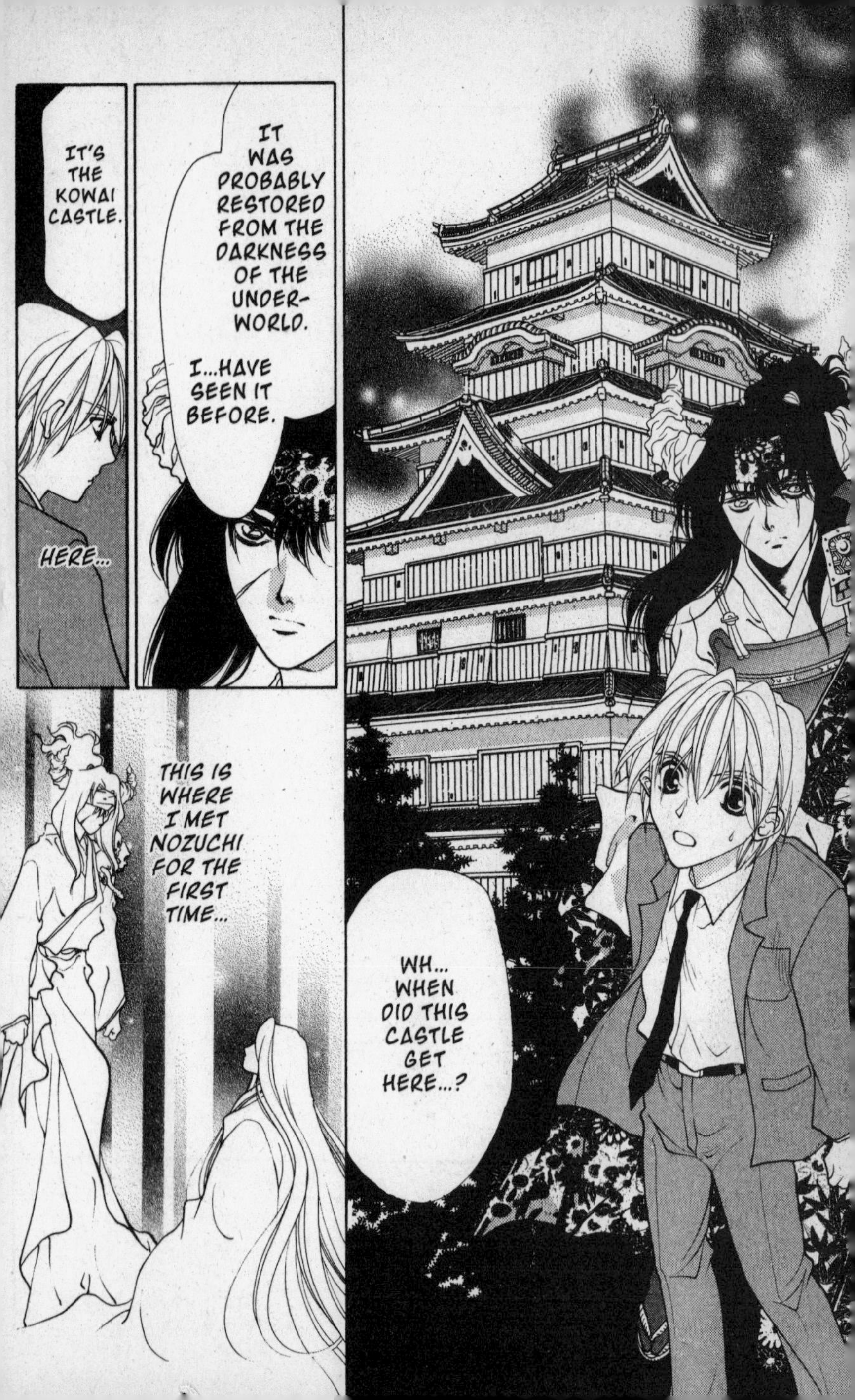
WH... WHEN DID THIS CASTLE GET HERE...?
IT WAS PROBABLY RESTORED FROM THE DARKNESS OF THE UNDER-WORLD.
I...HAVE SEEN IT BEFORE.
IT'S THE KOWAI CASTLE.
HERE...
THIS IS WHERE I MET NOZUCHI FOR THE FIRST TIME...

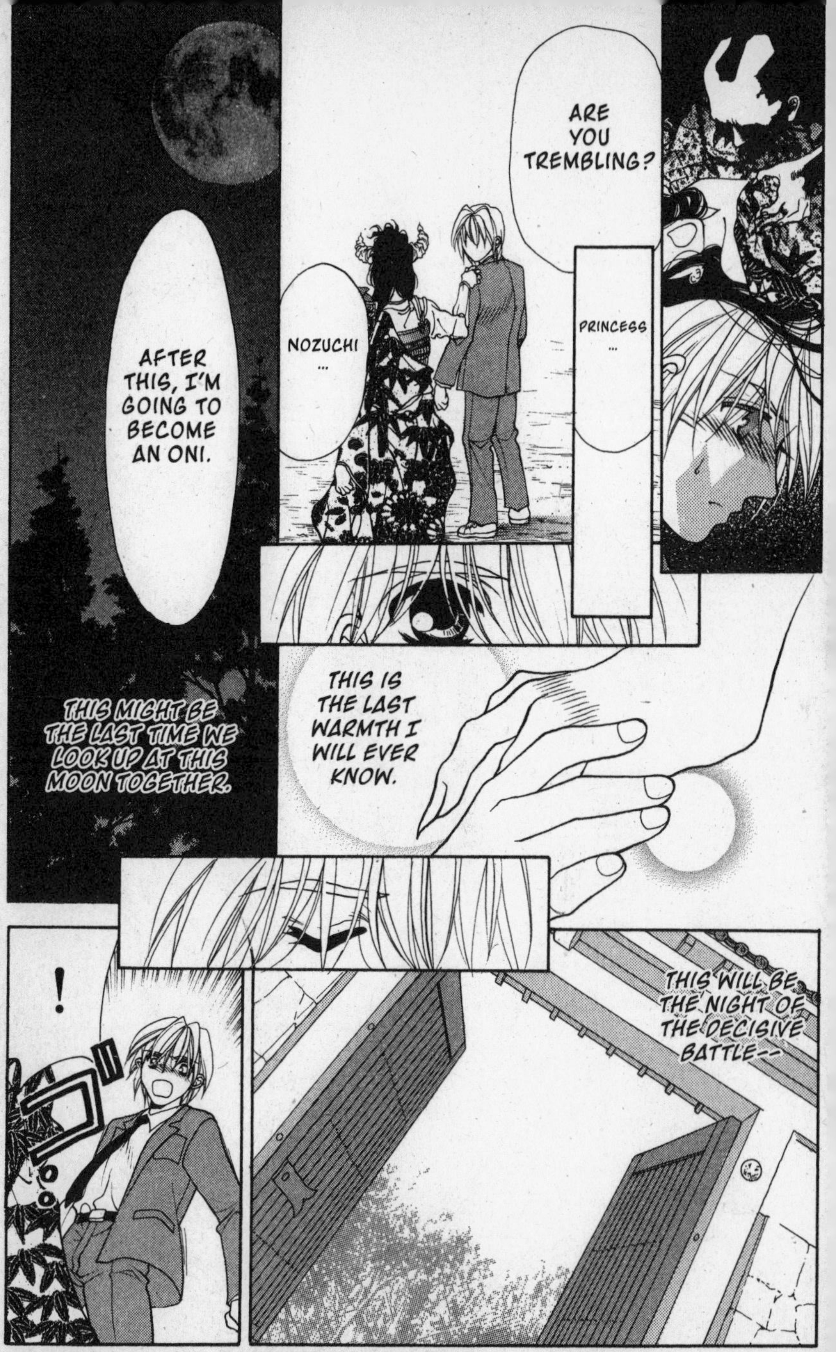
ARE YOU TREMBLING?
PRINCESS ...
NOZUCHI ...
AFTER THIS, I'M GOING TO BECOME AN ONI.
THIS IS THE LAST WARMTH I WILL EVER KNOW.
THIS MIGHT BE THE LAST TIME WE LOOK UP AT THIS MOON TOGETHER.
THIS WILL BE THE NIGHT OF THE DECISIVE BATTLE--
!

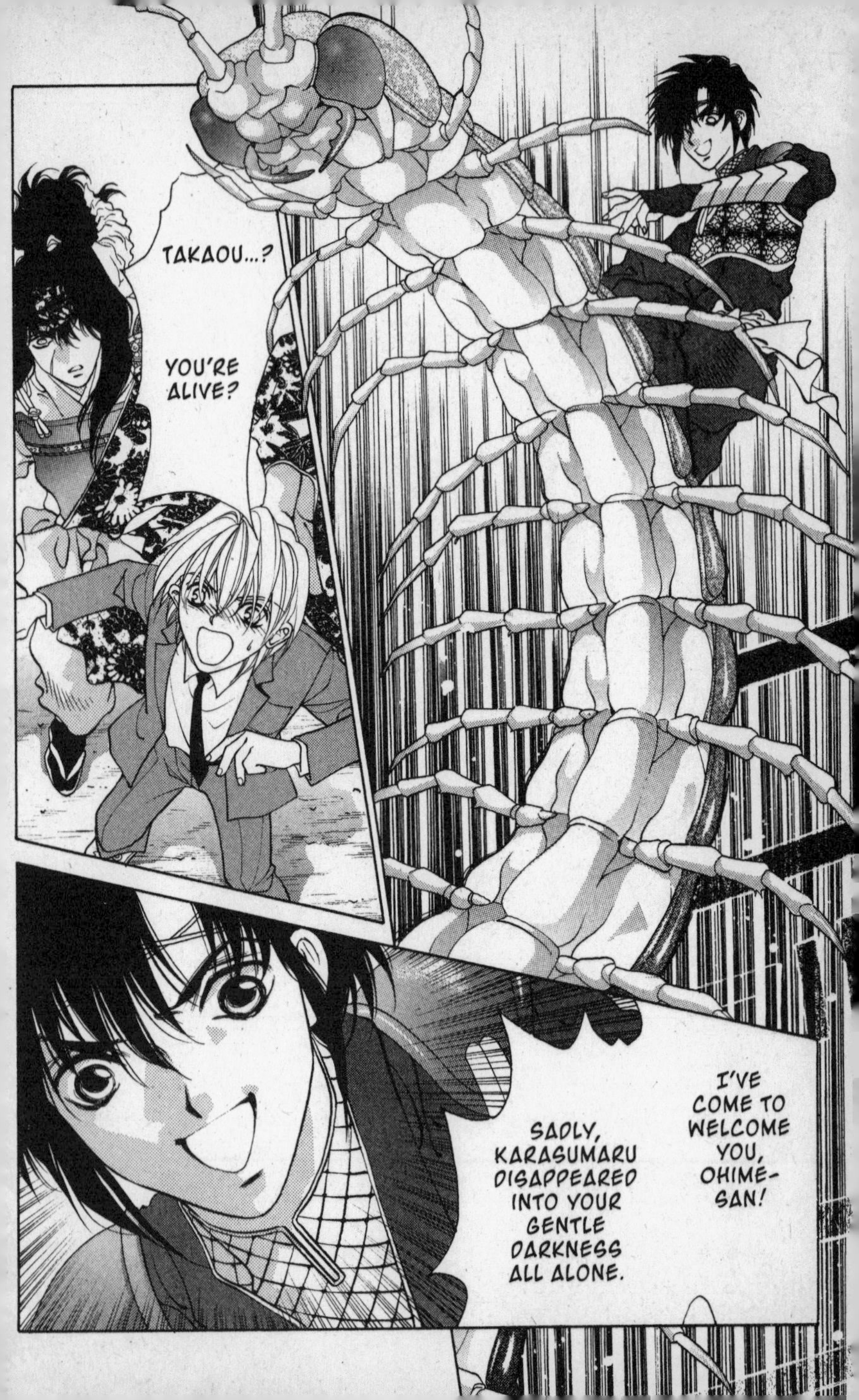
TAKAOU...?
YOU'RE ALIVE?
I'VE COME TO WELCOME YOU, OHIME-SAN!
SADLY, KARASUMARU DISAPPEARED INTO YOUR GENTLE DARKNESS ALL ALONE.

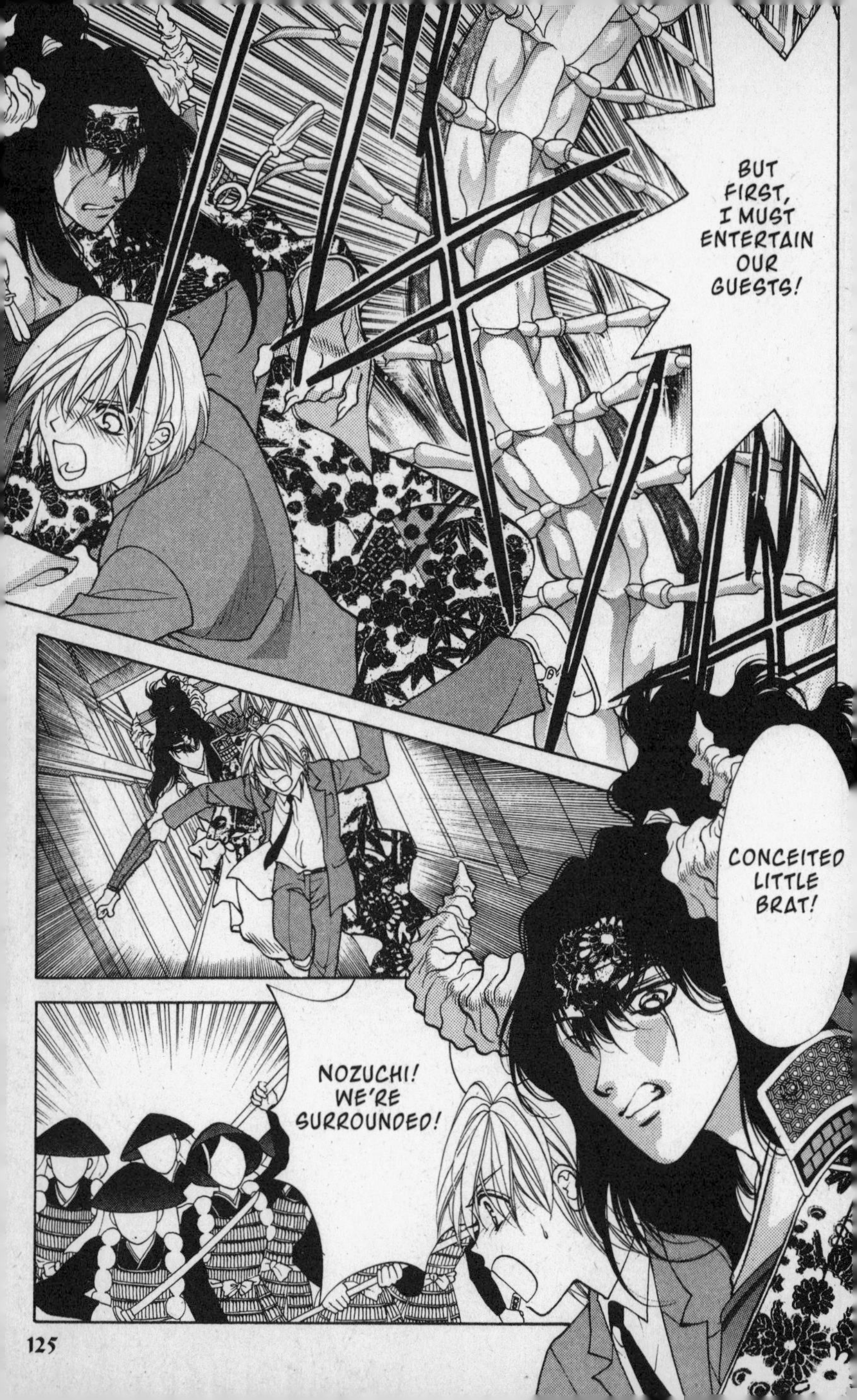
BUT FIRST, I MUST ENTERTAIN OUR GUESTS!
CONCEITED LITTLE BRAT!
NOZUCHI! WE'RE SURROUNDED!

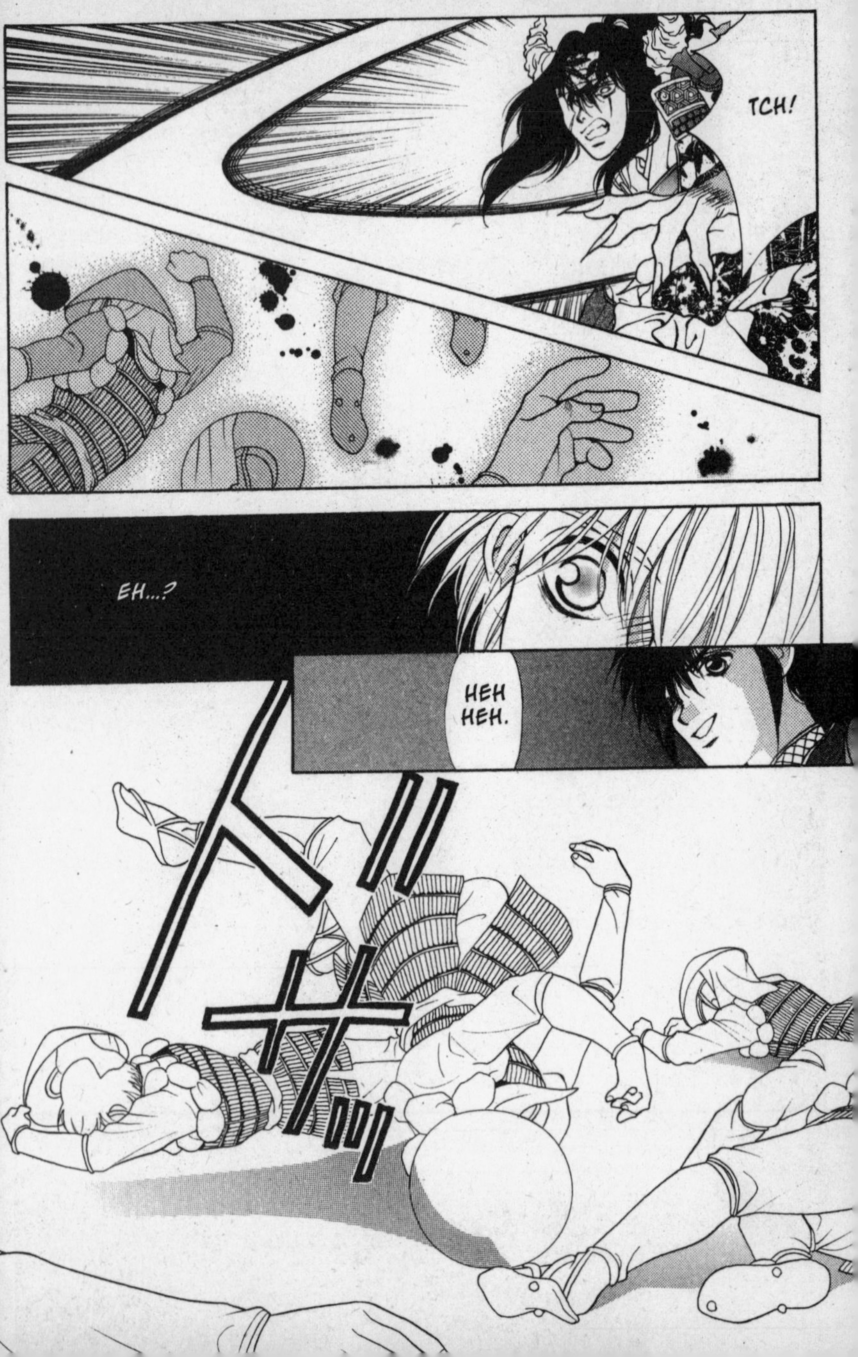
TCH!
EH...?
HEH HEH.
ドサッ

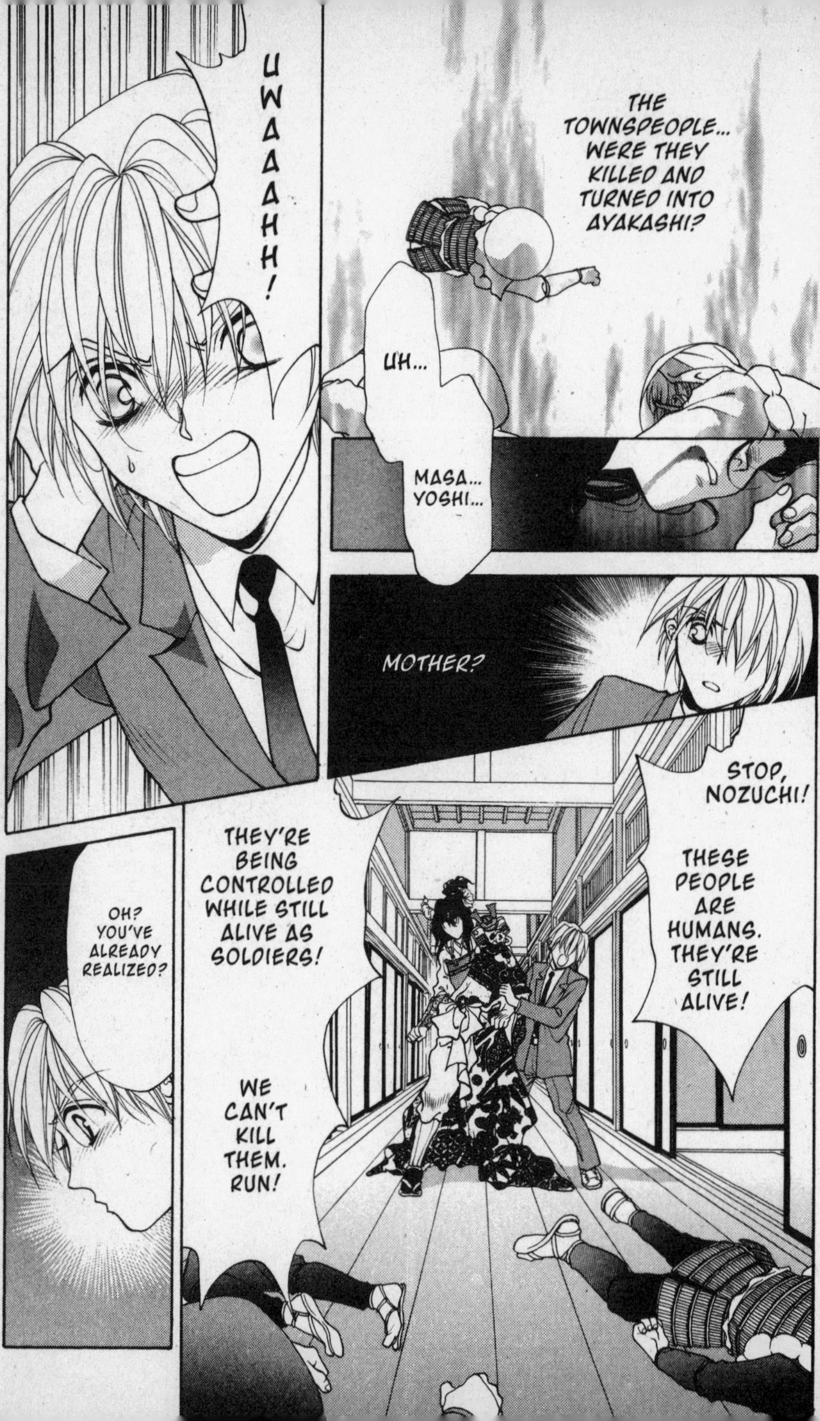
THE TOWNSPEOPLE... WERE THEY KILLED AND TURNED INTO AYAKASHI?
UH...
MASA... YOSHI...
MOTHER?
UWAAAAHH!
STOP, NOZUCHI!
THESE PEOPLE ARE HUMANS. THEY'RE STILL ALIVE!
THEY'RE BEING CONTROLLED WHILE STILL ALIVE AS SOLDIERS!
WE CAN'T KILL THEM. RUN!
OH? YOU'VE ALREADY REALIZED?

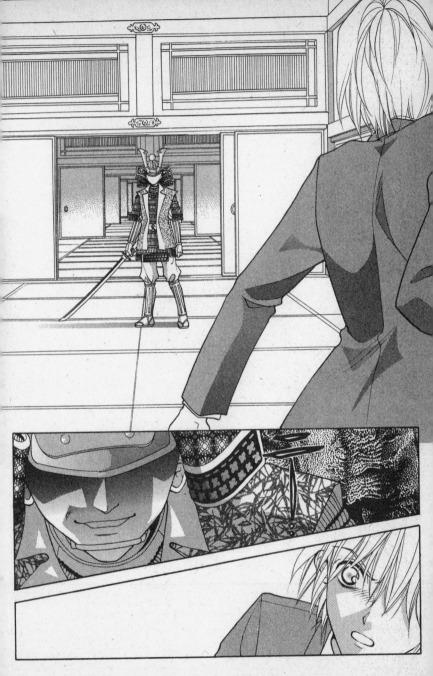

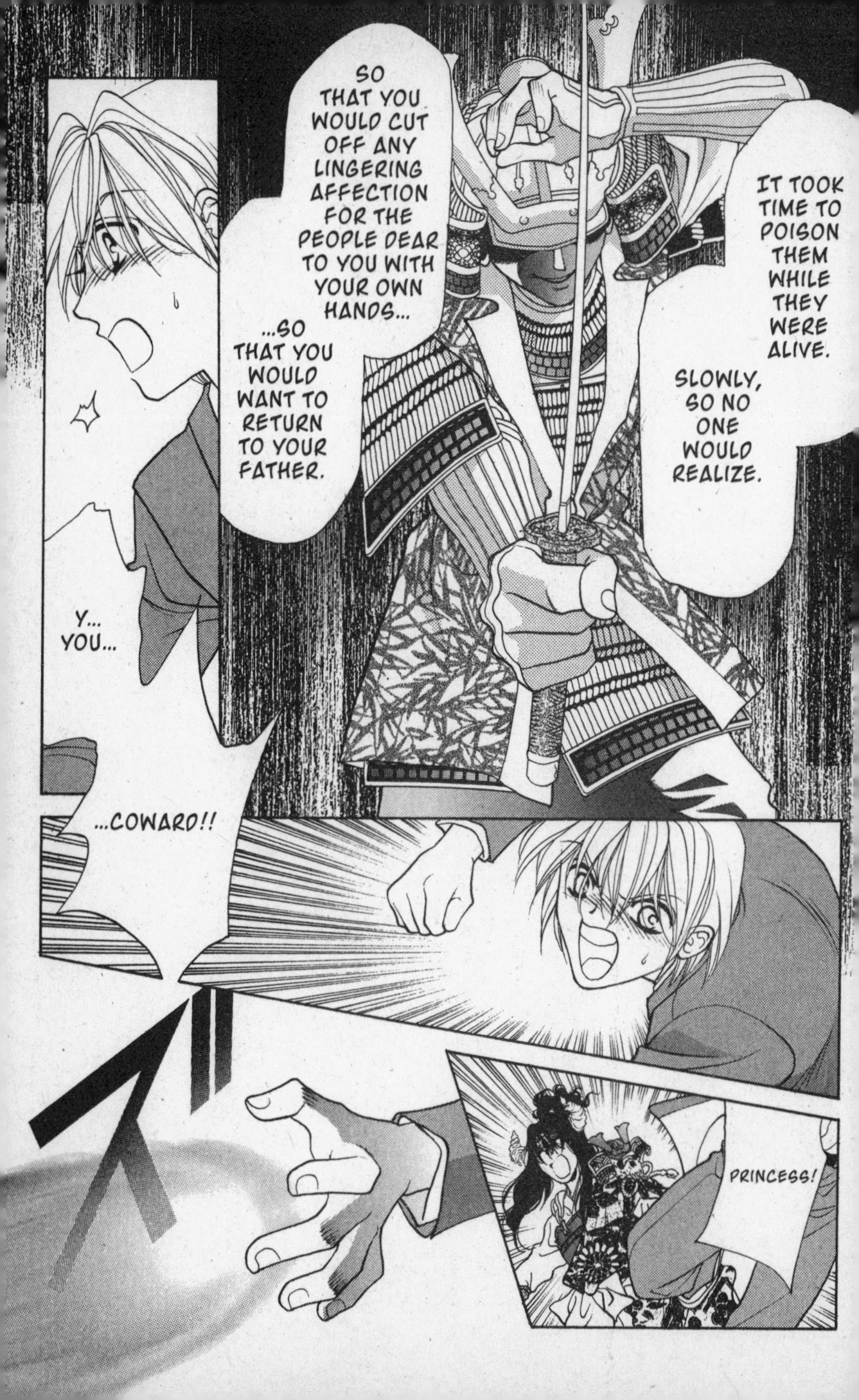
IT TOOK TIME TO POISON THEM WHILE THEY WERE ALIVE.
SLOWLY, SO NO ONE WOULD REALIZE.
SO THAT YOU WOULD CUT OFF ANY LINGERING AFFECTION FOR THE PEOPLE DEAR TO YOU WITH YOUR OWN HANDS...
...SO THAT YOU WOULD WANT TO RETURN TO YOUR FATHER.
Y... YOU...
...COWARD!!
PRINCESS!

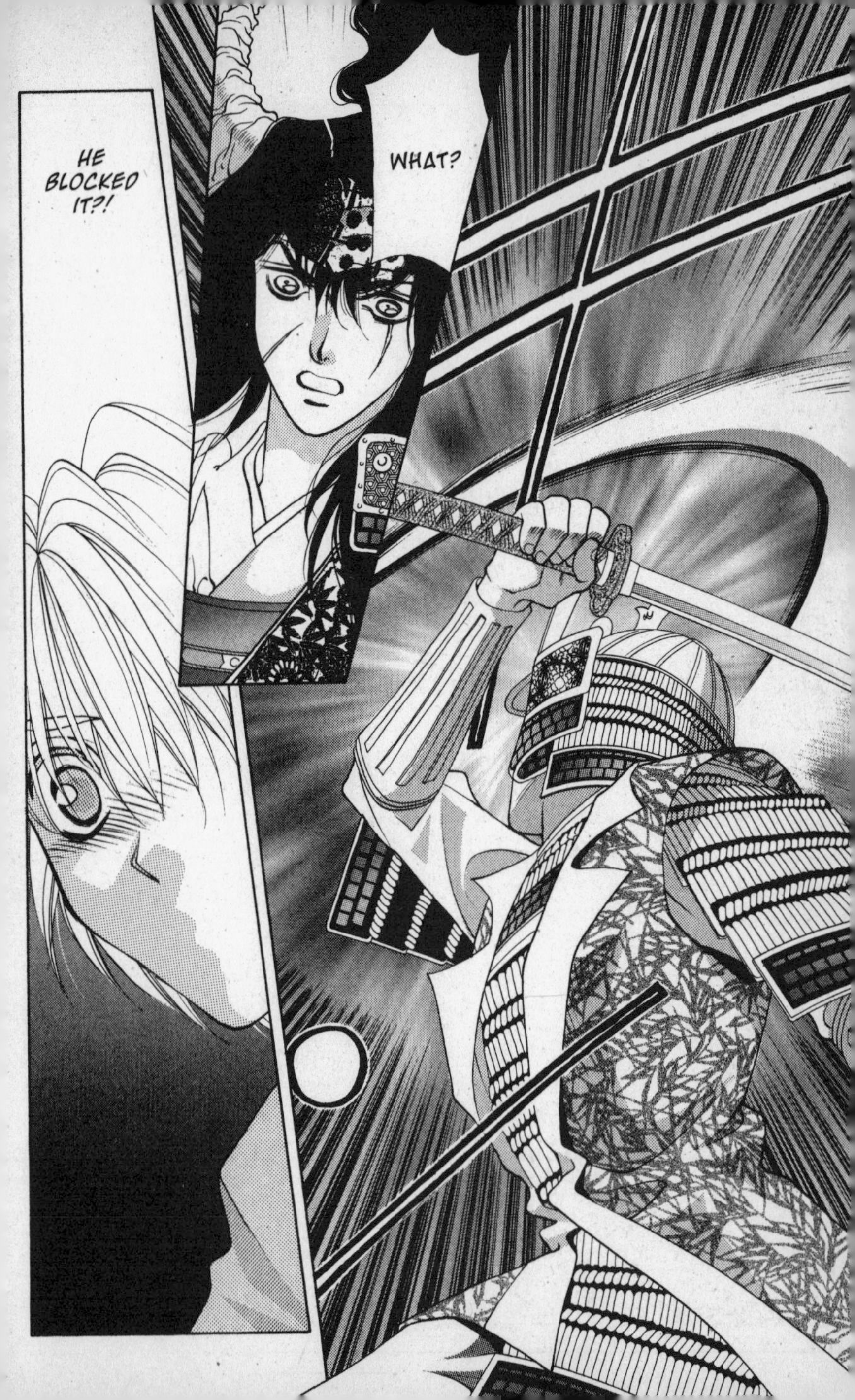
WHAT?
HE BLOCKED IT?!

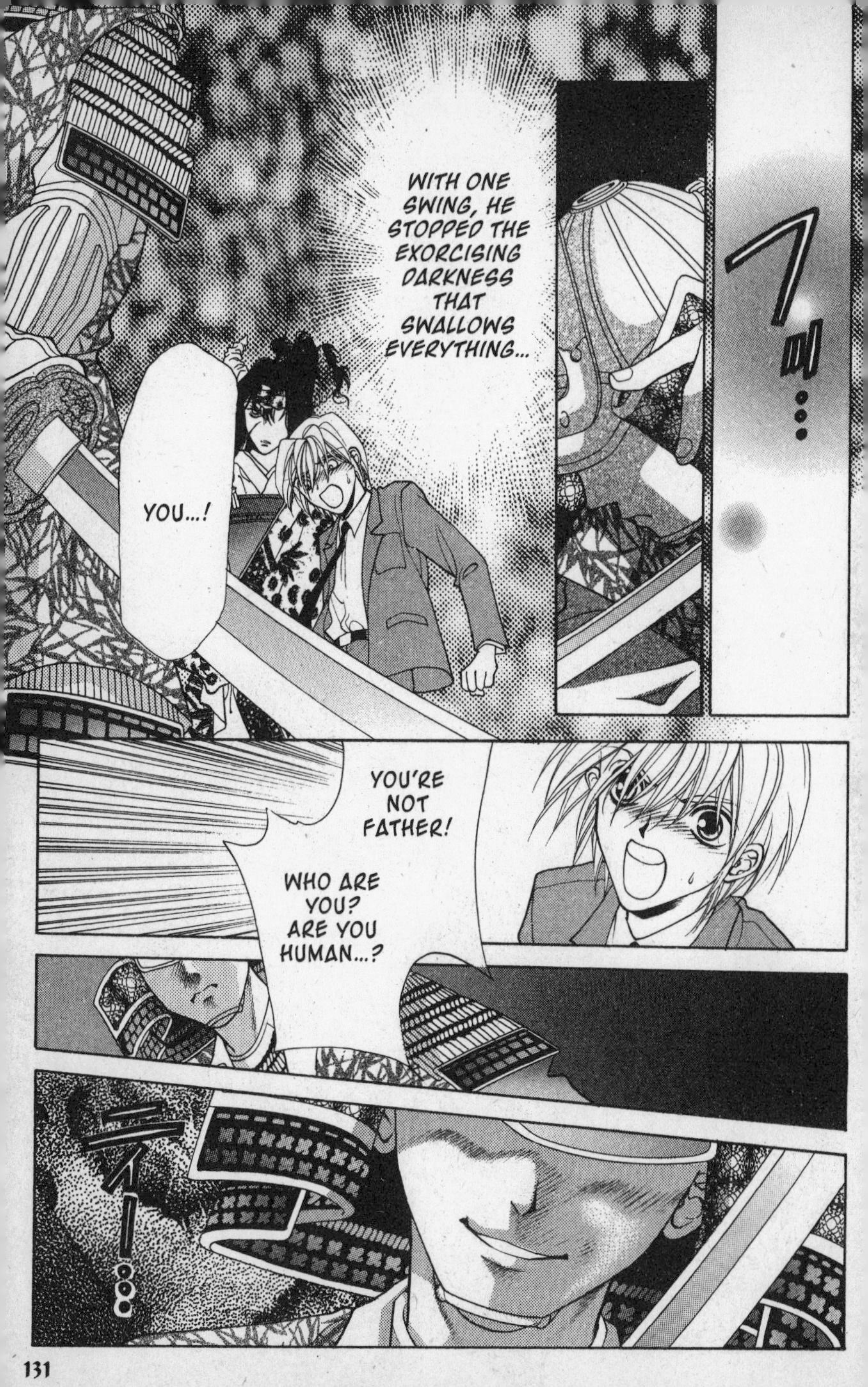
WITH ONE SWING, HE STOPPED THE EXORCISING DARKNESS THAT SWALLOWS EVERYTHING...
YOU...!
YOU'RE NOT FATHER!
WHO ARE YOU? ARE YOU HUMAN...?

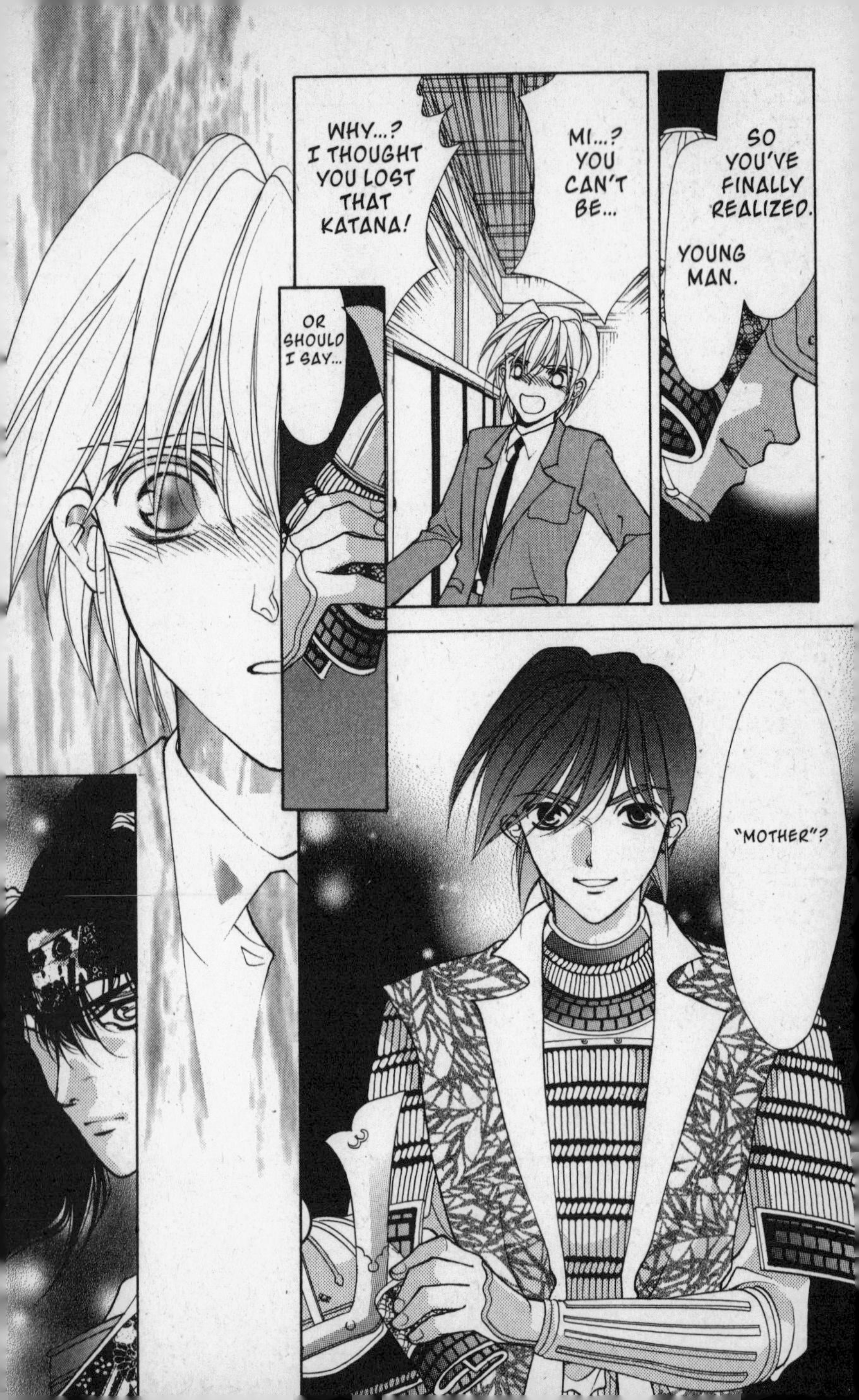
SO YOU'VE FINALLY REALIZED.
YOUNG MAN.
MI...? YOU CAN'T BE...
WHY...? I THOUGHT YOU LOST THAT KATANA!
OR SHOULD I SAY...
"MOTHER"?

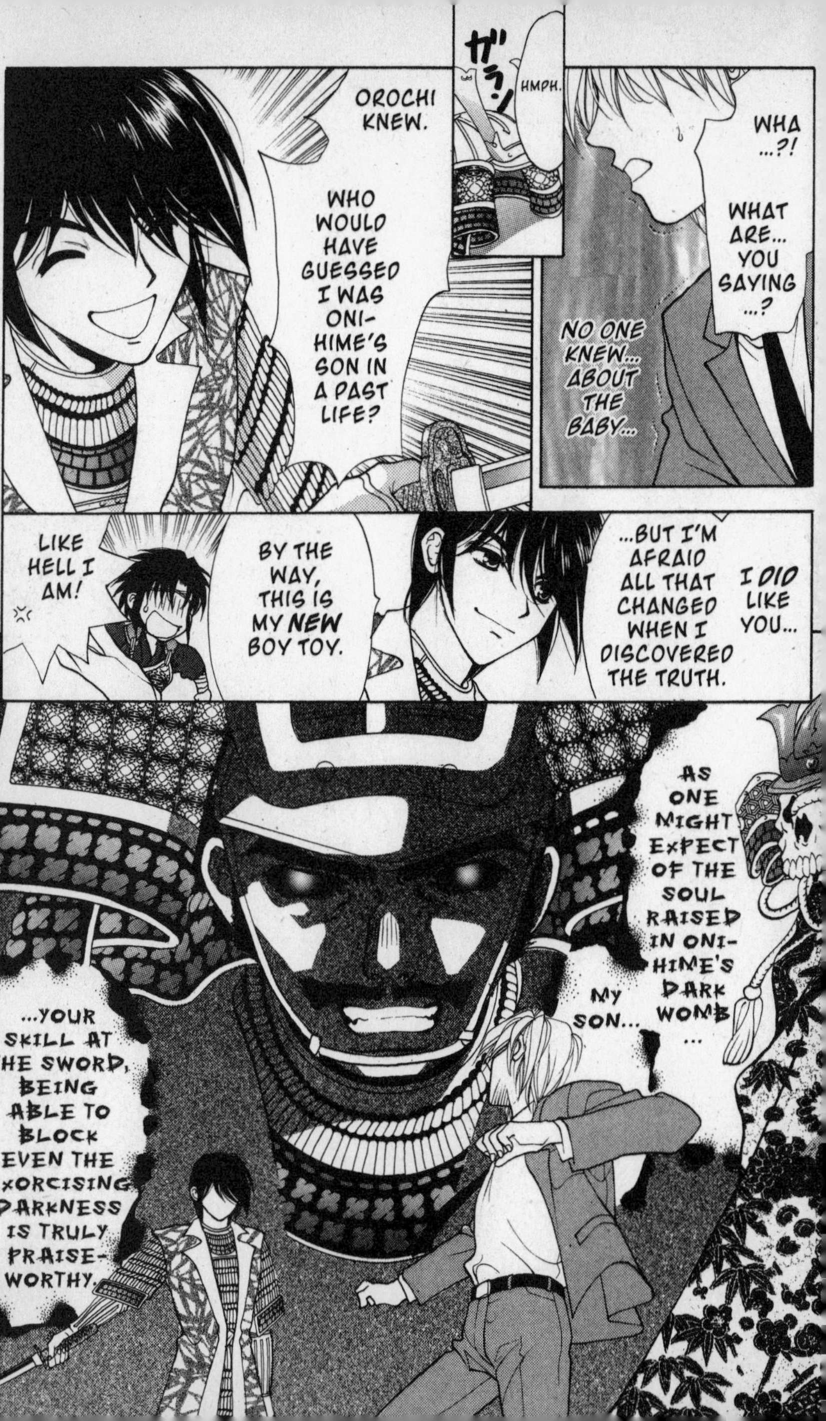
WHA ...?!
WHAT ARE... YOU SAYING ...?
NO ONE KNEW... ABOUT THE BABY...
ガラン
HMPH.
OROCHI KNEW.
WHO WOULD HAVE GUESSED I WAS ONI-HIME'S SON IN A PAST LIFE?
I *DID* LIKE YOU...
...BUT I'M AFRAID ALL THAT CHANGED WHEN I DISCOVERED THE TRUTH.
BY THE WAY, THIS IS MY **NEW** BOY TOY.
LIKE HELL I AM!
AS ONE MIGHT EXPECT OF THE SOUL RAISED IN ONI-HIME'S DARK WOMB ...
MY SON...
...YOUR SKILL AT THE SWORD, BEING ABLE TO BLOCK EVEN THE EXORCISING DARKNESS IS TRULY PRAISE-WORTHY.

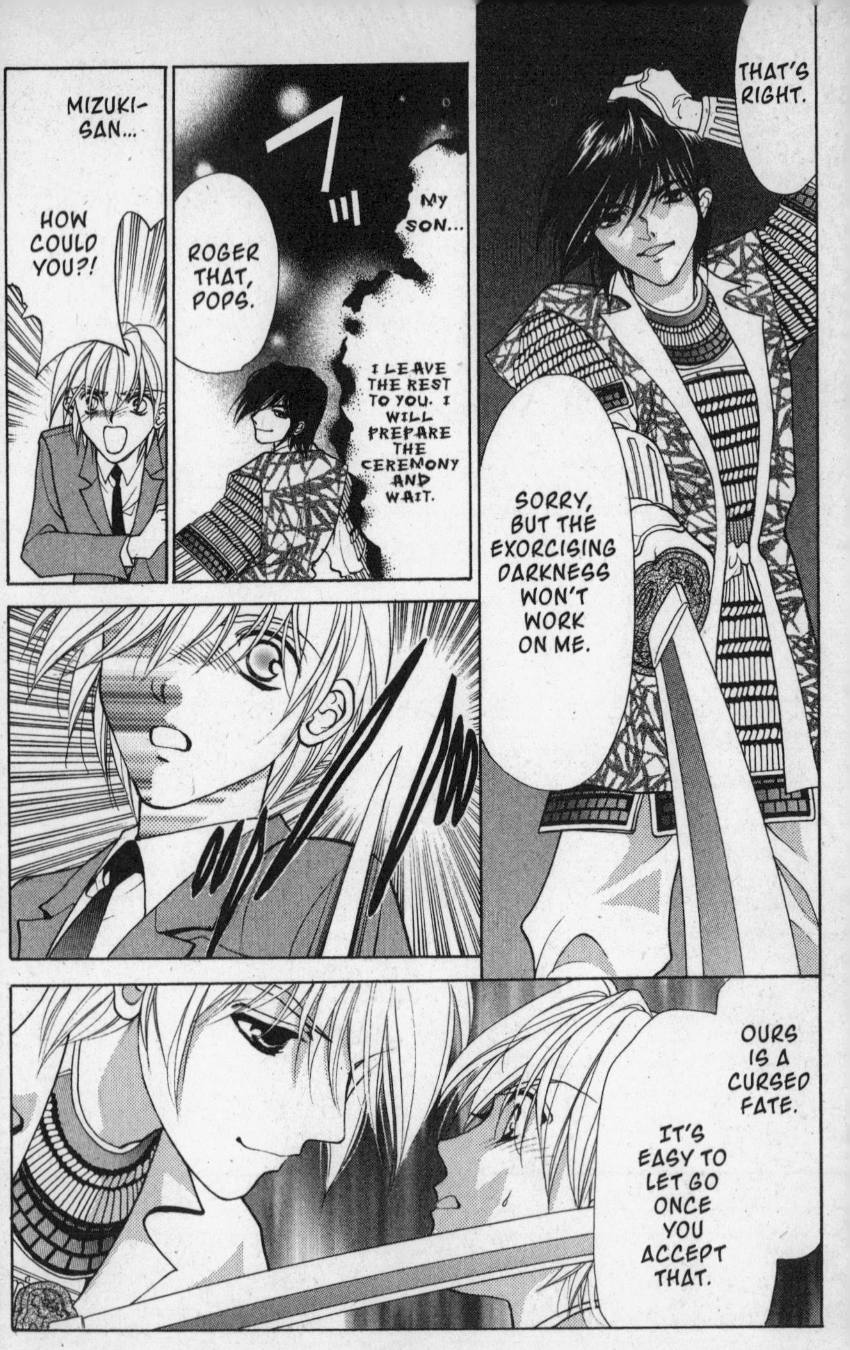

THAT'S RIGHT.
SORRY, BUT THE EXORCISING DARKNESS WON'T WORK ON ME.
MY SON...
ROGER THAT, POPS.
I LEAVE THE REST TO YOU. I WILL PREPARE THE CEREMONY AND WAIT.
MIZUKI-SAN...
HOW COULD YOU?!
OURS IS A CURSED FATE.
IT'S EASY TO LET GO ONCE YOU ACCEPT THAT.

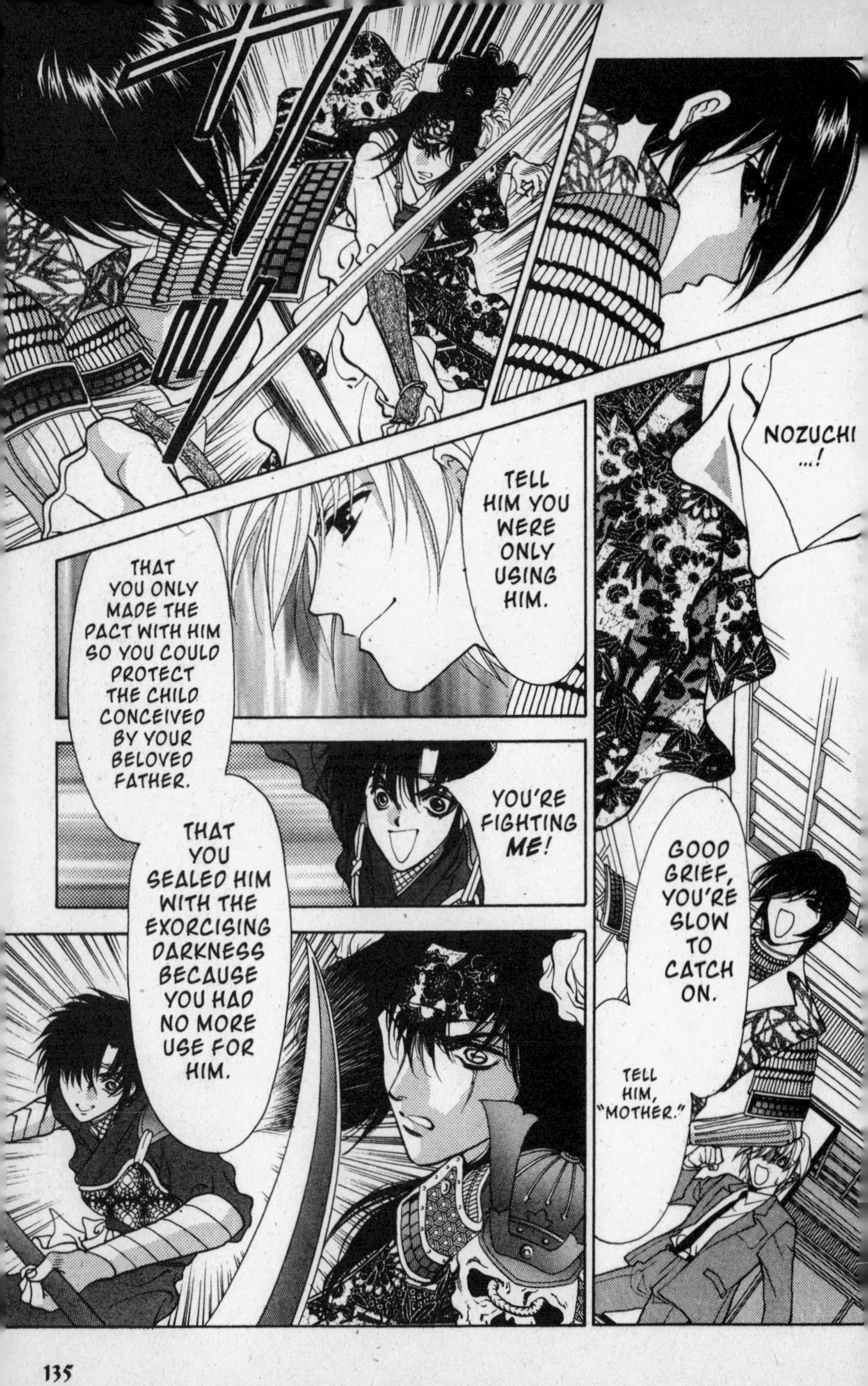
NOZUCHI ...!
GOOD GRIEF, YOU'RE SLOW TO CATCH ON.
TELL HIM, "MOTHER."
TELL HIM YOU WERE ONLY USING HIM.
THAT YOU ONLY MADE THE PACT WITH HIM SO YOU COULD PROTECT THE CHILD CONCEIVED BY YOUR BELOVED FATHER.
YOU'RE FIGHTING *ME*!
THAT YOU SEALED HIM WITH THE EXORCISING DARKNESS BECAUSE YOU HAD NO MORE USE FOR HIM.

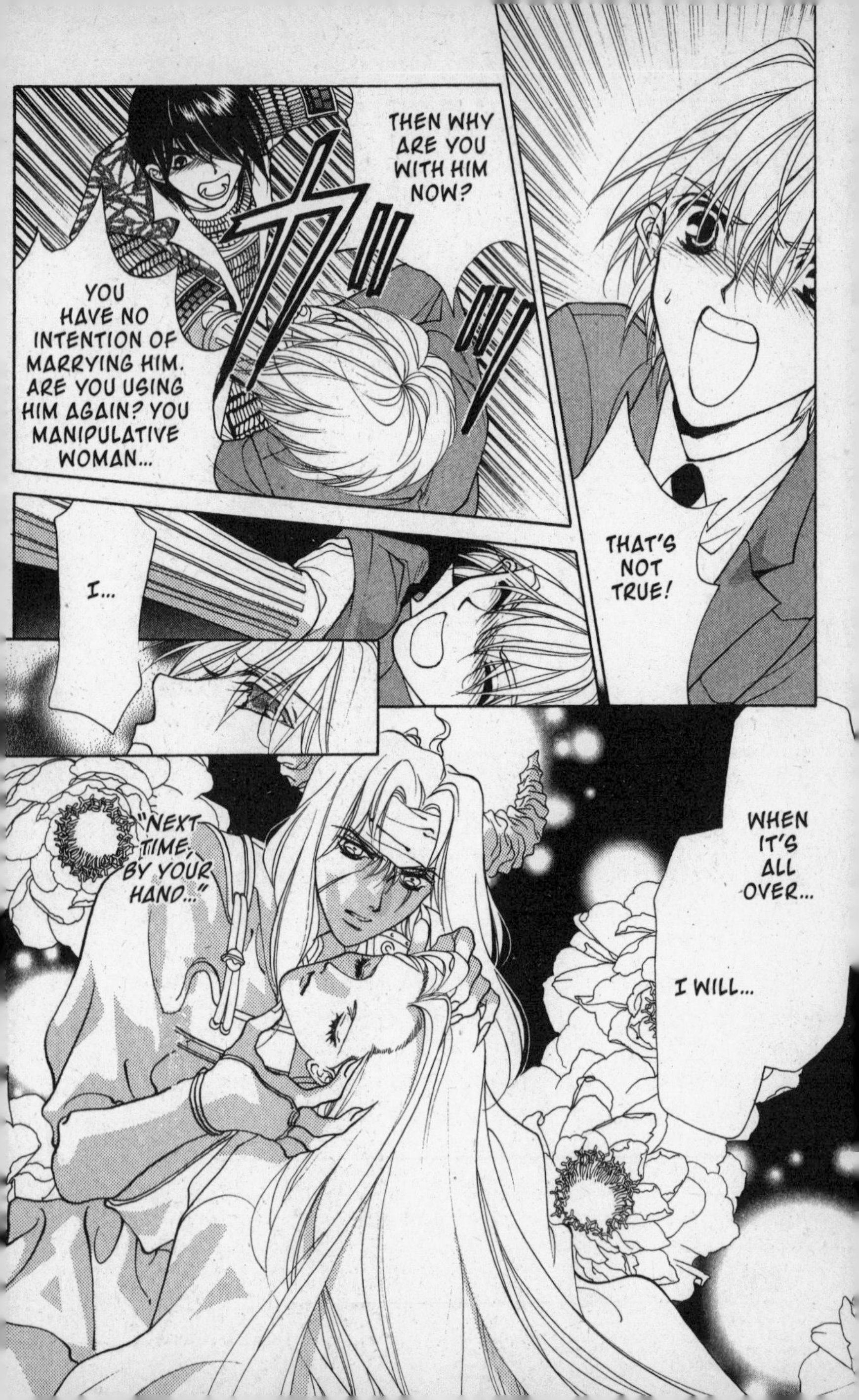
THAT'S NOT TRUE!
THEN WHY ARE YOU WITH HIM NOW?
YOU HAVE NO INTENTION OF MARRYING HIM. ARE YOU USING HIM AGAIN? YOU MANIPULATIVE WOMAN...
I...
WHEN IT'S ALL OVER...
I WILL...
"NEXT TIME, BY YOUR HAND..."

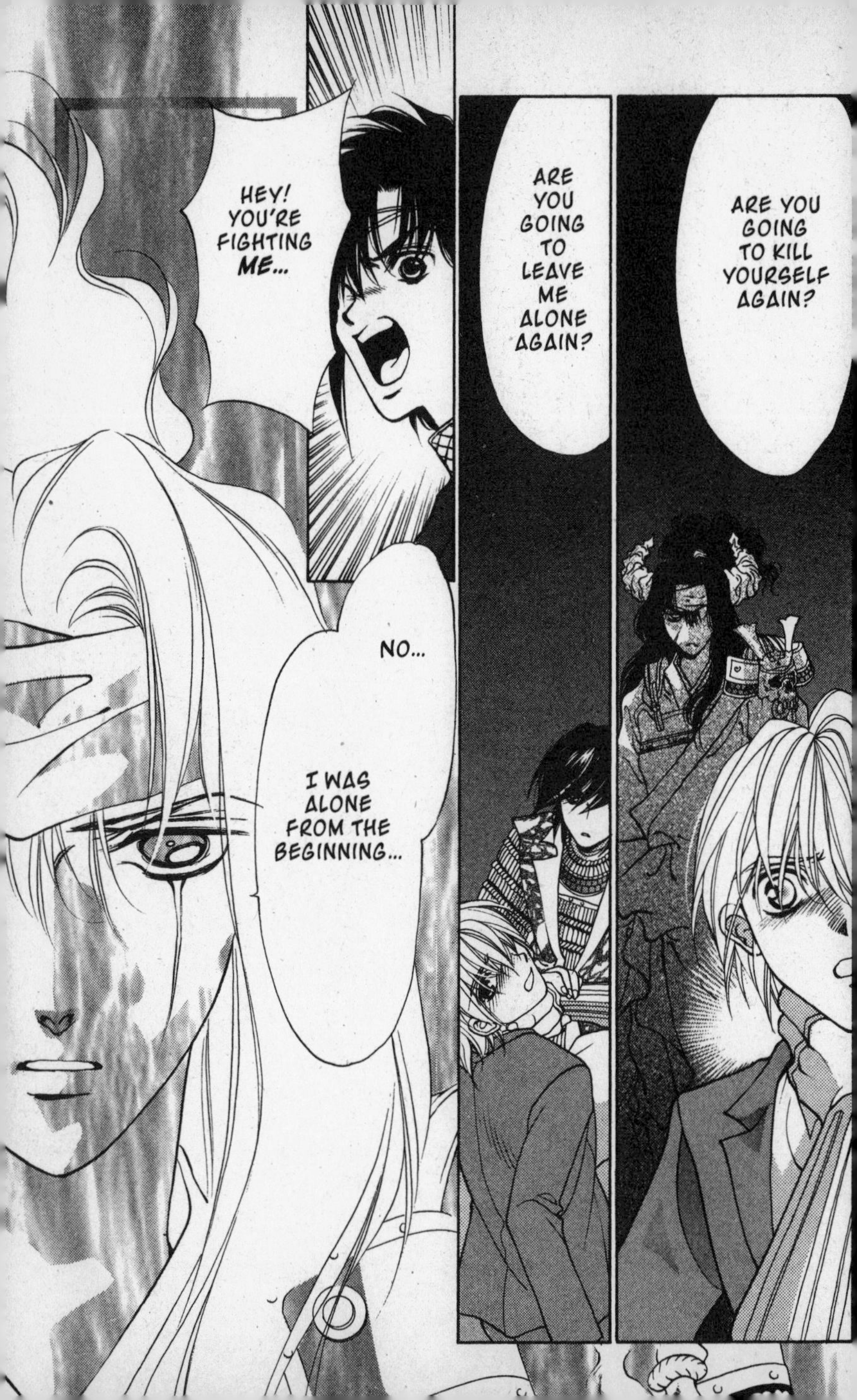
ARE YOU GOING TO KILL YOURSELF AGAIN?
ARE YOU GOING TO LEAVE ME ALONE AGAIN?
HEY! YOU'RE FIGHTING ME...
NO...
I WAS ALONE FROM THE BEGINNING...

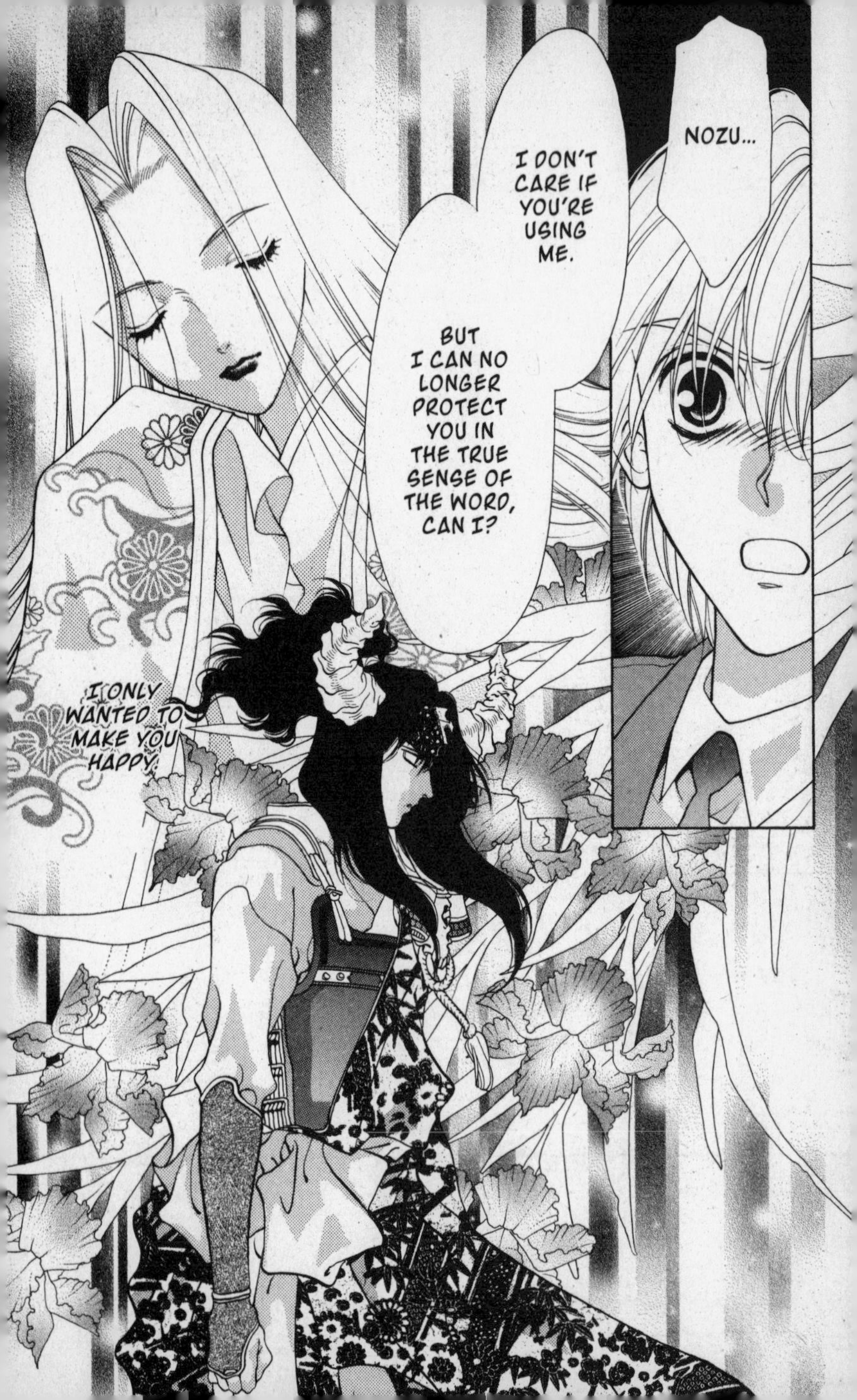
NOZU...
I DON'T CARE IF YOU'RE USING ME.
BUT I CAN NO LONGER PROTECT YOU IN THE TRUE SENSE OF THE WORD, CAN I?
I ONLY WANTED TO MAKE YOU HAPPY.

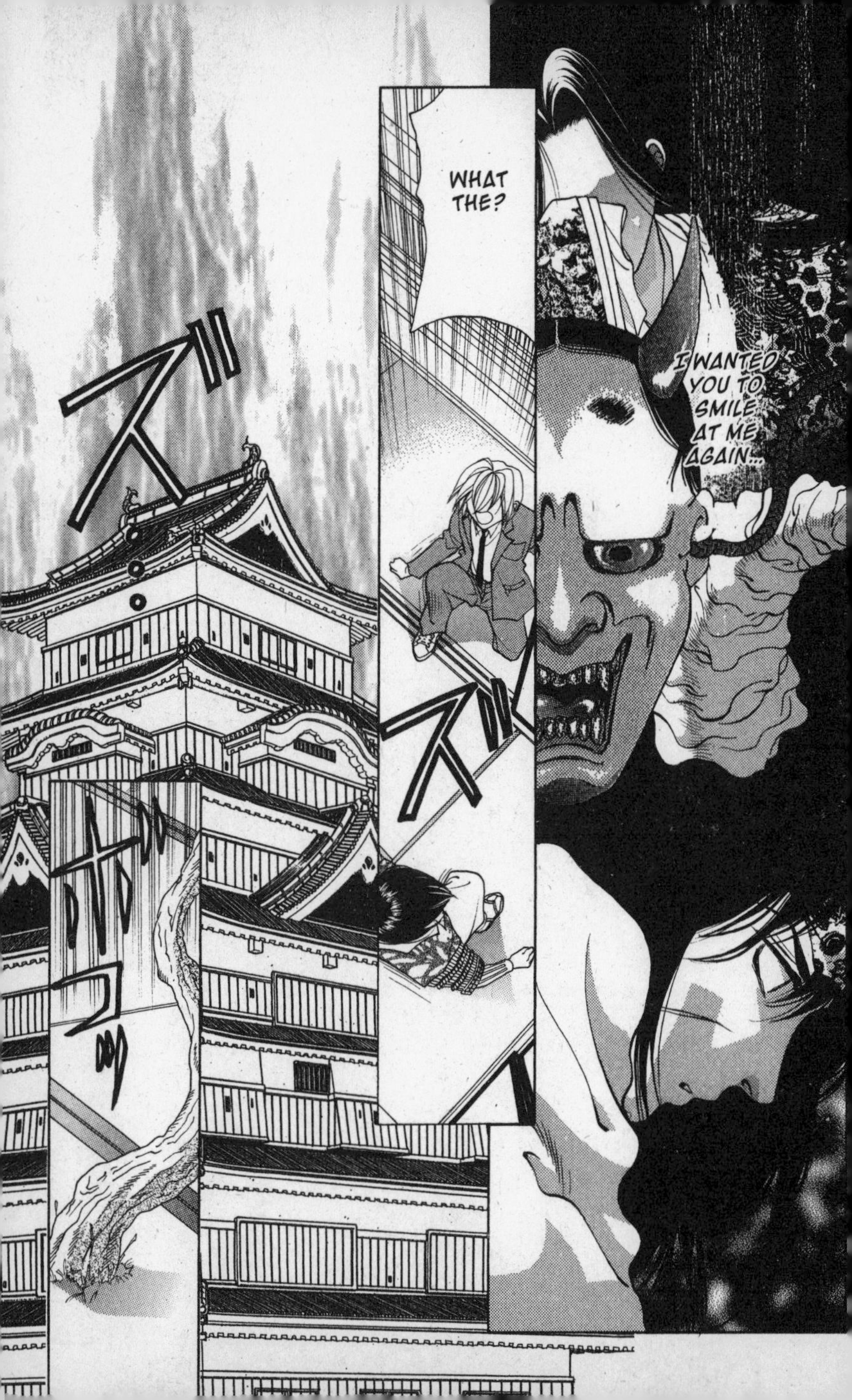
I WANTED YOU TO SMILE AT ME AGAIN...
WHAT THE?

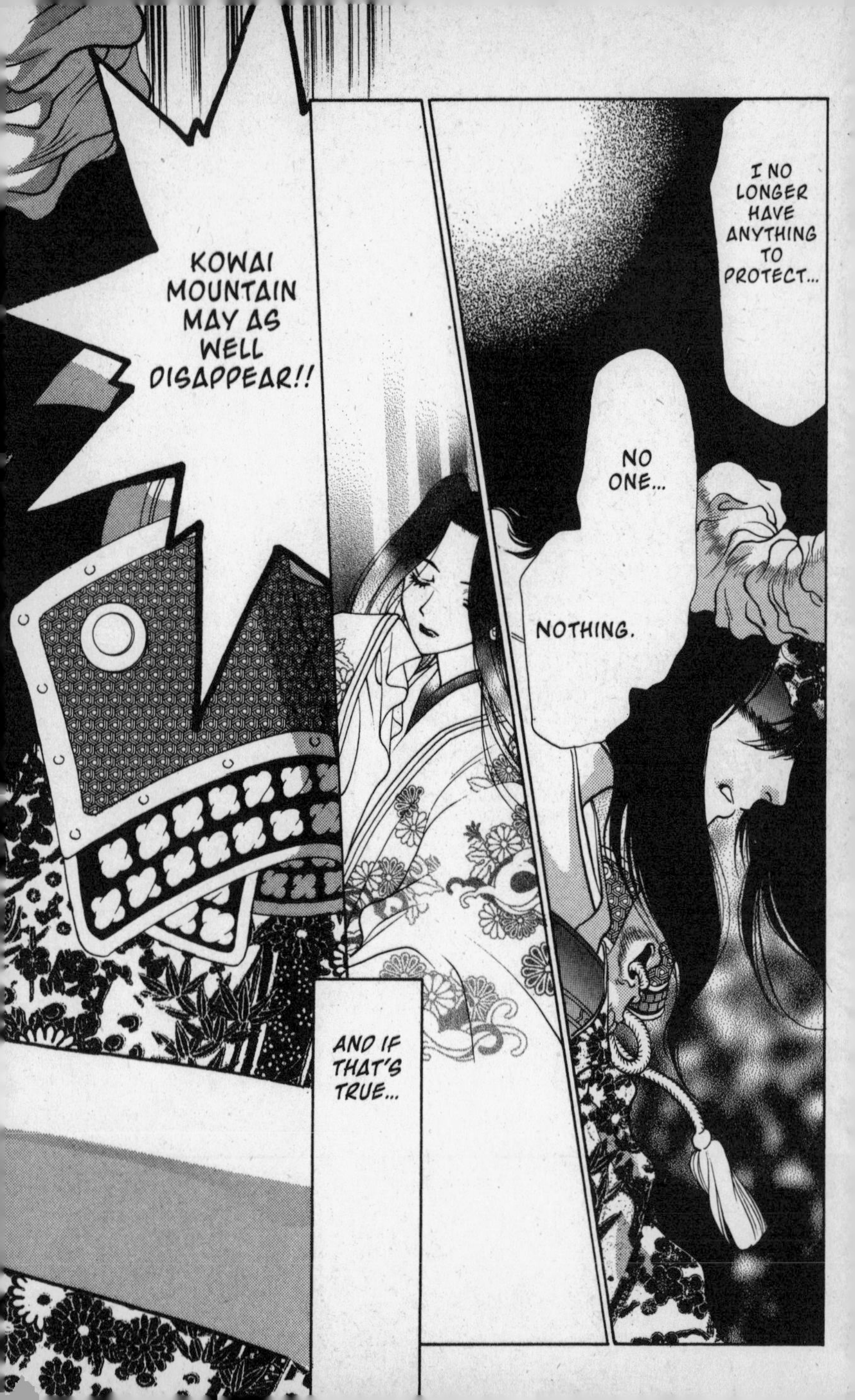
I NO LONGER HAVE ANYTHING TO PROTECT...
NO ONE...
NOTHING.
AND IF THAT'S TRUE...
KOWAI MOUNTAIN MAY AS WELL DISAPPEAR!!

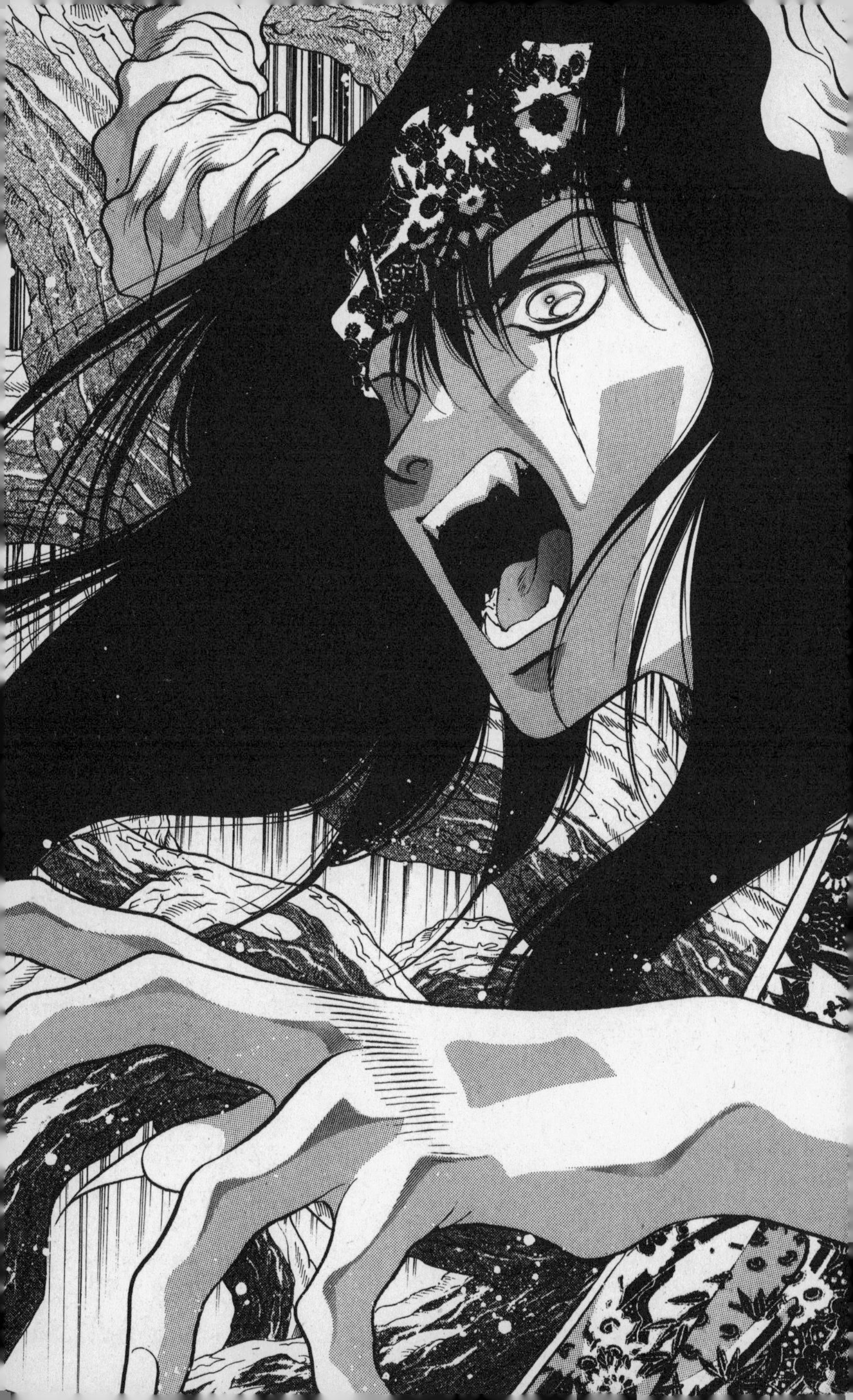

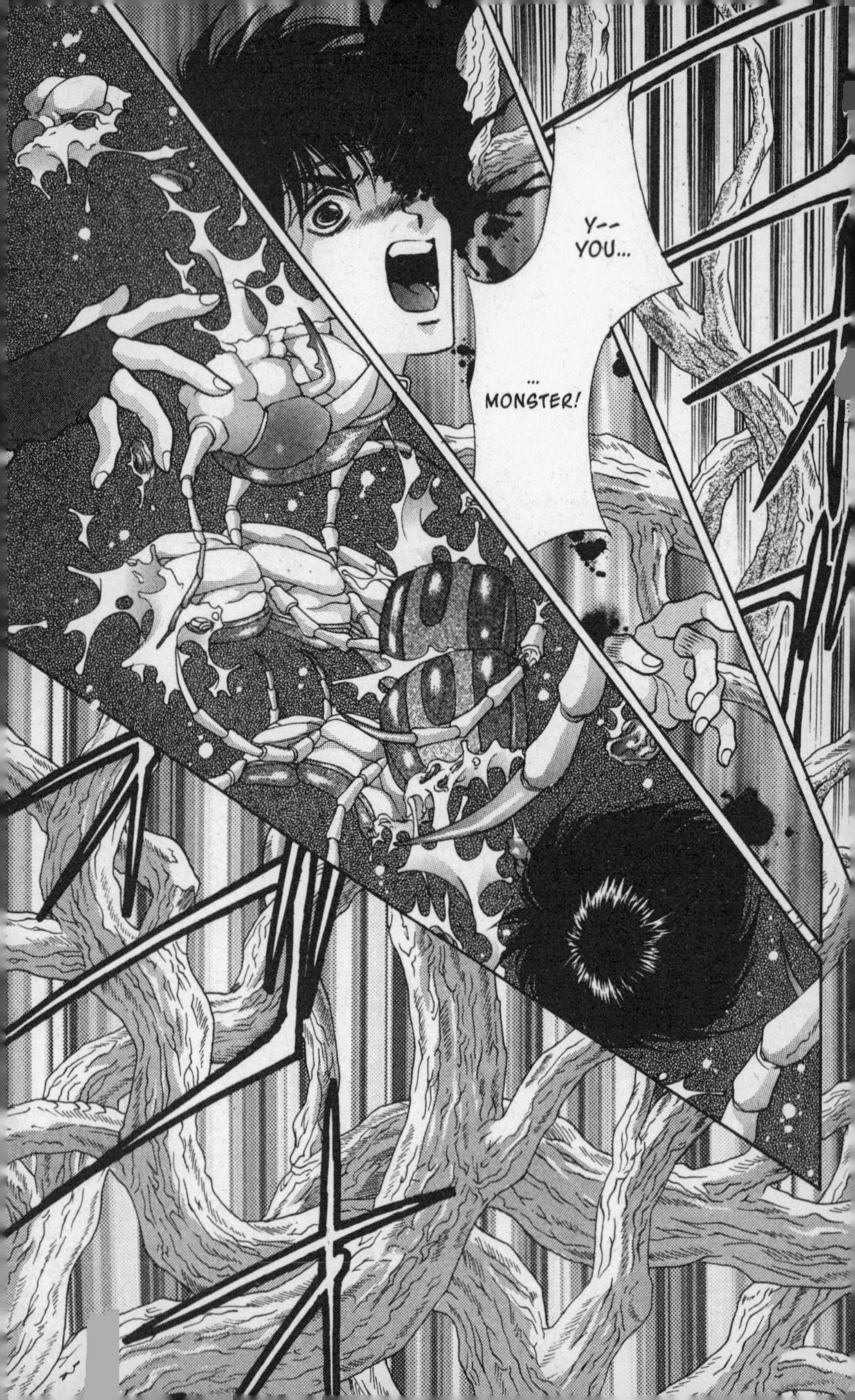
Y-- YOU...
... MONSTER!

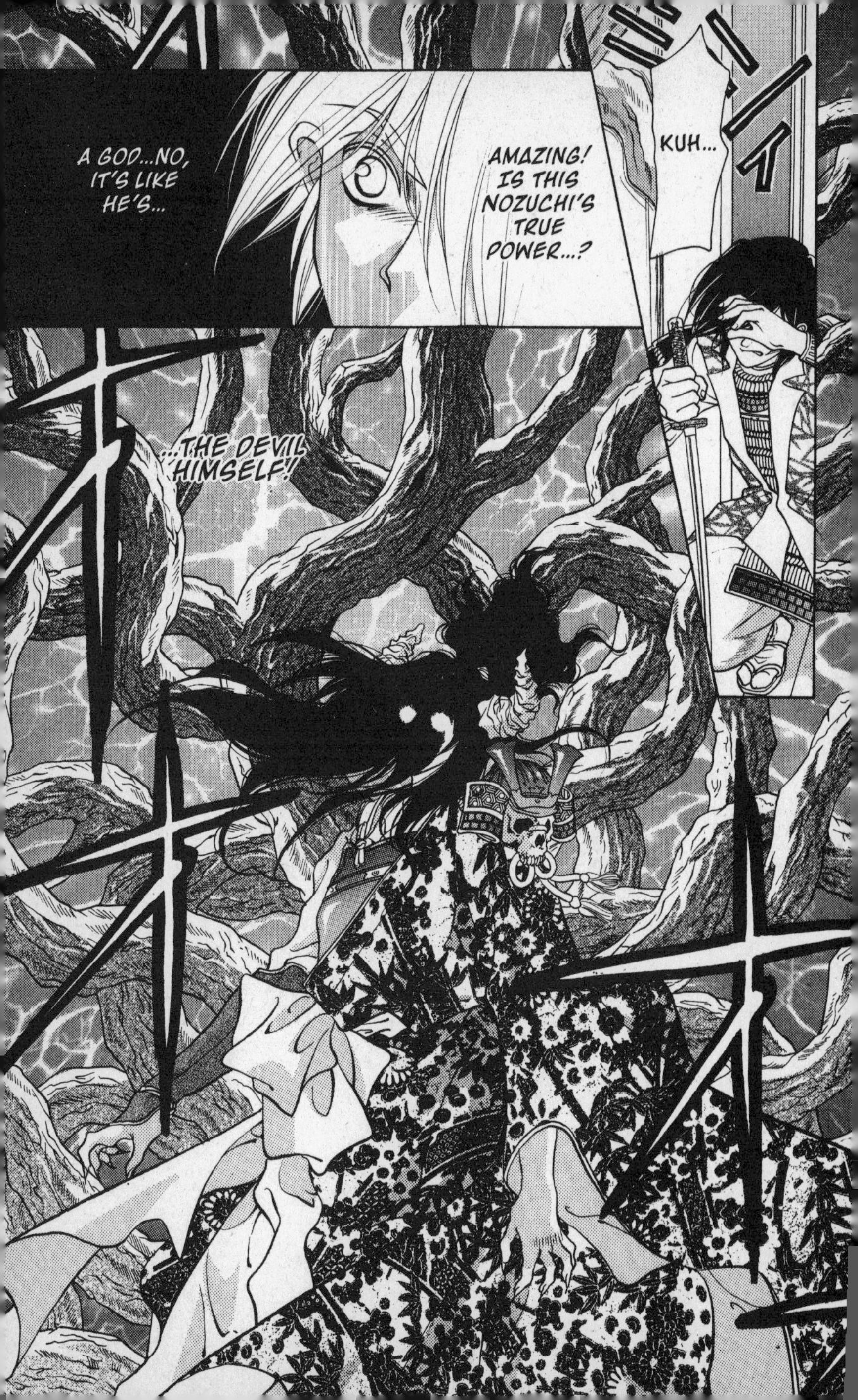
KUH...
AMAZING! IS THIS NOZUCHI'S TRUE POWER...?
A GOD...NO, IT'S LIKE HE'S...
...THE DEVIL HIMSELF!

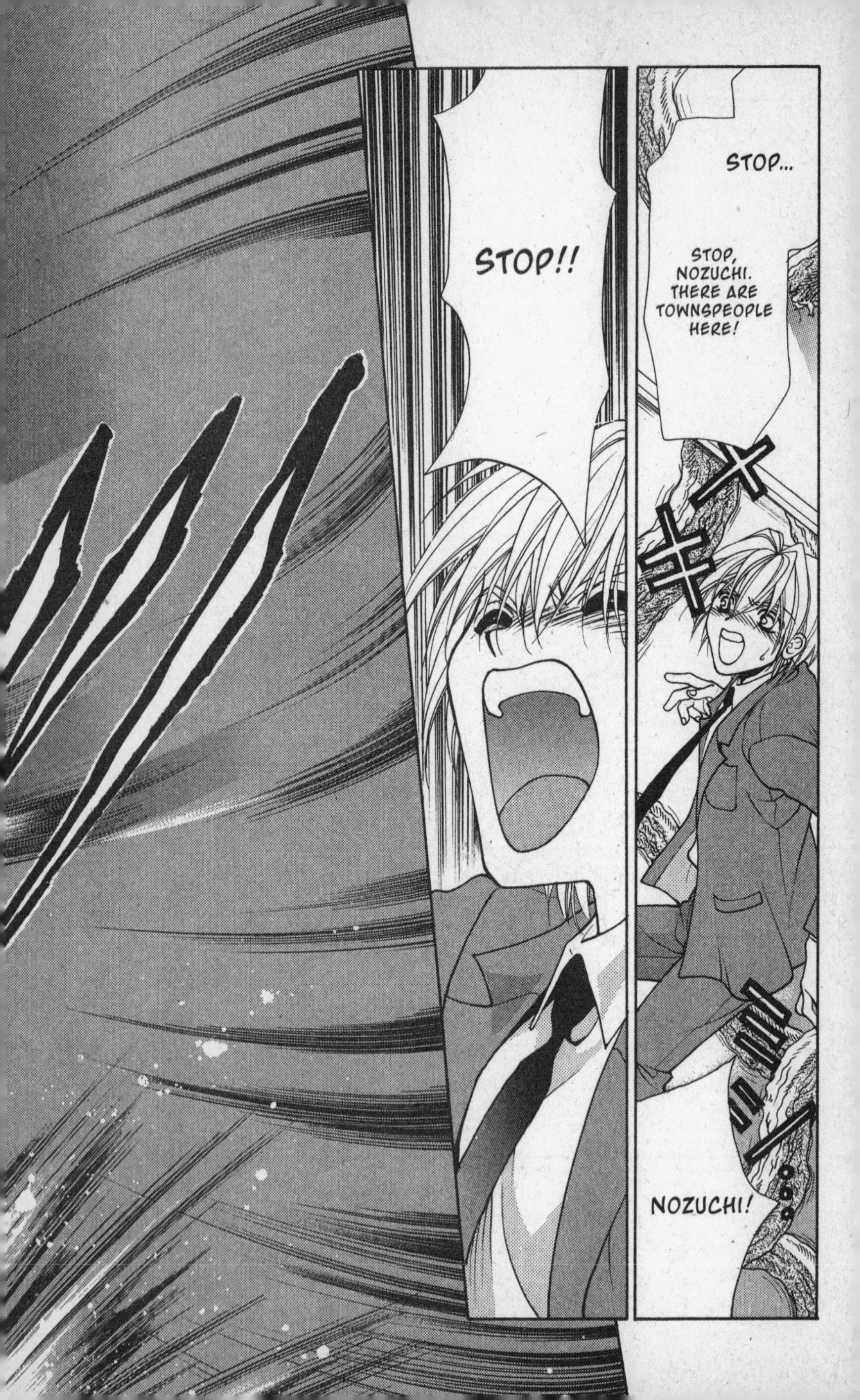
STOP...
STOP, NOZUCHI. THERE ARE TOWNSPEOPLE HERE!
NOZUCHI!
STOP!!

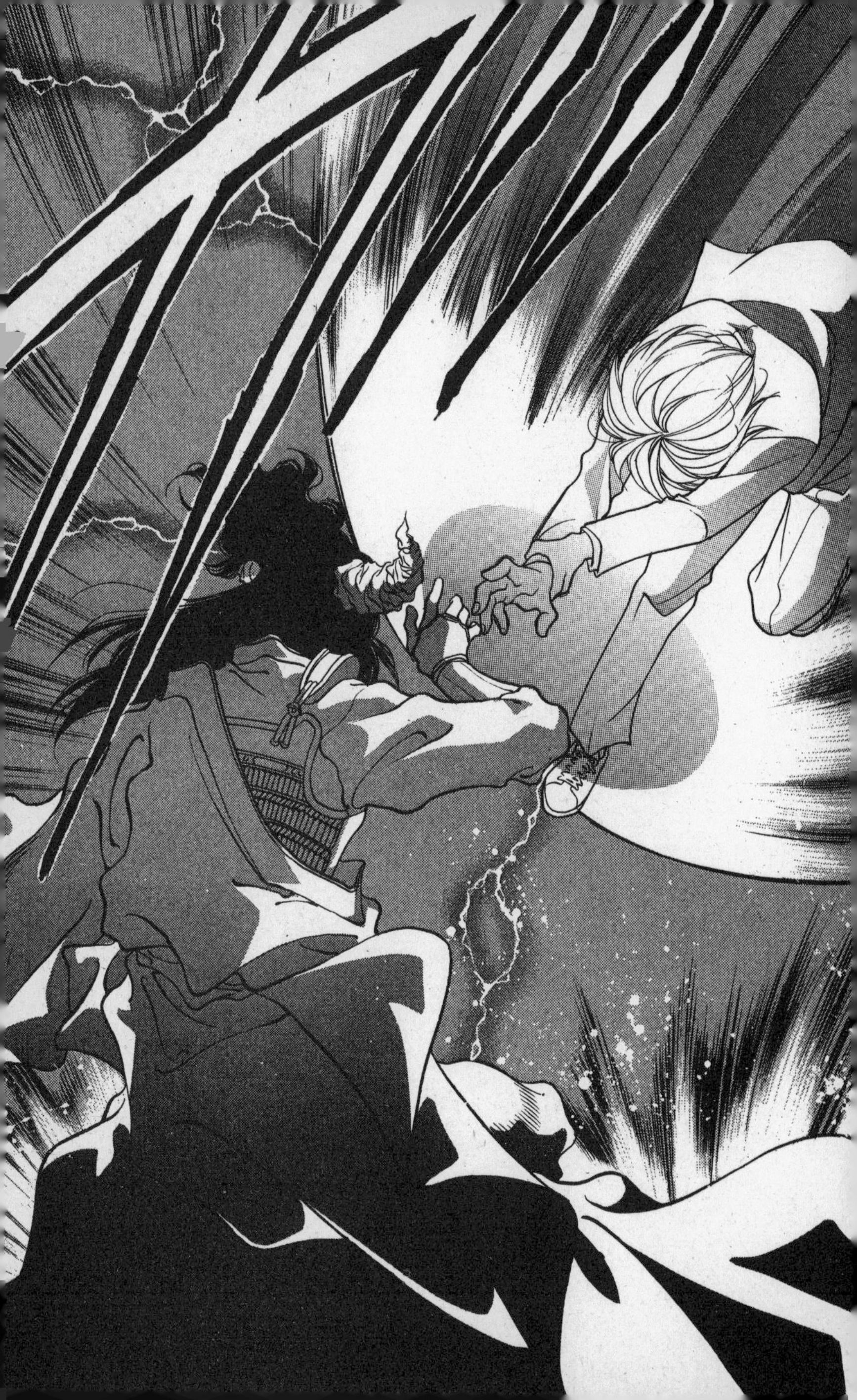

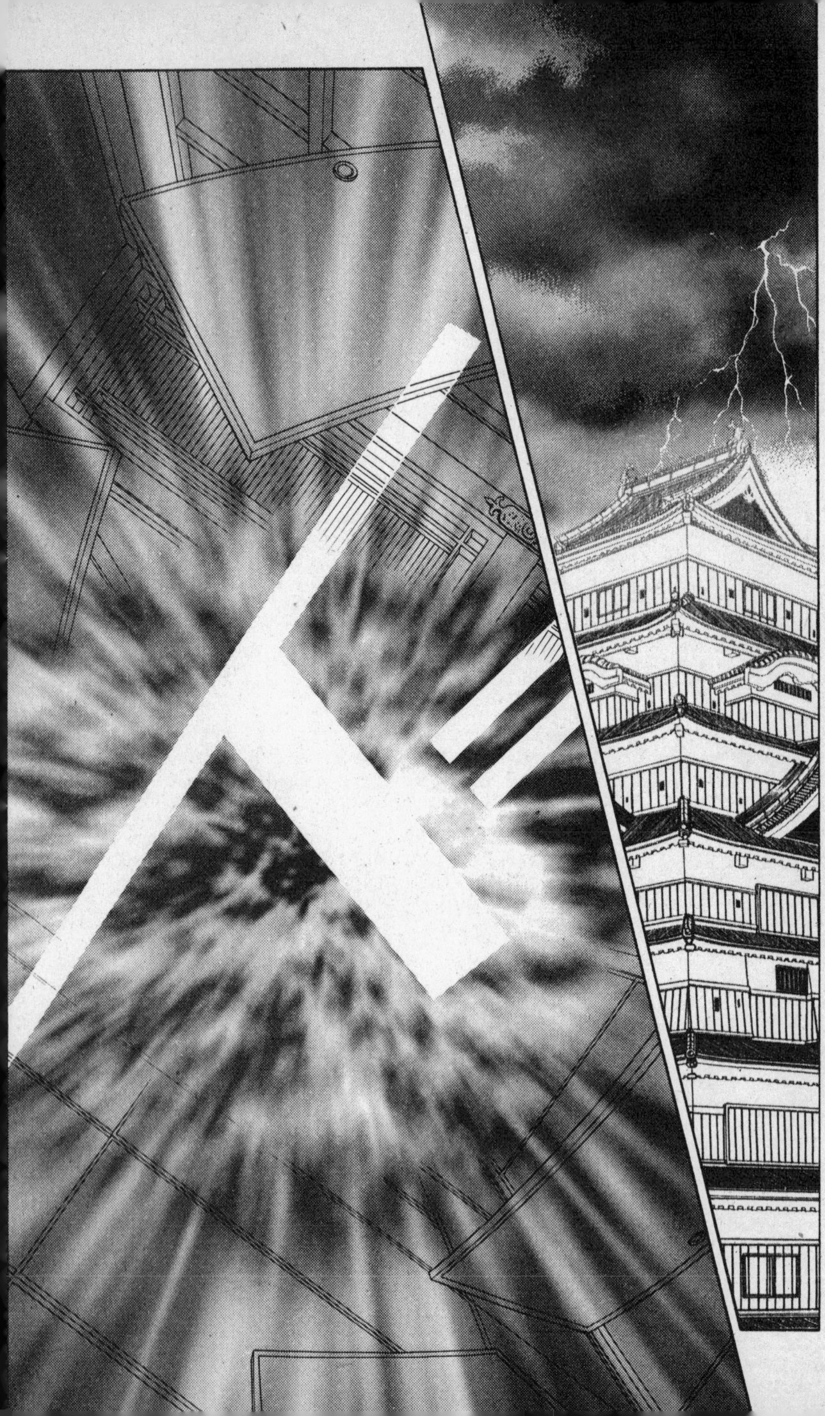

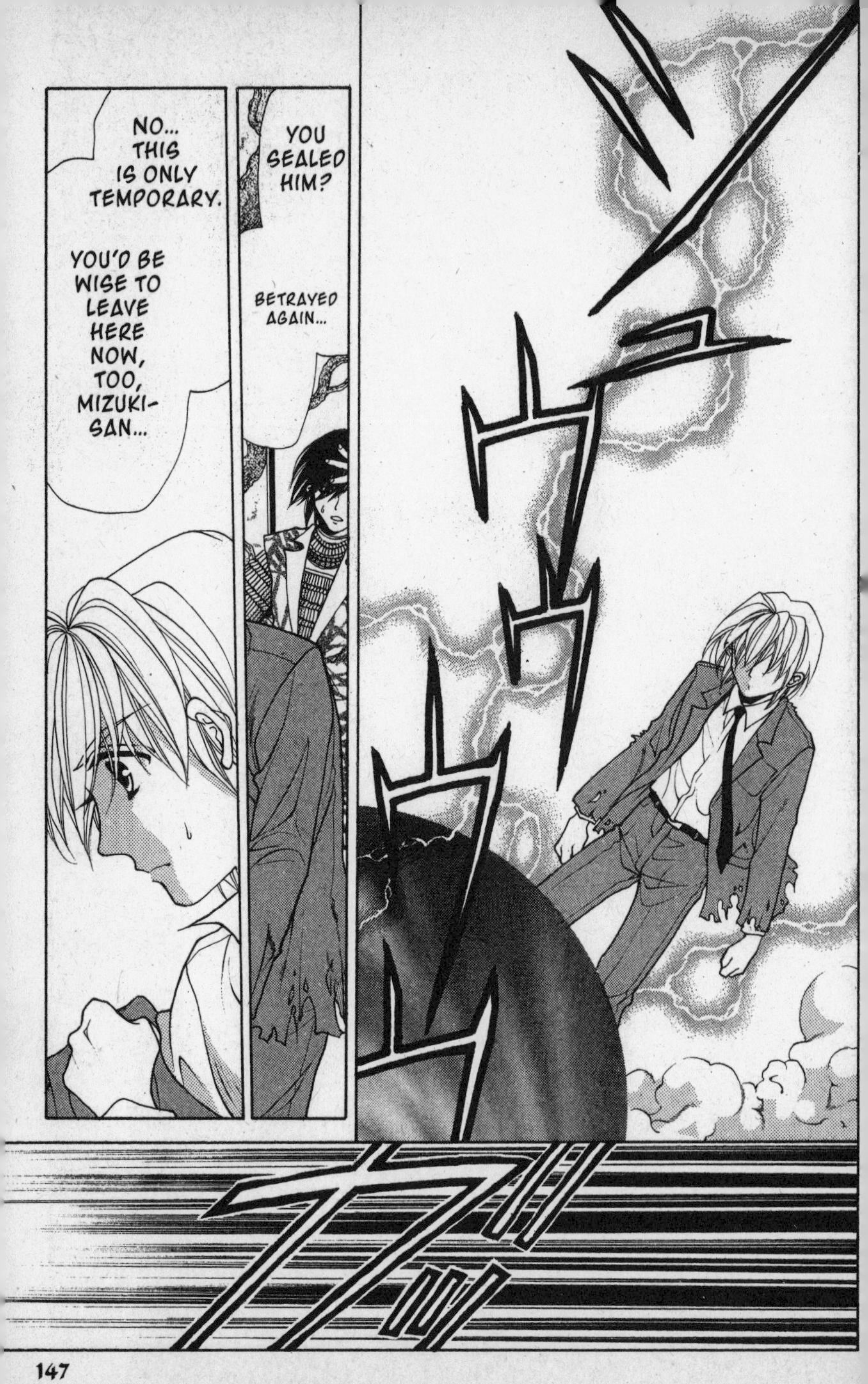
YOU SEALED HIM?
BETRAYED AGAIN...
NO... THIS IS ONLY TEMPORARY.
YOU'D BE WISE TO LEAVE HERE NOW, TOO, MIZUKI-SAN...

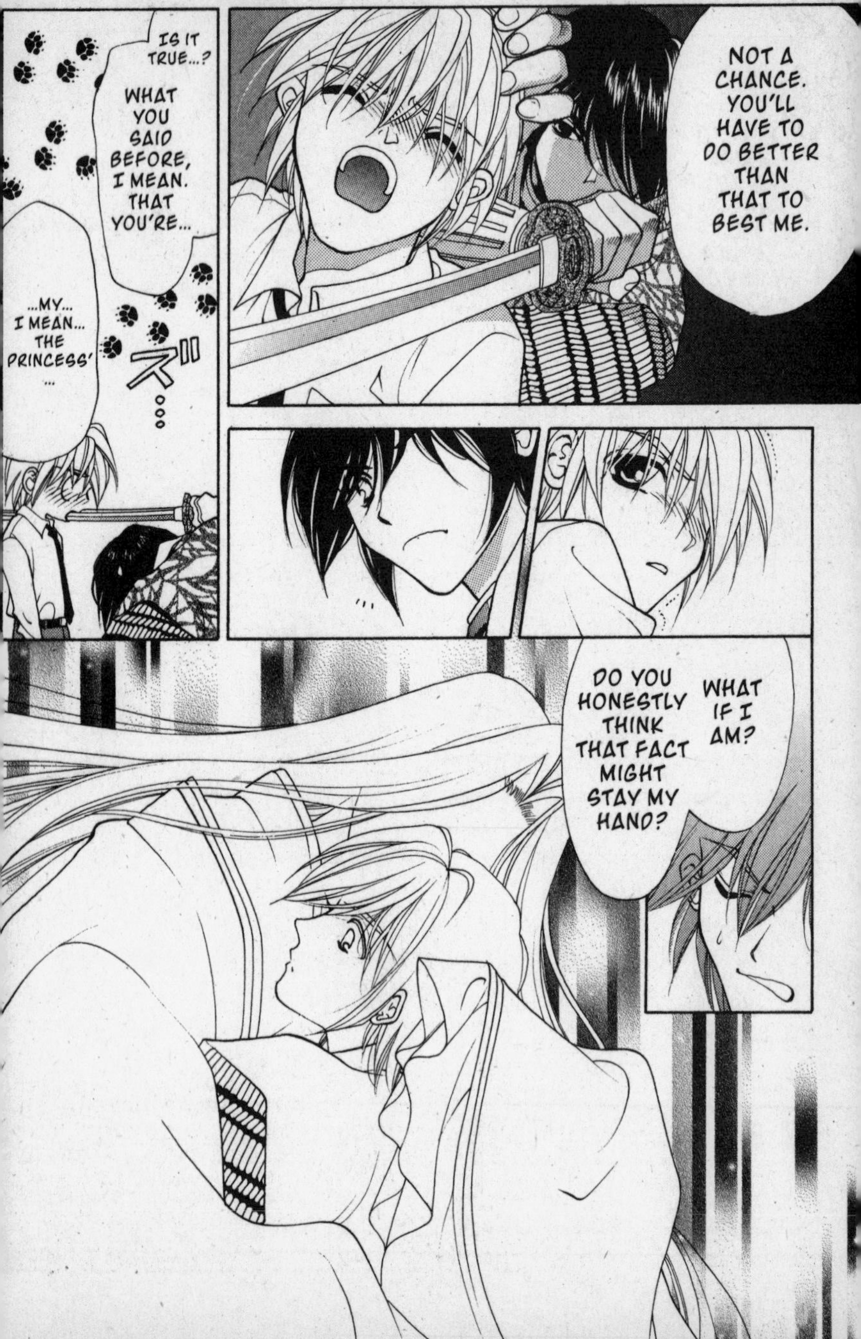
NOT A CHANCE. YOU'LL HAVE TO DO BETTER THAN THAT TO BEST ME.
IS IT TRUE...?
WHAT YOU SAID BEFORE, I MEAN. THAT YOU'RE...
...MY... I MEAN... THE PRINCESS' ...
WHAT IF I AM?
DO YOU HONESTLY THINK THAT FACT MIGHT STAY MY HAND?

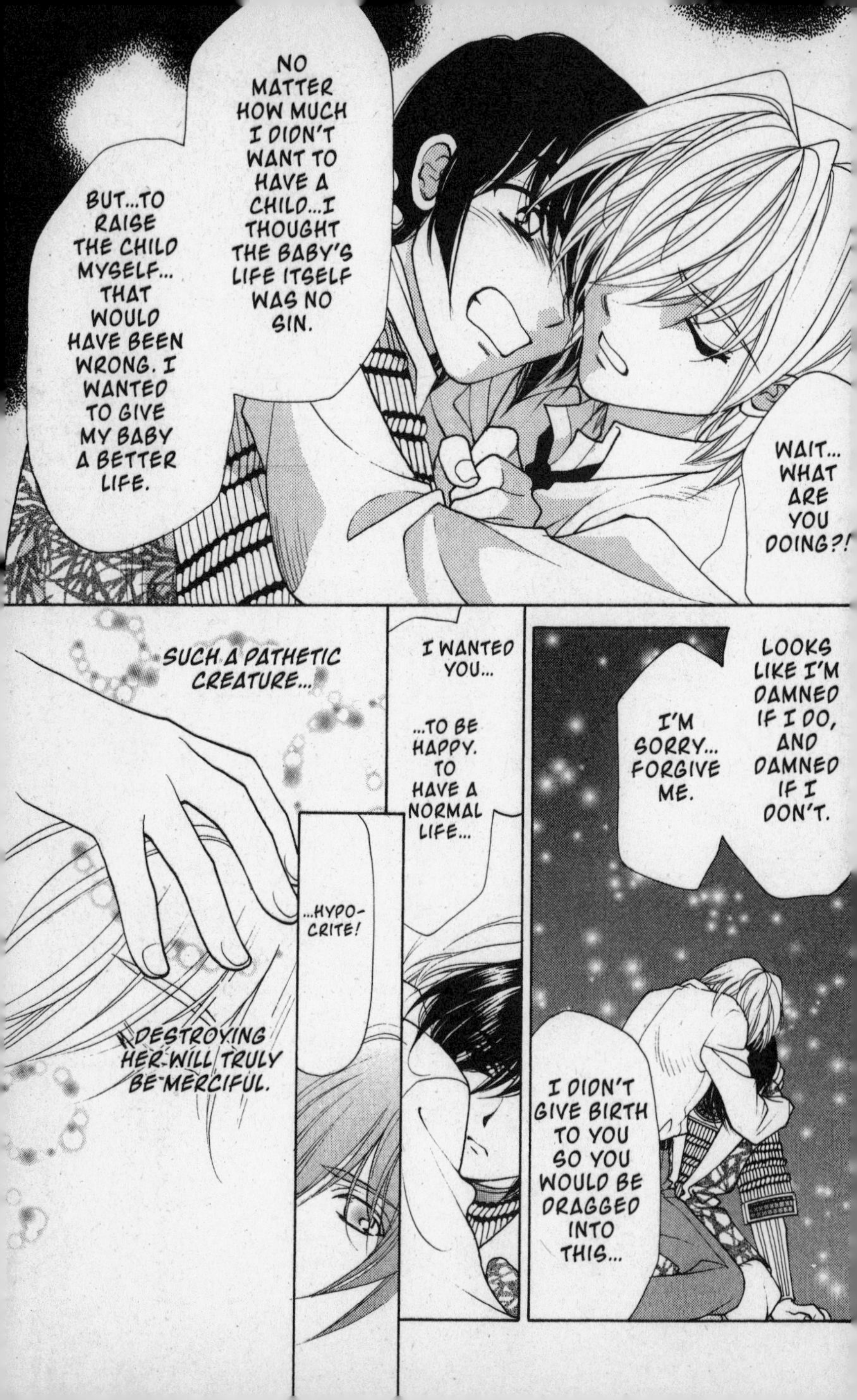
NO MATTER HOW MUCH I DIDN'T WANT TO HAVE A CHILD...I THOUGHT THE BABY'S LIFE ITSELF WAS NO SIN.
BUT...TO RAISE THE CHILD MYSELF... THAT WOULD HAVE BEEN WRONG. I WANTED TO GIVE MY BABY A BETTER LIFE.
WAIT... WHAT ARE YOU DOING?!
LOOKS LIKE I'M DAMNED IF I DO, AND DAMNED IF I DON'T.
I'M SORRY... FORGIVE ME.
I DIDN'T GIVE BIRTH TO YOU SO YOU WOULD BE DRAGGED INTO THIS...
I WANTED YOU...
...TO BE HAPPY. TO HAVE A NORMAL LIFE...
...HYPOCRITE!
SUCH A PATHETIC CREATURE...
DESTROYING HER WILL TRULY BE MERCIFUL.

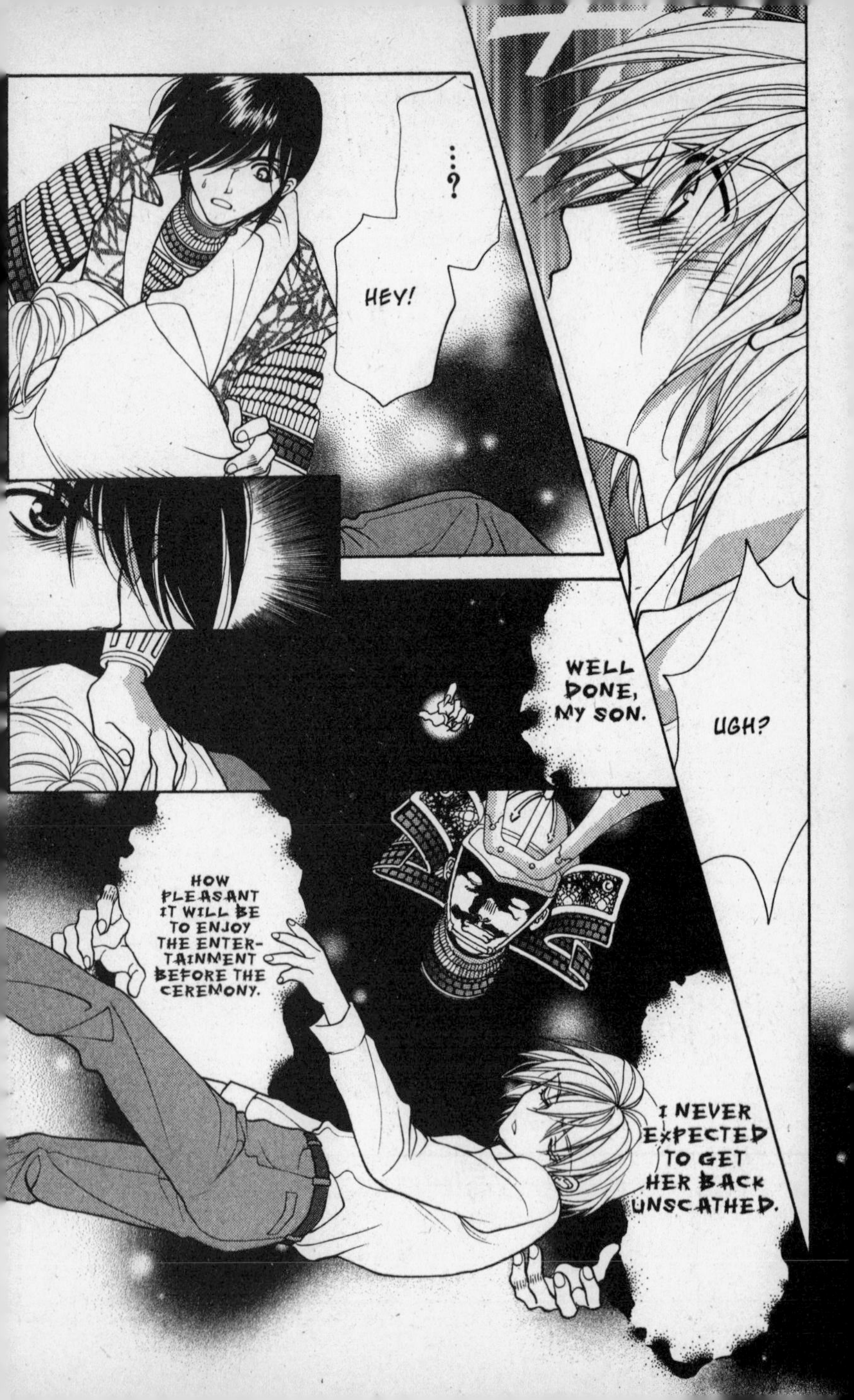
UGH?
...?
HEY!
WELL DONE, MY SON.
I NEVER EXPECTED TO GET HER BACK UNSCATHED.
HOW PLEASANT IT WILL BE TO ENJOY THE ENTER-TAINMENT BEFORE THE CEREMONY.

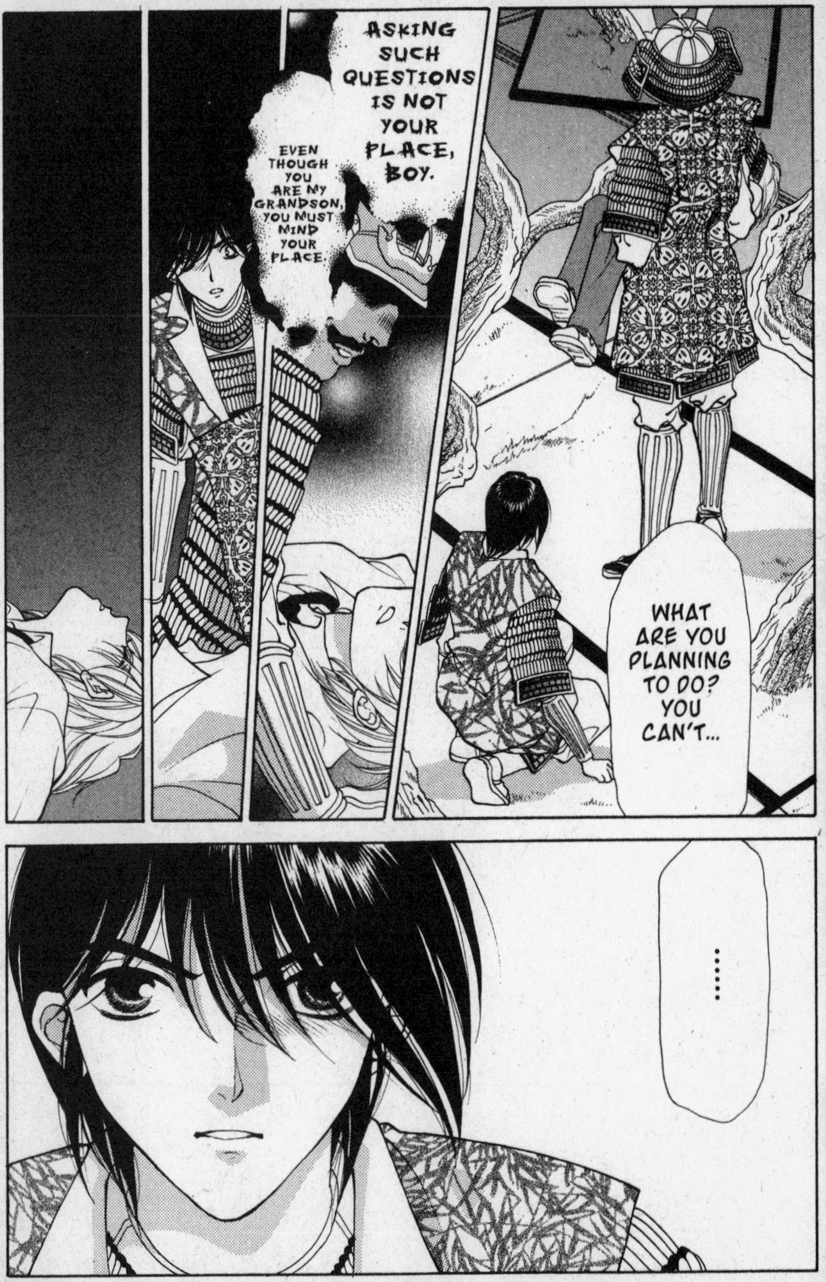
WHAT ARE YOU PLANNING TO DO? YOU CAN'T...
ASKING SUCH QUESTIONS IS NOT YOUR PLACE, BOY.
EVEN THOUGH YOU ARE MY GRANDSON, YOU MUST MIND YOUR PLACE.
......

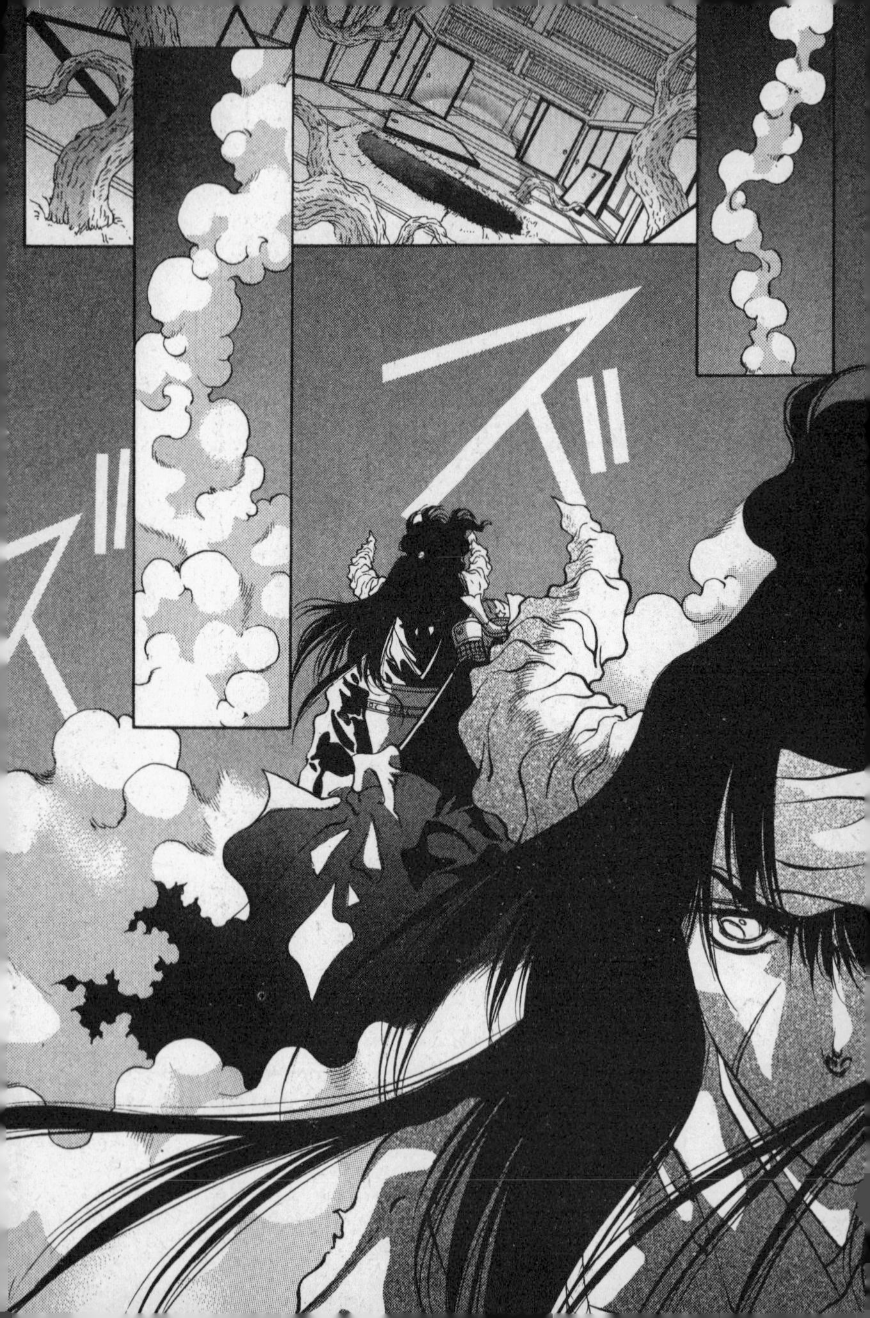
ズ
ズ

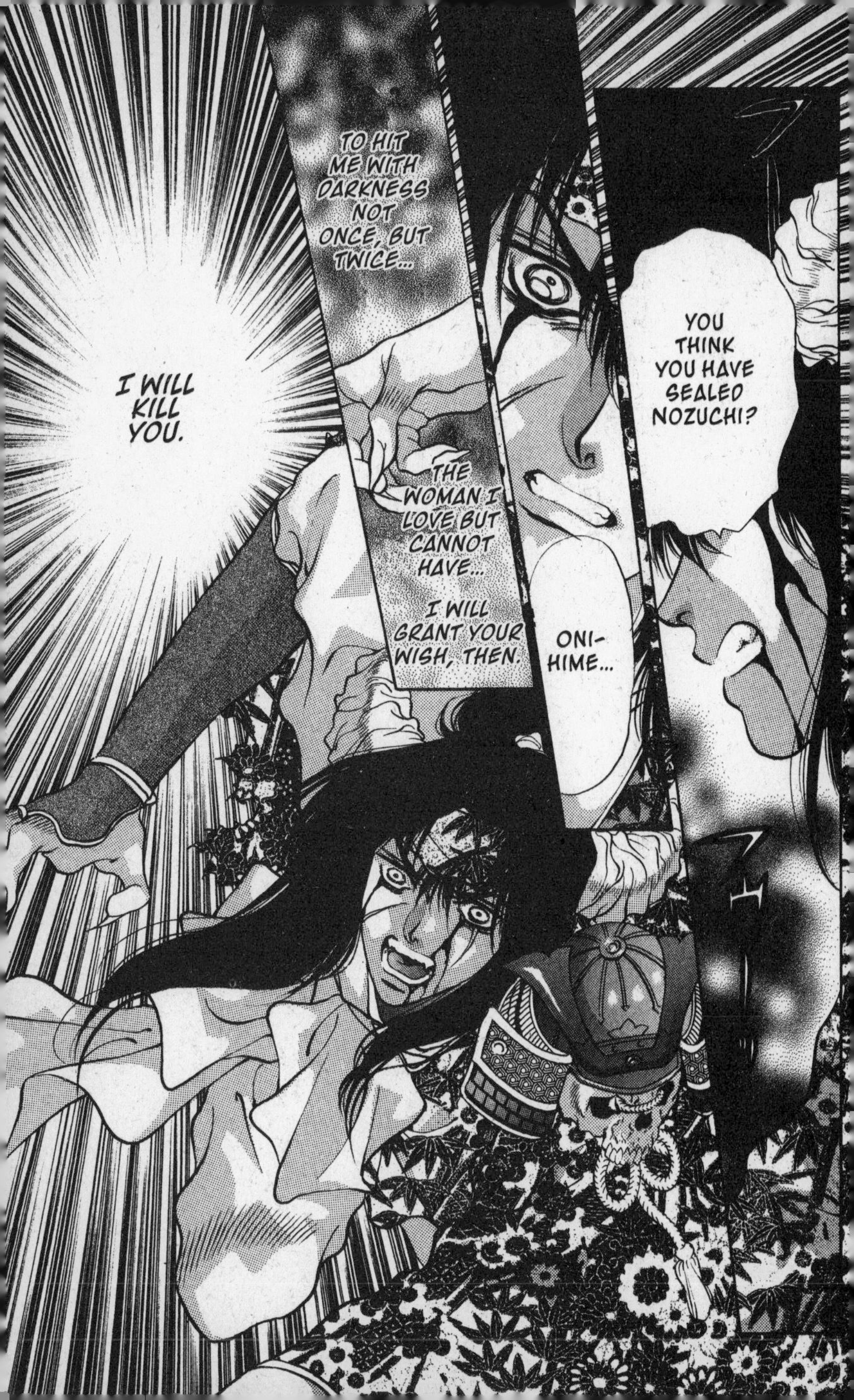
YOU THINK YOU HAVE SEALED NOZUCHI?
ONI-HIME...
TO HIT ME WITH DARKNESS NOT ONCE, BUT TWICE...
THE WOMAN I LOVE BUT CANNOT HAVE...
I WILL GRANT YOUR WISH, THEN.
I WILL KILL YOU.

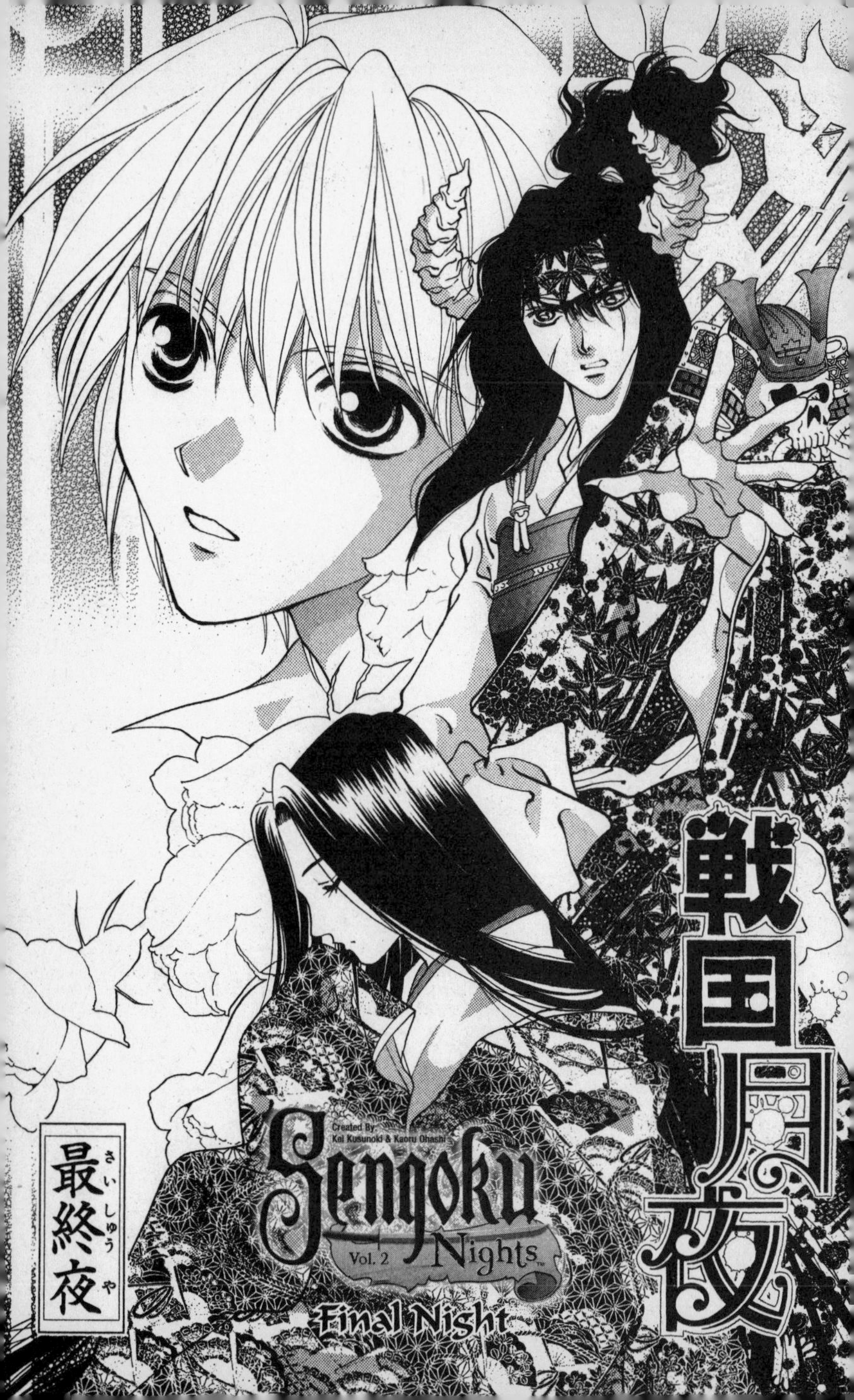
戦国月夜
Sengoku Nights
Vol. 2
Created By
Kei Kusunoki & Kaoru Ohashi
最終夜
Final Night

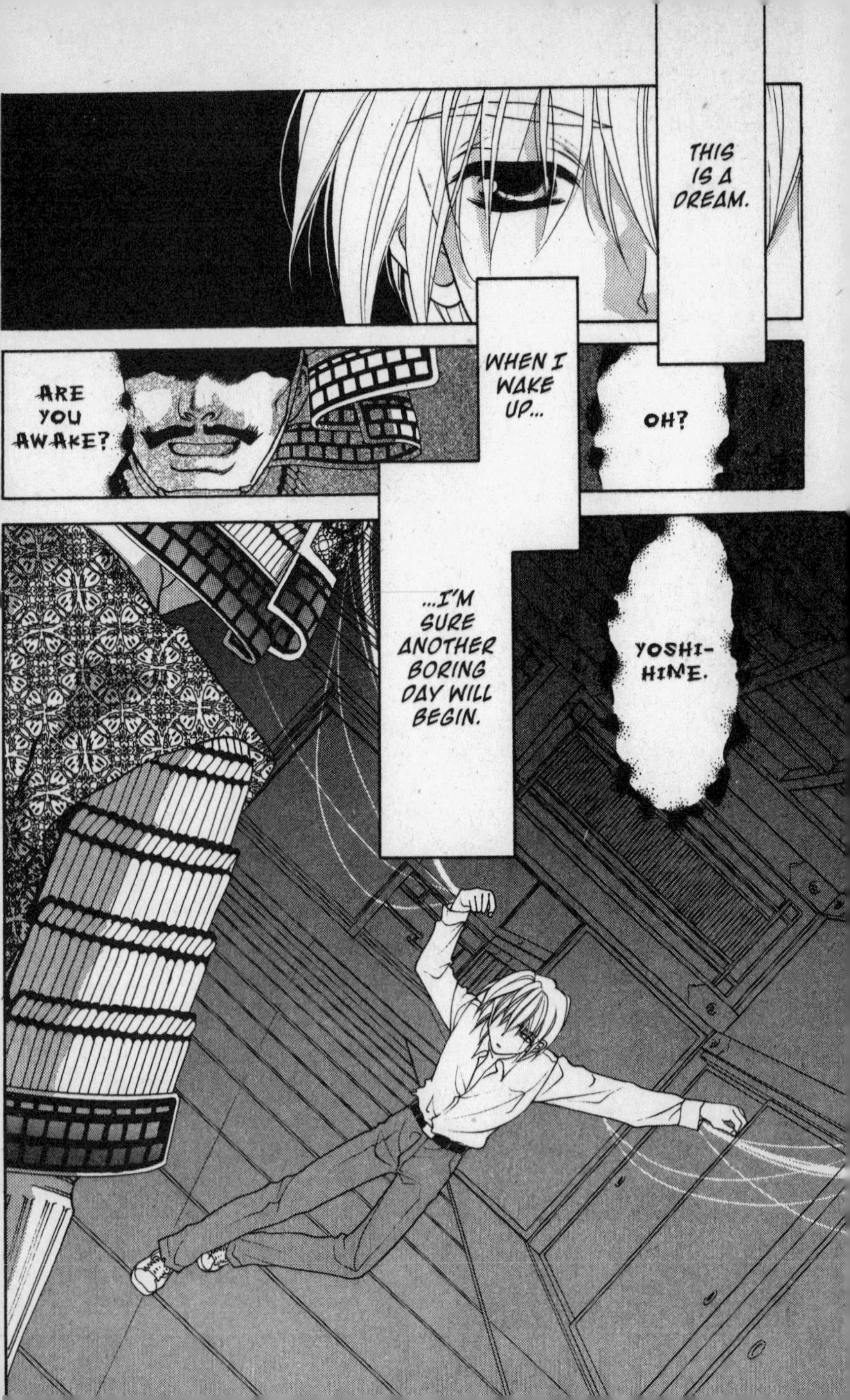
THIS IS A DREAM.
OH?
WHEN I WAKE UP...
ARE YOU AWAKE?
YOSHI-HIME.
...I'M SURE ANOTHER BORING DAY WILL BEGIN.

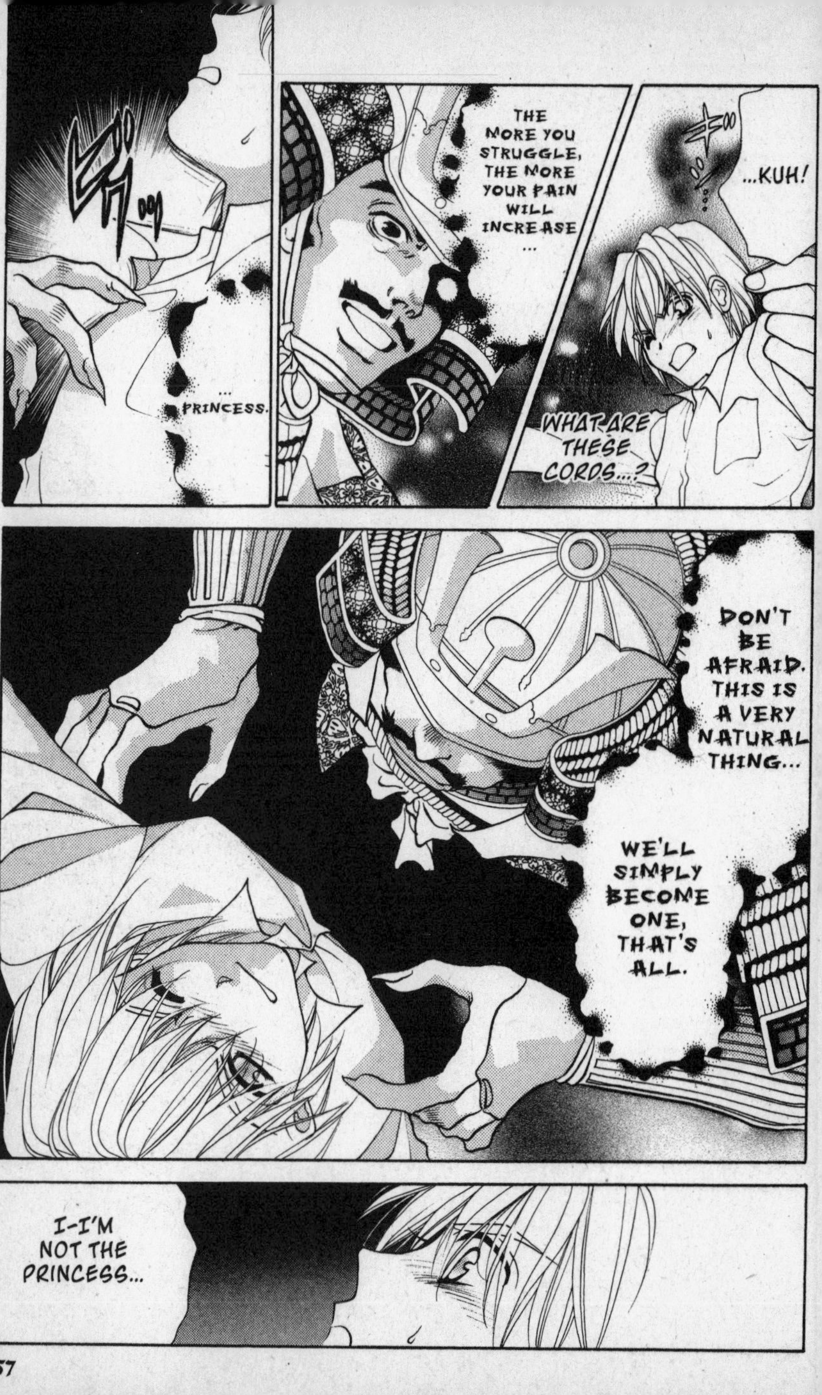
...KUH!
WHAT ARE THESE CORDS...?
THE MORE YOU STRUGGLE, THE MORE YOUR PAIN WILL INCREASE ...
... PRINCESS.
DON'T BE AFRAID. THIS IS A VERY NATURAL THING...
WE'LL SIMPLY BECOME ONE, THAT'S ALL.
I-I'M NOT THE PRINCESS...

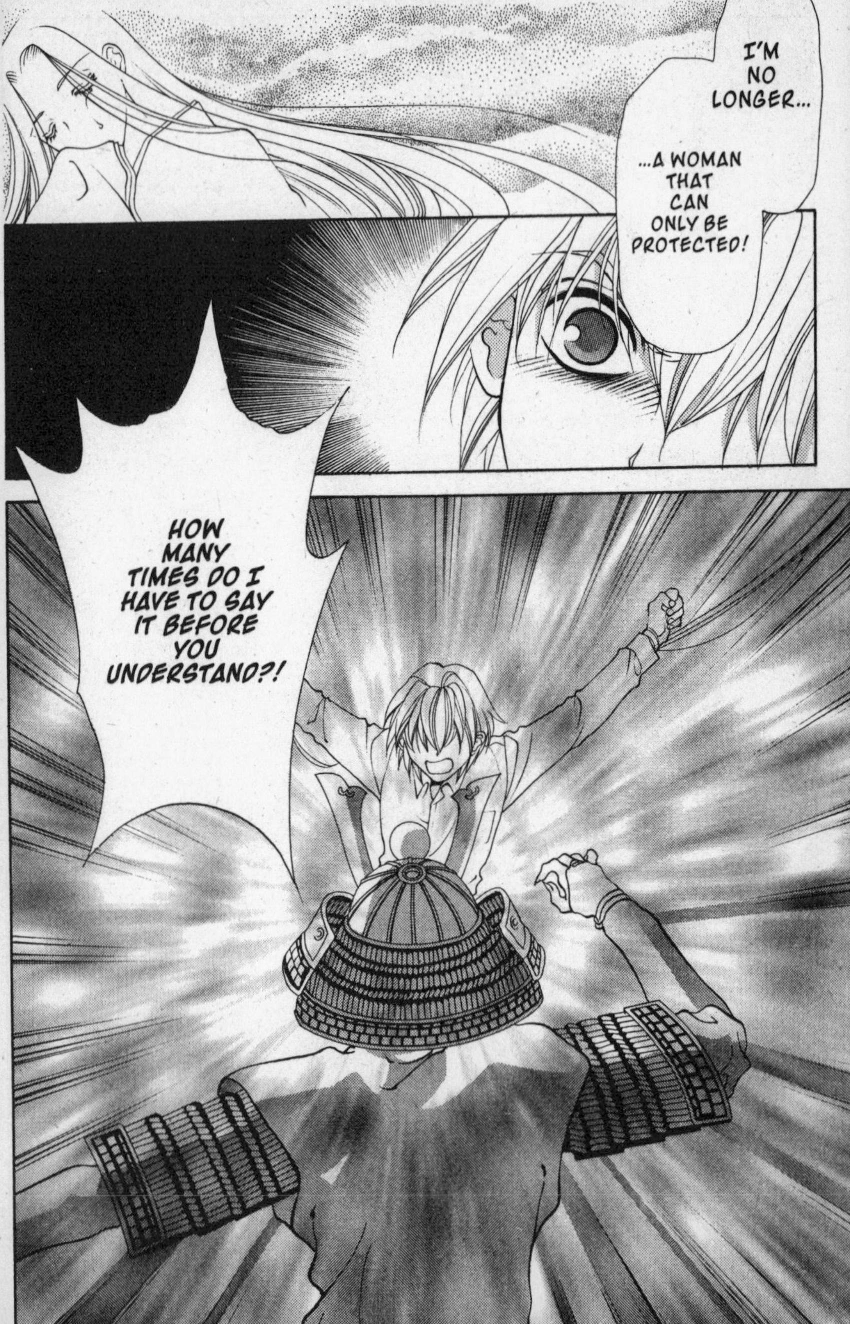
I'M NO LONGER...
...A WOMAN THAT CAN ONLY BE PROTECTED!
HOW MANY TIMES DO I HAVE TO SAY IT BEFORE YOU UNDERSTAND?!

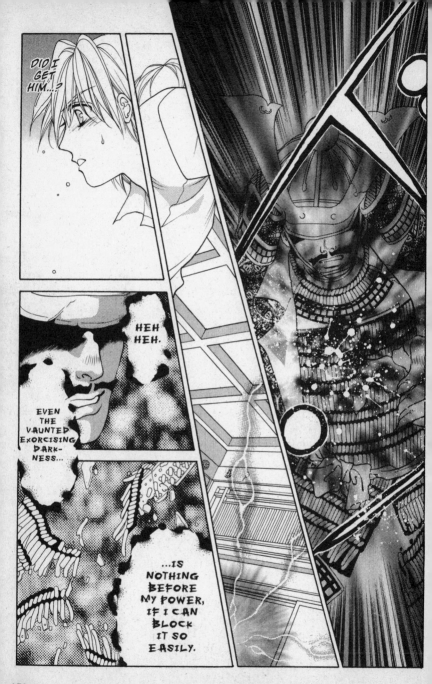

DID I GET HIM...?

HEH HEH.

EVEN THE VAUNTED EXORCISING DARKNESS...

...IS NOTHING BEFORE MY POWER, IF I CAN BLOCK IT SO EASILY.

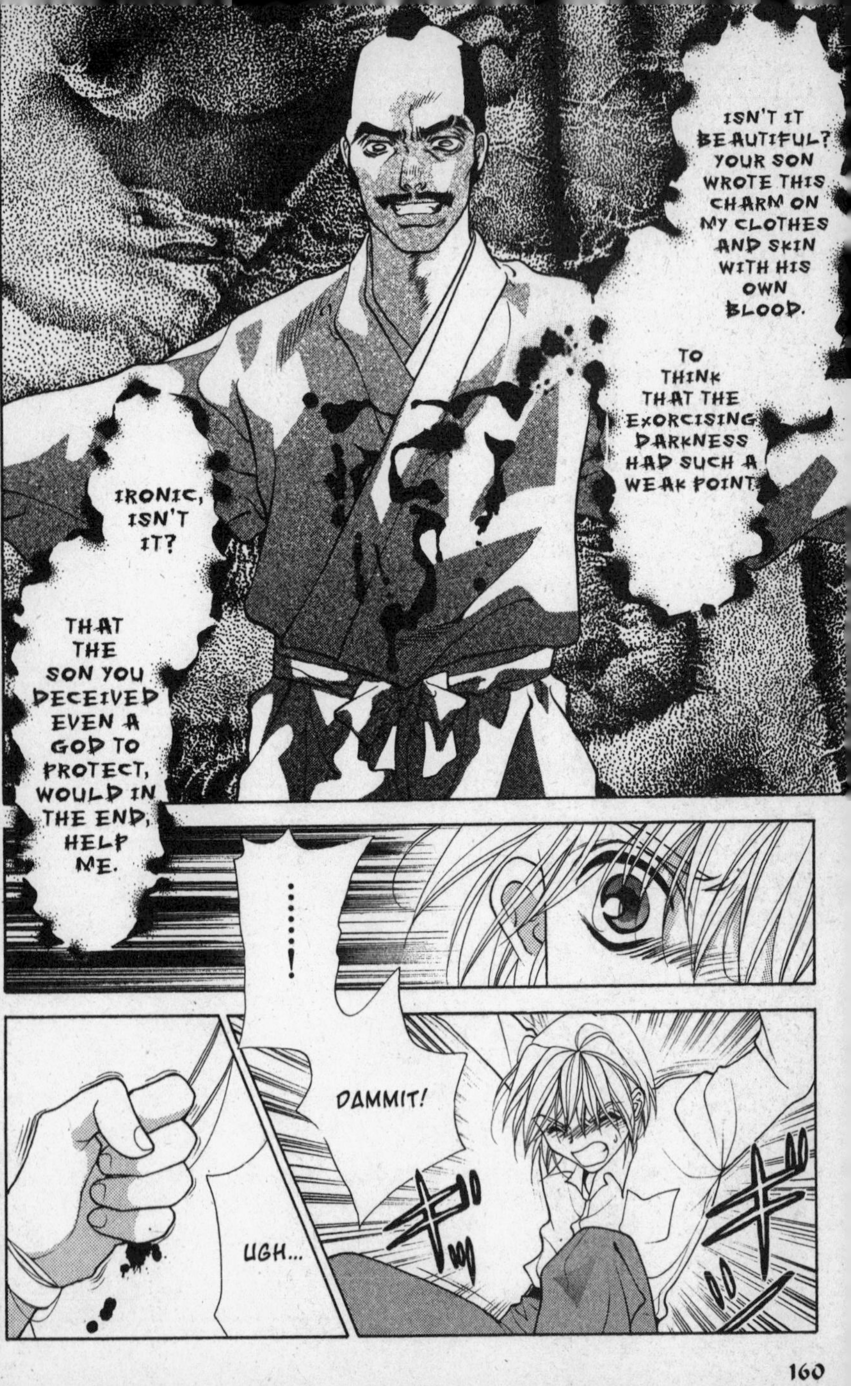
ISN'T IT BEAUTIFUL? YOUR SON WROTE THIS CHARM ON MY CLOTHES AND SKIN WITH HIS OWN BLOOD.
TO THINK THAT THE EXORCISING DARKNESS HAD SUCH A WEAK POINT.
IRONIC, ISN'T IT?
THAT THE SON YOU DECEIVED EVEN A GOD TO PROTECT, WOULD IN THE END, HELP ME.
......!
DAMMIT!
UGH...

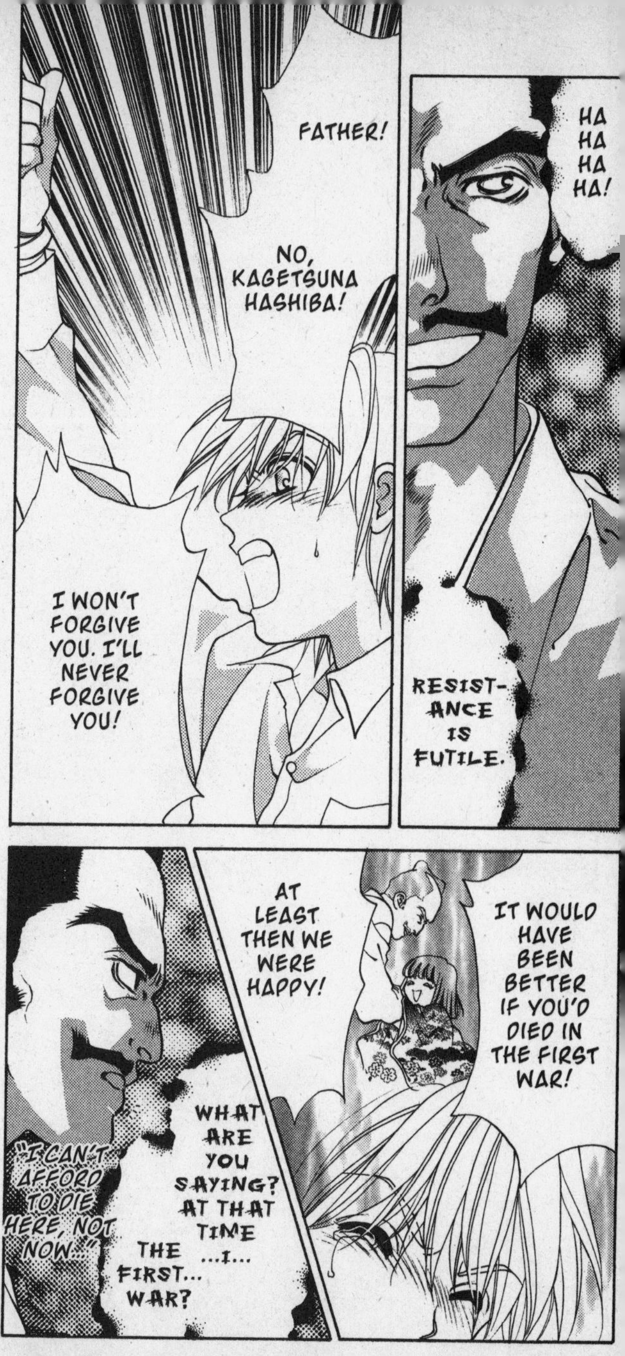
HA HA HA HA!
RESISTANCE IS FUTILE.
FATHER!
NO, KAGETSUNA HASHIBA!
I WON'T FORGIVE YOU. I'LL NEVER FORGIVE YOU!
IT WOULD HAVE BEEN BETTER IF YOU'D DIED IN THE FIRST WAR!
AT LEAST THEN WE WERE HAPPY!
WHAT ARE YOU SAYING? AT THAT TIME ...I...
THE FIRST... WAR?
"I CAN'T AFFORD TO DIE HERE, NOT NOW..."
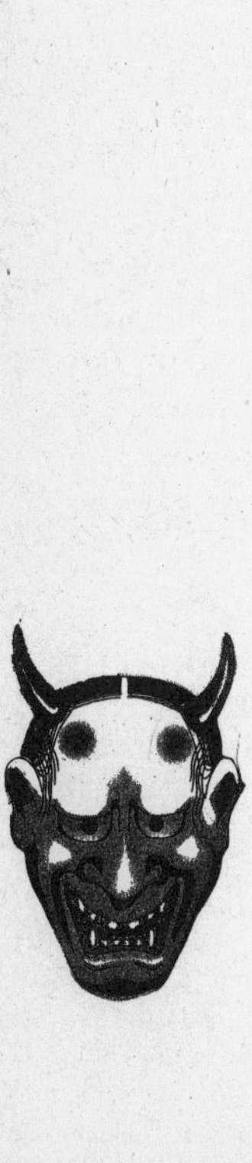

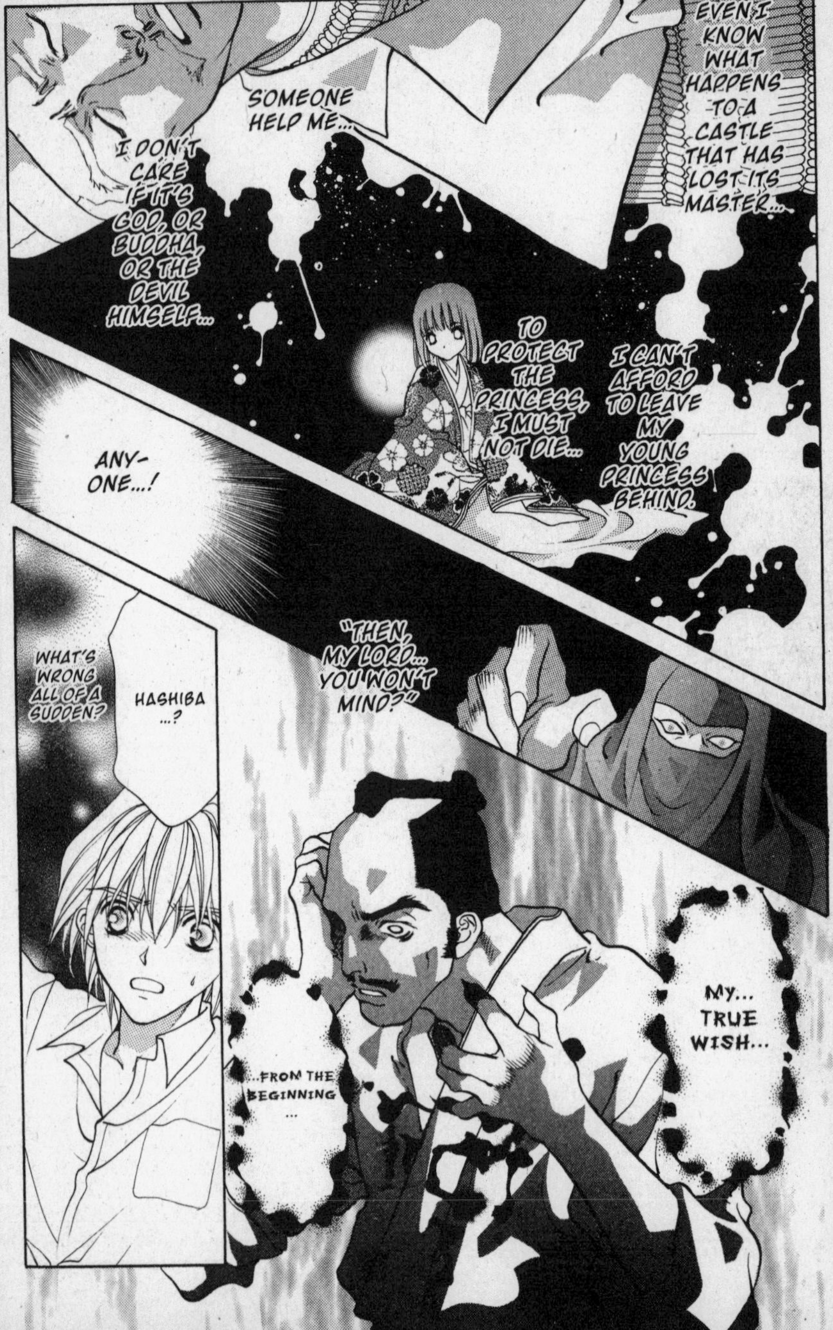
EVEN I KNOW WHAT HAPPENS TO A CASTLE THAT HAS LOST ITS MASTER...
SOMEONE HELP ME...
I DON'T CARE IF IT'S GOD, OR BUDDHA, OR THE DEVIL HIMSELF...
I CAN'T AFFORD TO LEAVE MY YOUNG PRINCESS BEHIND.
TO PROTECT THE PRINCESS, I MUST NOT DIE...
ANY-ONE...!
"THEN, MY LORD... YOU WON'T MIND?"
MY... TRUE WISH...
...FROM THE BEGINNING...
HASHIBA ...?
WHAT'S WRONG ALL OF A SUDDEN?

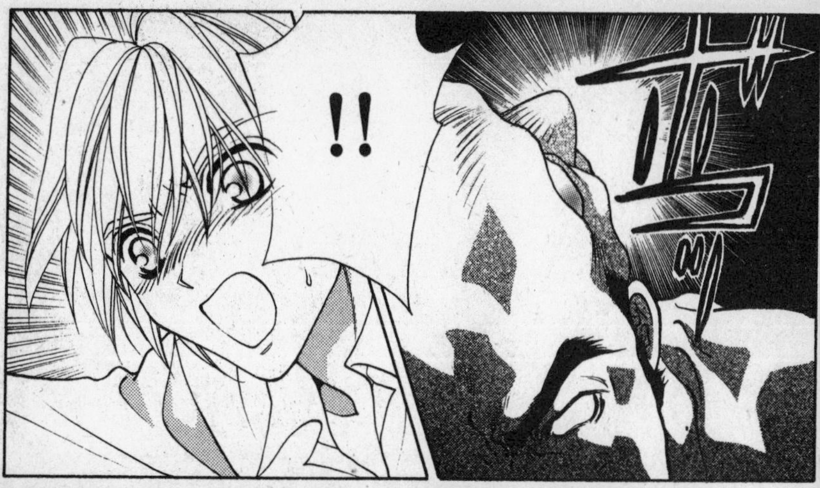
!!

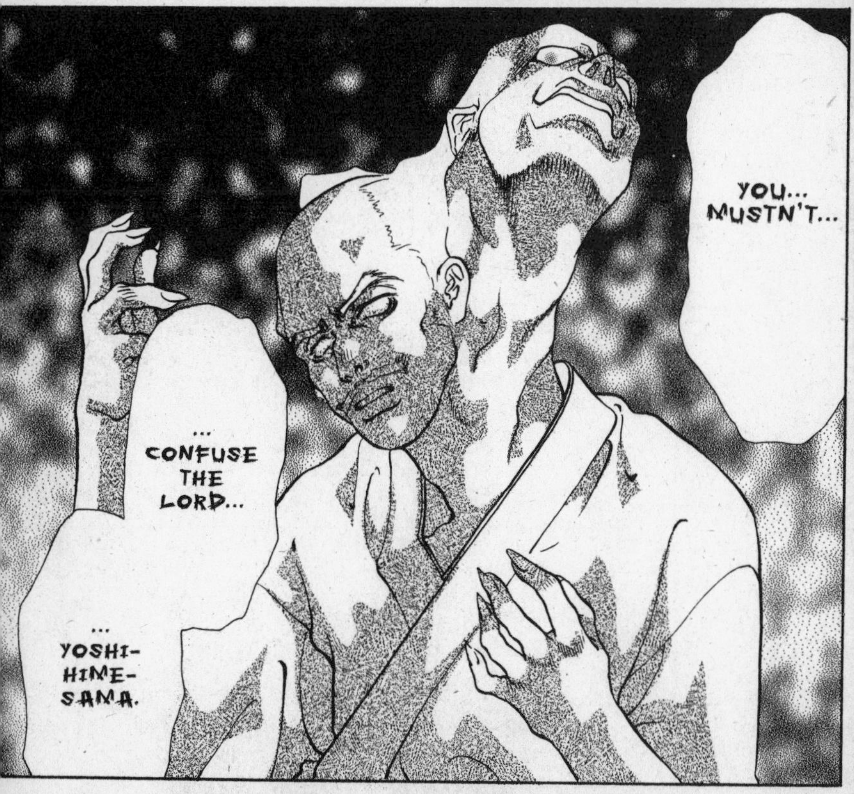
YOU... MUSTN'T...
...CONFUSE THE LORD...
...YOSHI-HIME-SAMA.

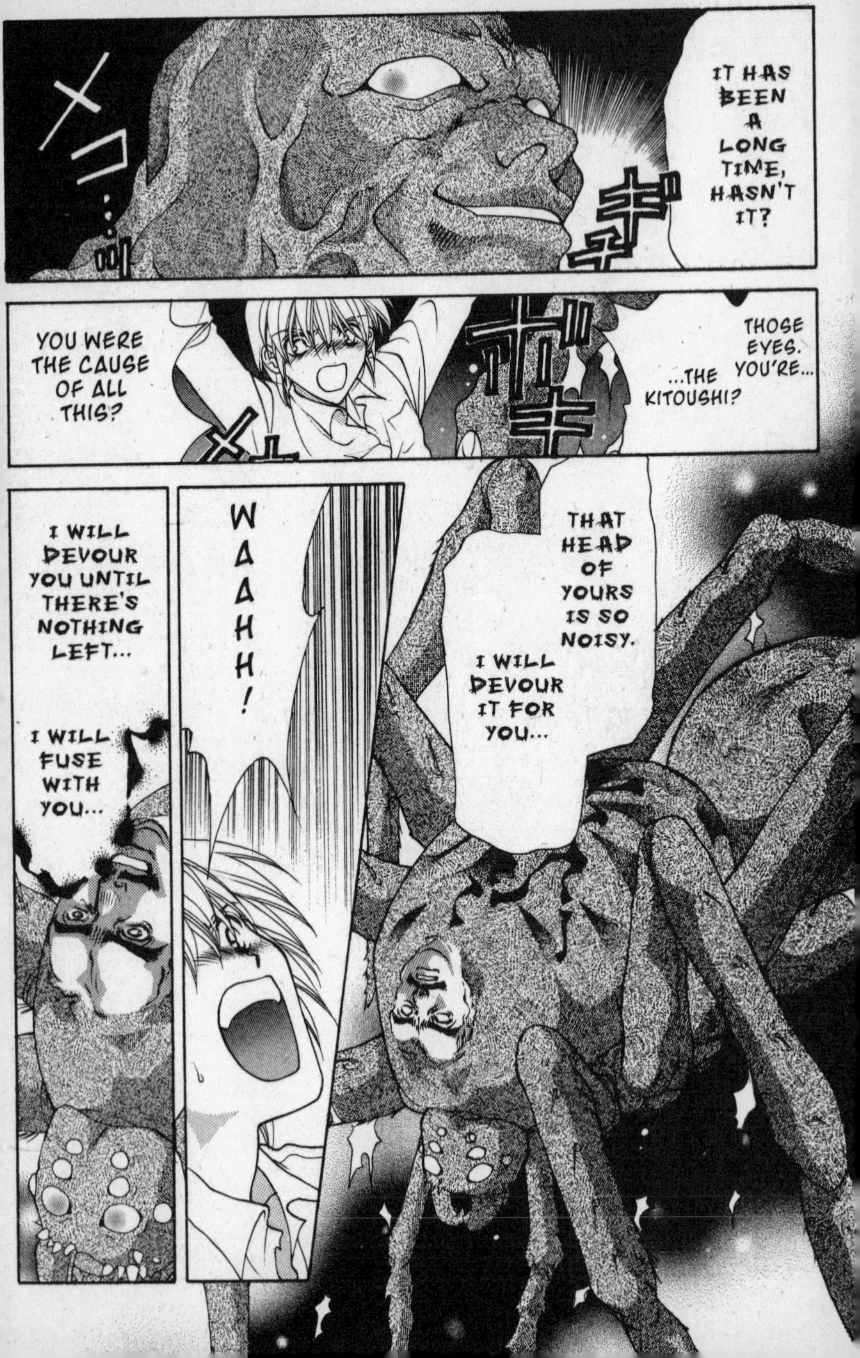
IT HAS BEEN A LONG TIME, HASN'T IT?
THOSE EYES. YOU'RE...
...THE KITOUSHI?
YOU WERE THE CAUSE OF ALL THIS?
THAT HEAD OF YOURS IS SO NOISY.
I WILL DEVOUR IT FOR YOU...
WAAHH!
I WILL DEVOUR YOU UNTIL THERE'S NOTHING LEFT...
I WILL FUSE WITH YOU...

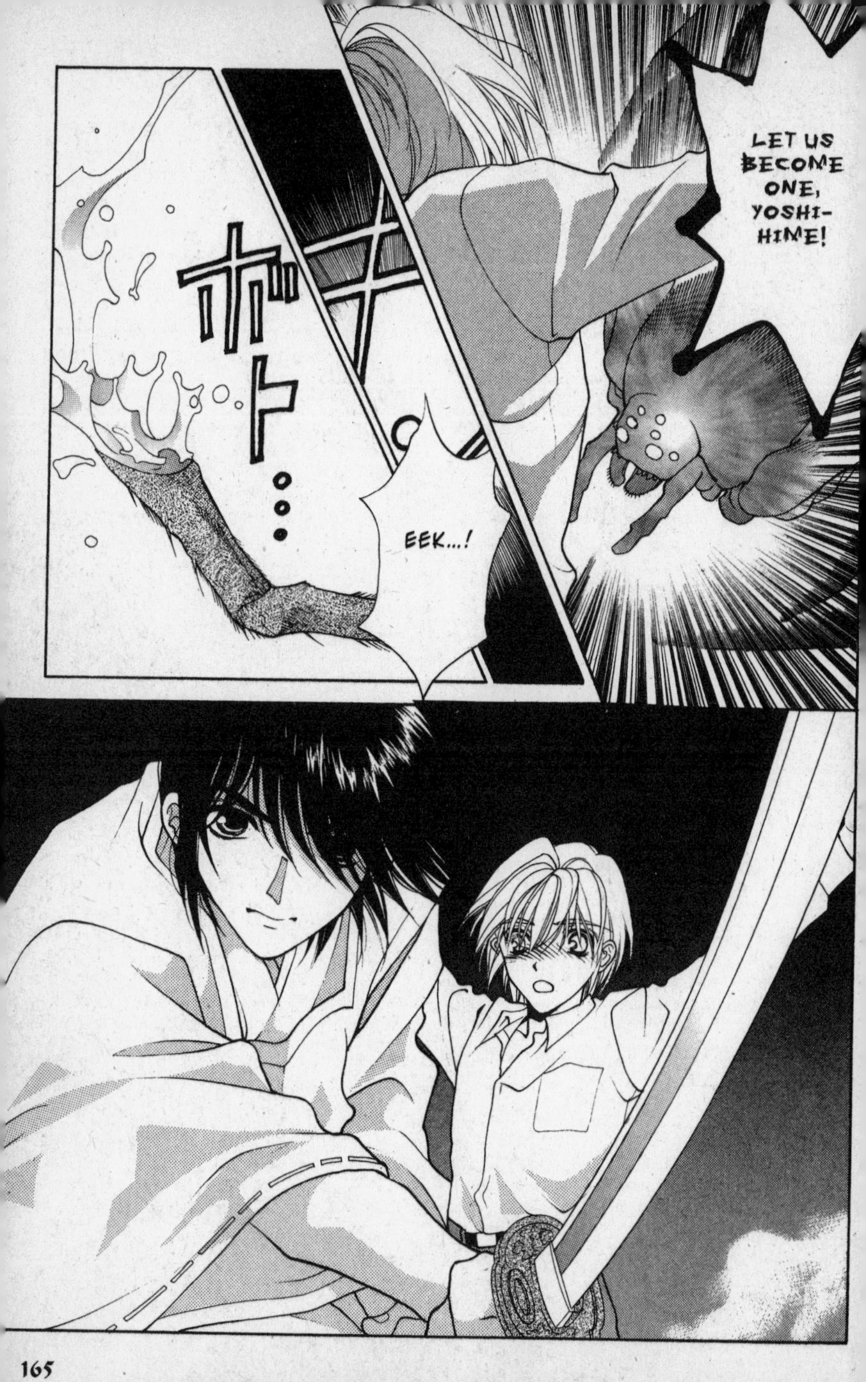
LET US BECOME ONE, YOSHI-HIME!
EEK...!
ボト…

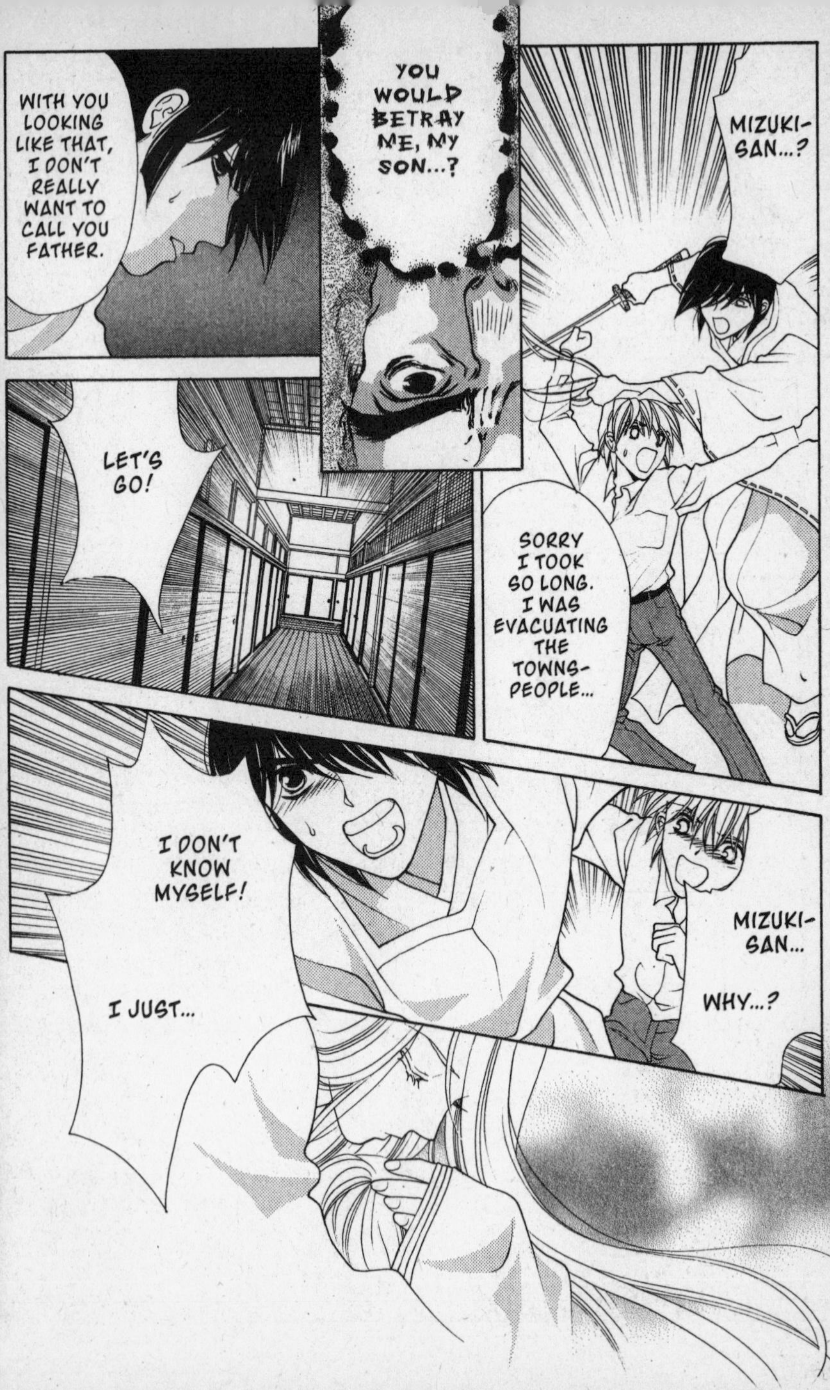
MIZUKI-SAN...?
SORRY I TOOK SO LONG. I WAS EVACUATING THE TOWNS-PEOPLE...
YOU WOULD BETRAY ME, MY SON...?
WITH YOU LOOKING LIKE THAT, I DON'T REALLY WANT TO CALL YOU FATHER.
LET'S GO!
MIZUKI-SAN...
WHY...?
I DON'T KNOW MYSELF!
I JUST...

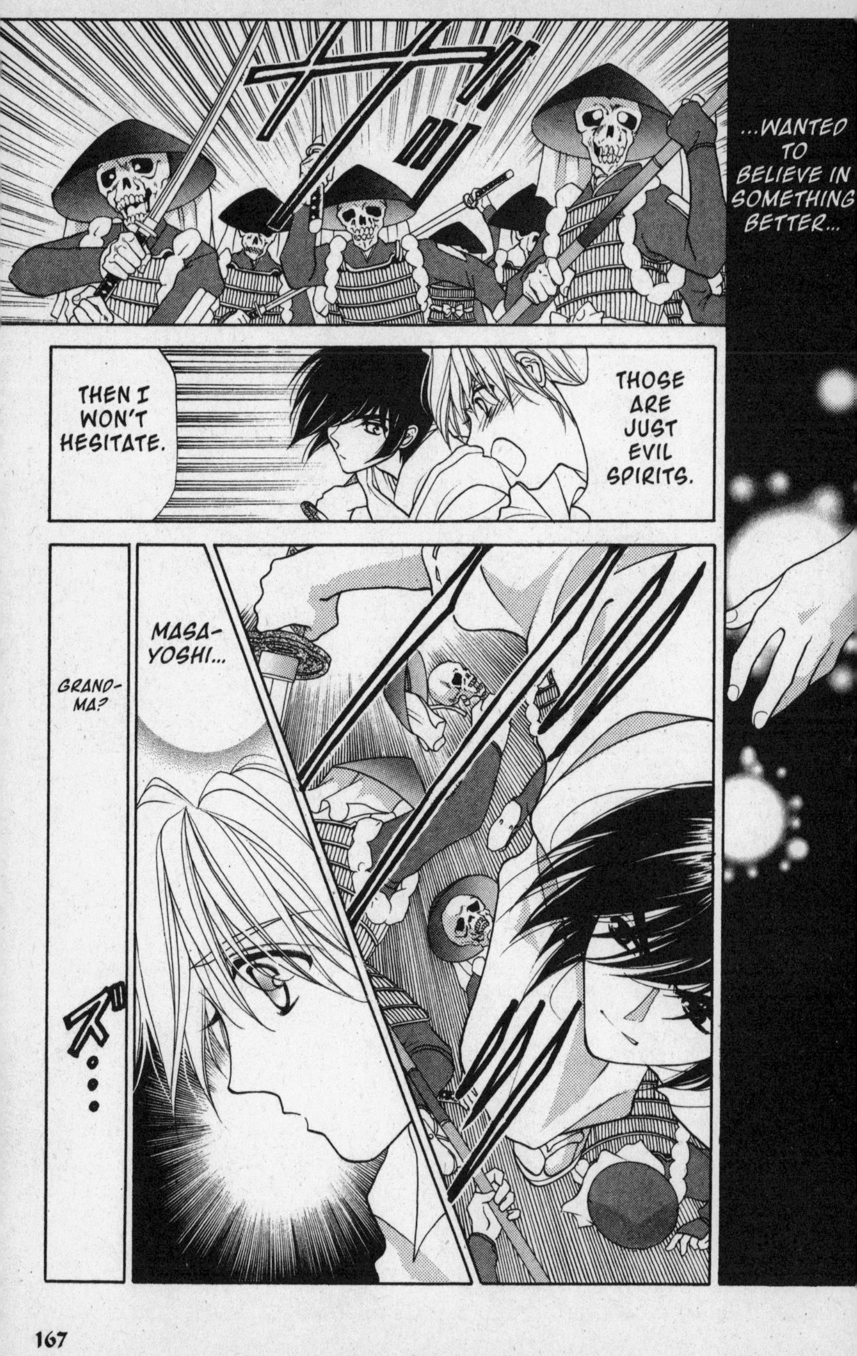
...WANTED TO BELIEVE IN SOMETHING BETTER...
THOSE ARE JUST EVIL SPIRITS.
THEN I WON'T HESITATE.
MASA-YOSHI...
GRAND-MA?

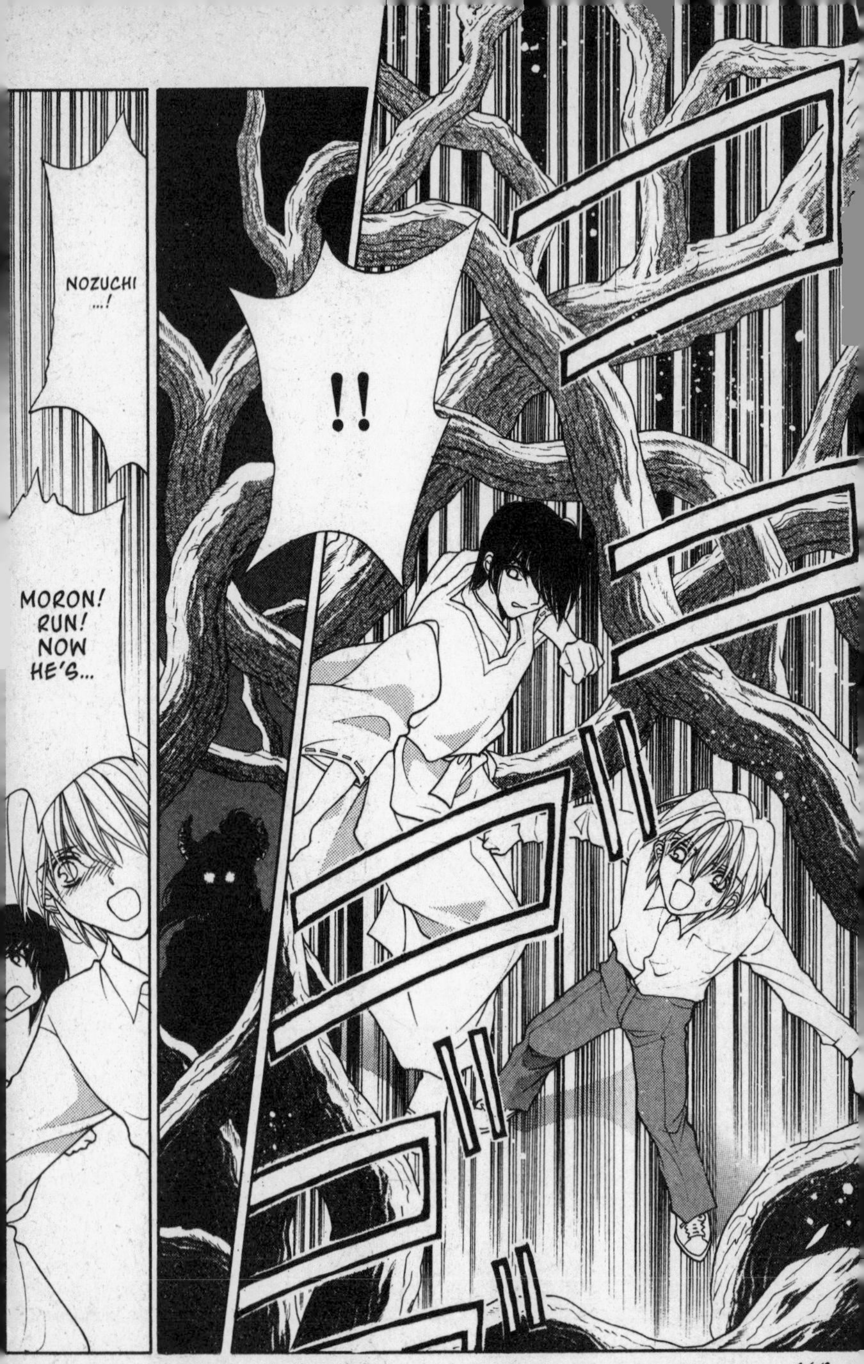
!!
NOZUCHI ...!
MORON! RUN! NOW HE'S...

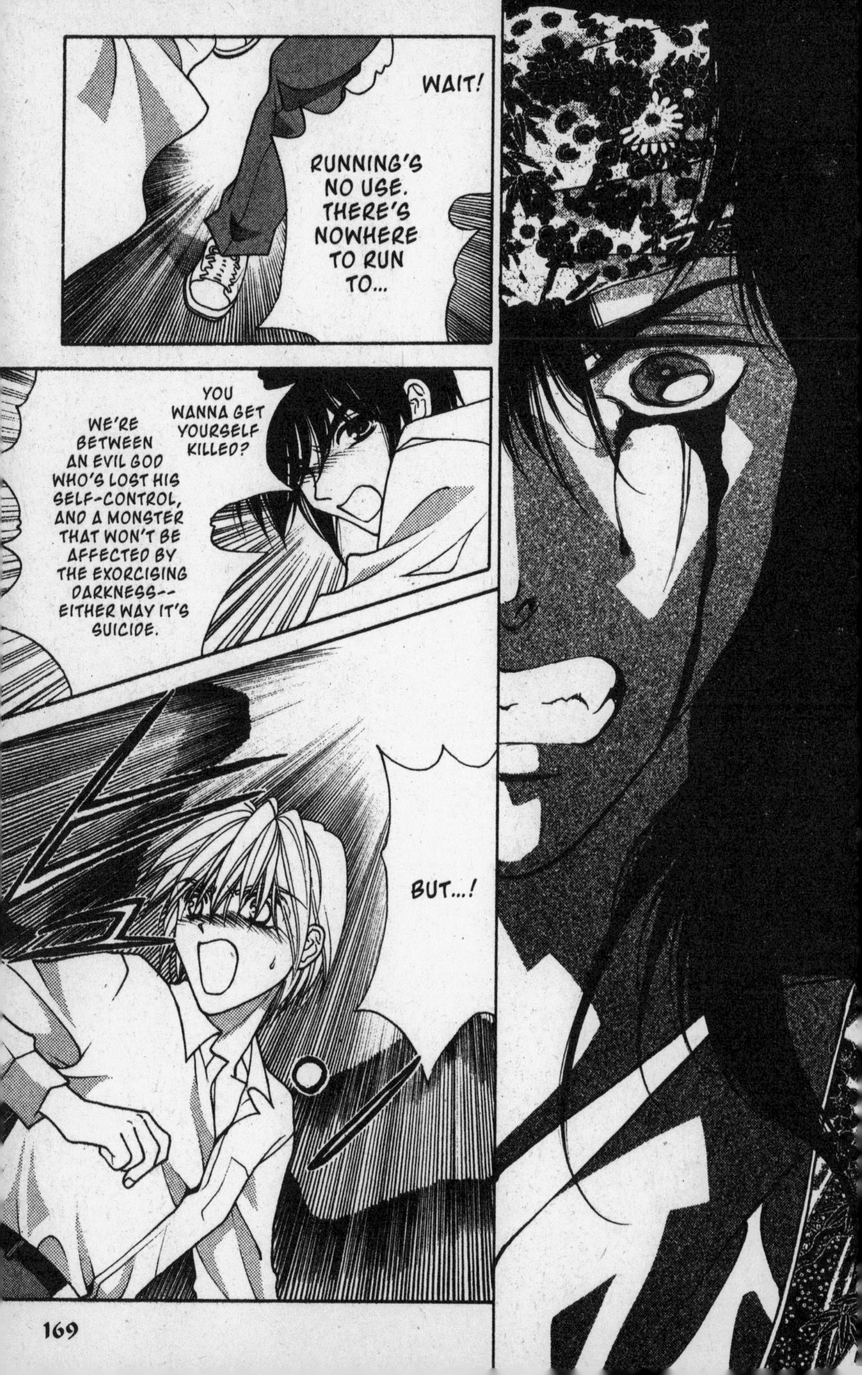
WAIT!
RUNNING'S NO USE. THERE'S NOWHERE TO RUN TO...
YOU WANNA GET YOURSELF KILLED?
WE'RE BETWEEN AN EVIL GOD WHO'S LOST HIS SELF-CONTROL, AND A MONSTER THAT WON'T BE AFFECTED BY THE EXORCISING DARKNESS--EITHER WAY IT'S SUICIDE.
BUT...!

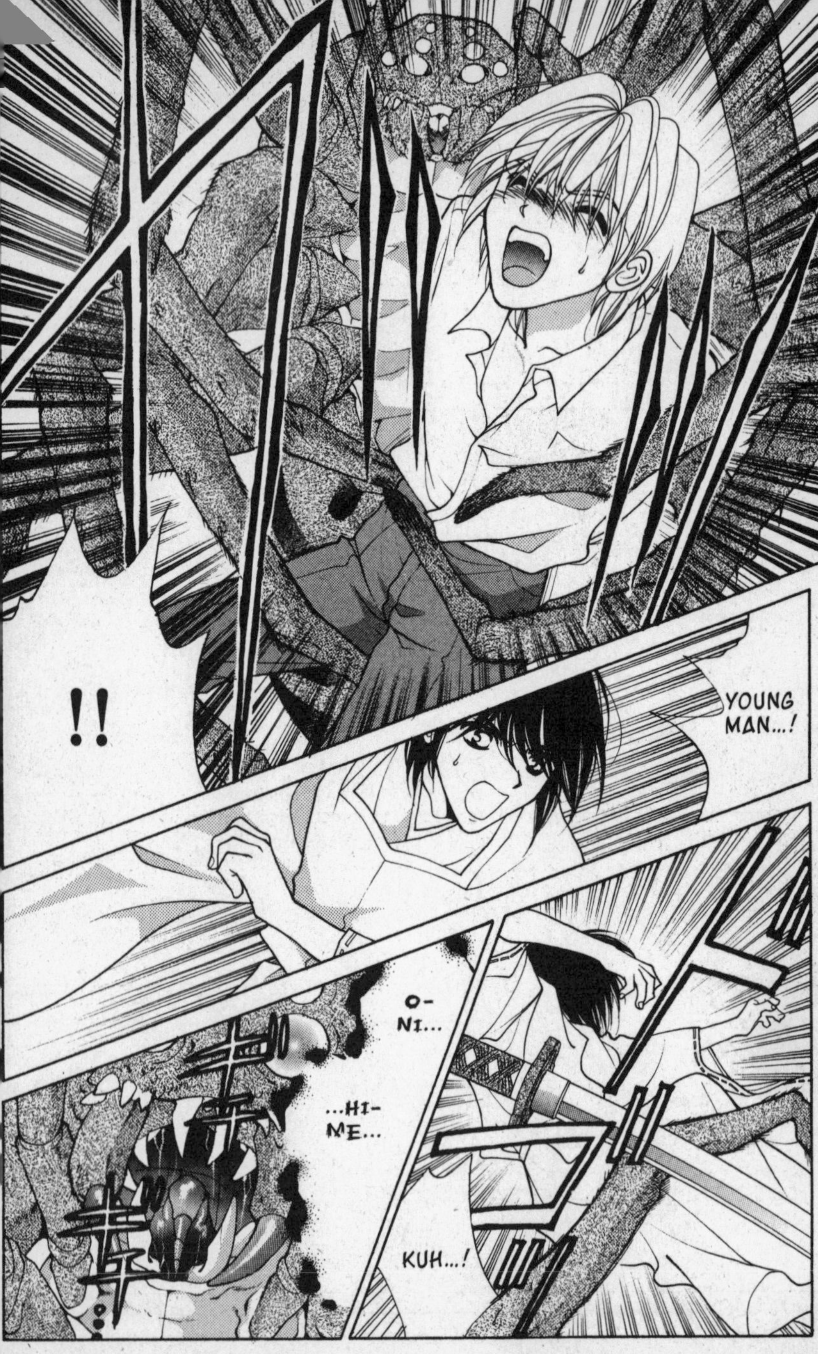
!!
YOUNG MAN...!
KUH...!
O-NI...
...HI-ME...

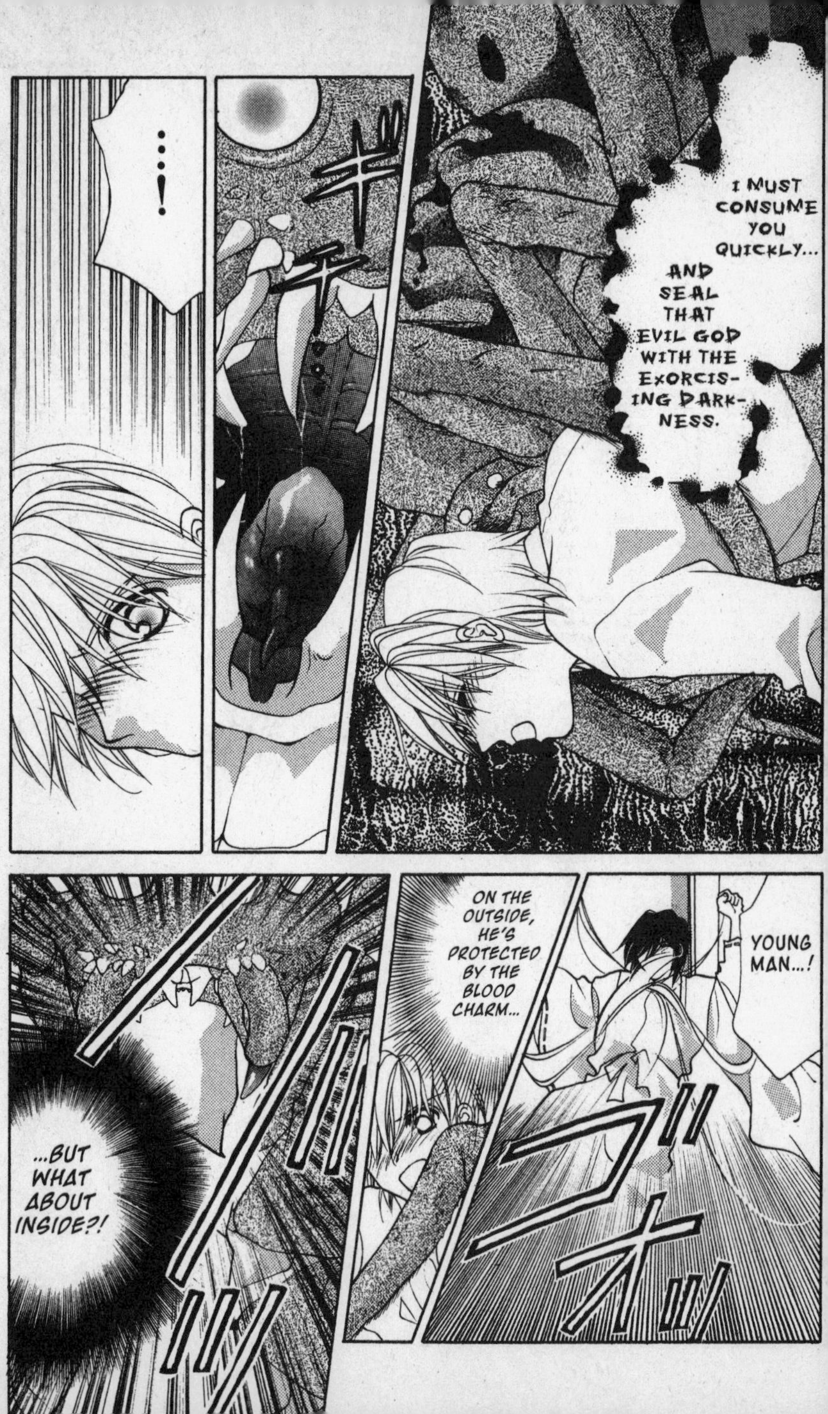

I MUST CONSUME YOU QUICKLY...
AND SEAL THAT EVIL GOD WITH THE EXORCISING DARKNESS.
...!
YOUNG MAN...!
ON THE OUTSIDE, HE'S PROTECTED BY THE BLOOD CHARM...
...BUT WHAT ABOUT INSIDE?!

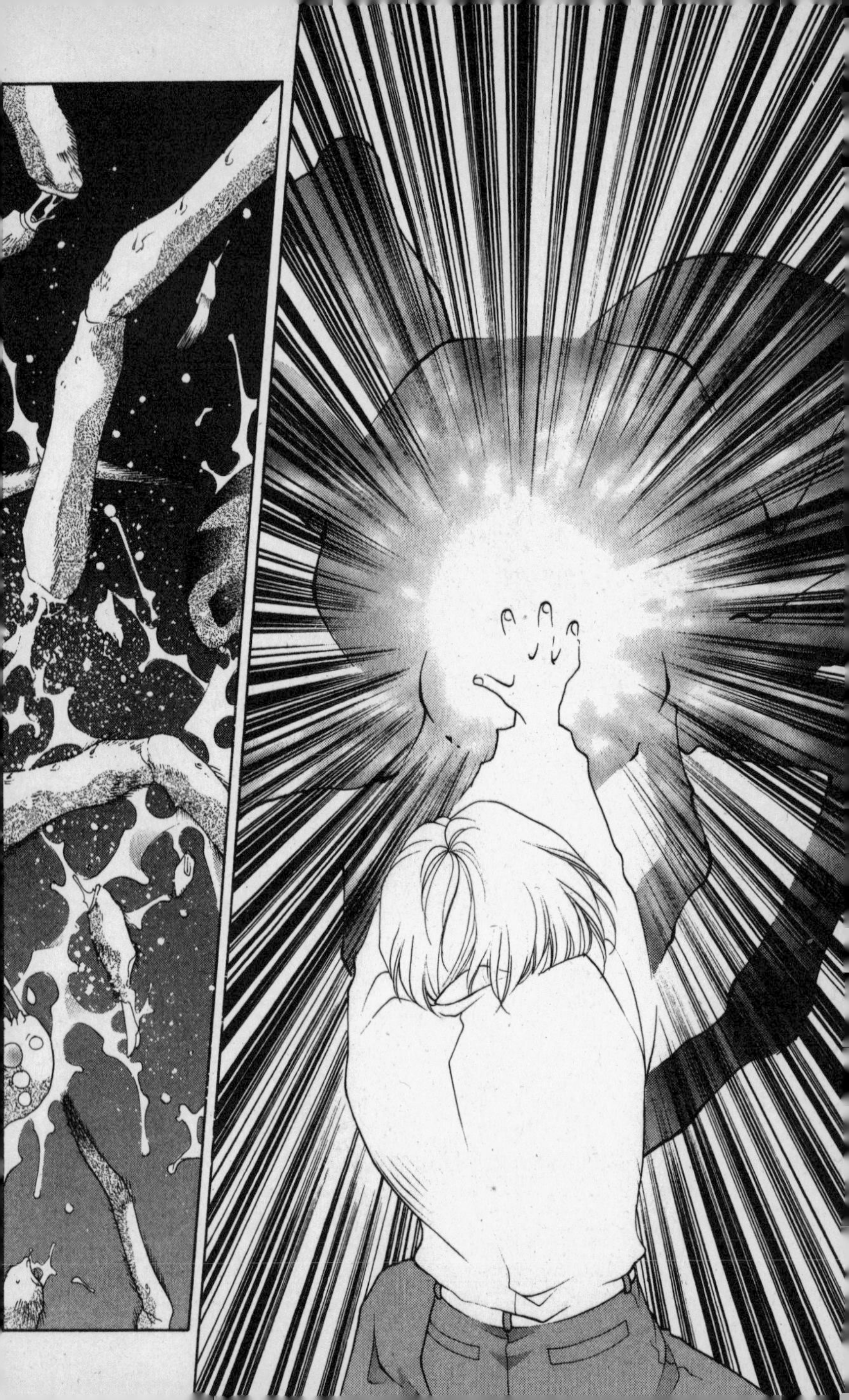

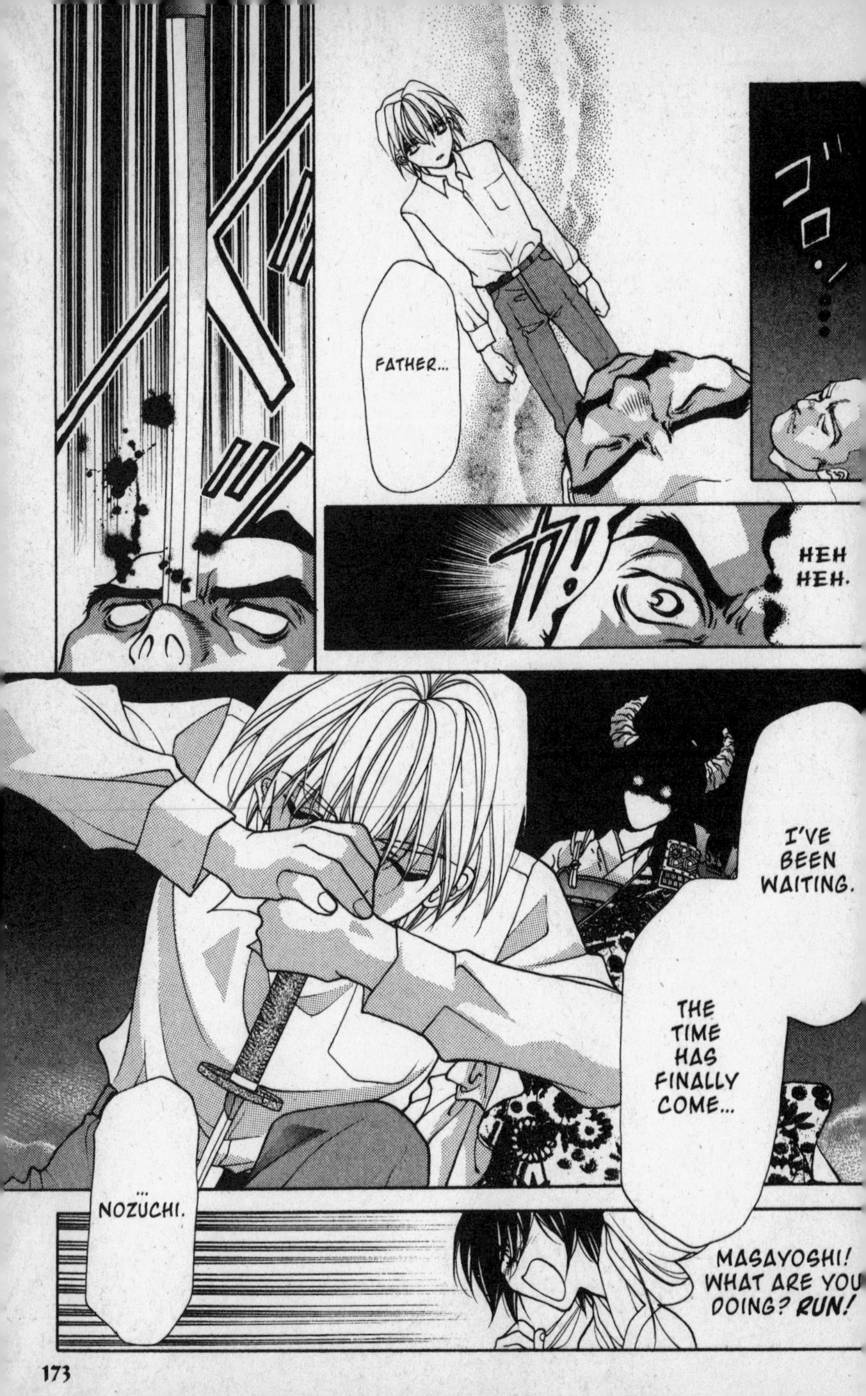
FATHER...
カッ!
HEH HEH.
I'VE BEEN WAITING.
THE TIME HAS FINALLY COME...
... NOZUCHI.
MASAYOSHI! WHAT ARE YOU DOING? RUN!

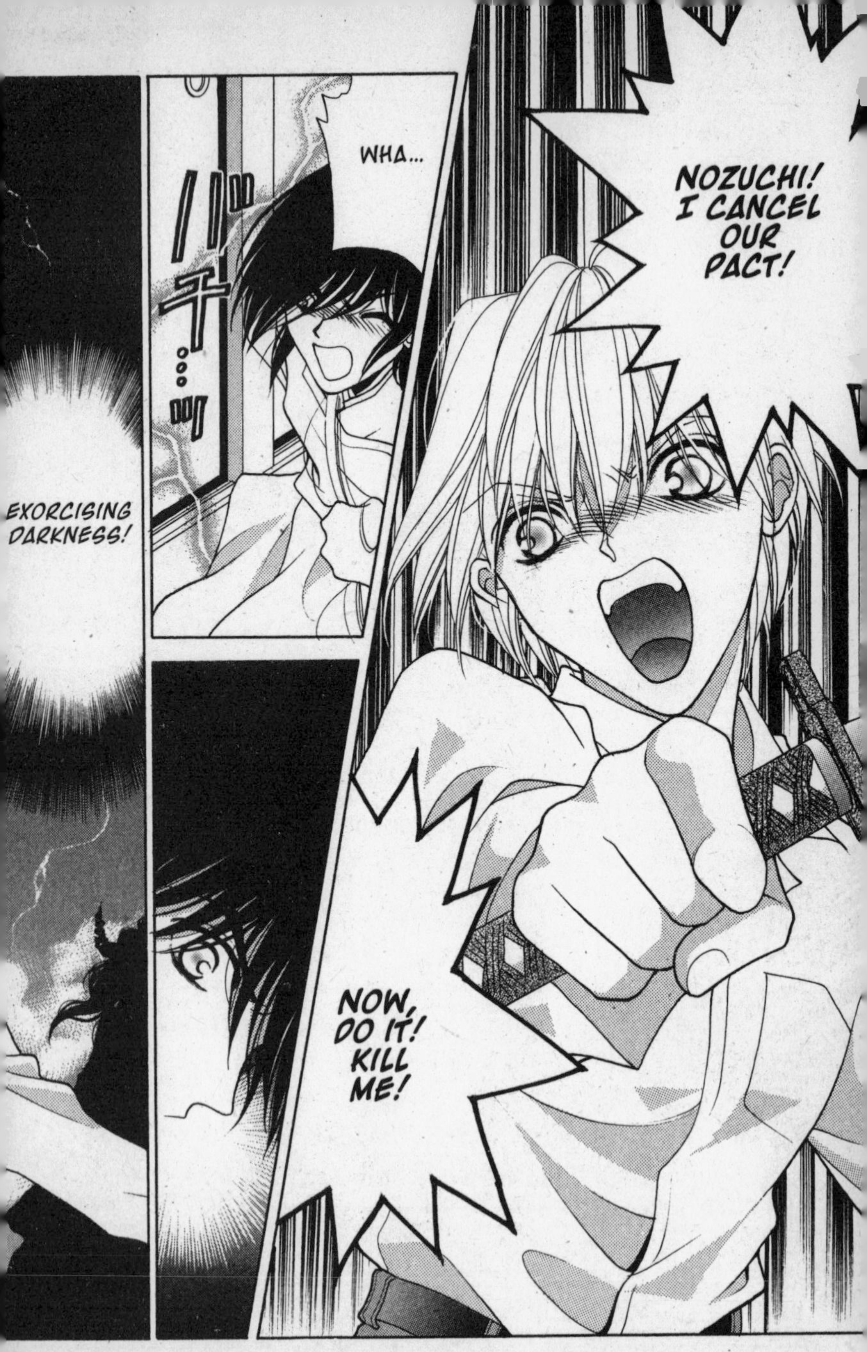
NOZUCHI! I CANCEL OUR PACT!
NOW, DO IT! KILL ME!
WHA...
EXORCISING DARKNESS!

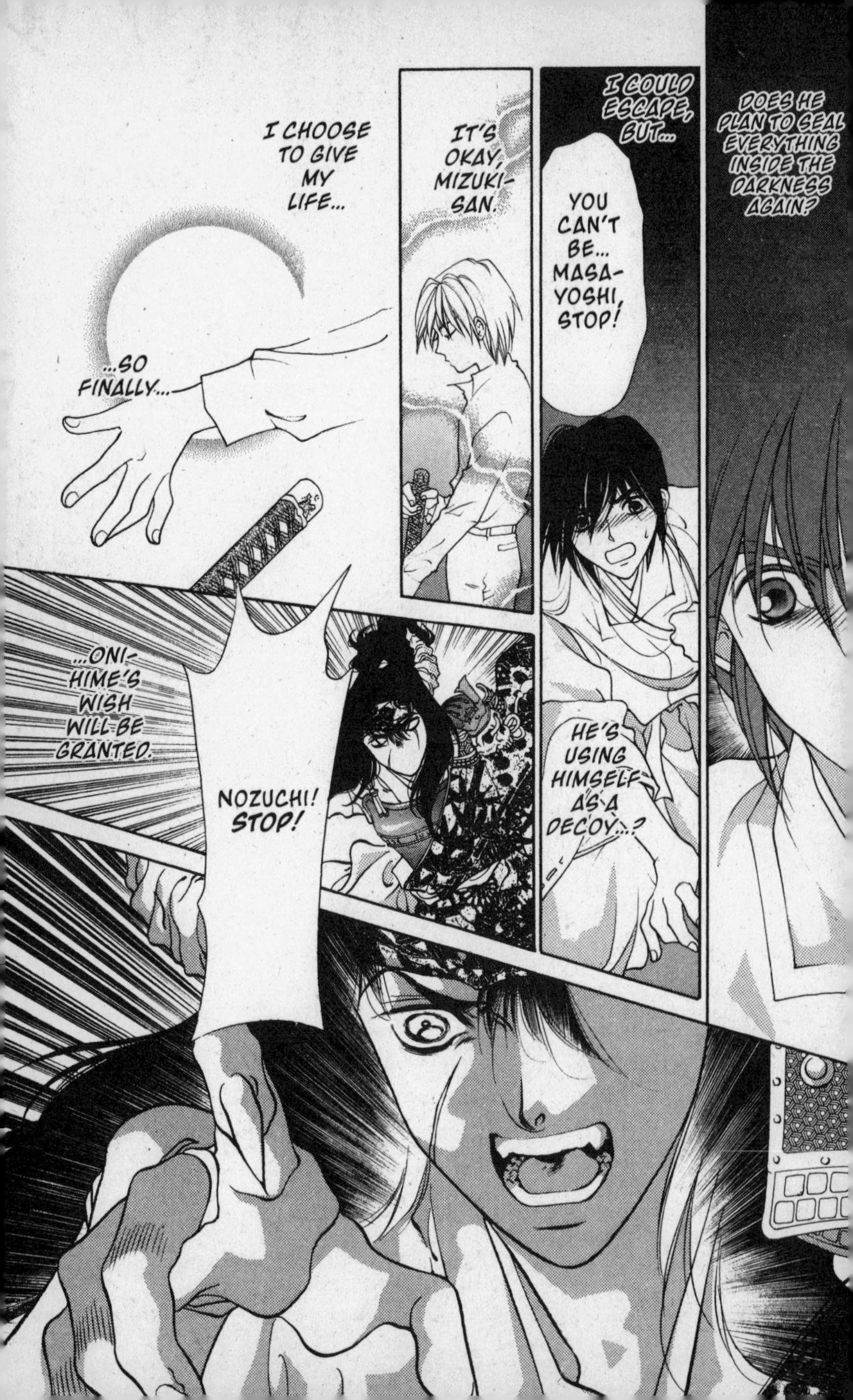
DOES HE PLAN TO SEAL EVERYTHING INSIDE THE DARKNESS AGAIN?
I COULD ESCAPE, BUT...
YOU CAN'T BE... MASA-YOSHI, STOP!
HE'S USING HIMSELF AS A DECOY...?
IT'S OKAY, MIZUKI-SAN.
I CHOOSE TO GIVE MY LIFE...
...SO FINALLY...
...ONI-HIME'S WISH WILL BE GRANTED.
NOZUCHI! STOP!

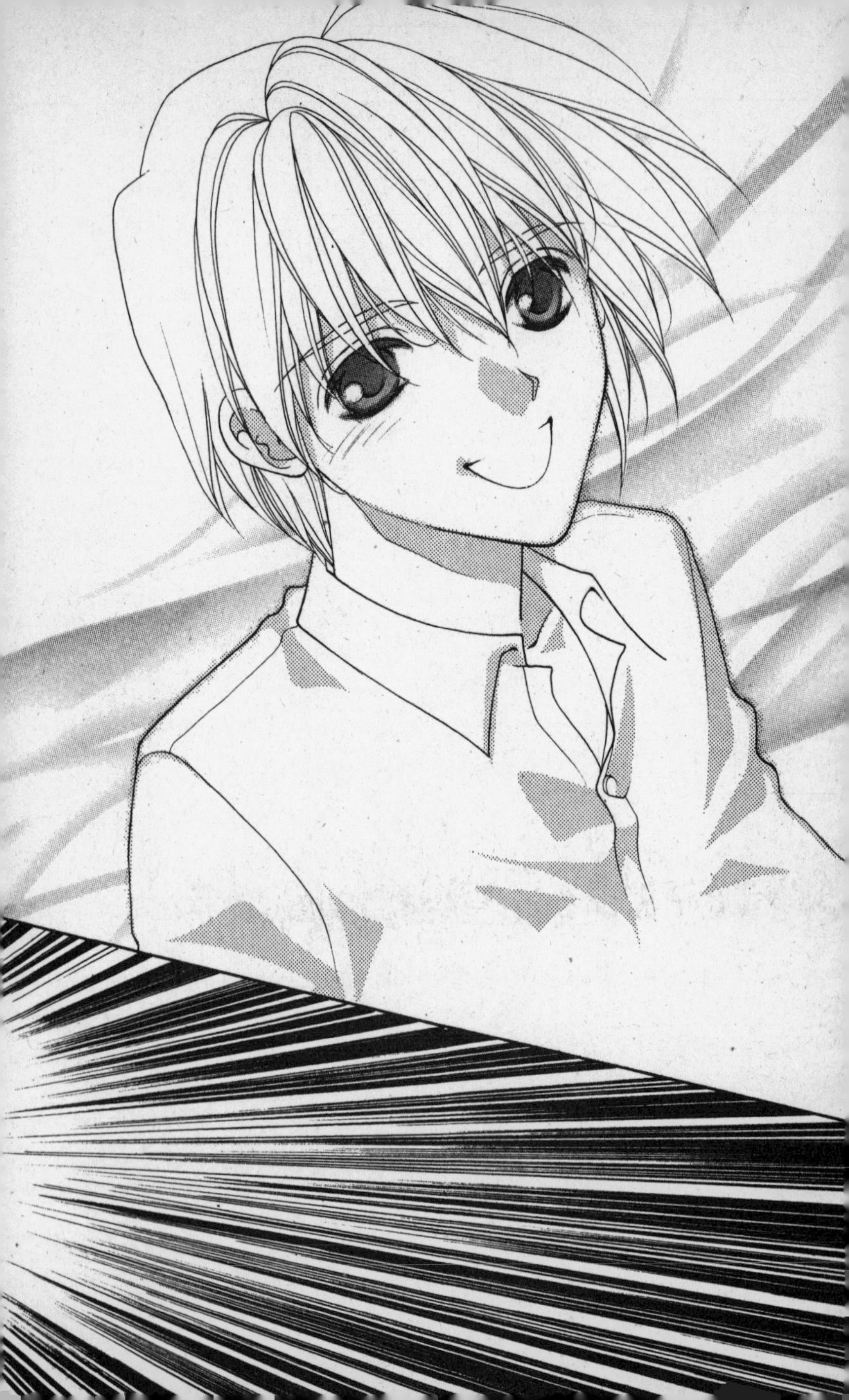

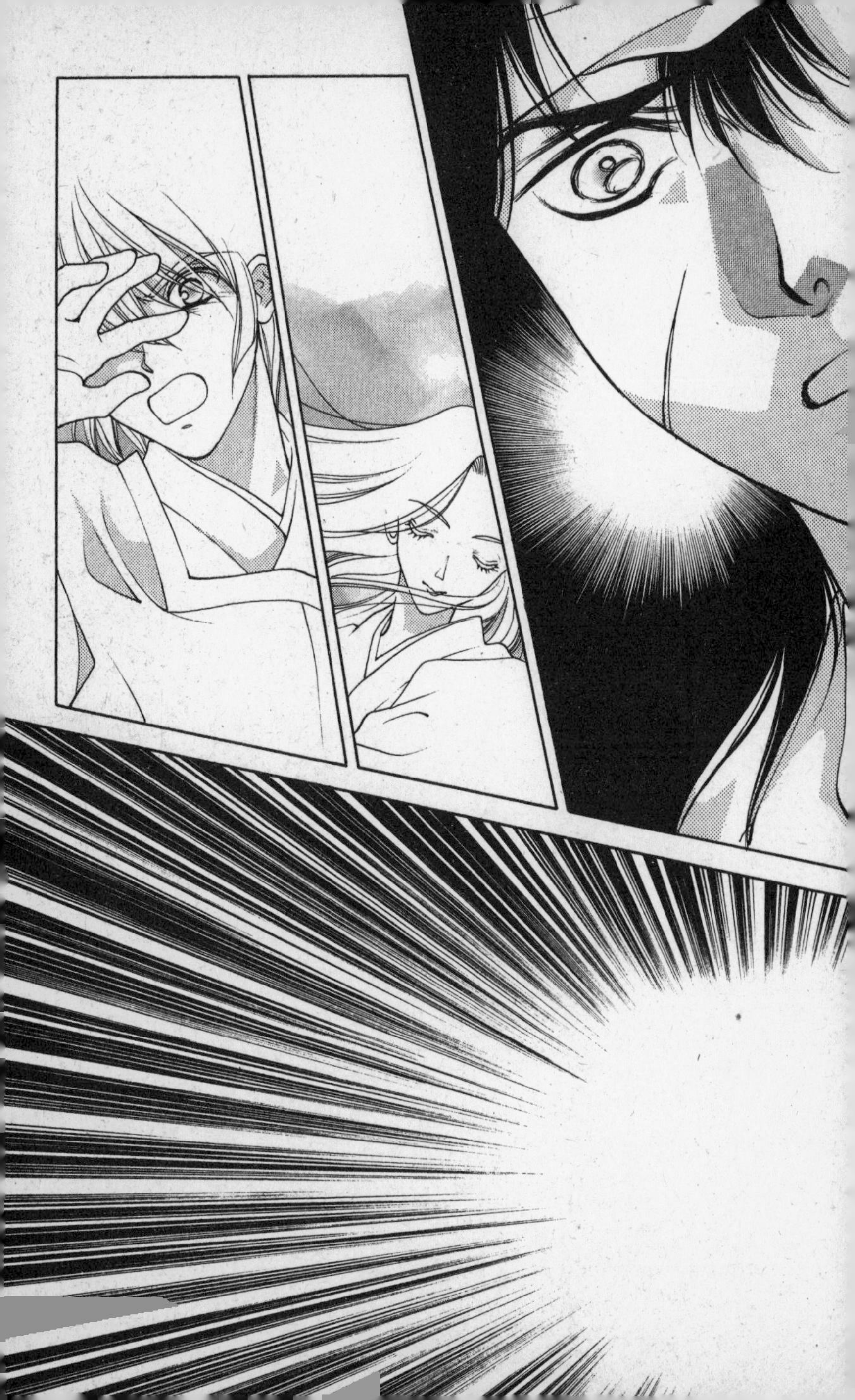

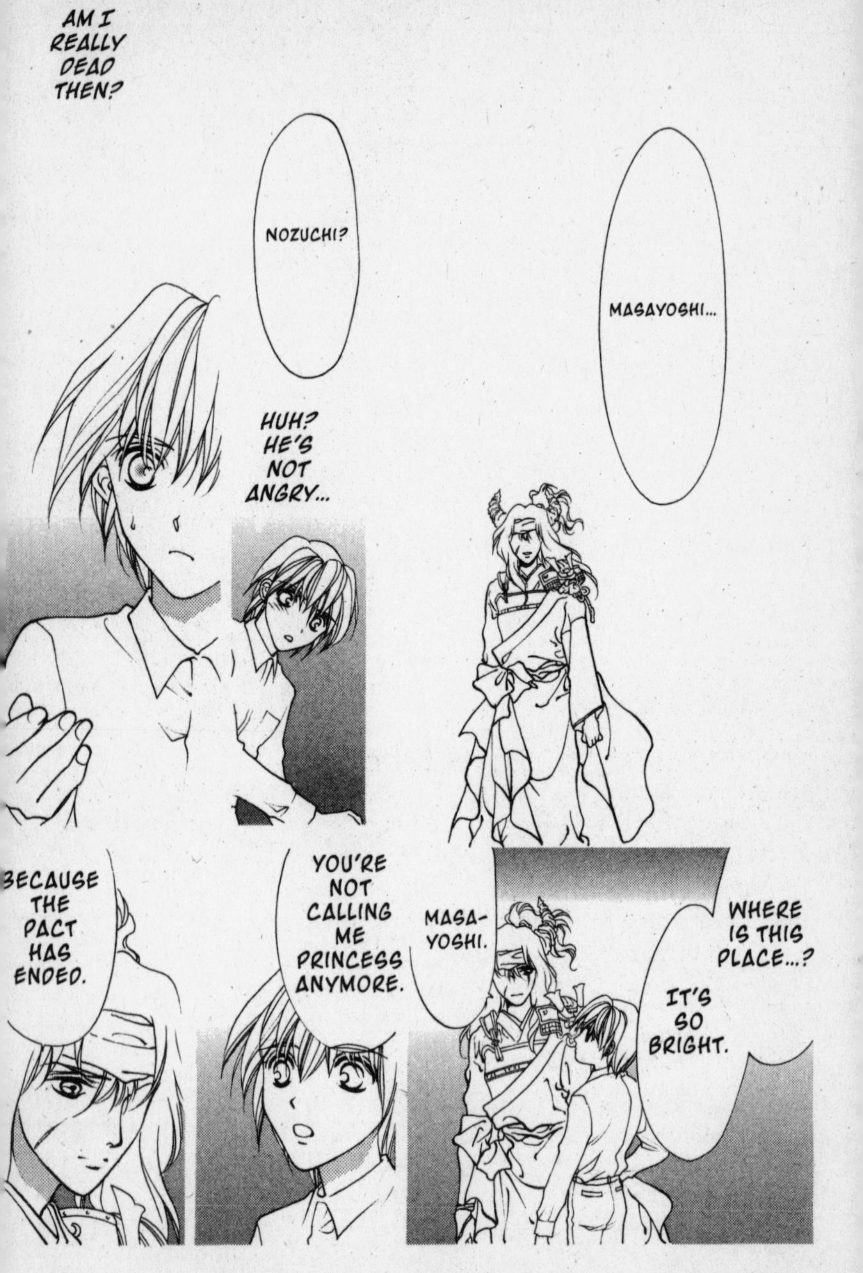
MASAYOSHI...
AM I REALLY DEAD THEN?
NOZUCHI?
HUH? HE'S NOT ANGRY...
WHERE IS THIS PLACE...?
IT'S SO BRIGHT.
MASA-YOSHI.
YOU'RE NOT CALLING ME PRINCESS ANYMORE.
BECAUSE THE PACT HAS ENDED.

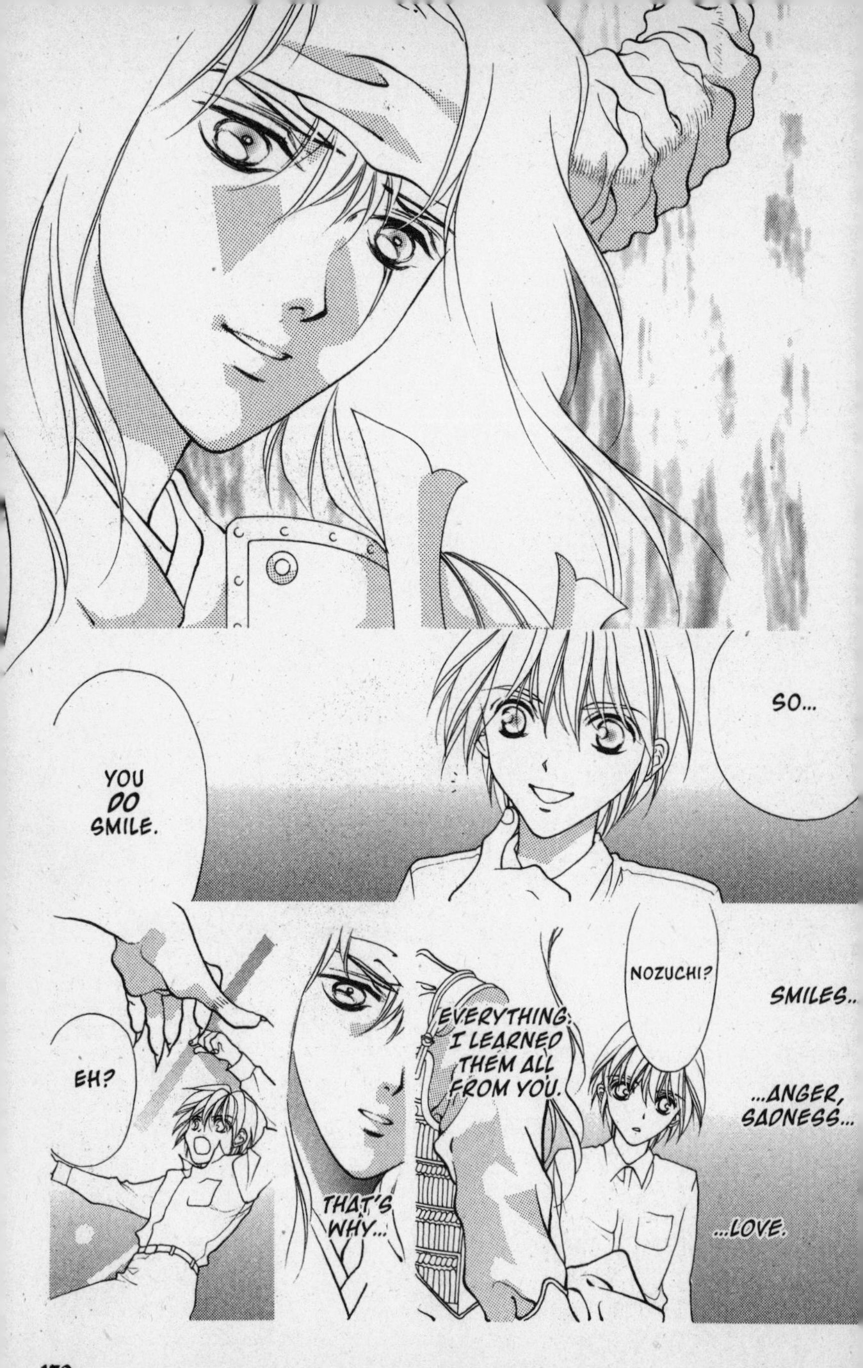
SO...
YOU DO SMILE.
SMILES...
...ANGER, SADNESS...
...LOVE.
NOZUCHI?
EVERYTHING I LEARNED THEM ALL FROM YOU.
THAT'S WHY...
EH?

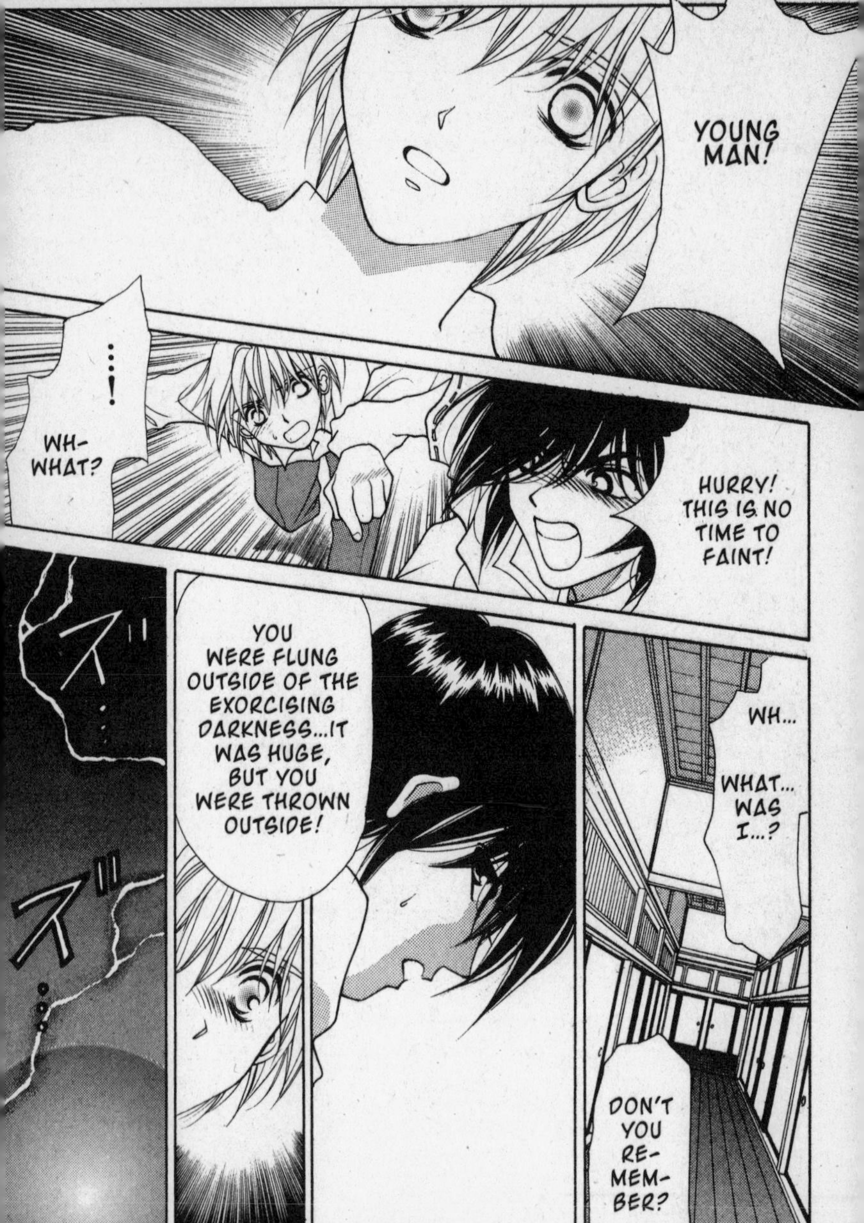
YOUNG MAN!
HURRY! THIS IS NO TIME TO FAINT!
...!
WH-WHAT?
WH...
WHAT... WAS I...?
DON'T YOU RE-MEM-BER?
YOU WERE FLUNG OUTSIDE OF THE EXORCISING DARKNESS...IT WAS HUGE, BUT YOU WERE THROWN OUTSIDE!
ズ…
ズ…

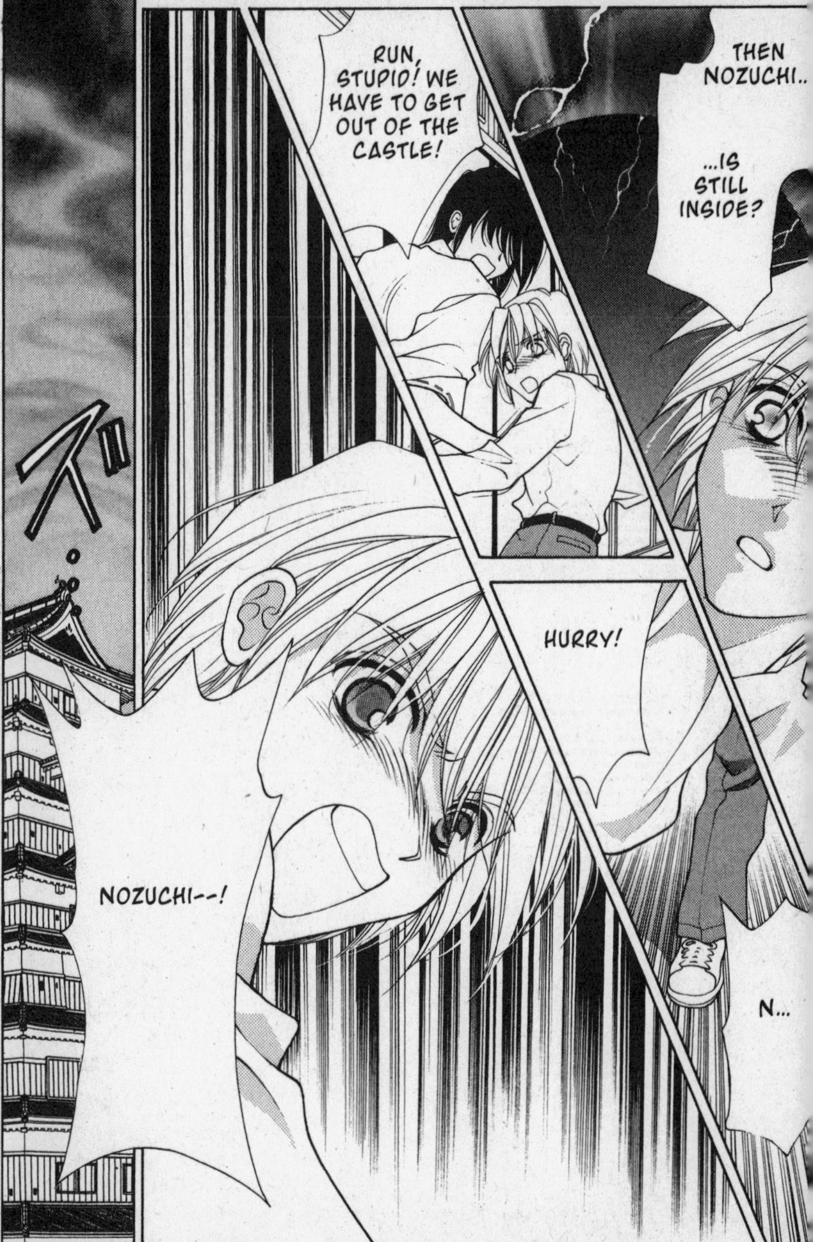
THEN NOZUCHI..
...IS STILL INSIDE?
N...
RUN, STUPID! WE HAVE TO GET OUT OF THE CASTLE!
HURRY!
NOZUCHI--!

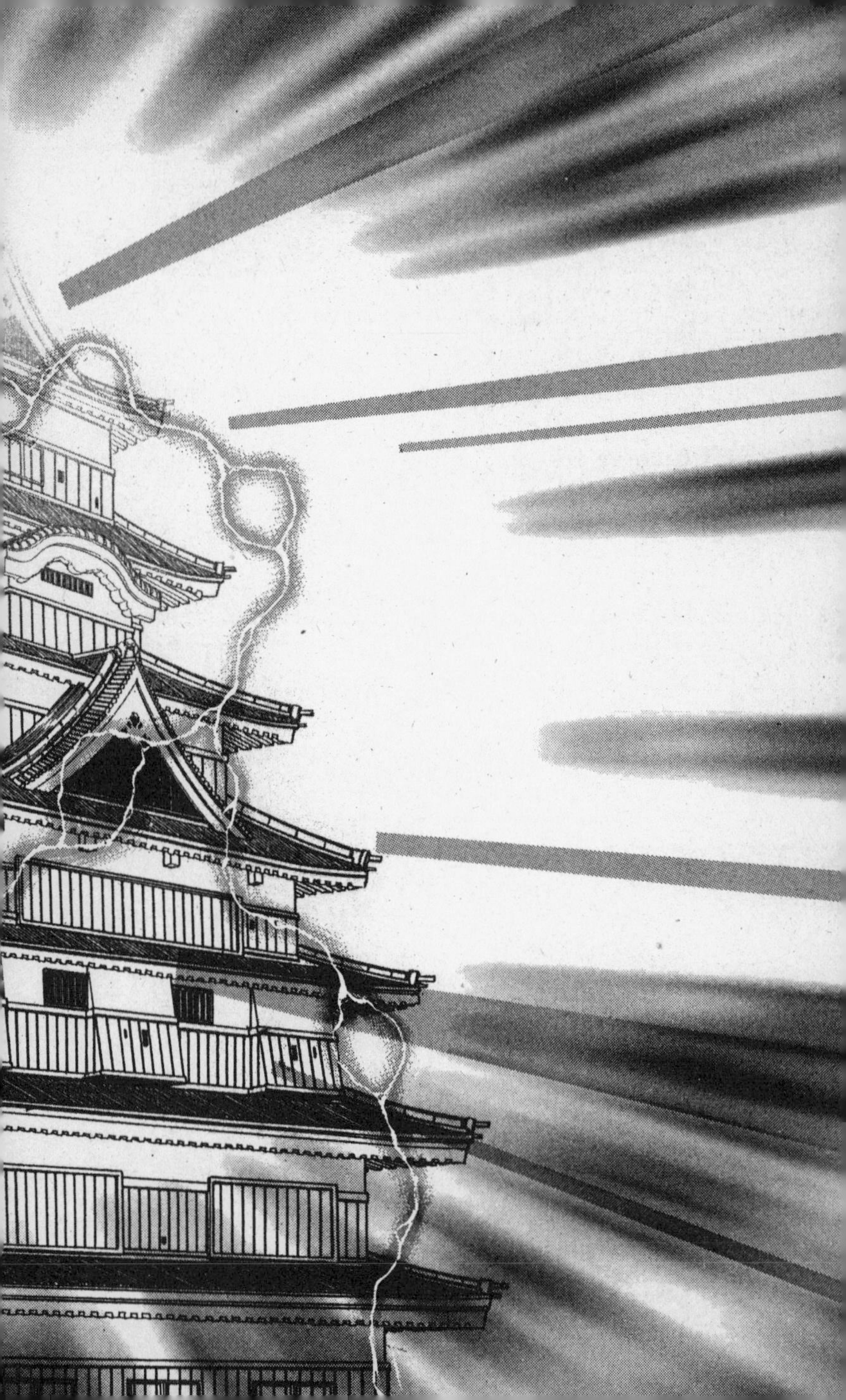

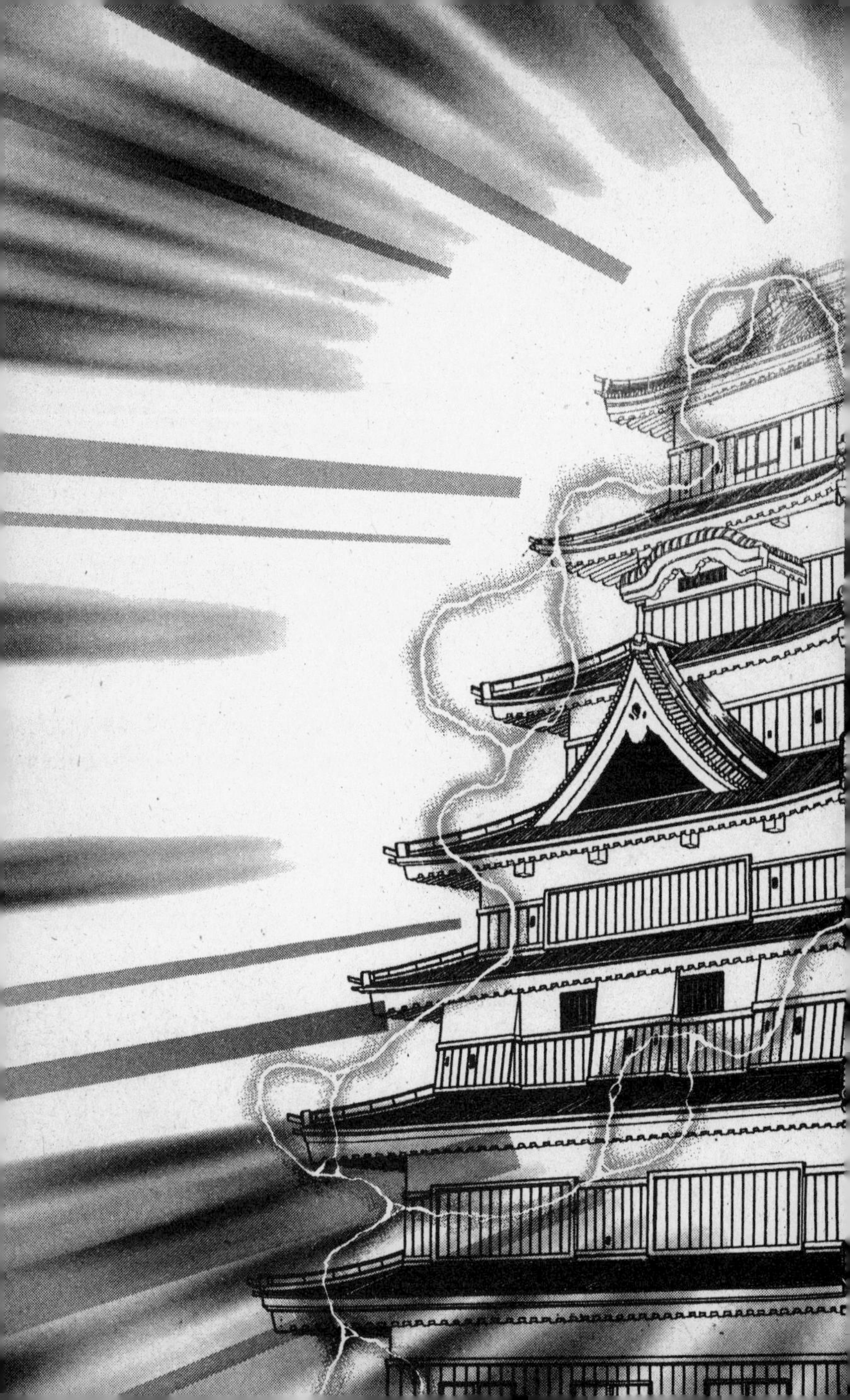

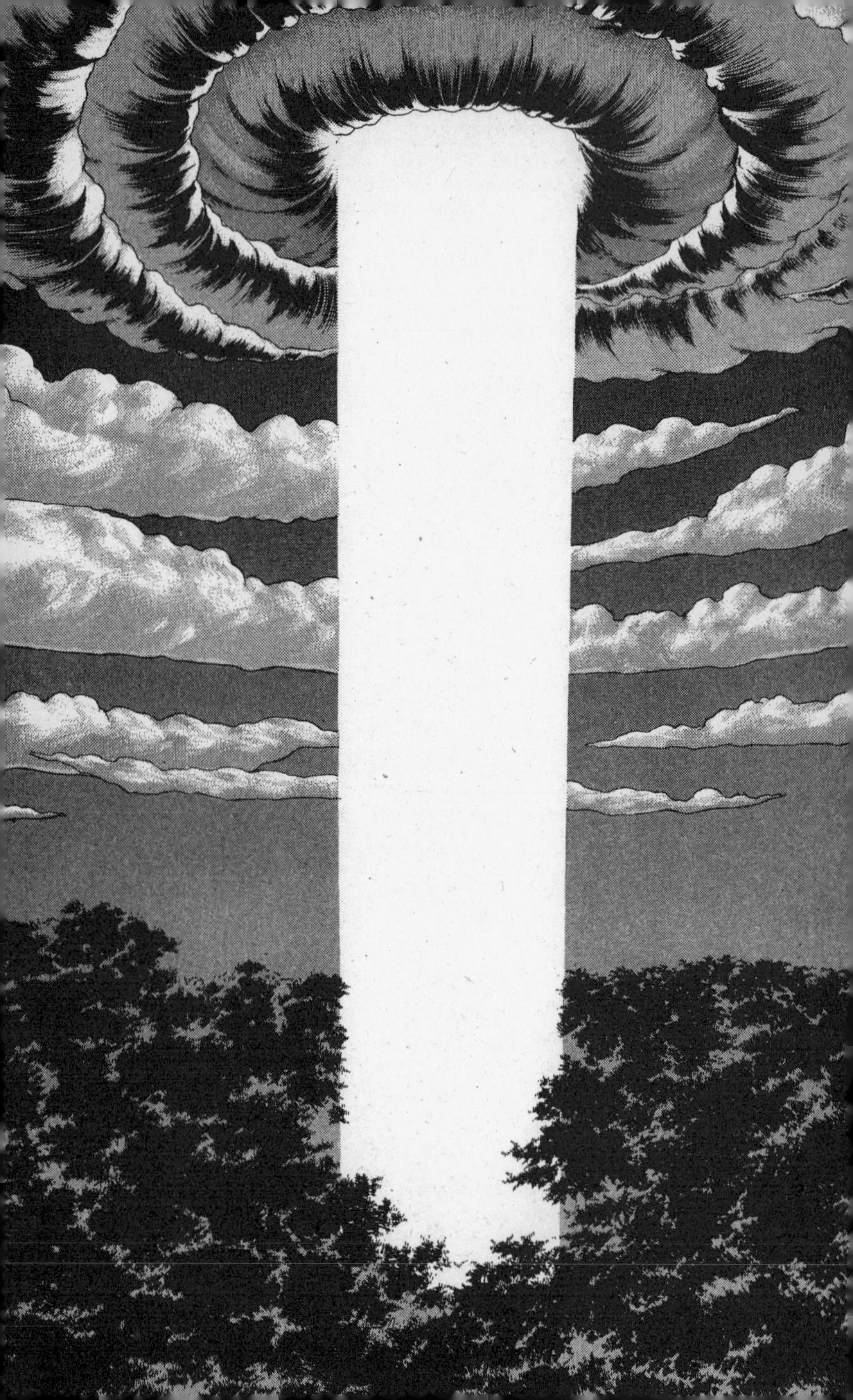

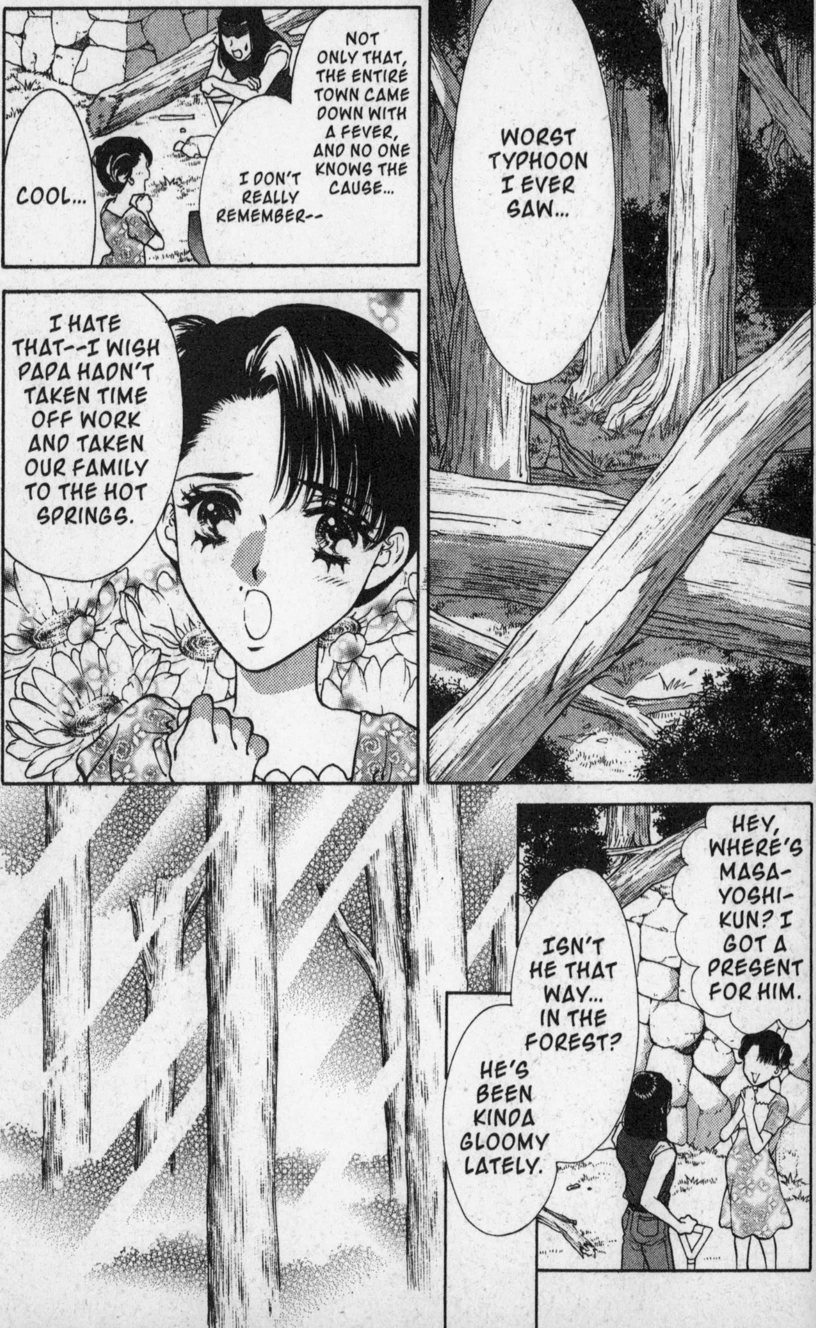
WORST TYPHOON I EVER SAW...
NOT ONLY THAT, THE ENTIRE TOWN CAME DOWN WITH A FEVER, AND NO ONE KNOWS THE CAUSE...
I DON'T REALLY REMEMBER--
COOL...
I HATE THAT--I WISH PAPA HADN'T TAKEN TIME OFF WORK AND TAKEN OUR FAMILY TO THE HOT SPRINGS.
HEY, WHERE'S MASA-YOSHI-KUN? I GOT A PRESENT FOR HIM.
ISN'T HE THAT WAY... IN THE FOREST?
HE'S BEEN KINDA GLOOMY LATELY.

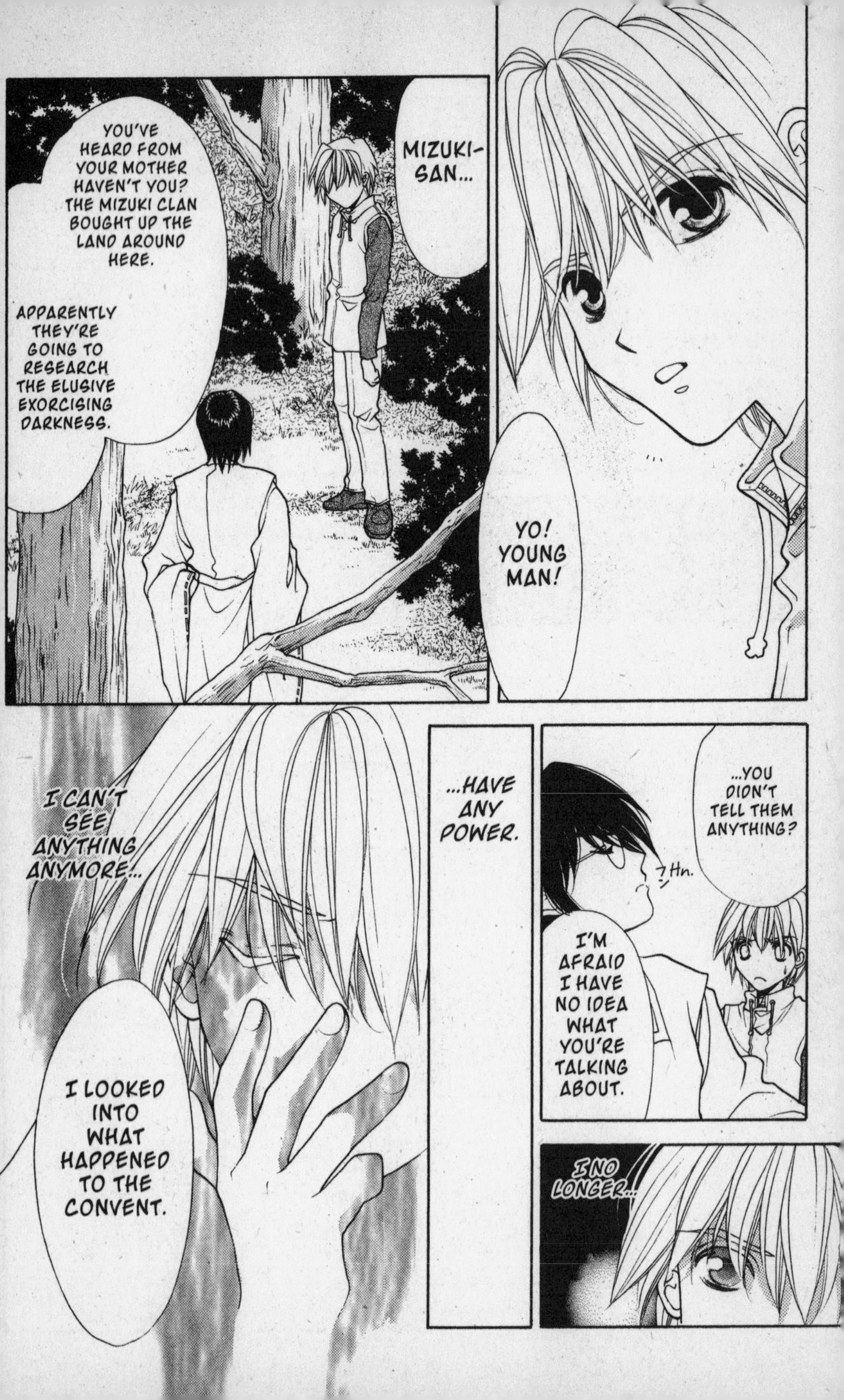
...
YO! YOUNG MAN!
MIZUKI-SAN...
YOU'VE HEARD FROM YOUR MOTHER HAVEN'T YOU? THE MIZUKI CLAN BOUGHT UP THE LAND AROUND HERE.
APPARENTLY THEY'RE GOING TO RESEARCH THE ELUSIVE EXORCISING DARKNESS.
...YOU DIDN'T TELL THEM ANYTHING?
Hn.
I'M AFRAID I HAVE NO IDEA WHAT YOU'RE TALKING ABOUT.
I NO LONGER...
...HAVE ANY POWER.
I CAN'T SEE ANYTHING ANYMORE...
I LOOKED INTO WHAT HAPPENED TO THE CONVENT.

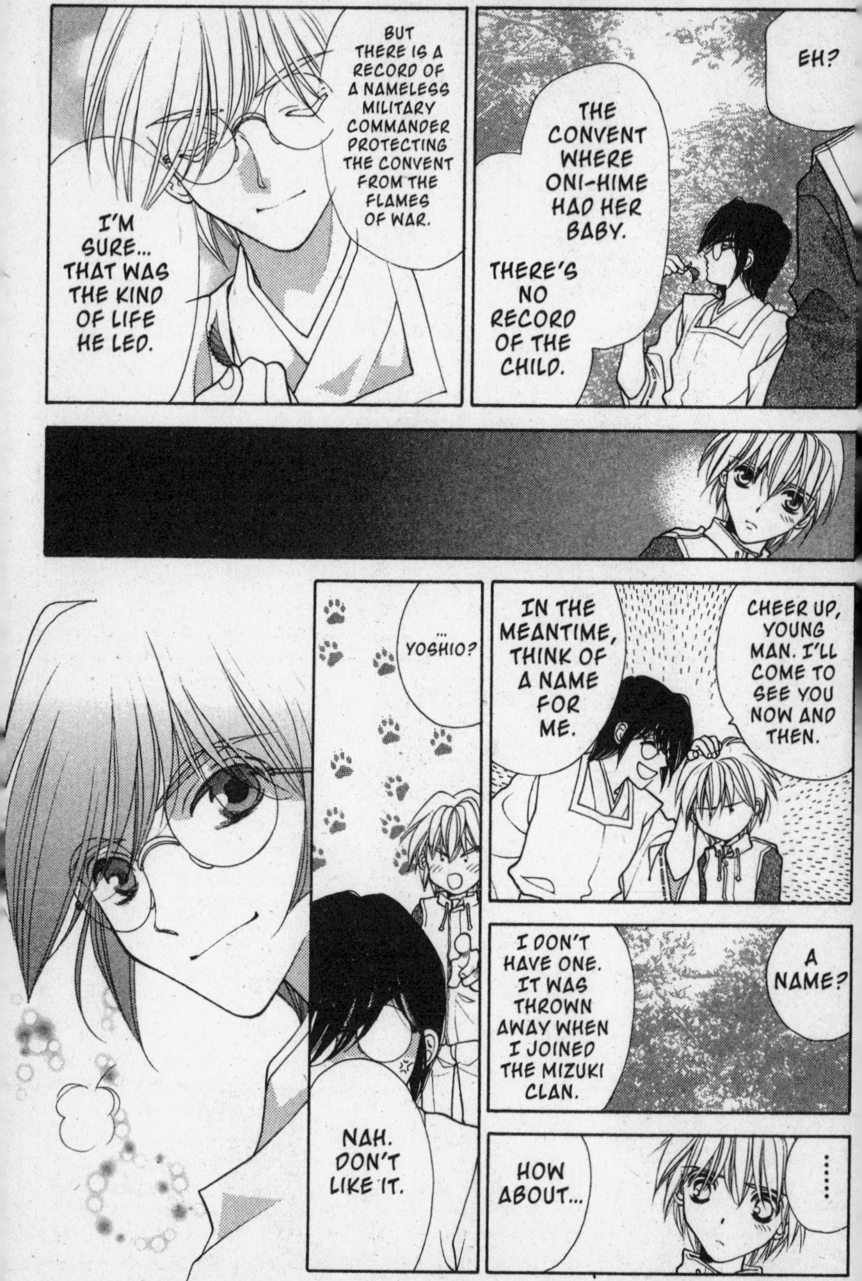
EH?
THE CONVENT WHERE ONI-HIME HAD HER BABY.
THERE'S NO RECORD OF THE CHILD.
BUT THERE IS A RECORD OF A NAMELESS MILITARY COMMANDER PROTECTING THE CONVENT FROM THE FLAMES OF WAR.
I'M SURE... THAT WAS THE KIND OF LIFE HE LED.
CHEER UP, YOUNG MAN. I'LL COME TO SEE YOU NOW AND THEN.
IN THE MEANTIME, THINK OF A NAME FOR ME.
A NAME?
I DON'T HAVE ONE. IT WAS THROWN AWAY WHEN I JOINED THE MIZUKI CLAN.
......
HOW ABOUT...
... YOSHIO?
NAH. DON'T LIKE IT.

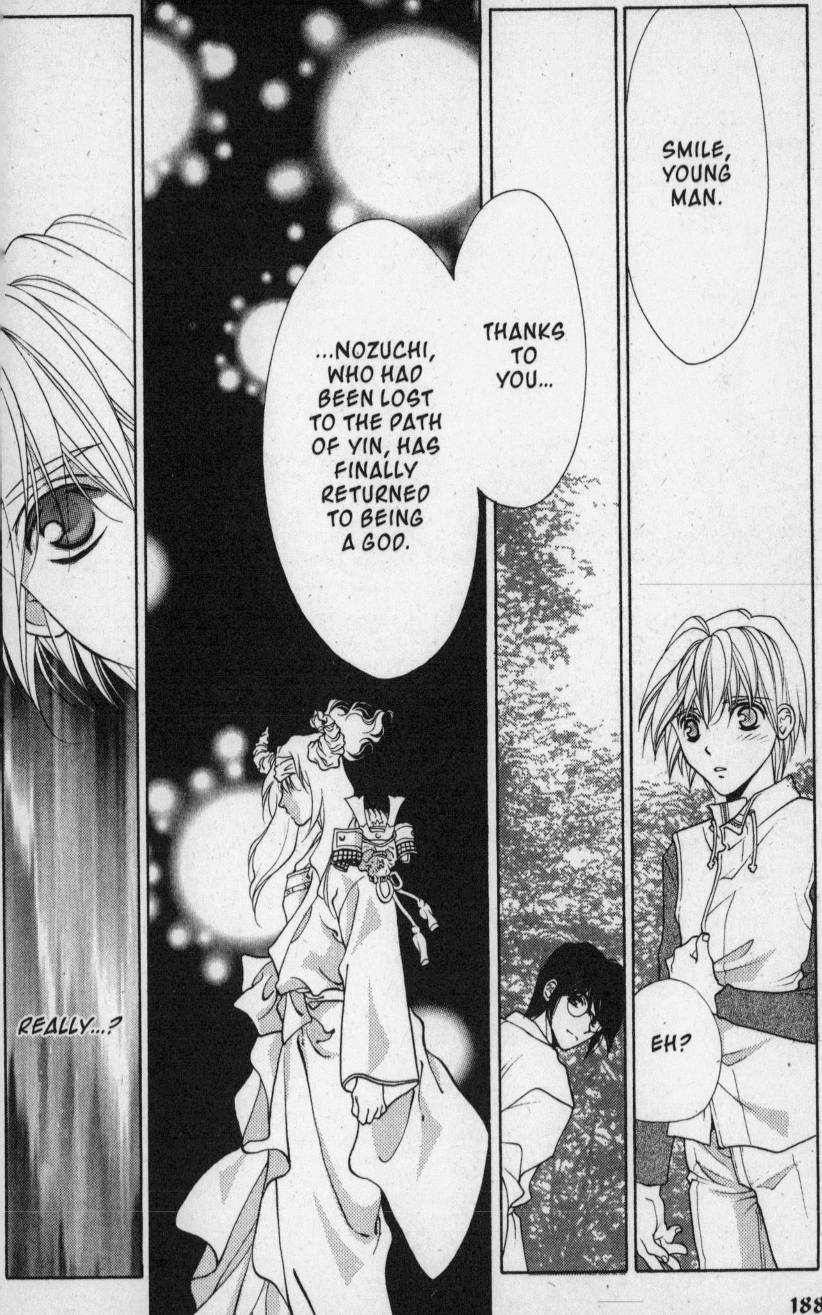
SMILE, YOUNG MAN.
EH?
THANKS TO YOU...
...NOZUCHI, WHO HAD BEEN LOST TO THE PATH OF YIN, HAS FINALLY RETURNED TO BEING A GOD.
REALLY...?

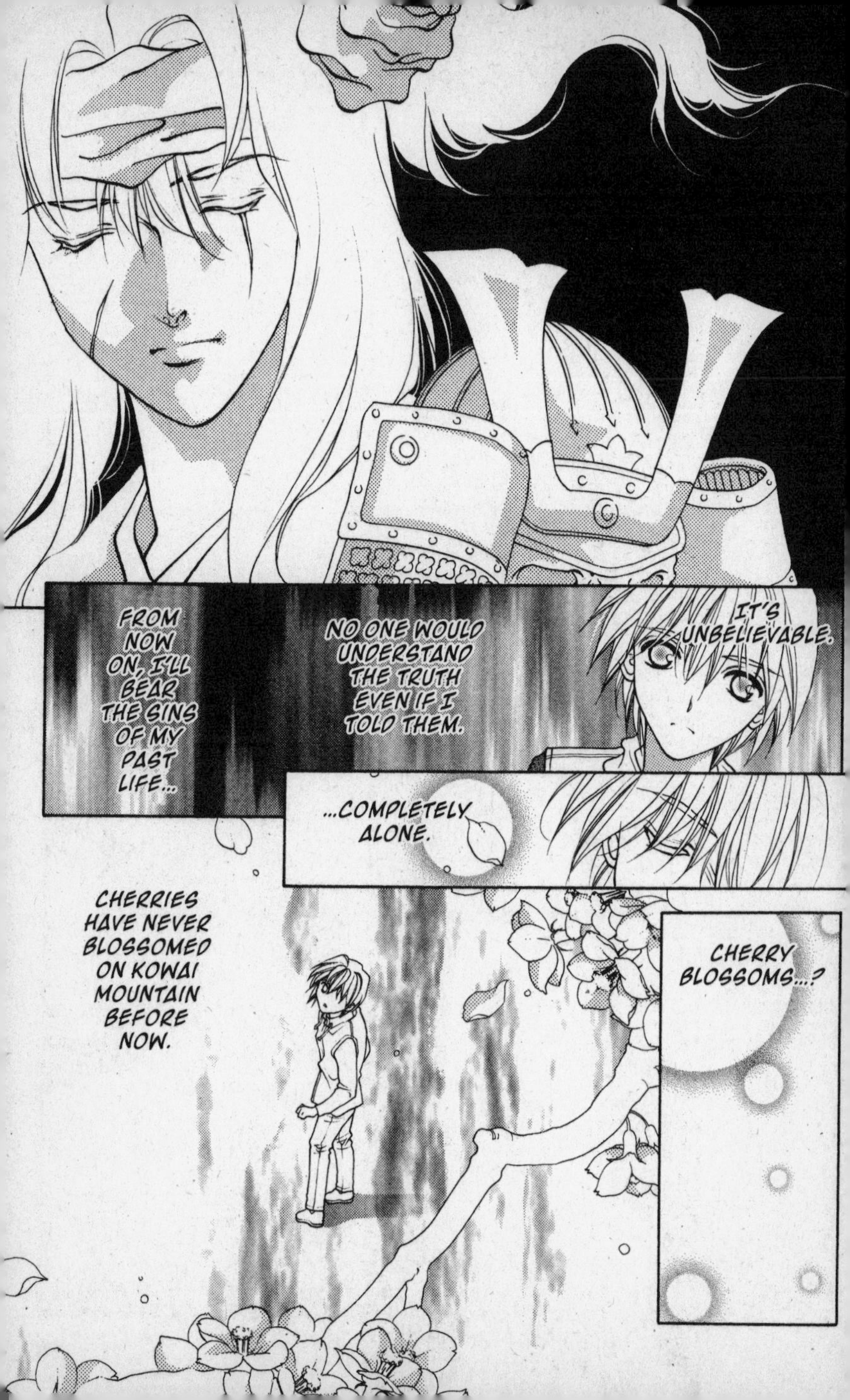
IT'S UNBELIEVABLE.
NO ONE WOULD UNDERSTAND THE TRUTH EVEN IF I TOLD THEM.
FROM NOW ON, I'LL BEAR THE SINS OF MY PAST LIFE...
...COMPLETELY ALONE.
CHERRY BLOSSOMS...?
CHERRIES HAVE NEVER BLOSSOMED ON KOWAI MOUNTAIN BEFORE NOW.

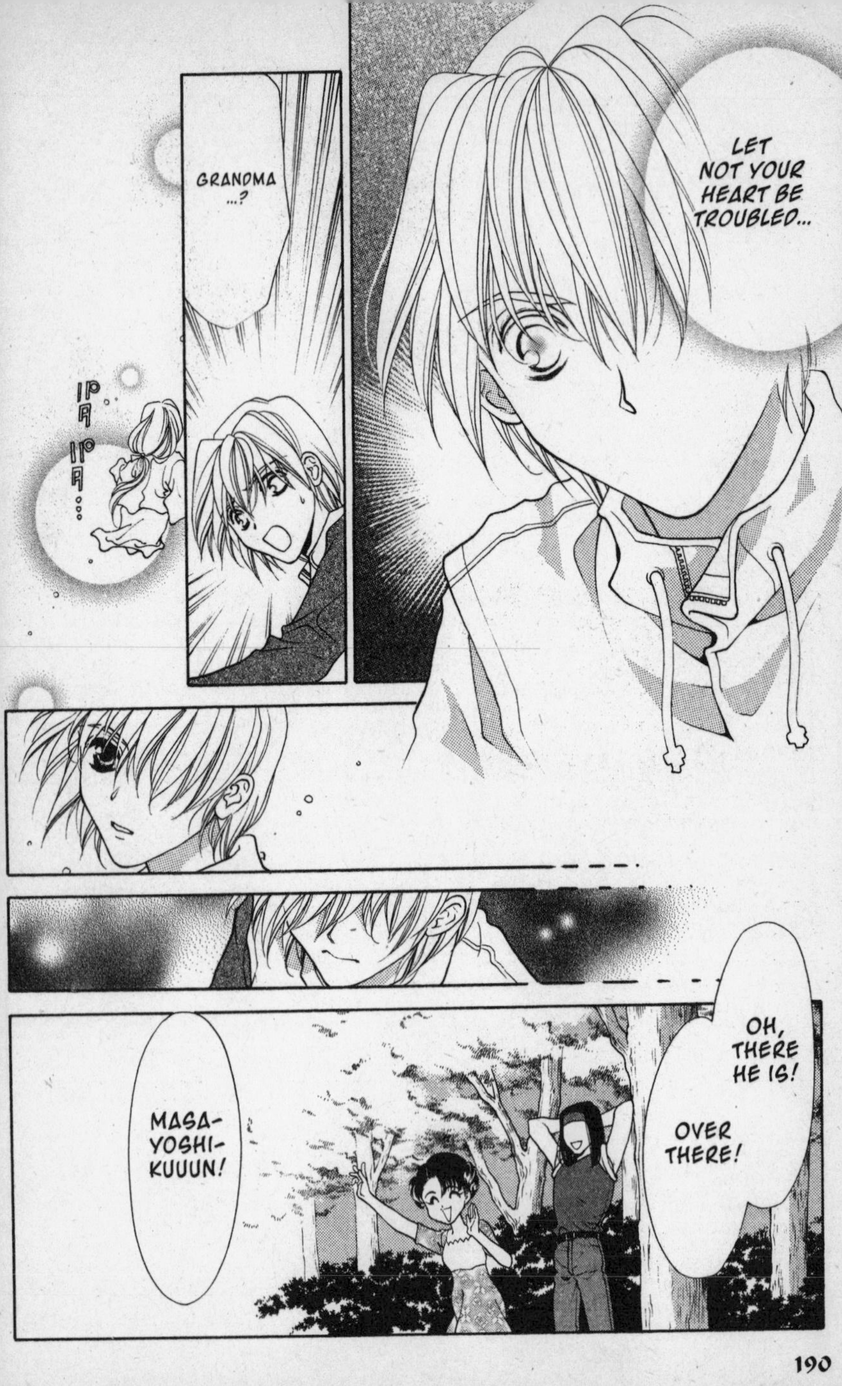
LET NOT YOUR HEART BE TROUBLED...
GRANDMA ...?
OH, THERE HE IS!
OVER THERE!
MASA-YOSHI-KUUUN!

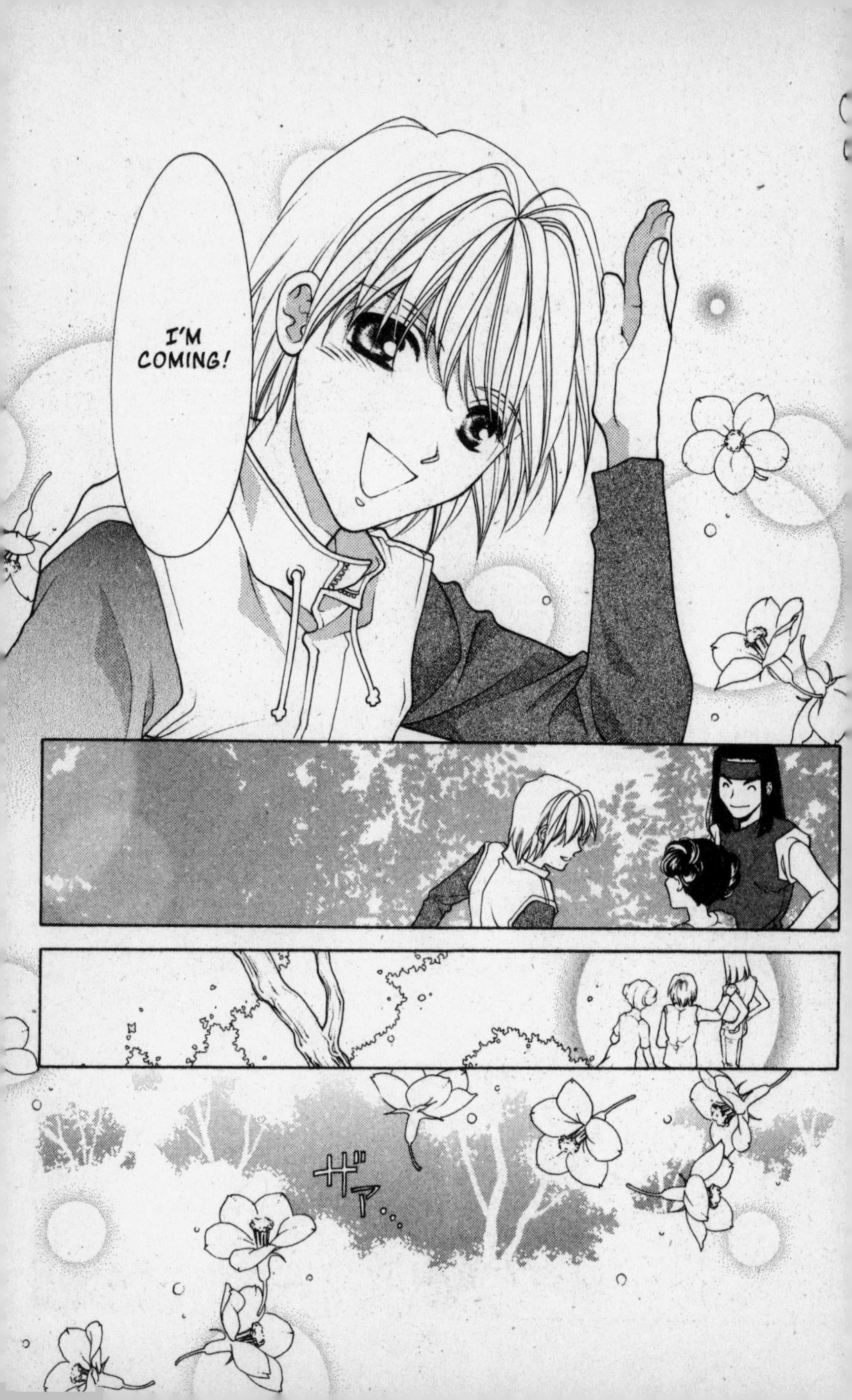
I'M COMING!
ザァ…

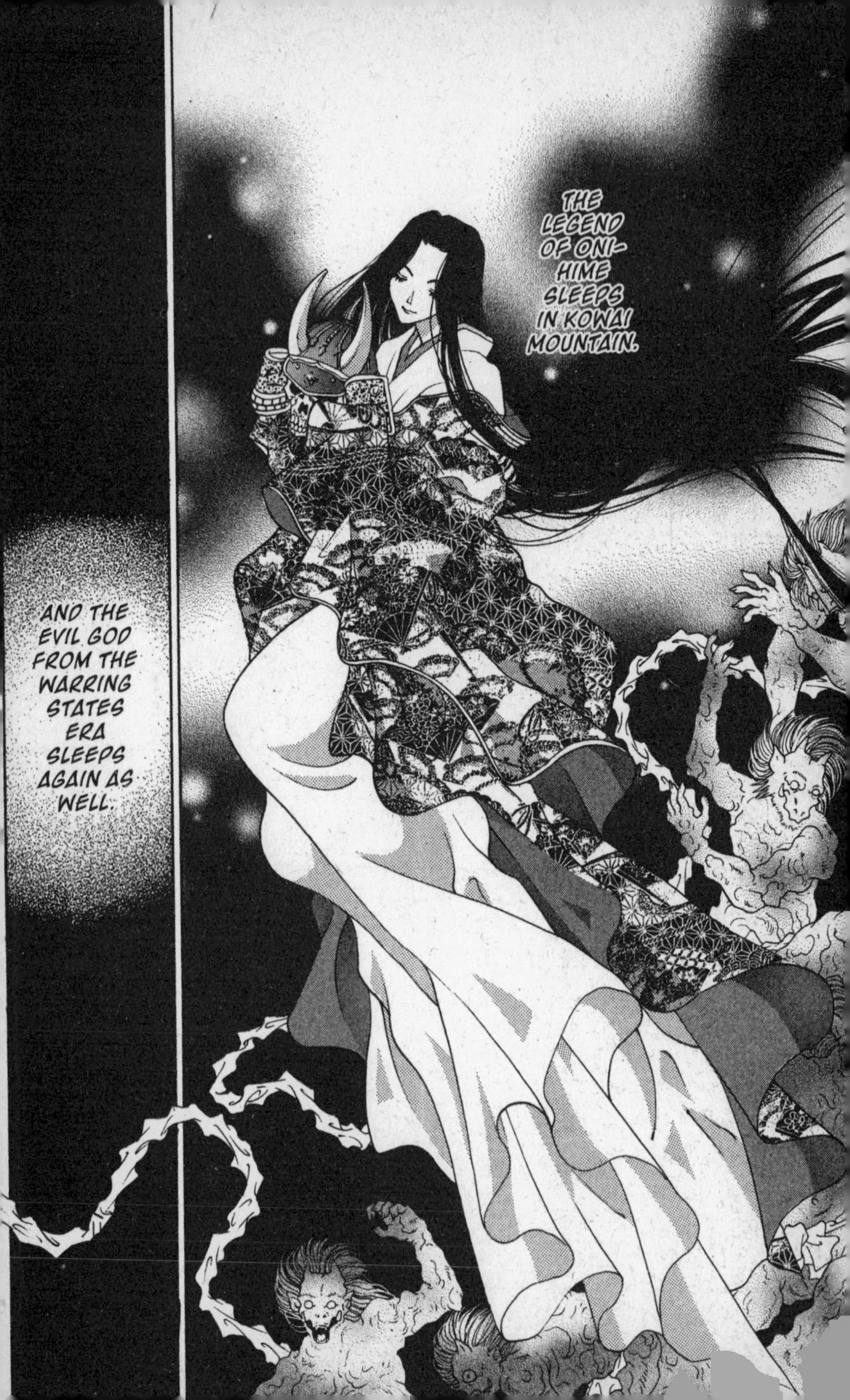
THE LEGEND OF ONI-HIME SLEEPS IN KOWAI MOUNTAIN.
AND THE EVIL GOD FROM THE WARRING STATES ERA SLEEPS AGAIN AS WELL.

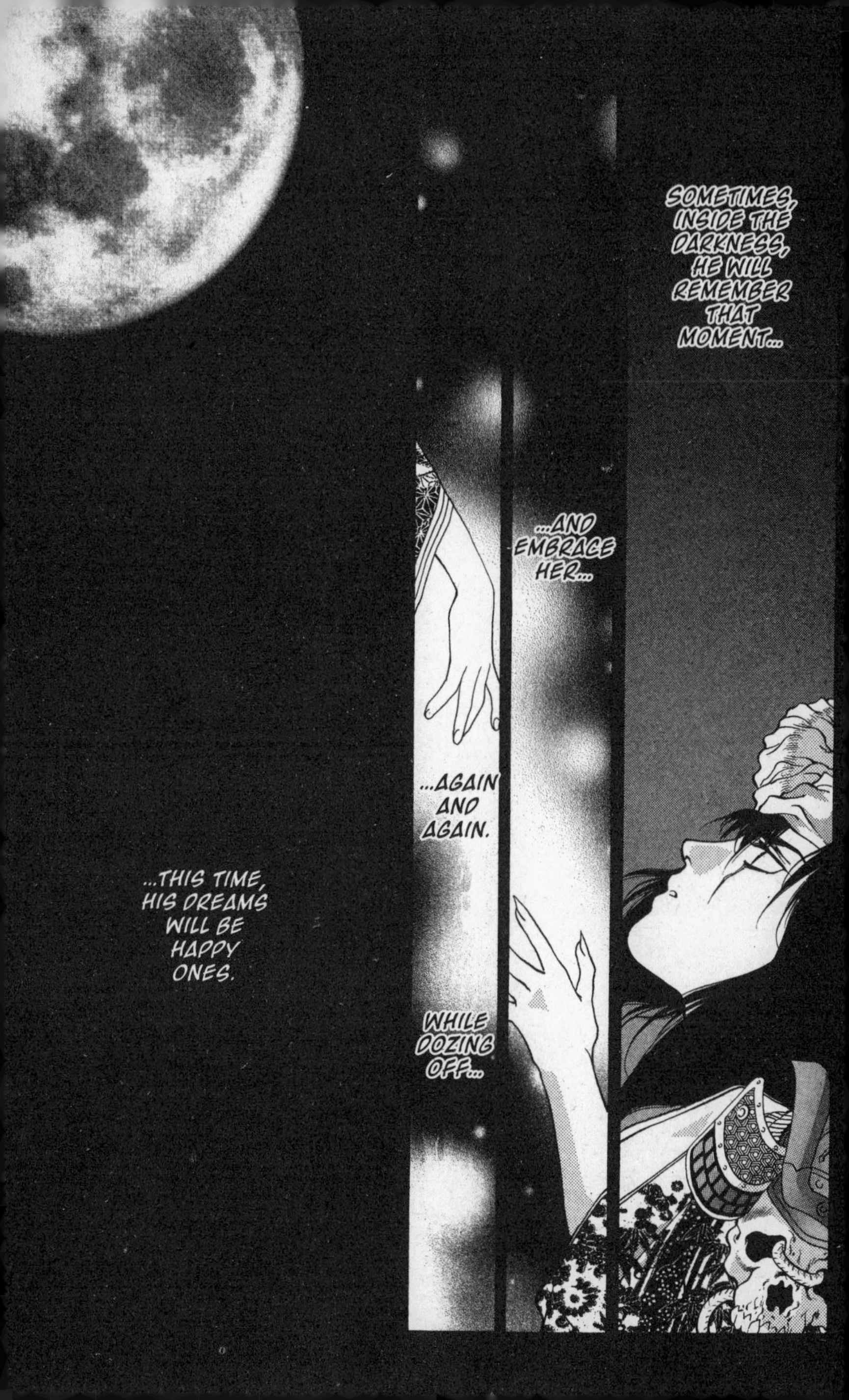
SOMETIMES, INSIDE THE DARKNESS, HE WILL REMEMBER THAT MOMENT...
...AND EMBRACE HER...
...AGAIN AND AGAIN.
WHILE DOZING OFF...
...THIS TIME, HIS DREAMS WILL BE HAPPY ONES.

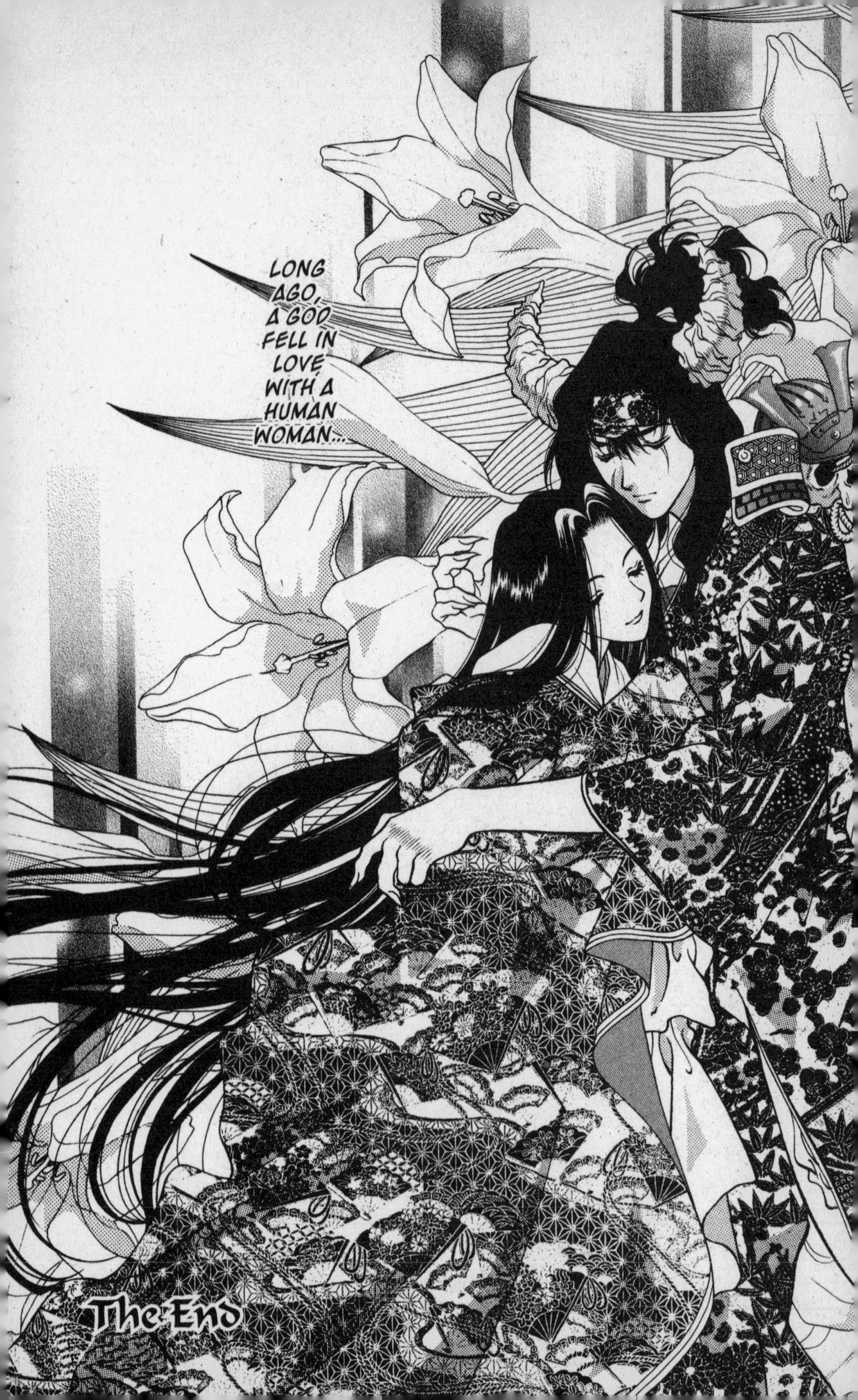
LONG AGO, A GOD FELL IN LOVE WITH A HUMAN WOMAN...
The End

It's finally ended!

The first long-running series that the sisters have collaborated on! How did you like *Sengoku Nights*? Originally it was only going to be five chapters, but it was so popular, it turned into two volumes! Lucky! ♡

It started out pretty light, but it got pretty intense! It was really hard to work on when we were busy... When you're doing a collaboration, it really is hard to work on if you're not always together. There were so many times we had to stop work because our timing was off. There were also times when we'd have our assistants draw just the costumes first, and they'd be invisible people (laugh).

Hmm...but, well, I guess it was fun.

We might do another collaboration. Since we've kind of gotten the hang of it.

Please support us!! ♡

AND COME SEE OUR HOMEPAGE!
HTTP://WWW.NGY1.1ST.NE.JP/~K2OFFICE

THERE'S A SENGOKU NIGHTS PAGE AND IMAGE MELODIES. (WE GOT THEM AS PRESENTS)

NOW, ENJOY OUR ASSISTANTS' SENGOKU NIGHTS, 'KAY?

Created By: Kei Kusunoki & Kaoru Ohashi

Sengoku Nights Vol. 2

In charge of names:
Kaoru Ohashi

Character design:
Kei Kusunoki

Nozuchi, Grandma, Yoshino, and the enemy characters were almost all drawn by Kei Kusunoki

Masayoshi, Mizuki, Princess, parents, Shishiou, and the mob characters were almost all drawn by Kaoru Ohashi

Assistants:
Jimmy-chan, Oshizu-chan, Mahhii, Aya-chin, Waka-chan

Our first monochrome CG! We still have a lot to learn...

At last, a novel debut!
By Jimmy-chan

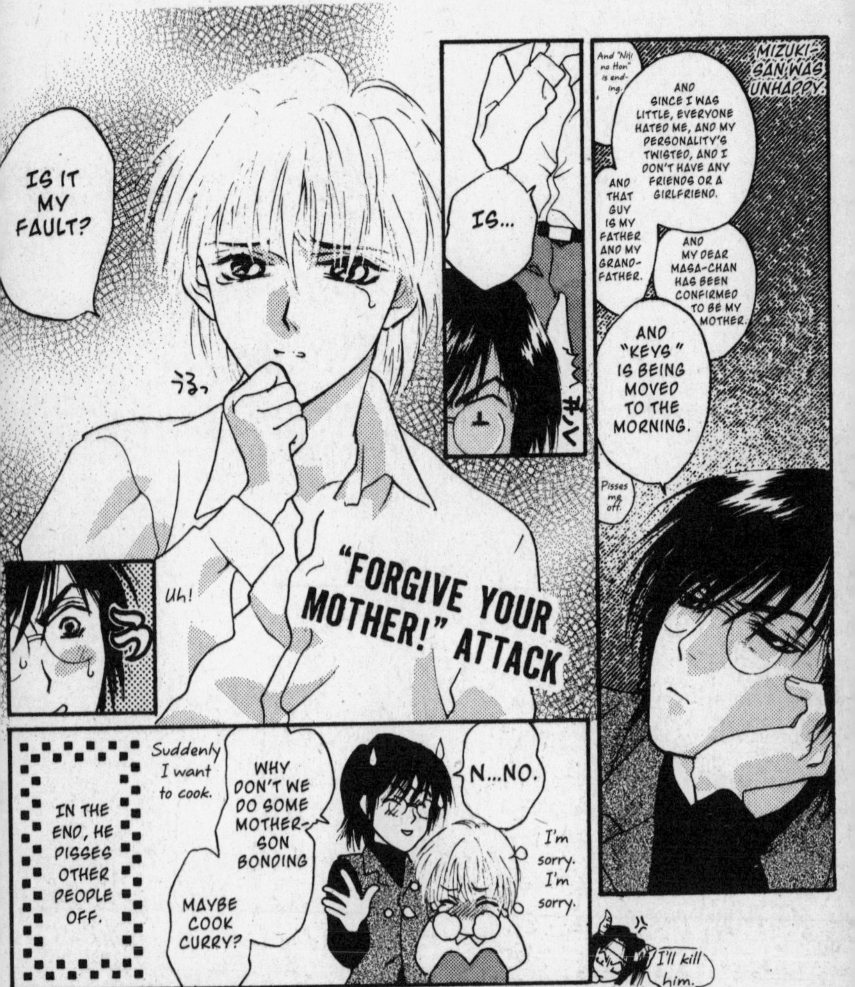
MIZUKI-SAN WAS UNHAPPY.
And "Niji no Hon" is ending.
AND SINCE I WAS LITTLE, EVERYONE HATED ME, AND MY PERSONALITY'S TWISTED, AND I DON'T HAVE ANY FRIENDS OR A GIRLFRIEND.
AND THAT GUY IS MY FATHER AND MY GRANDFATHER.
AND MY DEAR MASA-CHAN HAS BEEN CONFIRMED TO BE MY MOTHER.
AND "KEYS" IS BEING MOVED TO THE MORNING.
Pisses me off.
IS...
IS IT MY FAULT?
"FORGIVE YOUR MOTHER!" ATTACK
Uh!
N...NO.
I'm sorry. I'm sorry.
WHY DON'T WE DO SOME MOTHER-SON BONDING
MAYBE COOK CURRY?
Suddenly I want to cook.
IN THE END, HE PISSES OTHER PEOPLE OFF.
I'll kill him.

Nozu-Nozu

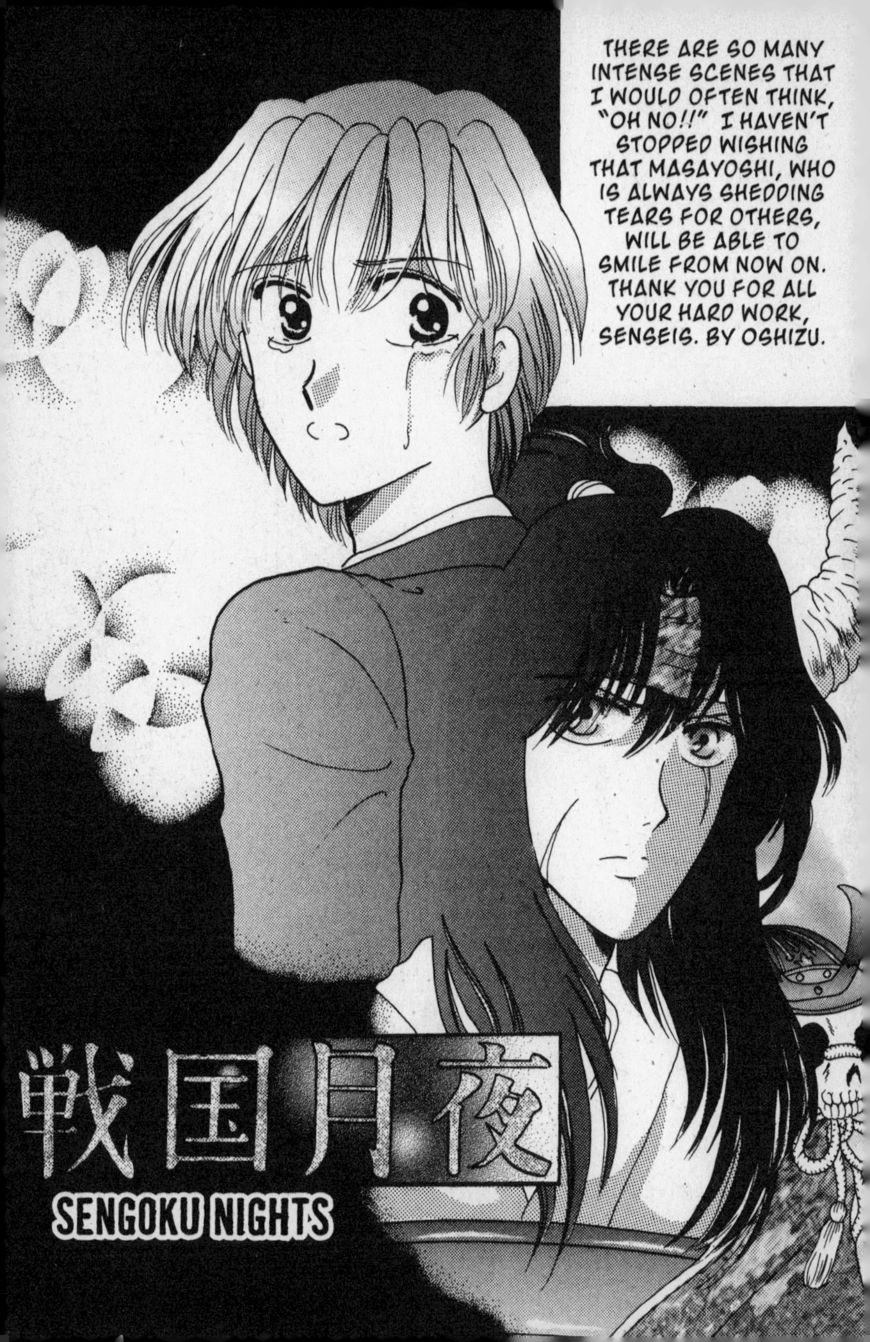
THERE ARE SO MANY INTENSE SCENES THAT I WOULD OFTEN THINK, "OH NO!!" I HAVEN'T STOPPED WISHING THAT MASAYOSHI, WHO IS ALWAYS SHEDDING TEARS FOR OTHERS, WILL BE ABLE TO SMILE FROM NOW ON. THANK YOU FOR ALL YOUR HARD WORK, SENSEIS. BY OSHIZU.
戦国月夜
SENGOKU NIGHTS

By Mahhii

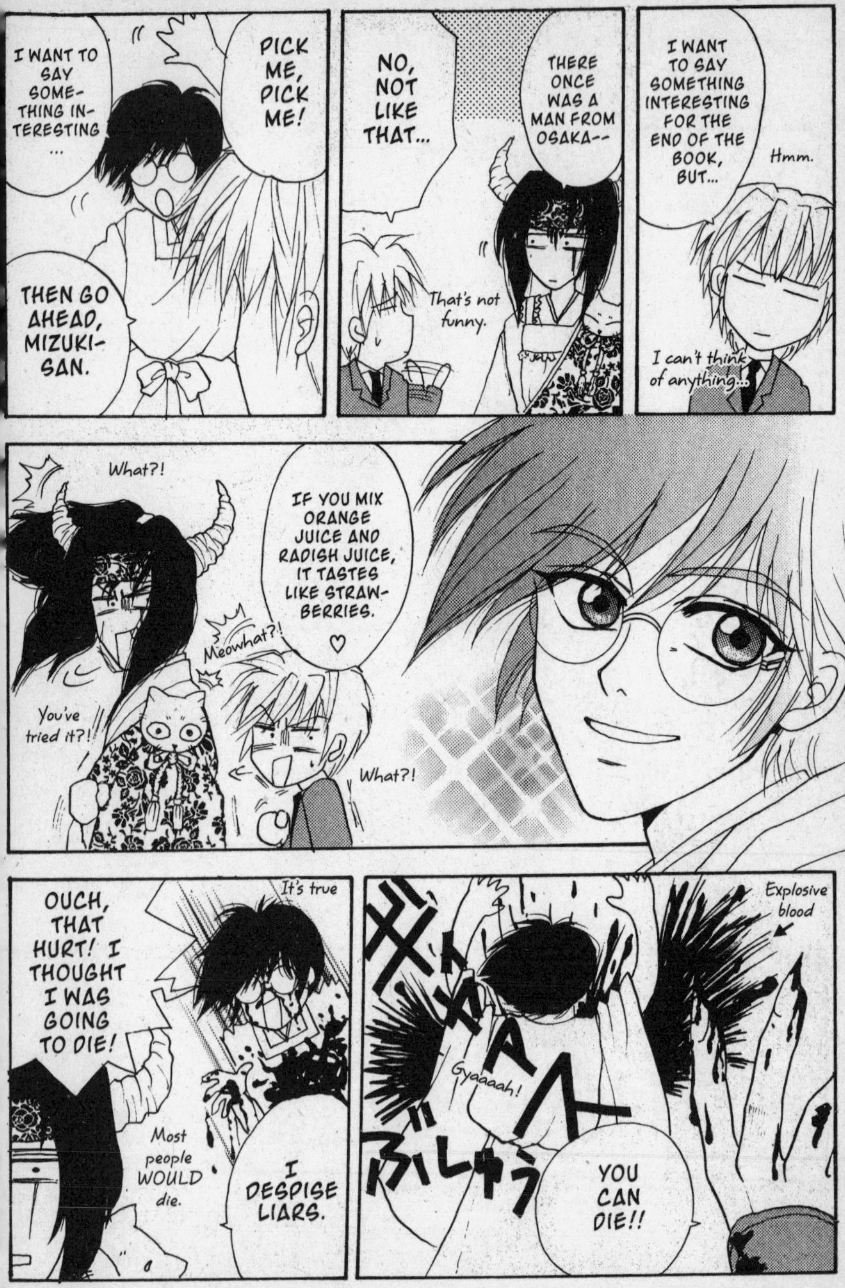
I WANT TO SAY SOMETHING INTERESTING FOR THE END OF THE BOOK, BUT...
Hmm.
I can't think of anything...
THERE ONCE WAS A MAN FROM OSAKA--
NO, NOT LIKE THAT...
That's not funny.
PICK ME, PICK ME!
I WANT TO SAY SOME-THING IN-TERESTING ...
THEN GO AHEAD, MIZUKI-SAN.
IF YOU MIX ORANGE JUICE AND RADISH JUICE, IT TASTES LIKE STRAW-BERRIES. ♡
What?!
Meowhat?!
You've tried it?!
What?!
Explosive blood
Gyaaaah!
YOU CAN DIE!!
It's true
OUCH, THAT HURT! I THOUGHT I WAS GOING TO DIE!
I DESPISE LIARS.
Most people WOULD die.

Goodbye, Nozuchi... *sniffle*...
by Aya-chin

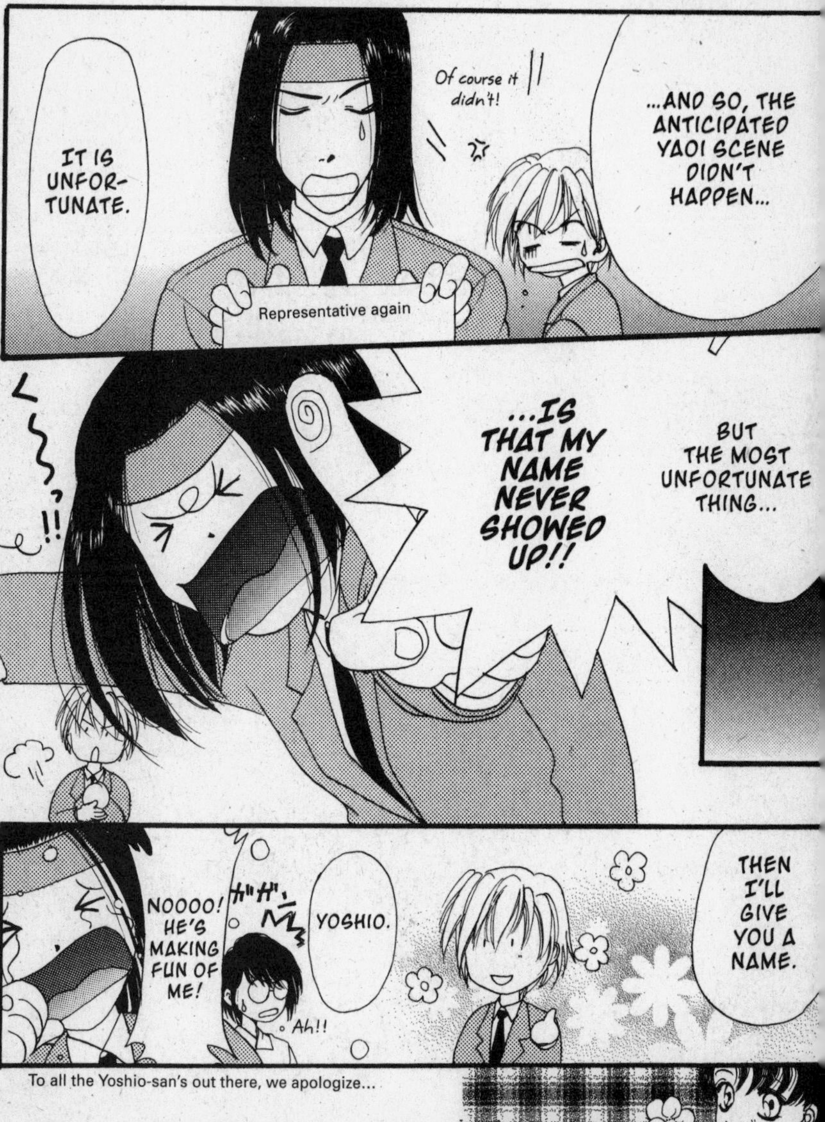
...AND SO, THE ANTICIPATED YAOI SCENE DIDN'T HAPPEN...
Of course it didn't!
Representative again
IT IS UNFORTUNATE.
BUT THE MOST UNFORTUNATE THING...
...IS THAT MY NAME NEVER SHOWED UP!!
THEN I'LL GIVE YOU A NAME.
YOSHIO.
Ah!!
NOOOO! HE'S MAKING FUN OF ME!

To all the Yoshio-san's out there, we apologize...

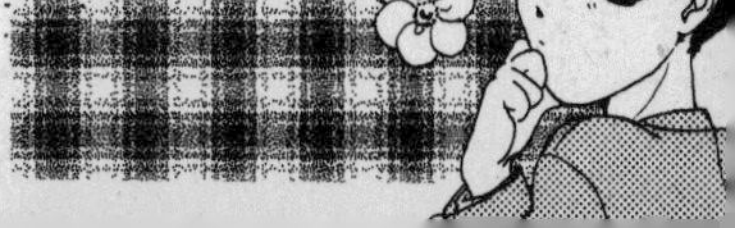

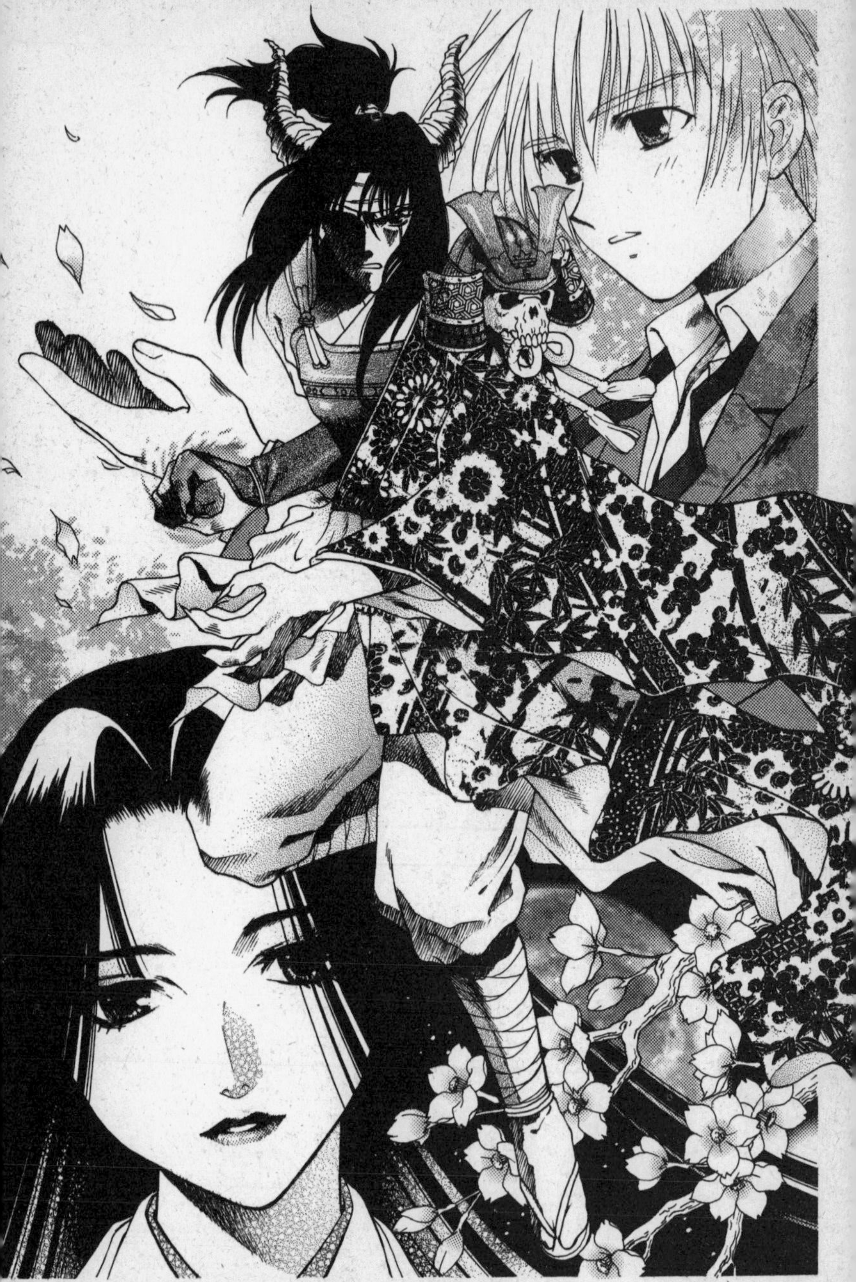

By Wakako

TOKYOPOP SHOP

THIS FALL, TOKYOPOP CREATES A FRESH, NEW CHAPTER IN TEEN NOVELS...

For Adventurers...

Witches' Forest: The Adventures of Duan Surk

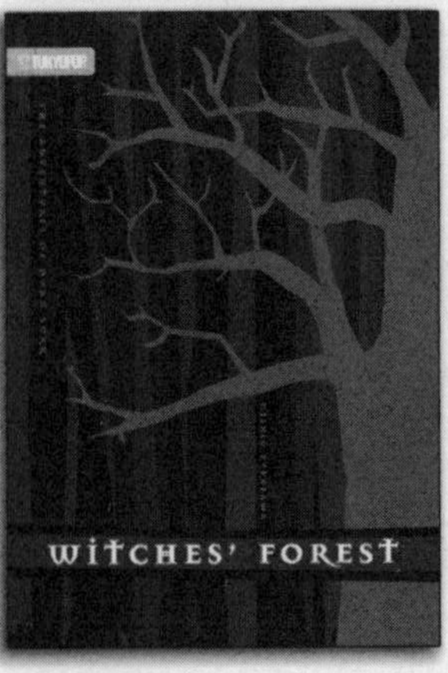
TOKYOPOP
witches' forest

By Mishio Fukazawa

Duan Surk is a 16-year-old Level 2 fighter who embarks on the quest of a lifetime—battling mythical creatures and outwitting evil sorceresses, all in an impossible rescue mission in the spooky Witches' Forest!

BASED ON THE FAMOUS *FORTUNE QUEST* WORLD

For Dreamers...

Magic Moon

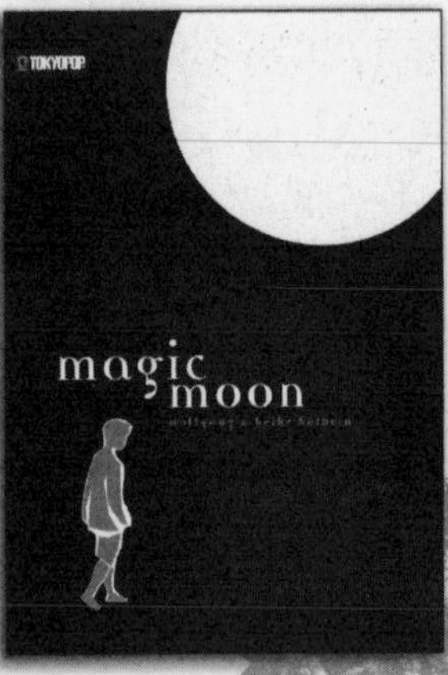
TOKYOPOP
magic moon

By Wolfgang and Heike Hohlbein

Kim enters the engimatic realm of Magic Moon, where he battles unthinkable monsters and fantastical creatures—in order to unravel the secret that keeps his sister locked in a coma.

THE WORLDWIDE BESTSELLING FANTASY *THRILLOGY* ARRIVES IN THE U.S.!

TOKYOPOP PRESENTS

For Believers...

Scrapped Princess:
A Tale of Destiny

By Ichiro Sakaki

A dark prophecy reveals that the queen will give birth to a daughter who will usher in the Apocalypse. But despite all attempts to destroy the baby, the myth of the "Scrapped Princess" lingers on...

THE INSPIRATION FOR THE HIT ANIME AND MANGA SERIES!

For Thinkers...

Kino no Tabi:
Book One of The Beautiful World

By Keiichi Sigsawa

Kino roams the world on the back of Hermes, her unusual motorcycle, in a journey filled with happiness and pain, decadence and violence, and magic and loss.

THE SENSATIONAL BESTSELLER IN JAPAN HAS FINALLY ARRIVED!

that I'm not like other people...

Ayumu struggles with her studies, and the all-important high school entrance exams are approaching. Fortunately, she has help from her best bud Shii-chan, who is at the top of the class. But when the test results come back, the friends are surprised: Ayumu surpasses Shii-chan's scores and gets into the school of her choice—without Shii-chan! Losing her friend is so painful for Ayumu that she starts cutting herself to ease her sorrow. Finally, Ayumu seeks comfort in a new friend, Manami. But will Manami prove to be the friend that Ayumu truly needs? Or will Ayumu continue down a dark path?

LIFE
Volume 1
Keiko Suenobu

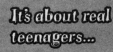

It's about real teenagers...

It's about real high school...

It's about real life.

LIFE
BY KEIKO SUENOBU

Ordinary high school teenagers...
Except that they're not.

READ THE ENTIRE FIRST CHAPTER ONLINE FOR FREE:

STOP!

This is the back of the book.
You wouldn't want to spoil a great ending!

This book is printed "manga-style," in the authentic Japanese right-to-left format. Since none of the artwork has been flipped or altered, readers get to experience the story just as the creator intended. You've been asking for it, so TOKYOPOP® delivered: authentic, hot-off-the-press, and far more fun!

DIRECTIONS

If this is your first time reading manga-style, here's a quick guide to help you understand how it works.

It's easy... just start in the top right panel and follow the numbers. Have fun, and look for more 100% authentic manga from TOKYOPOP®!